Judging

CLARENDON LAW SERIES

RECENT TITLES IN THE SERIES

The Conflict of Laws
5th Edition
ADRIAN BRIGGS

Discrimination Law
3rd edition
SANDRA FREDMAN

War
ANDREW CLAPHAM

Land Law
3rd edition
ELIZABETH COOKE

Competition Law and Antitrust
DAVID J. GERBER

The United Kingdom Constitution
An Introduction
N.W. BARBER

Introduction to Company Law
3rd edition
PAUL DAVIES

Bentham and the Common Law Tradition
2nd edition
GERALD J. POSTEMA

Law and Values in the European Union
STEPHEN WEATHERILL

Personal Property Law
4th edition
MICHAEL BRIDGE

The Idea of Arbitration
JAN PAULSSON

The Anthropology of Law
FERNANDA PIRIE

Law and Gender
JOANNE CONAGHAN

The Concept of Law
3rd Edition
H.L.A. HART

With a Postscript edited by Penelope
A. BULLOCH AND JOSEPH RAZ

With an Introduction and Notes by
LESLIE GREEN

Administrative Law
5th edition
PETER CANE

An Introduction to the Law of Trusts
3rd edition
SIMON GARDNER

Natural Law and Natural Rights
2nd edition
JOHN FINNIS

Employment Law
2nd edition
HUGH COLLINS

International Law
VAUGHAN LOWE

Civil Liberties
CONOR GEARTY

Intellectual Property
MICHAEL SPENCE

Policies and Perceptions of Insurance Law in the Twenty-First Century
2nd edition
MALCOLM CLARKE

Philosophy of Private Law
WILLIAM LUCY

Law in Modern Society
DENIS GALLIGAN

An Introduction to Tort Law
2nd edition
TONY WEIR

Equity
2nd edition
SARAH WORTHINGTON

Atiyah's Introduction to the Law of Contract
6th edition
STEPHEN A. SMITH AND P.S. ATIYAH

Unjust Enrichment
2nd edition
PETER BIRKS

An Introduction to Family Law
2nd edition
GILLIAN DOUGLAS

Criminal Justice
LUCIA ZEDNER

Contract Theory
STEPHEN A. SMITH

Public Law
ADAM TOMKINS

Personal Property Law
3rd edition
MICHAEL BRIDGE

Judging

ROSS CRANSTON
Professor of Law, London School of Economics and Political Science, UK

OXFORD
UNIVERSITY PRESS

OXFORD
UNIVERSITY PRESS

Great Clarendon Street, Oxford, OX2 6DP,
United Kingdom

Oxford University Press is a department of the University of Oxford.
It furthers the University's objective of excellence in research, scholarship,
and education by publishing worldwide. Oxford is a registered trade mark of
Oxford University Press in the UK and in certain other countries.

Published in the United States of America by Oxford University Press
198 Madison Avenue, New York, NY 10016, United States of America.

British Library Cataloguing in Publication Data
Data available

Library of Congress Control Number: 2025940560

ISBN 9780198987987 (pbk.)
ISBN 9780198858881 (hbk.)

DOI: 10.1093/9780191890994.001.0001

Printed and bound by
CPI Group (UK) Ltd., Croydon, CR0 4YY

FSC
www.fsc.org
MIX
Paper | Supporting
responsible forestry
FSC® C013604

The manufacturer's authorised representative in the EU for product safety is
Oxford University Press España S.A. of Parque Empresarial San Fernando de Henares,
Avenida de Castilla, 2—28830 Madrid (www.oup.es/en or product.safety@oup.com).
OUP España S.A. also acts as importer into Spain of products made by the manufacturer.

For Hazel and Molly

Preface

Judging is work, often demanding work, work which can have a significant impact on people's lives, relationships, and property. Others undertake demanding work, and their decision-making can appreciably affect people's lives. The distinctive work of judging is the impartial resolution of disputes and the maintenance of the rule of law. By contrast with others engaged in dispute resolution, judging is performed by a specialist cadre, the judges, who comprise a separate branch of the state, standing alongside the others, the legislature and the executive government. A corollary of dispute resolution by judges is that it occurs within the context of applying the rights and duties contained in a society's laws. Judges doing this work independently, impartially, and with integrity enhance public confidence in the administration of justice and further the rule of law.

In common law countries, dispute resolution by senior judges can involve enunciating and developing the law. This is one aspect of how the work of judging varies with the position which a judge occupies. At one end of the spectrum there are the relatively few apex court judges, who exercise this important function of lawmaking when deciding the limited number of cases they consider each year. Along the spectrum are the many hundreds of judges whose speedy and impartial resolution of large numbers of disputes of a widely differing character is of immediate importance to the parties involved. There are judges hearing high volume, relatively straightforward applications, judges conducting trials, judges sitting in problem-solving courts, and judges considering appeals in intermediate appellate courts. The work of all these judges, as well as that of apex court judges, contributes to the legitimacy of the judiciary as a whole. The work of each is fundamental to the rule of law.

This book is about the work of judging—the values underlying judges' work and what judges actually do in practice. It attempts to capture the essence of judging, wherever judges are placed in the judiciary. For most litigants whose cases reach court, the end point will be the decision of a judge, perhaps relatively low in the judicial hierarchy or, in a few cases, a judge in the senior courts. For such litigants, these are the judges at the heart of the legal system, not those in the apex court. Even when, exceptionally, a case reaches the apex court, it will generally have begun with a judge elsewhere in the system, and the foundations for how the apex judges decide it will have been laid there.

There are boundaries to the book's coverage. It is about the civil, not the criminal, law. It is limited to the experience of judging in a selected number of common law countries. It is written mainly from an English perspective, with examples taken from Australia, Canada, India, and the United States. A great deal of legal writing about judging, broadly conceived, centres on critiquing the substance of judicial decisions, especially those of apex and intermediate appellate courts, and on a theoretical analysis of how this occurs or, at least, should occur. While both appraising the merits of specific judicial decisions, and a jurisprudential analysis of legal developments, are important, a theme of this book is that it is time more attention was given to the reality of most judicial work, and the context in which it is undertaken. The fact is that judging is an intense and practical activity, and unless of a scholarly bent, or in an apex court, common law judges have little time or inclination to explore legal theories. As a former chief justice of Australia noted, in so far as judges develop a philosophy of judicial decision-making, they generally do so in the light of their experience as judges.[1]

While the book does not dwell on legal theories, it does have recourse to the social sciences. The internalization by the judge of judicial values, and the judge's socialization into the accepted norms of judging, are areas where the social sciences can contribute to our understanding of the world of the judge. A closely related area is the tendency of the judge to conform to judicial norms because of the positive reputation which this can earn from other judges, the profession, and the public. What social psychologists have over many years uncovered about cognitive bias is a recurring theme. It contributes to an understanding of the judge's work in matters like fact-finding, as well as in the use of mental short-cuts and rules of thumb in making intuitive decisions, especially against a backdrop of 'getting through' a heavy caseload. Social science theory can also throw light on the variations between judges in judicial decision-making, on the social forces at play when judges sit with other judges on a panel hearing a case, and on the impact of a judge's background, beliefs, and attitudes on their decision-making.

The book underlines that judges work within a social context. A full account of the environment within which they do this would include matters

[1] Sir Anthony Mason, 'The Art of Judging' (2008) 12 Southern Cross ULR 33, 37.

such as their role in facilitating access to justice, in resolving disputes alongside those such as arbitrators, mediators, and community leaders, and in ensuring that the other branches of the state act lawfully. The social context on which the book focuses in considering the work of judges is the values that judiciaries have set for themselves—independence, impartiality, and integrity. Whatever position a judge occupies, a paramount feature of their work is the expectation that they will perform it consistently with those values. Even if judges are not always conscious of these values as they go about their everyday work, the institutional patterns and work practices of judging should give effect to them. It should be the context in which judges work. For these values to be effective, however, there needs to be a commitment to them on the part of each individual judge and their internalization so they become second nature.

Judicial independence, the first value, is to ensure that judges can decide cases in accordance with their legal merits, free from improper pressures and inducements from both outside the judiciary and within. Protections against these pressure and inducements are embedded in constitutions, statutes, soft law, and understandings, but importantly also depend for their efficacy on the judge's 'state of mind', along with the support given by the bar, the political class, and society. The other side of the coin to judicial independence is judicial accountability. That takes various forms, including that judges decide cases in accordance with law, hear them in open court, and explain their conclusions in publicly available, reasoned decisions. The second value, impartiality, protects against decisions based on the biases of the judge and the identity of the parties, although in everyday practice it is concerned with the bearing that a judge's interests, associations, opinions, and previous contact with a party may appear to have on a case.

Integrity, the third value, connotes adherence to the content of judicial virtue. In the book this value includes principles governing a judge's behaviour in court—acting fairly, competently, and diligently, exhibiting respect, patience, and decorum, and according equal concern and respect to all. By contrast with other professions, however, judges are not only held to high standards of behaviour at work, they must also accept considerable restrictions on their activities away from the bench and, in some respects, for the rest of their lives. Integrity, independence, and impartiality are the values which the judiciary of England and Wales identify as fundamental.[2] The

[2] eg, *Guide to Judicial Conduct* (London, Courts and Tribunals Judiciary, 2023); *The Lady Chief Justice's Report 2024* (London, Judiciary of England and Wales, 2024).

same three fundamental values are adopted elsewhere.[3] Other jurisdictions add additional values to these three, such as respect, diligence, competence, and equality.[4] As we have seen, these can be, and in England (and elsewhere) are, subsumed by the value of integrity.

As well as spelling out the meaning and implications of these three values of independence, impartiality, and integrity, Part I of the book covers how they are secured in practice, and the norms of behaviour signified by them for judicial work. Each of these values is crucial to public confidence in both the judges and the judiciary as a whole. The commitment to them has both individual and institutional dimensions. The individual judge must embrace these values and manifest them through their everyday work in court and in their lives in the outside world. Public confidence also derives from the ethos of the judiciary as a whole and its attentiveness to, and compliance with, these values. The individual commitment of the judge is interrelated to that of the judiciary as an institution. The individual judge must have a commitment to these values, but that needs underpinning by structural and other features of the judiciary as an institution to secure and further them. As well as this judge–judiciary interrelatedness, there is also an interrelatedness involving society: judges and the judiciary as an institution must act in a way which accords with these values to earn public confidence, but these values will only flourish with support from society—the political class, the legal profession, opinion leaders, influencers, and civil society organizations. Public support in a community for an independent, impartial, and virtuous judiciary needs nurturing.

Part II of the book is concerned with the practice of judging. The judge's work has changed since the mid twentieth century. While dispute resolution remains the core, judges these days undertake a range of additional functions. Managing cases is just one aspect. Increases in the population, in economic activity, in migration, and in rights consciousness have all stimulated more disputes and a consequent pressure on judges to manage the courts' caseloads. As a result, the pace of litigation can no longer be dictated by the parties, and along with court administrators judges now manage the flow of litigation, both through routinization in the processing of straightforward,

[3] eg, Council of Chief Justices of Australia and New Zealand, *Guide to Judicial Conduct, Third Edition (Revised)* (Sydney, AIJA, 2023).

[4] *Bangalore Principles of Judicial Conduct* (Vienna, United Nations, 2018); Canadian Judicial Council, *Ethical Principles for Judges* (Ottawa, CJC, 2021).

simple cases, and the tailored handling of the more complex. Along with managing cases, judges now have a larger role in managing courts, as well as engaging with their local communities and the wider society. At the time of writing there is an important discussion about the role of generative artificial intelligence. It is unclear what the implications of AI for judging will be, but again that will produce changes in the practice of judging and how judges work.

The practice of judging in Part II of the book begins with what is called the legal and policy framework governing how judges are appointed and their terms and conditions of service. These have a bearing on the practice of judging—the competence, efficiency, and application with which the work of judging is performed—as well as the strength of the commitment of those appointed to judicial values and to the standards of judicial behaviour. They also contribute to public confidence in the judiciary, as does the selection of judges more reflective of society. The discussion then turns to what is called judgecraft, the specific skills needed for judging, in addition to legal ability and legal skills. Practical judging often begins and ends with the facts of a particular case since, once these are settled the law being relatively straightforward a conclusion can often follow as a matter of course. As well as the skills of fact-finding, judges need judgecraft to make speedy decisions 'on the papers', without an oral hearing; to deliver *ex tempore* (immediate) judgments; to manage cases with 'litigants in person' (known as 'pro se' parties in the US, 'self-representing' parties in other jurisdictions), who lack legal representation, often because public funding has been withdrawn; and to write clear, concise, and persuasive judgments.

The book's final chapter concerns judicial decision-making. It canvasses contentions that the individual judge can be affected in their decision-making by psychological factors, their relations with others, and their social beliefs, as well as their different conceptions of the task. Notwithstanding the reality of these influences as regards the individual judge, judicial decision-making must accord with judicial values, including the value of fidelity to law. Judicial decisions must be legally motivated, so that the judge's conclusions are based in legal principle, the parties' submissions, and the facts of a case. In practice, judicial decision-making proceeds routinely and without difficulty. Judges interpret legislation and apply precedent relevant to the facts of a case. On occasions, judges face more difficult choices and challenging issues, but the acceptable methodology of common law judging enables these to be approached in a practical way so that judicial power is exercised responsibly even if there are disagreements about outcome and the path to it.

In preparing the book I have built up many debts. For a period of just over nine years I was privileged to be a judge of the High Court of England and Wales, and sat as a part-time judge before and after that. During that time I learnt much about judging from conversations with, and observations of, my colleagues, for which I am grateful. I have also benefited from legal visits abroad, conferences organized by the Commonwealth Magistrates' and Judges' Association, and participation in judicial training in various parts of Africa and the Pacific. In 2022 I profited from a seminar involving English and Australian judges, held under the auspices of the Australian Academy of Law, and from separate meetings with Australian judges. Although the work of judges in civil law countries can differ markedly from that in common law systems, I learnt much from assignments for the European Commission with the judiciaries of central and eastern Europe and Turkey.

A number of academic and judicial colleagues have been generous in assisting me with the book: Gabrielle Appleby, Peter Applegarth, Michael Blackwell, Bill Blair, Neil Duxbury, Chris Maxwell, Vivien Rose, and John Thomas. They have saved me from error, and suggested many improvements. I am especially appreciative of the efforts of Sarah Worthington, who challenged me to rethink both the structure and analysis of the book. None, however, share any responsibility for the mistakes, misunderstandings, and misinterpretations in the text. I am as ever thankful to the Law School at the London School of Economics, to its dean, David Kershaw, and to my colleagues there for furnishing me with a supportive and interdisciplinary environment. As with my previous books, the librarians at the Royal Courts of Justice and the LSE were characteristically helpful. Aditi Malik assisted with some Indian references. I must acknowledge the patience of Oxford University Press in waiting for the manuscript. In particular I am grateful to Jamie Berezin who commissioned it, and to Charlotte Kershaw, Charlotte Holloway, Victoriya Sherly, and Amanda Anstee, who guided it to final publication.

Brief Contents

Detailed Contents

PART II. PRACTICE

Table of Cases

UNITED KINGDOM

COURT OF JUSTICE OF THE EUROPEAN UNION

EUROPEAN COURT OF HUMAN RIGHTS

INTERNATIONAL CRIMINAL TRIBUNAL FOR THE FORMER YUGOSLAVIA (ICTY)

NATIONAL COURTS

Australia

Canada

Ghana

India

Ireland

Kenya

Malawi

New Zealand

Special Court for Sierra Leone

Singapore

South Africa

United States of America

Table of Legislation

Statutory Instruments

United States

INTERNATIONAL INSTRUMENTS

PART I
VALUES

1
Independence

I Introduction

States almost universally claim to act in accordance with the rule of law, whatever the reality. The rule of law entails a legal system with independent, impartial, and non-corrupt judges, laws which are clear, publicly available, and in accordance with the constitution and human rights, and a court system which is fair, accessible, and efficient, and which protects human, contractual, property, and other legal rights. The rationale for judicial independence is to enable judges to adjudicate cases impartially, fairly, and according to their legal merits, and to insulate the judges from improper pressure or inducements which derive directly or indirectly from others. Claims about the rule of law and judicial independence mean nothing if they do not accord with the reality. Central to public confidence in the judges is whether judicial independence is effectively recognized and given effect to in practice. Judicial independence contributes to the legitimacy of decision-making by judges, public acceptance of their rulings, and the rule of law.

Judicial independence is especially important when the judge is reviewing the exercise of power by the executive government against individuals, or adjudicating a dispute between individuals and the executive government. Judges independent of political influences must keep the state from illegality and the abuse of power. The judicial role in upholding human rights and freedoms acquires an added force when those involved are unpopular with the executive government or the public. As well as their role in such public law and human rights matters, independent judges provide an assurance of impartial decision-making in private law disputes involving contracts, property, and civil wrongs. Threats to judicial independence in this context can emanate from interests outside government such as business. In political systems with different levels of government such as federalism or devolution, an independent judiciary can act as an impartial arbiter of disputes between the various centres of political power.

Judging. Ross Cranston, Oxford University Press. © Ross Cranston 2025.
DOI: 10.1093/9780191890994.003.0001

Judicial independence has acquired a variety of meanings, and discussions of it can descend into platitudes or acquire a sloganeering quality. Section II of the chapter outlines how international bodies have elaborated judicial independence as a value. It then turns to how the many facets of judicial independence can be organized under broad categories, elaborated in the chapter. One of these is a division between external and internal independence, depending on the origins of threats to judicial independence, whether from outside the judiciary or from inside. Structural independence, discussed in sections III and IV of the chapter, addresses the measures designed to insulate the individual judge and the judiciary as an institution from these threats. What is termed behavioural independence in section V is concerned with the social and cultural protections for independence. Then section VI of the chapter turns to judicial accountability, the other side of the coin to judicial independence. An independent judiciary is not unfettered, and judges must account for the exercise of judicial power. Independence, accountability, and the legitimacy of judicial power run together.

II Principles and Practice

A meeting of international jurists in New Delhi in 1959 stated: 'An independent Judiciary is an indispensable requisite of a free society under the Rule of Law.'[1] That seminal statement has been built on in international instruments drawn up by governmental and non-governmental bodies. Their formulation of the principles of judicial independence, summarized in this section, is a useful stating point. While certain core principles in these international instruments are essential to judicial independence, the importance of the different aspects understandably varies over time and between societies. The discussion therefore turns to how the different dimensions to judicial independence can be categorized and so better understood.

(A) An International Value

The principles governing judicial independence are contained in a number of international instruments. Perhaps most importantly, in 1985 the UN

[1] International Commission of Jurists, *The Rule of Law in a Free Society. A Report on the International Congress of Jurists* (ICJ 1960).

General Assembly endorsed The Basic Principles on the Independence of the Judiciary.[2] These define judicial independence as judges making decisions 'impartially, on the basis of facts and in accordance with the law, without any restrictions, improper influences, inducements, pressures, threats or interferences, direct or indirect, from any quarter or for any reason'. They then spell out a very broad canvass for judicial independence: there shall be no inappropriate or unwarranted interference with the judicial process; judicial selection shall safeguard against appointments for improper motives; the law must secure the security, adequate remuneration, and conditions of service of judges and guarantee their pensions; judges must have guaranteed tenure; promotion must be based on objective factors; the assignment of cases is a matter of internal judicial administration; and disciplinary action against judges must be procedurally fair, in accordance with established standards, and subject to independent review.[3]

At the outset the UN Basic Principles place the obligation on states to guarantee their judges' independence.[4] As highlighted in this first paragraph and as is evident in other paragraphs, the UN Basic Principles impose obligations on member states to further and guarantee judicial independence through law, administration, and practice. Principle 7 underlines one particular obligation: the duty of each member state to provide adequate resources to enable the judges to perform their functions properly. The UN Basic Principles recognize that judges have freedom of speech and may form judges' associations.[5] However, they also recognize that judges have obligations along with these various rights, notably that they must act impartially and independently, in other words must resist threats, pressure, inducements, or blandishments. Principle 6 also obliges them to ensure that judicial proceedings are conducted fairly and that the rights of parties are respected. In exercising freedom of speech, the UN Basic Principles make clear that judges must conduct themselves so as to preserve the dignity of their office and the independence and impartiality of the judiciary as an institution.

Aspects of the UN Basic Principles are replicated and expanded upon in other international instruments. In the Commonwealth of Nations (formerly the British Commonwealth), comprising over fifty states, there are the

[2] UNGA Res 40/ 32 (29 November 1985) and UNGA Res 40/ 146 (13 December 1985) (hereafter UN Basic Principles).

[3] ibid 4, 10–14, 17–20.

[4] ibid 1.

[5] ibid 8–9. See pp. 135, 190 below.

so-called *Latimer House Principles*.[6] In addressing judicial independence, they deal as do the UN Basic Principles with matters such as judicial appointments, financial security, the adequate funding of the judiciary, and the disciplining of judges. Unlike them, the *Latimer House Principles* add that with the appointment of judges appropriate consideration must be given to the need for the progressive attainment of gender equity and the removal of other historic factors of discrimination.[7] Moreover, an Annex underlines the need for a 'culture of judicial education' and for adequate funding for judicial training. Importantly, the *Latimer House Principles* acknowledge the principle of judicial accountability: judges are accountable to the constitution and to the law, which they must apply honestly, independently, and with integrity.[8] Both the principles of judicial independence and judicial accountability, they add, 'underpin public confidence in the judicial system and the importance of the judiciary as one of the three pillars upon which a responsible government relies'.[9]

In 2010 the Council of Europe—the body responsible for the European Convention on Human Rights (ECHR)—adopted its Recommendation CM/Rec(2010)12, 'Judges: Independence, Efficiency and Responsibilities'.[10] Drawing on ECHR fair trial rights in article 6.1, the Recommendation highlights the essential role of judges in ensuring the safeguarding of human rights and fundamental freedoms. Judicial independence, it says, is an inherent element of the rule of law and indispensable to judges' impartiality and to the functioning of the judicial system. It underlines the point that judicial independence is not a privilege of the judges but a guarantee of respect for human rights and fundamental freedoms. The Recommendation elaborates on the basic principle of judicial independence providing, for example, that cases must not be withdrawn from a judge without valid, objective, and transparent reasons; that in protecting judicial independence states must introduce sanctions against persons seeking to influence judges in an improper manner; and that apart from giving reasons judges should

[6] *Commonwealth (Latimer House) Principles on the Three Branches of Government* (Commonwealth Secretariat 2009) (hereafter *Latimer House Principles*). On the *Latimer House Principles* see *Ayers-Caesar v Judicial and Legal Service Commission* [2025] UKPC 15 [5], [32] (Lord Reed) (PC, Trinidad and Tobago).

[7] Para (IV)(a). See pp. 162–164 below.

[8] Para (VII)(b). See also *ELI-Mount Scopus European Standards of Judicial Independence* (European Law Institute 2024) Standard 3, comment (e) (hereafter *ELI-Mount Scopus European Standards*).

[9] Para (VII)(b).

[10] (Council of Europe 2011).

not otherwise be obliged to justify their decisions.[11] The Recommendation also states that governments and legislatures should avoid the criticism of judgments and should refrain from actions that would undermine both judicial independence and public confidence in the judiciary.[12]

(B) Framing Judicial Independence

The international and regional instruments just outlined sketch judicial independence in very broad terms. Judicial independence is a value with many parts. The discussion of judicial independence in the rest of the chapter seeks to give order to these different parts by orienting them around three main aspects: firstly, the threats to judicial independence, and secondly and thirdly, the structural and behavioural protections to counter these threats. Before each of these is developed at length, this section offers a brief overview.

First, the threats to judicial independence lead to a simple division of subject matter under the heads of external independence and internal independence. External independence focuses on what has traditionally been thought of as the rationale for judicial independence—the need to secure the judiciary against external threats, inducements, and improper influences, notably but not exclusively from the executive government. As an example, the guarantee of judicial independence in the UK's Constitution Reform Act 2005 contains a duty on the lord chancellor (the minister for justice) and other ministers of the executive government to uphold the independence of the judiciary, and imposes a specific obligation that they 'must not seek to influence particular judicial decisions through any special access to the judiciary'.[13] Internal independence refers to the freedom of a judge in performing judicial duties to be 'independent of judicial colleagues in respect of decisions that the judge is obliged to make independently'.[14] Historically, internal independence has not attracted the same attention as external independence, but it is now recognized as a crucial aspect of judicial independence.

The second dimension concerns what can be termed the structural protections of judicial independence. These can be divided depending on whether the protections are for the individual judge (individual independence) or the

[11] Appendix, paras 9, 14–15.
[12] Appendix, para 18.
[13] Constitution Reform Act 2005, ss 3(1), 3(5).
[14] *Bangalore Principles of Judicial Conduct* (United Nations 2018) Value 1, para 1.4.

judiciary as a whole (institutional independence).[15] Structural protections for the individual judge encompass what have historically been the well-established protections of the judge's independence—security of tenure and strong protection from dismissal for senior judges (except for misbehaviour), financial security through judicial salaries and pensions which in general cannot be reduced, and immunity from being sued when performing judicial functions. Institutional independence turns on constitutional arrangements and values, as well as the freedom of the judiciary collectively through its leadership judges to decide on court procedures and practices, the allocation of judges to particular work, and the assignment and listing of cases.

Thirdly, it is widely recognized that structural independence is insufficient, and that in practice judicial independence depends heavily on behavioural factors—on the individual judge in performing the judicial role irrespective of threats and inducements, and on society in supporting the judges when doing this. This leads to a division between what can be termed personal independence and cultural independence. Personal independence concentrates on the conduct of judges in making decisions and justifying them in the reasons they give. A judge without much in the way of structural protections of independence may behave in a fiercely independent manner and exhibit real courage in the face of outside or internal threats and inducements. By contrast a judge in a judiciary with strong structural protections of independence may nevertheless dissemble in deciding a case to win the approval of other judges, the executive government, the legislature, or the public. As to what is called cultural independence, this recognizes that the strength of judicial independence turns on a variety of social and political factors, including norms, conventions, and understandings on the part of the political class, opinion leaders, and the public. Historically in some societies the principle of judicial independence has been widely accepted and is well entrenched in the social and political culture. In others it has failed to take root in the society's culture.

(C) External Independence: Outside Threats and Inducements

External independence is concerned with improper threats to the independence of judges from outside the judiciary. In some contexts, the threats may

[15] *Valente v The Queen* [1985] 2 SCR 673 [20] (Le Dain J for the court).

be overt and immediate; in others, they may be subtle and insidious. Threats of physical violence and arrest respectively were a reality facing the chief justice of Zimbabwe in 2001 and the chief justice of Papua New Guinea in 2012 for decisions which had displeased the executive government. The extreme case is where judges are killed for what they have done as judges—for example, in Ghana in 1982, where three High Court judges were abducted from their homes and killed (believed to have been by agents of the government); in Northern Ireland in 1987, where the IRA murdered an appeal court judge and his wife; and in Italy in 1992, where a judge was assassinated by the Mafia when pursuing organized crime. A responsibility of the UN's Special Rapporteur on the independence of judges and lawyers is to report on attacks around the world on the independence of judges, lawyers, and prosecutors.[16] That aim of supporting judges exposed to threats to their independence or their person is shared by the two leading international membership organizations of judges, the International Association of Judges, founded in Salzburg in 1953, and the Commonwealth Magistrates' and Judges' Association, founded in 1970.

External independence, the Council of Europe's Venice Commission says, 'shields the judge from influence by other state powers and is an essential element of the rule of law'.[17] External influence on judges can take the form of financial or other inducements such as the payment of a bribe, as well as improper pressure, threats, or hints both to the individual judge deciding a case as well as the judiciary as an institution. Traditionally the threats to judicial independence were thought of as emanating from the executive government. A European example from 2008 led to the resignation of the Belgian government after the First President of the Court of Cassation raised questions about the backdoor intervention by the minister of justice at the Court of Appeal of Brussels in a controversial claim by the shareholders of Fortis Bank, what had been Belgium's largest bank, against its acquisition by the French bank, BNP Paribas.[18] However, threats can come from non-governmental sources such as commercial parties, organized crime, and terrorists who have an interest in the outcome of private litigation, prosecutions, and other matters such as applications by law enforcement bodies to

[16] eg, UN Human Rights High Council, 53rd session, 18 July 2023, A/HRC/RES/53/12.

[17] 'Report on the Independence of the Judicial System Part I: The Independence of Judges' adopted by the Venice Commission at its 82nd Plenary Session (Venice, 12–13 March 2010) para 56.

[18] Marc Bossuyt, 'The Independence of the Judiciary in Belgium' in Shimon Shetreet (ed), *The Culture of Judicial Independence* (Brill Nijhoff 2014) 140–143.

the courts to order the seizure of their assets. As well, pressure on judicial independence may originate with the media and interest groups.

Governments may seek to curb judicial independence as regards the decisions of judges on matters which are politically and economically sensitive. Decisions which most directly attract a government's interest concern election outcomes and its continuation in power. That was brought home with the controversial decision of the US Supreme Court in *Bush v Gore*[19] which meant the election of one presidential candidate over another without the recount ordered by the Florida Supreme Court in that decisive state. In Britain there has been a long tradition of election courts, where petitions challenging election results in individual constituencies are heard by High Court judges with little fanfare.[20] That mechanism was incorporated into the constitutions of Commonwealth countries on their independence from Britain and assumed enhanced importance in countries with presidential constitutions. There has been a long history in many of these countries of judges dismissing petitions challenging the outcome of presidential elections on technical grounds. Whatever the legalities, the courts have in effect provided cover for the continuation in power by authoritarian regimes despite vote-rigging. For the first time in Africa, in 2017 the Kenyan Supreme Court bravely nullified a presidential election because the irregularities in the way it was conducted substantially affected the outcome. The court ordered fresh elections within sixty days, as provided for in the constitution, and the election was rerun.[21]

Various avenues can be utilized by a government to bring judges into line with its goals of fixing elections, suppressing opposition figures, curbing the media, seizing assets, or benefiting supporters. Appointments are one. Known sympathizers can be appointed to the bench or promoted. Assurances of support may be obtained from candidates before appointment, especially in crucial areas such as the outcome of presidential elections and justiciable issues touching on the government's key policies. Appointment may be combined with court packing, especially of the apex court, so that the number of judges is increased and vacancies then filled by those who will toe the government's line. The populist government in power in Poland until 2023 used the appointment and promotion process from around 2015 to mould

[19] 531 US 98 (2000).

[20] The Parliamentary Elections Act 1868 was the earliest provision.

[21] *Raila Odinga v IEBC* [2017] KESC 42, [2017] eKLR [400]–[403]. See also *Mutharika v Chilima (Constitutional Appeal No. 1 of 2020)* [2020] MWSC 1 (Malawian presidential election nullified). cf *Mahama v Electoral Commission* [2021] GHASC 12 (Ghanian presidential election upheld).

the judiciary. It captured the nominating body for judges established under the Polish constitution so that its judicial membership was elected by the lower house of the legislature rather than by the judiciary. The issue went to the Court of Justice of the European Union (CJEU) which held that the transformation in the appointment process cast doubt on the judicial independence and impartiality of the Polish judiciary, which are required by EU law for courts in member states like Poland.[22]

Dismissal or the possibility of dismissal of judges is another tool for governments seeking to shape judicial decision-making. Four examples suffice. The first concerns Malaysia in the 1980s, where the courts had ruled against the government in cases concerning freedom of the press, the standing of citizens to challenge state action, habeas corpus, and sedition. The situation came to a head in 1988 when the Lord President of the Supreme Court and some of his colleagues were removed from office. The crisis had long-term repercussions for the standing of the Malaysian judiciary and public confidence in it. The second example is the suspension in 2007, and later removal from office, of Iftikhar Chaudhry CJ of Pakistan. Under him the Supreme Court had upset the military regime with decisions in public interest litigation (including rulings against the privatization of Pakistan Steel Mills and the deregulation of price controls for oil and sugar) and favouring those illegally detained in the war on terror. Chaudhry CJ was reinstated in 2009 after mass protests by lawyers, although for other reasons later lost the support of his judicial colleagues.

Thirdly, there was the removal in 2013 of Bandaranayake CJ by the Sri Lankan government after a Supreme Court decision that government legislation was unconstitutional. On the election of a new government she was restored to office but then retired. Finally, from about 2014 the governing party in Türkiye (Turkey) began asserting an unprecedented degree of control over the judiciary to ensure that government measures for suppressing internal opposition and criticism were effective. Following an attempted coup in July 2015 the control intensified. Judges perceived to have affiliations to interests other than the governing party were purged. Around 3,000 judges and prosecutors, including two judges of the Constitutional Court and more than 160 judges of the Court of Cassation and the Supreme Administrative

[22] Case C-718/21 *Krajowa Rada Sądownictwa (Keeping a judge in office)* EU:C:2023:1015, [2024] 3 CMLR 14 (GC). See also Case C-824/18 *AB v Krajowa Rada Sądownictwa* EU:C:2021:153, [2021] 3 CMLR 5, [2022] 4 WLR 36 [17], [126]–[139] (GC).

Court, were taken into police custody and subsequently placed in pre-trial detention.[23]

There are more circuitous methods for a government to remove judges than through outright dismissal. The populist Polish government which lost power in 2023 adopted various measures to neutralize judges whose agenda might not coincide with its own. This was associated with a political discourse suggesting that the existing judiciary was inefficient as well as an elite which did not share the values of 'the people'. One aspect was the Law on the Supreme Court of 8 December 2017, which reduced the retirement age for judges from seventy to sixty-five, although it empowered the country's president to authorize a judge to continue beyond sixty-five for up to a further six years. The result was that some one-third of the court's judges, including the first president of the Supreme Court, had to leave office with immediate effect.

The European Commission challenged the Polish law before the CJEU. After holding that judicial independence is enshrined as a principle of European Union law, the court concluded that the Polish law had breached this principle.[24] Judges' security of tenure was not absolute, but exceptions had to be legitimate, compelling, proportionate, and not raise reasonable doubt as to the court's imperviousness to external factors.[25] The forced retirement of large numbers of judges demonstrated that the real objective was to reconstruct the bench—not a legitimate aim.[26] Moreover, the court concluded, the law was disproportionate in not offering transitional provisions or early retirement.[27] While a power to extend a judge's term was not objectionable in itself, the CJEU decided that, in this context, it was.[28]

As well as these tools of appointing and removing judges, non-conforming judges may be vulnerable to unjustified disciplinary measures. Then there is 'telephone justice'. The term not only indicates judges being directly informed about the desired outcome for a case, but it is also a metaphor for the use of signalling devices and informal networks of influence. Court presidents will sense what is expected and assign (or reassign) cases to secure the outcome favoured by the government or the influential politician, official, or businessperson. Either way judicial independence is systematically

[23] *Alparslan Altan v Turkey* App no 12778/17 (ECtHR, 16 April 2019) [14].
[24] Case C-619/18 *Commission v Poland* EU:C:2019:531, [2020] 1 CMLR 6 (GC).
[25] ibid [76], [79].
[26] ibid [78]–[90].
[27] ibid [91]–[96].
[28] ibid [124].

undermined and judges deprived of the authority to decide cases on their legal merits. There are also the more subtle means to create subservient judges to achieve a government's goals. One is through rewards for loyalty to the regime, for example, benefits for themselves and their families in the form of housing, transport, education, and foreign travel.

(D) Internal Independence: The Role of Other Judges

Judicial independence involves the independence of the judge not only from external forces but also from those originating inside the judiciary as from other, especially more senior, judges. At one level this can constitute no more than occasioning a stifling conformity of outlook and approach. At another level it can be unknown to the judge, at least for a period, that they have a black mark against them and will not sit on certain cases or be promoted. At yet another level it can be as insidious as judges being pressured by other judges or by judges in leadership positions regarding decisions on case management, the outcome of cases, or the reasons justifying these. If judges succumb, they will not be making a decision independently.

Internal independence only goes so far. As the international instruments on judicial independence outlined earlier make clear, judges have duties as well as rights. Not only must they resist pressures and inducements, but they must also act diligently, efficiently, and without self-interest in the performance of their judicial functions. Internal independence does not confer power on the individual judge over court administration. Judges (perhaps after negotiation) must ultimately accept decisions on the assignment and listing of cases.[29] They must also decide the cases allocated to them and produce orders and judgments within a reasonable time or the period laid down by leadership judges. We see in Chapter 4 how judges can face sanction if they fail to do this.[30]

An aspect of internal independence is that there should be no criticism of the judgments of other judges, except in the context of an appeal. The *Commentary on the Bangalore Principles* spells out some other implications of internal independence: judicial decision-making is a judge's sole responsibility, including when sitting in a collegiate court, although the *Commentary* adds that judges might find it helpful to consult colleagues on a hypothetical

[29] See *Chandler v Judicial Council*, 398 US 74 (1970).
[30] PP. 177, 188 below.

basis on difficult points.[31] Moreover, except by way of reasons or other lawful procedures, the *Commentary* states that a judge is not obliged to report on the merits of a case to other judges, and any court inspection system should not concern itself with the correctness of particular decisions.[32] Having the court rather than any named judge give judgment—accepted practice with courts like the CJEU—means that a judge can push hard internally for controversial decisions without the threat that their stance can be attributed to them by their home country or others.[33]

When judges do give separate judgments, internal independence includes how within limits they can express them. A simple, but telling example occurred with the famous dissent of Lord Atkin in *Liversidge v Anderson*,[34] where the majority held that a court could not review a detention order under wartime emergency regulations. The head of the judiciary, Lord Simon LC, who had not sat on the case, saw Atkin's draft dissenting judgment and recommended that he remove a satirical passage from it. There Atkin had written that the only authority which supported how the majority interpreted the regulations was Humpty Dumpty in Lewis Carroll's novel *Through the Looking-Glass, and What Alice Found There*. Even after a renewed attempt by Simon to have the 'jibe' removed, Atkin refused.

There are a number of cases in the jurisprudence of the European Court of Human Rights (ECtHR) concerning presiding (or other) judges exerting pressure on a judge to influence their decision. In these the ECtHR has held that a court's independence and impartiality required by article 6.1 ECHR is jeopardized in the absence of sufficient safeguards against this.[35] Proof of actual pressure affecting the outcome of a case is not necessary: there is a violation if legitimate doubts are raised about a judge's independence or impartiality. However, the Strasbourg court is realistic in recognizing that presiding (and senior) judges must have management powers to run their courts, which may risk the internal independence of the judges of their court: it is impossible to eliminate that risk completely.[36]

The factual context of the ECHR cases relates to presiding judges improperly allocating or reassigning cases, or to presiding judges improperly

[31] *Commentary on the Bangalore Principles of Judicial Conduct* (UNODC 2007) paras 39–40 (hereafter *Commentary on the Bangalore Principles*).
[32] ibid, paras 41–42.
[33] See p. 234 below.
[34] [1942] AC 206.
[35] *Parlov-Tkalčić v Croatia* App no 24810/06 (ECtHR, 22 December 2009) [86].
[36] ibid [91].

changing a judge's legal status. An example of both occurring was the removal of a judge of the Moscow City Court from hearing a high-profile corruption case and her subsequent dismissal as a judge. At one point she publicly accused the president of the court of subjecting her to pressure about the case.[37] The ECtHR held that there had been a breach of her right to freedom of expression in article 10 ECHR since she was alleging an important matter of public interest—that pressure on judges was common. It observed that the problem she raised had to be treated seriously if the Russian judicial system was to maintain its independence and enjoy public confidence.[38]

III Structural Independence: The Judge

Protecting the individual judge's independence, the first aspect of structural independence, was established in the Act of Settlement 1700 as regards tenure and salary. It provided that a judge's commission was held during good behaviour, and their salaries 'ascertained and established', but upon the address of both Houses of Parliament it may be lawful to remove them. These protections in the Act of Settlement still have force for the individual independence of the judge in protecting against interference with their tenure and their financial security. Experience demonstrates that additional protections for the individual judge are needed, notably protections against unjustified disciplinary measures, forced transfer to less desirable posts, and demotion or effective dismissal by the reorganization or abolition of their court. To these can be added safeguards against other threats—of being sued by disgruntled litigants, being harassed by government agencies (for example, the threat of an unjustified tax audit), and being intimidated by litigants and others about their decision-making.[39]

(A) Security of Tenure

Since the Act of Settlement 1701, supplemented by the Commissions and Salaries of Judges Act 1760, security of tenure has been the primary legal

[37] *Kudeshkina v Russian Federation* (2011) 52 EHRR 37.
[38] ibid [94]. Dissenting judgments observed that judges should exercise restraint in their public statements.
[39] PP. 60, 62–64 below.

protection of judicial independence in England and Wales.[40] Senior judges hold their commissions subject only to good conduct and removal by an address of both Houses of Parliament.[41] The Act of Settlement conferred a lifetime appointment on judges, but the fixed retirement ages subsequently introduced do not affect the principle of security of tenure. Judges lower in the hierarchy, those sitting in special courts, and tribunal judges have never had the protection enjoyed by senior judges.[42] Thus the lord chancellor may remove circuit and district judges for misbehaviour or incapacity, with the agreement of the chief justice.[43] There is now an additional step to removal for senior judges in Scotland: the Scottish parliament needs to have received a recommendation from an investigatory tribunal that removal is appropriate.[44]

Judicial independence through security of tenure is protected along similar lines in the constitutions of Commonwealth countries. In India Supreme Court judges have tenure until retirement age and cannot be removed except on the order of the president made after an address by each House of Parliament, supported by a majority of the total membership of each House and by a majority of not less than two-thirds of the members of that House present and voting.[45] Section 177 of the South African constitution provides that a judge may be removed from office if the Judicial Service Commission finds that the judge is grossly incompetent or is guilty of 'gross misconduct', and the National Assembly supports removal by a resolution adopted by at least two-thirds of its members. Australia has the parliamentary address procedure derived from the Act of Settlement for senior judges at both federal and state level. Senior judges in New South Wales have an additional protection similar to that in Scotland in that they cannot be removed through the address procedure unless there is a report recommending that course from the conduct division of the Judicial Commission, which is headed by the chief justice.[46] In the United States, Supreme Court and federal judges hold office during good behaviour.[47] Impeachment by Congress is the avenue for removal of a judge for misbehaviour. That involves a trial in the Senate once the House of Representatives adopts the articles of impeachment.

40 12 & 13 William III c 2, s 3, par 7.
41 Constitutional Reform Act 2005, ss 33; Senior Courts Act 1981, s 11(3)–(3A).
42 *McCawley v The King* [1920] AC 691 (PC, Australia).
43 Courts Act 1971, s 17(4).
44 Scotland Act 1998, s 95(6)–(10); Judiciary and Courts (Scotland) Act 2008, ss 35–39.
45 s 124(4).
46 Judicial Officers Act 1986, s 41.
47 US Constitution, Art III, Section 1.

Security of tenure is also written into international instruments such as the UN Basic Principles and regional instruments such as the ECHR. Principle 12 of the UN Basic Principles requires that judges, whether appointed or elected, must have guaranteed tenure until a mandatory retirement age or until the expiration of their term of office, and principle 18 provides that they are subject to suspension or removal only for reasons of incapacity or behaviour that renders them unfit to discharge their duties. The principles of judicial independence, including security of tenure, are built in as central features of the UN's rule of law indicators.[48] The Grand Chamber of the ECtHR has interpreted article 6.1 to include the principle of the irremovability for judges during their term of office, which 'is in general considered as a corollary of judges' independence—which is a prerequisite to the rule of law . . .'.[49] Consistently with what the court has said, it has been held that exceptions are only acceptable if justified by a legitimate objective, proportionate in light of that objective, and not such as to undermine public confidence.[50]

(B) Financial Security

A further aspect of judicial independence is protection from adverse interference with a judge's remuneration, principally by reducing it. The reasoning is that this is for the benefit of the institution and the community, not simply for the individual judge. In the *Federalist Papers*, No 79, Alexander Hamilton opined that, next to life tenure, nothing could contribute more to the independence of the judges than a fixed provision for their support. In the general course of human nature, he added, 'a power over a man's subsistence amounts to a power over his will'.[51] The *Commentary on the Bangalore Principles of Judicial Conduct* underlines the point: one of the conditions for judicial independence is financial security, the right to a salary and a pension, established by law, which is not subject to arbitrary interference by the executive in a manner that could affect judicial independence.[52] In the *Universal Charter of the Judge*, the International Association of Judges expresses the

[48] *United Nations Rule of Law Indicators, Implementation Guide and Project Tools* (2011) 5, 7, 70–71.
[49] *Guðmundur Andri Ástráðsson v Iceland* App no 26374/18 (ECtHR, 1 December 2020) [239].
[50] On the operation of security of tenure provisions in England see p. 172 below.
[51] *The Federalist Papers*, No 78 (Penguin 1987) 442–43 (hereafter *The Federalist Papers*).
[52] *Commentary on the Bangalore Principles* (n 31) para 26(b).

point this way: judges must receive sufficient remuneration to secure true economic independence, which must not depend on the results of the judge's work and must not be reduced during his or her judicial service.[53]

Protection against the reduction of judicial salaries was contained in the Commissions and Salaries of Judges Act 1760. The modern legislation for fixing judicial salaries in England now states that the lord chancellor, in agreement with the relevant minister, may increase a judge's salary but not reduce it.[54] Therefore a level of protection is afforded in that a reduction in judicial salaries lies in the hands of Parliament, not the executive. Elsewhere protection against a reduction in judicial remuneration is entrenched in constitutional instruments, either expressly or by implication. Article III, section 1 of the US constitution provides that the compensation of judges shall not be diminished during their continuance in office.[55] To similar effect are express provisions in other constitutions, for example section 125 of the Indian constitution, section 176(3) of the South African constitution, and section 72(iii) of the Australian constitution. There is no equivalent provision in the Canadian constitution, but in the *Provincial Judges' Case* in 1997 the Supreme Court held that an implied principle of judicial independence protected the salaries of judges.[56]

None of this means that a reduction of judicial salaries can never be justified. The *ELI-Mount Scopus European Standards of Judicial Independence* provide as an exception to the principle of non-reduction when there is a serious economic crisis in the judge's country, provided that any reduction is temporary, not directed against judges collectively or specific judges, and applies in the same terms to all sectors of public service.[57] In other words, in fairness and solidarity the judiciary should share the burden of a serious economic crisis with others. Such an occasion was the Great Depression in the 1930s, when the UK Parliament passed the National Economy Act 1931. It enabled the executive government to effect economies in government expenditure, including by reducing the renumeration 'of persons in His Majesty's Service'. The National Economy (Statutory Salaries) Order 1931 provided for an abatement of 20 per cent in the salary of a High Court

[53] International Association of Judges, *The Universal Charter of the Judge* (revised edn, IAJ 2017) art 8-1.

[54] Constitutional Reform Act 2005, s 34(4) (Supreme Court judges); Senior Courts Act 1981, s 12(3) (High Court/Court of Appeal judges); Administration of Justice Act 1973, s 9(3) (Scottish, Northern Ireland and District judges); Courts Act 1971, s 18(2)(d) (circuit judges).

[55] *United States v Will*, 449 US 200 (1980).

[56] *Reference re Remuneration of Judges of the Provincial Court (PEI)* [1997] 3 SCR 3.

[57] *ELI-Mount Scopus European Standards* (n 8) 10.5.

judge, a lesser abatement for less senior judges. As a matter of law, Professor Holdsworth argued, the Act did not apply to the judges since they were not in His Majesty's Service.[58] Others took a contrary view. The judges resisted the reduction, and in communications with the government invoked judicial independence and the deleterious effects on their standing and future recruitment to the bench. The reduction took effect but in 1934, when the immediate crisis had eased, their earlier salaries were restored.

The 2008 Global Economic Crisis led several countries to reduce judicial salaries, along with those of other public officials. Portugal was one. In exchange for EU financial assistance, the country was compelled to reduce what was regarded as an excessive budget deficit. This it did, in part, by reducing as from October 2014 the remuneration of members of the legislature, the executive, and the judiciary. From January 2016 the measures were gradually moderated and finally repealed in October that year. Nevertheless, the Portuguese judges' association challenged the reductions as infringing the principle of judicial independence enshrined in the Portuguese constitution and EU law. On a reference from the Supreme Administrative Court of Portugal, the CJEU held that the receipt by judges of a level of remuneration commensurate with the importance of their functions constituted a guarantee essential to judicial independence.[59] However, judicial independence was not impaired by the Portuguese measures which were dictated by EU austerity conditions, applied widely in the public sector, and were on their face temporary in nature.[60]

Salary reductions are impossible, even in a financial crisis, where the constitution prohibits it. Like Portugal, Ireland was also hard hit by the 2008 Global Financial Crisis. The remuneration of public officials was reduced, but for judges this was prohibited under article 35.5 of the Irish Constitution. While many Irish judges voluntarily relinquished a portion of their salary, a new government in 2011 proposed to formalize the position through a constitutional amendment. In November 2011 article 35.5 was added to the Irish Constitution by a 79.7 per cent majority of those voting in the necessary referendum. The high support for the measure indicated the public view that fairness demanded that judges, like others, should share the burden. New article 35.5.3 provides, in somewhat vague terms, that where reductions are

[58] W S Holdsworth, 'Constitutional Position of the Judges' (1932) 48 LQR 25.

[59] Case C-64/16 *Associação Sindical dos Juízes Portugueses* EU:C:2018:117, [2018] 3 CMLR 553 [45] (GC).

[60] ibid [46]–[51].

made by law to those whose remuneration is paid out of public money, and that law states that those reductions are in the public interest, provision may also be made for reductions to the remuneration of judges. Pursuant to the constitutional amendment, the Oireachtas quickly enacted the Financial Emergency Measures in the Public Interest (Amendment) Act 2011, which reduced judicial salaries significantly.

(C) Discipline, Transfers, and Court Reorganization

Suspending or removing a judge on trumped up disciplinary charges can be a quicker way to influence judicial decisions than attempting to change the composition of the judiciary by manipulating appointments and promotions. It can have a chilling effect on the independence of the whole judiciary. If the judge fails to carry out their duties in a proper manner or otherwise misconducts themselves, they are properly subject to disciplinary procedures. However, as the *Universal Charter of the Judge* provides, disciplinary action must not compromise genuine judicial independence. For this reason the *Charter* provides that judicial discipline must be conducted in accordance with law and established procedures and take account of objective and relevant considerations. The procedures should involve, it suggests, an independent authority with a majority of judges or an equivalent body like a court. There must be due process, the judge may be represented, and decisions must be reasoned and subject to review.[61] With judicial independence in mind, this protection of judges against arbitrary discipline or removal runs through other codes as well. Impeaching judges before the legislature would not accord with these standards, not least because it would involve trial by a political body.

Disciplinary threats can take various forms. As part of its campaign to mould a compliant judiciary, the Polish government in December 2017 increased the potential for political influence in judicial discipline. That was through the composition of the appointing body for judges of the new disciplinary chamber of the Supreme Court. The CJEU concluded that this disciplinary regime failed to guarantee the independence and impartiality of the disciplinary chamber and thus undermined judicial independence. It held that there would be reasonable doubts as to the imperviousness of the

[61] *Universal Charter of the Judge* (n 53) art 7. For procedures for judicial discipline see pp. 174–178 below.

chamber to external influences, in particular the direct or indirect influence of the Polish legislature and executive and with respect to its neutrality.[62] Moreover, the definition of disciplinary offences was such as to potentially include 'incorrect decisions', thereby undermining judicial independence and the rule of law in Poland.[63]

Judicial transfer as a disciplinary technique has the advantage for executive governments that it can be less obvious than dismissal and the motive behind it can be camouflaged. Article 3.4 of the Council of Europe's *European Charter on the Statute for Judges* provides that a judge may not be appointed to another judicial office or assigned elsewhere, even by way of promotion, without having freely consented, except where transfer is by way of a disciplinary sanction, results from the lawful alteration of the court system, or is a temporary assignment to reinforce a neighbouring court. Unsurprisingly, both the International Commission of Jurists and the Venice Commission reported adversely on the use of transfer in Türkiye after 2016 as a hidden form of disciplinary sanction and a means to marginalize judges and prosecutors perceived as unsupportive of government interests. The forced transfer of judges, without a fair hearing and due process safeguards, was a serious threat to judicial independence both said, since it was likely to have a severe chilling effect on independent judicial decision-making.[64]

An early if unusual example of transfer as a form of discipline for unpopular decisions was Sir Edward Coke's advancement in 1613, against his will, from his position as chief justice of the Common Pleas to be chief justice of the King's Bench following a period of conflict with both the church and King. The move had been proposed to the King by the Attorney General, Francis Bacon, on the grounds that the lower fees of the new office would 'be thought abroad a kind of discipline to him for opposing himself in the king's causes'.[65] Coke was finally dismissed as a judge three years later after his decisions trenching on the royal prerogative. Transfers such as Coke's can threaten judicial independence, as much as removals. It is for this reason

[62] Case C-791/19 *European Commission v Republic of Poland (Disciplinary regime for judges)* EU:C:2021:596, [2022] 1 CMLR 15 [112]–[113] (GC).

[63] at [154]–[157].

[64] International Commission of Jurists, *Turkey: the Judicial System in Peril. A Briefing Paper* (ICJ 2016) 17–18; *Turkey: the Judicial System in Peril. A Briefing Paper* (ICJ 2019) 18; Venice Commission, Opinion No 875/2017 (Turkey) 27; Commissioner for Human Rights of the Council of Europe (Dunja Mijatović), *Report following her Visit to Turkey from 1 to 5 July 2019* (Council of Europe 2020) [116], [121].

[65] Allen D Boyer, 'Coke, Sir Edward (1552–1634)', *Oxford Dictionary of National Biography* (OUP 2004) vol 12, 451, 455.

that judges need in principle to agree to sit in a different court or division of a court.

A well-known occasion in India of forced transfers occurred in 1976. Sixteen High Court judges who had upheld the rights of detainees during the Emergency period 1975–1977 were informed that they were being moved to other courts. The media was forbidden to report on the transfers, but the names of another forty potential transferees were leaked with the implied threat that they should toe the line. One of the transferees, SH Sheth J of the Gujarat High Court, filed a writ petition against his transfer. The case reached the Supreme Court after the Emergency had ended and a new government had been elected.[66] The court held that the power to transfer had to be exercised in the public interest, which told against punitive transfers. Justices Bhagwati and Untwalia would have gone further. To protect judicial independence, they said, they would construe the power to transfer judges in article 222(1) of the Indian constitution as requiring the judge's consent as a precondition. No order was necessary in the case since after the hearing the parties reached a settlement.

Worse than transfer can be if a judge's court is restructured or its jurisdiction changed, so that in effect they are deprived of office or demoted. The IBA's *Minimum Standards of Judicial Independence* provide that in case of legislation reorganizing courts, serving judges should not be affected, except for their transfer to another court of the same status.[67] When the English High Court was constituted during the judicial reforms of the 1870s, the legislation made all senior judges members of the new court, except for those appointed at the higher level of the Court of Appeal.[68] Similarly, with the establishment of the Crown Court in the early 1970s and the court reorganization associated with it, all judges then hearing serious crime who were not High Court judges, and all county court judges, became circuit judges automatically, thus preserving their status and conditions.[69] If the reorganization of a particular court or tribunal is for genuine reasons, however, a decision not to appoint incumbent judges to the new body may be justified, despite the principle of judicial independence, if they cannot demonstrate the requisite fitness or qualities.[70]

[66] *Union of India v Sankal Chand Himatlal Sheth* 1977 AIR 2328, 1978 SCR (1) 423.
[67] (International Bar Association 1982) [20(b)].
[68] Supreme Court of Judicature Act 1873, s 5.
[69] Courts Act 1971, s 16, Sch 2, Pt 1.
[70] See *Attorney-General (New South Wales) v Quin* [1990] HCA 21, (1990) 170 CLR 1.

(D) Immunity from Suit

The principle of judicial immunity dates to the time of Coke.[71] The judge acting in their judicial capacity is protected from being sued for what they do or say, even if they are mistaken, wrong about the law, or lack authority to make an order. Since at least the beginning of the nineteenth century the justification for immunity from suit has been that it is essential to judicial independence. In an Irish case it was said that an action before a judge by a plaintiff for what another judge had done was in the nature of an appeal, an appeal from an equal to an equal, a solecism in the law, and that 'the Plaintiff's case is against the independence of the Judges'.[72] In 1868 in the Court of Exchequer, Kelly CB said that judicial immunity was 'not for the protection or benefit of a malicious or corrupt judge, but for the benefit of the public, whose interest it is that the judges should be at liberty to exercise their functions with independence, and without fear of consequences'.[73] As Lord Denning MR put it in the leading case on judicial immunity, each judge should be able to do their work 'in complete independence and free from fear'.[74] Immunity from civil liability when judges perform their judicial functions continues to be recognized as central to judicial independence.[75]

As well as protecting judicial independence, immunity from suit has other justifications. Without immunity, it is sometimes said, a judge's creativity would be frustrated for fear of provoking litigation by a bold decision. There are also the practical difficulties with allowing persons to challenge judicial acts. First, even if judges were to be indemnified against the cost of claims against them, there would still be the time, effort, and perhaps stress for them associated with defending an action. There is also the practical task facing a court in deciding whether a judge has acted in bad faith, since there would need to be a trial into the character of the judge's actions. Next, in an age of social media and crowd funding there is the danger of disgruntled litigants harassing judges or mounting collateral attacks on their judgments by suing the judge. Fourthly, public confidence in the judiciary might well be undermined if lawsuits against judges were a regular feature of the landscape. Finally, there is the principle of finality in litigation: judicial immunity

[71] *Floyd v Barker* (1607) 12 Co Rep 23, 77 ER 1305.
[72] eg, *Taaffe v Downes* (1815) 3 Moo PC 36n, 13 ER 15, 18.
[73] *Scott v Stansfield* (1868) 3 LR Ex 220, 223.
[74] *Sirros v Moore* [1975] QB 118, 136.
[75] See also *ELI-Mount Scopus European Standards* (n 8) Standard 9, comment (b).

furthers this public interest, which is best served by a single, final, decision after due process and appeal.

In English law senior judges have near absolute immunity from civil liability. Notwithstanding that a jury found that a judge of the Supreme Court of Trinidad and Tobago had acted oppressively and maliciously in committing the plaintiff to prison for contempt of court and imposing excessive bail, it was held that the judge had immunity.[76] It is only when judges act in bad faith, doing what they know they lack the power to do, that they can be liable in damages.[77] Immunity extends not only to judicial acts but also to defamatory words. When a county court judge said of a defendant before him, an accountant and scrivener, that he was 'a harpy, preying on the vitals of the poor', the Court of the Exchequer held that no action would lie against the judge, even if the words were spoken maliciously and were irrelevant to the matter before the court.[78] There would seem to be no justification for judges in lower courts not enjoying the same immunity as senior judges.[79]

The principle of immunity from suit is alive and well in other common law jurisdictions such as Australia, Canada, and New Zealand.[80] At the international level, principle 16 of the UN Basic Principles on the Independence of the Judiciary states that judges should enjoy personal immunity from civil suits for monetary damages for improper acts or omissions in the exercise of their judicial functions. In its summary of European and international standards, the European Network of Councils for the Judiciary restates principle 16, adding that judges should only have functional immunity—immunity for acts done in the course of their judicial function, or such immunity as necessary to protect their independence against the threat of wrongful arrest.[81] None of this means that judges are not accountable for their actions. The corrupt judge or the judge perverting the course of justice is as subject to criminal prosecution as the lay person. As we shall see below there are now procedures for making complaints against judges for misconduct and

[76] *Anderson v Gorrie* [1895] 1 QB 668.

[77] *In re McC (A Minor)* [1985] AC 528, 540 (Lord Bridge).

[78] *Scott v Stansfield* n 73.

[79] See *Queensland v Mr Stradford (a pseudonym)* [2025] HCA 3, discussing Australian and English authorities.

[80] ibid; *MacKeigan v Hickman* [1989] 2 SCR 796; *Gazley v Lord Cooke of Thorndon* [1999] 2 NZLR 668; *Stump v Sparkman* 435 US 349 (1978).

[81] *Independence and Accountability of the Judiciary, ENCJ Report 2013-2014*, Appendix B, 61.

for disciplinary action to be taken against them.[82] The real difficulty of immunity from suit is that litigants and others may not obtain compensation or other relief for any loss caused by the aberrant judge.[83]

There have long been critics of the present framework for judicial immunity. One avenue for reform is to place a question mark over the near absolute immunity afforded to senior judges. In 1869 Cockburn CJ expressed the belief that judges would not fail to discharge their duties faithfully and fearlessly if the immunity were abolished, and that there were cases 'in which judicial opportunity might be so perverted and abused for the purpose of injustice as that . . . the authors of such wrong ought to be responsible to the parties wronged'.[84] Reform proposals in this regard follow the path of recommending a qualified immunity protecting, say, the judge making good faith errors, but not those abusing their power or acting maliciously, recklessly, or corruptly. A second avenue for reform is to provide some means of recompense to the party or witness when a judge has clearly gone wrong. Whatever the ambit of judicial immunity, public funds should be available for those suffering loss from a judicial wrong. There is no threat to judicial independence in the way of paying compensation.

IV Structural Independence: The Judiciary

Structural independence—the structural protections of judicial independence—concern not only the individual judge but also the judiciary collectively, in other words what can be described as institutional independence. The Canadian Supreme Court has said that this two-pronged understanding of individual and institutional independence is a recognition that judges are not only charged with the fair and just adjudication of individual cases but that they also have a constitutional role in protecting values such as the rule of law and equality before the law, and in preserving democratic processes.[85]

82 P. 175 below.
83 But see *SW v United Kingdom* (2021) 73 EHRR 18. See pp. 117–118 below.
84 *Dawkins v Lord Paulet* (1869) LR 5 QB 94, 110.
85 *The Queen v Beauregard* [1986] 2 SCR 56 [23]–[24].

(A) Constitutional and Statutory Protection

Constitutional protection of judicial independence takes different forms in different jurisdictions. Judicial independence can appear expressly as a constitutional value.[86] Alternatively, it may be implied in a jurisdiction's constitution.[87] Written constitutions may also provide for a separation of powers amongst the three branches of the state—the executive, legislative, and judicial—which may underpin the constitutional protection of judicial independence. These constitutional provisions may fashion a body of autochthonous jurisprudence for each jurisdiction. Even where judicial independence is strongly entrenched constitutionally, as in the United States, the judiciary, as Alexander Hamilton famously put it, is the weakest branch.[88] Judicial independence can be undermined by populist politicians using threats such as impeachment against judges. The separation of powers does not mean an absence of any relations between the judiciary and the other branches of government. There must be contact, at the least, on bread and butter issues such as funding the judiciary.[89]

In the UK the constitutional position of the judiciary lies historically in conventions, practices, and the common law. The legislature, the executive, and the judges each have their distinct province. A rationale of their separation is to prevent the concentration of power with the consequence that the freedom of the individual is under greater potential threat. Under the rule of law the lawmakers are subject to the ordinary law and issues about its application in individual cases is in the hands of the judges, a different branch of the state. The constitutional provision in the UK is that the judges interpret the law and verify that the powers asserted by the executive government accord with the substantive law, and that the way they are exercised conforms with common law standards of fairness.[90] The principle of judicial independence means that the judges must not be subject to improper influences from the legislature or the executive in performing these tasks.

In addition to these provisions there is a statutory provision in section 3(1) of the Constitutional Reform Act 2005, which imposes a duty on

[86] eg, Constitution of South Africa, s 165(2). See *S v Van Rooyen* [2002] ZACC 8; 2002 (5) SA 246.

[87] see Case C-192/18 *European Commission v Poland* EU:C:2019:924, [2020] 2 CMLR 4 [105]-[106] (GC).

[88] *The Federalist Papers* (n 51) 437.

[89] eg, See *MacKeigan v Hickman* (n 80) [84] (McLachlin J).

[90] *R v Secretary of State for the Home Department, ex parte Fire Brigades Union* [1995] 2 AC 513, 567 (Lord Mustill).

government ministers to uphold the principle of judicial independence. As well, section 3(5) obliges ministers not to seek to influence particular judicial decisions through any special access to the judiciary. The Act also creates a separate UK Supreme Court, which replaced the appellate committee of the House of Lords as the apex court in the UK. Since its establishment in the 1870s, the appellate committee comprised professional judges, but as part of Parliament its existence might have been perceived as an infringement of the principle that judges shall not only be independent of the other branches of government but also be seen to be independent. Justices of the UK Supreme Court who are life peers are disqualified from sitting or voting in the House of Lords until their retirement.[91] However, statute authorizes the chief justice of England and Wales to present written representations—such as an annual report—to Parliament, and to give oral evidence to parliamentary committees as part of the statutory duty to represent to Parliament the views of the judiciary.[92] An older statutory protection of the principle of judicial independence is that full-time judges are disqualified from being members of the House of Commons.[93] There are also parliamentary rules preventing ministers and MPs from attacking the character or motives of judges.[94]

If additional support for judicial independence in the UK were needed, it can be found in article 6.1 of the ECHR, which requires a fair hearing by an independent and impartial tribunal in the determination of civil rights and obligations and of criminal charges. According to the ECtHR, 'independence' in article 6.1 refers to the necessary personal and institutional independence required for impartial decision-making. Personal independence relates to the judge's state of mind of being impervious to external pressure, and institutional independence refers to safeguards from influence from other state powers. In considering whether a court can be treated as independent, the Strasbourg court has said that regard must be had to matters such as the manner of appointment of its judges and their terms of office, the existence of guarantees against outside pressures, and the question whether there is an appearance of independence.[95] Article 14 of the International Covenant on Civil and Political Rights is to similar effect as article 6.1.[96]

[91] Constitutional Reform Act 2005, s 137(3).

[92] ibid, ss 5, 7(2)(a).

[93] House of Commons Disqualification Act 1975, s 1(1)(a), Sch 1, Pt I.

[94] *Erskine May Parliamentary Practice* (25th edn, LexisNexis 2019) [21.23n].

[95] eg, *Findlay v United Kingdom* App no 22107/93 (1997) 24 EHRR 221 [73]; *Dolińska-Ficek and Ozimek v Poland* App nos 49868/19 and 57511/19 (ECtHR, 8 November 2021) [316].

[96] Human Rights Committee, 'General Comment No 32' in 'Right to Equality before Courts and Tribunals and to a Fair Trial' (23 August 2007) UN Doc CCPR/C/GC/32, section III.

(B) Operational Independence

Judicial independence turns, to an extent, on the judiciary's operational (or functional) autonomy. It is essential for judicial independence that the judges control matters which bear directly and immediately on the exercise of core judicial functions. The Canadian Supreme Court has defined these core operational responsibilities in relatively narrow terms.[97] They would include public access to court buildings and hearings, procedural rules and case management, the sittings of the court, the deployment of judges, the assignment of judges to hear cases, and the listing of cases for hearing. Independence in the performance of these core functions implies judges being able to direct administrative staff as they assist in carrying them out. A judiciary's self-government in relation to other operational features such as court administration or control over their budget is not an essential precondition to its independence.

Core functions: deployment, case assignment, and procedure

Operational independence justifies judges being in the driving seat as regards at least three core functions of judicial administration—the deployment of judges to areas of work, assigning particular cases to judges, and the procedures for hearing cases. All three bear directly and immediately on the key judicial function of deciding cases. The appearance of independence in relation to these core functions of judicial administration is as important as the reality: to ensure public confidence there must be no suggestion that these functions are being manipulated by an external source or internally to achieve a particular result in a case. The ad hoc assignment of a case to a different court than usual or to an ad hoc court without ordinary procedures is likely to cast a shadow over judicial independence.[98]

First, the core function of deployment. Arrangements for the deployment of judges in England and Wales is, as a matter of statute, in the hands of the chief justice.[99] By contrast in *Prokuratura Rejonowa*[100] the CJEU considered Polish legislation under which the minister for justice could, on the basis of criteria not made public, deploy a judge to a higher criminal court for a period and could, at any time, terminate the secondment without giving

97 *Valente v The Queen* [1985] 2 SCR 673 [49], [52].
98 See *Öcalan v Turkey* App no 46221/99 (2005) 41 EHRR 45 [112]–[118].
99 Constitutional Reform Act 2005, s 7(2)(c).
100 Case C-748/19 *Prokuratura Rejonowa v Mazowieckim* EU:C:2021:931 (GC).

reasons. The minister for justice was also the prosecutor general and so had power over both the public prosecutor and the seconded judge. The CJEU held that this gave rise to reasonable doubts as to the impartiality of seconded judges when deciding a case. It was open to doubt, the court added, whether during the period of a judge's secondment they were provided with the guarantees and the independence which all judges should normally enjoy in a state governed by the rule of law.[101]

Secondly, case assignment may have a bearing on the outcome of a case and thus judicial independence. When he was lord chancellor over a decade from 1895, Lord Halsbury packed panels in the House of Lords when it was hearing cases about trade unions and other matters. Lord Denning as Master of the Rolls in the 1960s and 1970s was said to have ensured that the court over which he presided had at least one other judge who would make a majority with him. The issue of case assignment has been much ventilated in relation to the Supreme Court of India. In 2018 the four senior judges of the court took the unusual step of calling a press conference where they questioned the assignment by the then chief justice of cases to different benches of the court. This was not the first, nor the last time that the unlimited power of the chief justice of India to assign (and reassign) cases has been criticized. Despite the criticism, the Supreme Court has held that to maintain its smooth operation a chief justice must be the 'master of the roster' and have the unreviewable discretion to assign cases.[102] The court has also rejected the suggestion that the power to roster cases should be placed in the hands of a collegium of senior judges instead of the chief justice alone.[103]

The UN Basic Principles provides that case assignment within a court is an internal matter of judicial administration.[104] This reflects the long-held common law view that listing is a judicial function. Neutrality in its performance is necessary because which judge is assigned to hear a case may matter to the result since judges can have different views of the legal merits of a case. In multi-judge courts, the judges assigned to hear a case may affect the outcome if they are closely divided.[105] Moreover, in the assignment of judges to hear cases, 'courts should not only be actually independent and impartial but . . . they should also be free of any appearance of the absence of those

[101] ibid [87].
[102] *Asok Pande v Supreme Court of India* (2018) 5 SCC 341.
[103] *Shanti Bhushan v Supreme Court of India* (2018) 8 SCC 396.
[104] UN Basic Principles (n 2) para 14.
[105] See *White v Chief Constable of South Yorkshire* [1999] 2 AC 455, 502, per Lord Hoffmann; *Bachan Singh v State Of Punjab*, AIR 1982 SC 1325, 1328, (1982) 3 SCC 24, 30, per Bhagwati J.

qualities'.[106] The same applies under the fair trial provisions of article 6.1 of the ECHR—appearances of independence are important. To be compatible with that article, the Strasbourg court has said that the assignment of a case must meet the requirements of objective independence and impartiality, be independent of the executive, and not be solely dependent on the discretion of the judicial authorities.[107] To protect internal judicial independence and a court's legitimacy, a relatively objective mechanism may be necessary such as random assignment.[108]

Third is the core function of determining a court's procedures, contained in the procedural rules, practice directions, and court guides for the conduct and management of litigation. Jeremy Bentham has been one of many to underline the importance to the justice system of procedural rules. Judges (and legal practitioners) know all too well that procedure looms large in the outcome of litigation. Procedural rules can have an impact on the substantive law. A simple example is the Practice Statement issued by the House of Lords in 1996, which reversed the effect of *London Tramways Co v London County Council* under which the House of Lords was bound by its previous decisions.[109] The Practice Statement indicated that the House of Lords would treat its previous decisions as normally binding, but that it would depart from them when it appeared right to do so.[110] That approach to previous rulings is regarded as part of the established jurisprudence for appeals in the UK Supreme Court.[111] The Practice Statement has had an impact on the substantive law in that, even when it has not expressly said so, the House of Lords, and its successor the UK Supreme Court, has felt free on occasion to vary or ignore its own precedents.

However, judicial independence does not justify a judicial monopoly over procedural matters: the executive government could justifiably decide that for reasons, say, of efficiency the courts need administrative rearrangement or should ensure tighter case management, or that to further access to justice there should be measures such as more extensive class (group) litigation or different rules regarding the award of costs or litigation funding.[112] In practice the details of any changes should generally be worked out after

[106] *Yiacoub v The Queen* [2014] UKPC 22, [2014] 1 WLR 2996 [10].
[107] *Pasquini v San Marino* App no 50956/16 (2020) 70 EHRR 10 [103], [110].
[108] P. 188 below.
[109] [1898] AC 375.
[110] Practice Statement (Judicial Precedent) [1966] 1 WLR 1234.
[111] *Austin v Southwark London Borough* [2010] UKSC 28, [2011] 1 AC 355 [24]–[25].
[112] eg, Civil Procedure Act 1997, s 3A; Access to Justice Act 1999, pt IV.

consultation with the judges to ensure their practicality and legitimacy. In Britain governments have generally respected the judiciary's operational independence in deciding on procedural rules and their reform. From the nineteenth century, major procedural changes have been, with government approval, judge-led.[113] Following the Constitutional Reform Act 2005, which confers leadership responsibilities on the chief justice, procedural reform in England and Wales has originated in the judiciary, although its implementation has sometimes required the government to facilitate a statutory base.[114]

Judicial administration and budgets

Broadly speaking there are three models for administering the judicial system—the executive (or ministry of justice) model, the judiciary model, and the partnership model. Apart from core matters such as case assignment, which is in the hands of the judges, in the executive model responsibility for judicial administration is mainly conferred on government officials, usually from the ministry of justice. In the judiciary model judges are entrusted with overall authority for the courts, although they delegate the day-to-day administration to their officials. Over time there has been a move in common law countries away from the executive model to confer on the judges a greater power over court administration.[115] The trend is most evident in apex courts, where their relatively small size facilitates the adoption of some type of judiciary model. An example is the UK Supreme Court.[116] Along the spectrum between the executive and judiciary models is what can be described as the partnership model, where responsibility is shared by the executive and judicial branches. In England and Wales a 'framework agreement' between the minister for justice and the chief justice places the management of the courts with a separate body, the courts service, which has judges on its board. It is answerable to both the minister for justice and chief justice: neither may intervene in the courts' day-to-day running.[117]

113 eg, Lord Woolf, *Access to Justice: Final Report to the Lord Chancellor on the Civil Justice System in England and Wales* (HMSO 1996).

114 Lord Justice Jackson, *Review of Civil Litigation Costs: Final Report* (TSO 2009), implemented by part 2 of the Legal Aid, Sentencing and Punishment of Offenders Act 2012 and changes in the Civil Procedure Rules.

115 eg, Courts Administration Service Act, SC 2002 c 8, s 8 (Canada); Federal Court of Australia Act 1976 (Cth) s 18A; Court Services Victoria Act 2014 (Vic) s 4; Judiciary and Courts (Scotland) Act 2008, s 60, Sch 3; Courts Service Act 1998 (Ireland).

116 Constitutional Reform Act 2005, ss 48, 49(1)–(2), 51.

117 HM Courts & Tribunals Service, *Framework Document* (Cm 8882, 2014).

An advantage of the move away from the executive model is said to be to improve the quality of judicial administration since judges are more attuned to what works and what will work. There are, however, disadvantages. One is the diversion of effort of senior judges from their adjudicative functions to management tasks. Another is that judges may not have management skills or the ability to decide on matters such as the adoption of new technology. Whatever the advantages and disadvantages, there is no evidence that the judiciary model of judicial administration is essential to judicial independence. In specific contexts greater administrative control may enable judges to resist any blandishments of the executive government. However, the historical experience in common law jurisdictions belies any universal truth that the executive model of judicial administration is inconsistent with judicial independence.

Judicial councils (or councils for the judiciary) have been promoted in parts of Europe with the aim of furthering judicial independence. They had existed in France and Italy, but after the fall of communism in the 1990s the European Union, the Council of Europe, and others recommended their adoption in central and east European countries on this basis. At least one-half of their members are judges elected on a representative basis by other judges, with other members coming from civil society. The typical council is responsible for the appointment, training, promotion, and disciplining of judges and for the administration of the courts.[118] Critics contend that in some jurisdictions judicial councils have been politicized while in others, where a court's president has won dominance, there is the perverse effect of institutional independence, but not independence for the individual judges.

An adequate budget is necessary for judges to perform judicial functions. In practice judiciaries are often a Cinderella of public services. The *Latimer House Principles* contain a typical statement of principle, that securing judicial independence means allocating adequate resources enabling the judiciary 'to operate effectively without any undue constraints which may hamper [it]'.[119] The Canadian Supreme Court has established that control over the judicial budget is not a necessary element of judicial independence since it does not bear sufficiently directly and immediately on the exercise by judges of their judicial functions.[120] Judiciaries with direct access to the

[118] eg, Council of Europe, *European Charter on the Statute for Judges* (1998) DAJ/DOC(98)23, principle 1.3; Council of Europe, 'Judges: Independence, Efficiency and Responsibilities', Recommendation CM/Rec(2010)12, paras 26–29 and Explanatory Memorandum (2011) paras 34–36.

[119] *Latimer House Principles* (n 6) IV(c).

[120] *Reference re Remuneration of Judges of Provincial Court of PEI* (n 56) [253].

legislature for their moneys or with control over their budgets are not, for that reason alone, more independent than those whose funding is channelled through their finance ministry or ministry of justice. Budgetary decisions would trench on judicial independence, however, if based on the discretionary decisions of officials (instead of being founded on objective and transparent criteria), or subject to political considerations (for example, a financial cut following an adverse judicial ruling).

(C) Boundaries to Extrajudicial Functions

The core function of the judge is to adjudicate disputes. In practice judges perform a variety of other functions. While many are non-controversial auxiliary functions, others may threaten judicial independence. This is a possibility where the executive seeks the appointment of a judge for a task to use, as a cover, the judiciary's reputation for independence, fair-mindedness, and integrity. In performing the task the judge may become too entangled with the other branches of government or attract public controversy because of its nature or the manner of its performance. Extrajudicial appointments can also give the appearance of partiality or the impression that a judge has a stake in interests other than the impartial resolution of disputes in court. It can be an unhappy experience for a judge conducting a public function if challenged, even unsuccessfully, in court proceedings for acting unfairly or in a biased manner.[121]

Extrajudicial assignments therefore have the potential to jeopardize the judiciary's image as an independent and impartial arm of the state. The judiciary's reputation for impartiality can be compromised in the eyes of the public and judicial independence undermined. Whether the appointment is in the public interest is beside the point. This was starkly underlined in *South African Association of Personal Injury Lawyers v Heath*[122] where the Constitutional Court of South Africa held that a judge could not serve as the head of a special investigation unit for corruption and improper conduct in state institutions. In doing so the Constitutional Court recognized the public benefit in confronting the threats to democracy these practices posed and the

[121] eg, *Chrétien v Gomery* 2010 FCA 283, 409 NR 193 (FCA, Canada); *Air New Zealand Ltd v Mahon* [1984] AC 808 (PC, NZ); *Godongwana v Pillay J* [2009] ZAECGHC 29 (HC, South Africa, Eastern Cape).

[122] [2000] ZACC 22; 2001 (1) SA 883.

positive role the judge would play. However, there was the partisan nature of the investigations and as part of that the litigation to be undertaken to recover losses to the state. Ultimately, said the court, the question was whether the judge would be performing functions incompatible with judicial office and, if so, whether that would be harmful to the judiciary as an institution or materially breach the required line with the executive 'to maintain the independence of the judiciary'.[123]

Auxiliary functions

Certain types of extrajudicial function are unexceptional and no threat to judicial independence. These may be termed auxiliary activities to recognize their closeness to the judicial function. Court management is one such function, along with judges serving on bodies responsible for the appointment, promotion, and disciplining of judges. Involvement in legal education is another, either formally through participation in supervisory bodies, or informally in part-time teaching at law schools. Since it was founded in 1965 the Law Commission in England and Wales has been chaired by a judge.[124] That has also been a practice with comparable law reform bodies elsewhere. The focus on these bodies tends to be on lawyer's law rather than more controversial topics involving social legislation. A further example is the Sentencing Council for England and Wales, which promotes greater consistency in sentencing practice. That is chaired by a judge and has a majority of judicial members.[125] None of these auxiliary activities should threaten the reality or appearance of judicial independence. They are ancillary to judging and enhance the law and the administration of justice through its modernization and the promotion of the competence and standing of the legal profession, including judges. Only occasionally do they attract public criticism.

Once one goes beyond auxiliary activities like these, there are questions about serving judges acting in other extrajudicial capacities. Depending on the context, this may not threaten the reality and public perception of independence. The participation of judges in boundary commissions is one such case.[126] In places like the UK, Canada, and New Zealand their role in keeping electoral boundaries up to date with population changes has generally been without controversy and ensures that this dimension of enhancing

[123] ibid [31], per Chaskalson P for the court.
[124] See now Law Commissions Act 1965, s 1(1A).
[125] Coroners and Justice Act 2009, Sch 15, paras 1–3.
[126] eg, Parliamentary Constituencies Act 1986, Sch 1, para 3(a).

representative democracy has legitimacy in the eyes of the public. Another example was the appointment of Lord Nolan, while still a judge, as the first chair of the Committee on Standards in Public Life, which scrutinizes the ethical standards of public officials in Britain. It was established at a point when there was much criticism of the conduct of the British political class. The seven principles of public life enunciated by the committee—selflessness, integrity, objectivity, accountability, openness, honesty, and leadership—are those long expected of judges. The importance of the committee's work has been universally acknowledged. No harm to the judiciary was caused by Nolan's appointment; it may even have enhanced its standing.

On the other hand, the appearance of judicial independence was threated when President Franklin D Roosevelt had as unofficial advisers those he had appointed to the US Supreme Court, notably Professor Felix Frankfurter. Along the spectrum is that, after the Second World War, Justice Jackson of the US Supreme Court took leave to be the chief prosecutor at the Nuremberg trials of Nazi war criminals. He was criticized by Harlan Stone CJ for undermining judicial independence, although others were supportive. Justice Arbour, then of the Ontario Court of Appeal, was lauded by Canadians when she served as chief prosecutor at the International Criminal Tribunals for Rwanda and the Former Yugoslavia. The Canadian parliament amended the Judges Act to enable her to take leave from her judicial duties to fulfil these roles.[127] Before the establishment of the UK Supreme Court, judges of the House of Lords sometimes participated in debates in the parliamentary chamber. Some of these debates involved issues of law or judicial administration and no harm was done. Others concerned matters of high political controversy.[128] The danger has largely passed since justices of the UK Supreme Court are no longer automatically appointed as members of the House of Lords.

Public inquiries: investigative and policy/advisory

A type of extrajudicial assignment is the appointment of judges to public inquiries and commissions.[129] Investigative inquiries are one type, where judges perform the sort of fact-finding they might undertake in court. Examples are inquiries into prominent or mass deaths or major disasters. It might be thought that these would be straightforward and could be

[127] Judges Act, RSC, 1985, c J-1, s 56.1(1)–(5).

[128] eg, Hansard, HL Deb 12 March 2001, vol 623, col 629.

[129] See also 309 below.

conducted without any threat to judicial independence. The continuing controversy surrounding the commission on the assassination of President Kennedy, chaired by Warren CJ of the US Supreme Court, puts paid to that belief.[130] Similarly in Britain there was media condemnation of the report by a judge in the House of Lords, Lord Hutton, into the death of a former UN weapons inspector, Dr Kelly, who had been publicly identified as the source of stories critical of the government's rationale for the invasion of Iraq.[131] Much of the criticism was because the Hutton report did not produce the outcome the media would have preferred, a condemnation of the prime minister and his government. Coronial inquiries by senior judges into the circumstances surrounding the deaths of Princess Diana and of ninety-seven football fans in the Hillsborough stadium disaster in 1989 received a more favourable reception.[132]

If investigative inquiries can attract controversy, it should not be surprising that this can be doubly so when serving judges undertake inquires which are more policy-oriented or advisory in nature. A well-known example in Britain is the Leveson Inquiry into the press, which was appointed in the wake of a scandal where journalists were revealed to have hacked telephones to access information for stories.[133] Sir Brian Leveson, a member of the Court of Appeal, recommended a statutory base for a new press complaints authority, which was widely criticized in the media and never adopted. Another example is Lord Justice Scott's inquiry into the sale of arms to Iraq in the 1980s.[134] It raised important issues about the accountability of ministers and the government to Parliament, but its impact was diminished because of allegations of inefficiencies and unfairness in its conduct (many by those in the firing line). Having a more positive impact was the Bloody Sunday inquiry, chaired by a sitting law lord, Lord Saville, into events in Northern Ireland on Sunday, 30 January 1972, when British soldiers fired on and killed thirteen people, injuring more, during a protest march.[135] Reception of Lord

[130] *Report of the President's Commission on the Assassination of President Kennedy* (US Government Printing Office 1964).

[131] *Report of the Inquiry into the Circumstances Surrounding the Death of Dr David Kelly CMG by Lord Hutton*, HC 247 (Stationery Office 2004).

[132] See *R (on the application of Al Fayed) v Assistant Deputy Coroner of Inner West London* [2008] EWHC 713 (Admin) and *R (on the application of Crompton) v South Yorkshire Police and Crime* Commissioner [2017] EWHC 1349 (Admin), [2018] 1 WLR 131, [15]–[17] respectively.

[133] *An Inquiry into the Culture, Practices and Ethics of the Press, Report*, HC 779 (Stationery Office 2012).

[134] *Report of the Inquiry into Exports of Defence Equipment and Dual-Use Goods to Iraq and Related Prosecutions* (HMSO 1996).

[135] *Report of the Bloody Sunday Inquiry* (2010, HC 29).

Scarman's report on the Brixton riots in 1981 was also positive and contributed to the enactment of the Police and Criminal Evidence Act 1984.[136]

For present purposes the issue is not whether serving judges conducting policy-oriented or advisory inquiries produce worthwhile or generally acceptable conclusions, but whether their participation might compromise their individual independence and that of the judiciary as a whole. The issue is not as acute where an inquiry is undertaken by a retired judge, but for the sitting judge there is the threat of criticism by the media or entanglement in political controversy, which may tarnish individual and institutional reputations. The Bloody Sunday inquiry confirmed criticism at the time of errors in an earlier inquiry into those events, conducted by the then chief justice of England and Wales, Lord Widgery.[137] In the process of conducting the inquiry a judge may opine on matters about which their court may later adjudicate. Using serving judges for such inquiries has the direct cost of taking judges away from judging. There is an added danger if judges become commentators on their reports, more so if they are advocates for the implementation of their recommendations. Advocacy undermines the appearance of independence and impartiality. Where boundaries to extrajudicial activities are drawn differs between jurisdictions.

Outside appointments: four approaches

Within that broad framework the approach to appointing judges varies in different jurisdictions. Protecting judicial independence is at the forefront of some of them. The first approach is absolutist, that judges are appointed to decide cases in court and extrajudicial roles outside the administration of justice are not permitted. The absolutist approach was established in the Australian state of Victoria a century ago when the government requested a judge to serve as a Royal Commissioner into a misuse of public funds. Irvine CJ informed the Attorney General that having consulted all the judges of his court none would be available to sit on non-judicial governmental bodies. The duty of the judges, he explained, was to adjudicate cases. Confining themselves to this function had meant that the judges had, except in rare cases, retained public confidence and not been drawn into public controversy. Though presenting on their face some features of a judicial character, Irvine CJ added, inquiries resulted 'only in findings of fact

[136] Lord Scarman, *Report on the Brixton Disorders of 10–12 April 1981* (Cmnd 8427, 1981).
[137] *Report of the Tribunal Appointed to Inquire into the Events on Sunday, 30 January 1972* (1972, HL 101, HC 220).

which were likely to become the subject of political debate'.[138] The position in the so-called Irvine memorandum was reasserted by all the judges of the Victorian Supreme Court in 1952. It is still the norm and sitting (but not retired) Victorian judges rarely accept appointment to public inquires.

The second is a 'separation of powers approach', focusing on the institutional independence of the judiciary and the condition that an extrajudicial appointment must not be incompatible with the reality and appearance of the judiciary's constitutionally guaranteed separateness. In recent times the High Court of Australia has evolved a specialized jurisprudence along these lines, which has tightened restrictions on extrajudicial appointments. *Wilson v Minister for Aboriginal and Torres Strait Islander Affairs*[139] is illustrative. There the High Court held that a government minister could not appoint a federal court judge to report on whether areas of land should be classified as First Nation heritage. Performance of a quasi-judicial function like this, it asserted, compromised public confidence in the integrity of the judge and the judiciary if it was integral or closely connected with the legislature or the executive; if the judge was subject to executive instruction or advice; or if the function would be exercised on political grounds. The court concluded, rather surprisingly, that the judge in this case was equivalent to a ministerial adviser, even if only in theory she was open to ministerial direction, liable to removal as inquirer, and reporting on matters political in character.[140]

The third is an approach which seeks to identify a list of appointments which are thought to jeopardize judicial independence. These may be general in character and offer, at most, guidance as to what is impermissible. The guidance may be supplemented by published advice on specific cases so that a list can be consolidated as to what is allowed or forbidden. The US *Code of Conduct* for federal judges is somewhat along these lines.[141] Canon 4 provides that a judge should not participate in extrajudicial activities that detract from the dignity of the judge's office, interfere with the performance of the judge's official duties, reflect adversely on the judge's impartiality, lead to frequent disqualification, or violate the specific limitations set out. Canon 4F then contains strict limitations to an appointment to a governmental committee or commission: it is only permissible if it concerns the law, the legal

[138] Irvine CJ's letter is set out in full in Mr Justice McInerney, 'The Appointment of Judges to Commissions of Enquiry and other Extra-Judicial Activities' in *Judicial Essays* (Law Foundation of NSW and Victoria 1974) 37.

[139] [1996] HCA 18, (1996) 189 CLR 1.

[140] ibid [25]–[26].

[141] *Code of Conduct for United States Judges*, Guide to Judiciary Policy, vol 2A, ch 2.

system, or the administration of justice, or if the appointment of a judge is required by federal statute. The commentary to Canon 4F provides that the appropriateness of accepting extrajudicial assignments must be assessed in light of the need to protect the courts from involvement in matters that may prove to be controversial. These code provisions are supplemented by the possibility of a judge seeking an advisory opinion from the Committee on Codes of Conduct established for that purpose.

Finally, there is the ad hoc approach in Britain. Possibly because of the judiciary's high reputation, the official attitude has been relatively sanguine about any damage to judicial independence and public confidence when judges are appointed to undertake public inquiries. It has long been assumed that the state will turn to judges at times of crisis to restore integrity or to provide reassurance. In 2004 the government stated that it was appropriate for judges to chair inquiries because their experience and position made them well suited to the role in analysing evidence, determining facts, and reaching conclusions.[142] The Judicial Office for England and Wales explained in one publication that judges may be called on to chair official reviews of events or decisions because of their impartiality and experience—inquiries investigating issues of serious public concern, and high-profile inquests to establish the causes of death of those who appear to have died by violent or unnatural means.[143] In practice in England approval of the chief justice is required. The limit to the appointment of a sitting judge tends to be availability, so that public inquiries in England are often conducted by retired judges.

V Behavioural Independence

There are two broad categories of behavioural independence, what can be described as personal independence and cultural independence. Personal independence is concerned with the state of mind of the judge—the courage of the judge to perform judicial functions, despite being subject to pressures, influences, threats, and temptations. What can be termed cultural independence encompasses the historical backing for the idea of judicial independence in a jurisdiction, and the conventions, traditions, and norms which bolster it. Both personal and cultural independence are underpinned by the supportive behaviour of political, professional, media, and civil society

142 Department of Constitutional Affairs, *Effective Inquiries* (CP 12/04, 2004) para 46.
143 *The Judicial System of England and Wales A Visitor's Guide* (Judicial Office, nd) 41–42.

organizations. In some jurisdictions personal and cultural independence may be more strongly protective in practice of judicial independence than the structural features encompassed by any adjudicative or institutional independence.

A simple example is that before the establishment of the UK Supreme Court in 2009 the judges (the law lords) in the apex court—the appellate committee of the House of Lords—could behave in a bold and independent manner. Especially with the growth of judicial review from the 1960s, they regularly decided claims against the interests of the government and other public bodies. However, the House of Lords as a court lacked institutional independence from the legislature since it was part of the second chamber of parliament. Nor was it institutionally independent of the executive government: a member of the cabinet, the lord chancellor, presided over its hearings until well into the twentieth century and was also head of the judiciary. The judicial independence of the law lords derived from their earlier careers as independent barristers, their background (with one or two exceptions) as professional judges, and the history, conventions, and norms which supported their role as independent judges.

(A) Personal Independence: The Judge's 'State of Mind'

Structural protections of judicial independence only go so far. Along with institutional independence, the ECtHR emphasizes the personal independence of the judge—the 'state of mind, which denotes a judge's imperviousness to external pressure as a matter of moral integrity'.[144] In other words the individual judge needs the strength of character to deflect improper influences and blandishments and to withstand pressures and threats. The structural protections may not be relevant to the operation of these forces or, if they are, will not be strong enough for the judge to resist them in their decision-making unless they have the moral integrity to do so. This quality is sometimes summed up as judicial courage. It derives in part from the judge's own character but also from their socialization. As law students, judges learn to take legal rules, legal ethics, and the rule of law seriously, albeit that they learn about uncertainty in the law and its application and the need for legal reform. At the bar or as part-time or full-time professional judges they

[144] eg, *Dolińska-Ficek and Ozimek v Poland* (n 95) [316].

further assimilate the understanding that judicial decision-making should not be arbitrary or ideological but should be justified by reasons grounded on legal principle. Judges will also have imbibed the crucial lesson that judicial independence demands integrity on their part and is not there to enable them to abuse the judicial role and diverge from accepted paradigms.

The challenges to a judge's personal independence and moral integrity are many and varied. They range from the subtle and informal to the blatant and hard-edged. First, the challenge may be largely internal to the judge. Even though judges have considerable autonomy they may not think and behave independently. A judge may have an attitude of mind that the job will be easier if despite doubts they accept the status quo or simply agree with their fellow judges rather than working through an issue themselves. Another example is if the judge owes appointment to a person or (political) movement, and then on the bench aligns with their interests when relevant issues arise. Further, a judge may decide a case strategically to win the approval of a particular audience—more senior judges, the executive, or the public. The temptation to do this may be accentuated if the judge is seeking promotion or faces reappointment or re-election.[145]

Apart from internal challenges, there are the external pressures on a judge's moral integrity. Some of these may derive from the general social milieu in which they live and work. A stark example was the position of those federal judges in southern US states, who had to dismantle desegregation in education following the US Supreme Court decisions in *Brown v Board of Education*.[146] The judges had to do this despite the opposition of the overwhelming majority of the white population, which abhorred the law which the judges had to implement. The role of one of these judges, Judge J Skelly Wright, a federal district judge in Louisiana from 1949 to 1962, has been highlighted. Together with his family, he faced social ostracism, vilification, and anonymous threats as he made court orders for desegregation in the face of state, local, and popular obstruction.

Then there are the specific challenges to the judge's personal independence. Financial inducements, including a bribe, are an obvious example.[147] As we have seen the threats from government include that if decisions involving its interests are unfavourable a judge may be dismissed, be transferred to a less desirable post, or forfeit any chance of advancement. Threats

[145] P. 154 below.
[146] 347 US 483 (1954), 349 US 294 (1955).
[147] PP. 129–132 below.

may be explicit but may be conveyed implicitly by, for instance, the treatment of other judges in a similar position. Threats follow predictably with the arrival of populist, authoritarian, or totalitarian regimes. It requires moral integrity for a judge to continue if they are not dismissed or do not resign. The historical experience is that many judges resist. In some contexts it has been possible to challenge changes to the judiciary with the support of judges' associations, the bar, civil society groups, and regional and international organizations. An example is the Polish judges who successfully invoked the support of European courts against the subversion of judicial independence by the populist Polish government in the period 2015–2023.[148]

Another possibility, as with the small number of 'liberal judges' in apartheid South Africa is that, with care, the judge may be able to interpret legal principles against state interests. The judge may know, however, that those decisions may be successfully appealed to a court stacked with government-supporting judges, and that one's freedom of manoeuvre may be compromised through judicial redeployment or case assignment. A third possibility is of the judge moving beyond dissent to mount opposition to the regime: in Nazi Germany and the countries it occupied, a few dissident judges acted for a time contrary to the law to protect individuals by persuading state officials to overlook matters, or, in a few cases, by manipulating or destroying evidence.

(B) Cultural Independence: Society's Support

Judicial independence is, in part, a relational concept, concerning the relationship of a judiciary to the society in which it works. The nature of the relationship between judges and their society, and the structural solutions to which it gives rise, vary over time and between jurisdictions. What can be termed a culture of judicial independence can develop historically. It comprises norms, conventions, traditions, and understandings which caution governments and others against measures threatening judicial independence. It will lead to different institutional forms in different jurisdictions. However, in broad terms it will involve the executive government and legislature accepting that they must not attempt to circumvent the structural protections of judicial independence or to influence the judge's adjudicative

[148] See pp. 10, 20 above.

independence. In addition, the executive government and legislature will accept the need to comply with court orders, even if they occasionally decide (if entitled to by constitutional arrangements) to reverse the effect of a legal decision by statute. Despite inevitable tensions, there should be a mutual respect between the three branches of the state. The societal expectation will be that judges decide cases free from outside interference.

Forging a culture of judicial independence can take time. In the UK it emerged in embryonic form from the struggle between the King and Parliament and the civil war of the seventeenth century. Security of tenure was recognized in the Act of Settlement 1701 but until 1760 judges still lost office on the death of a monarch. Senior judges continued their involvement in government. In the mid eighteenth century Lord Mansfield, known for enunciating important principles of English commercial law, sat in the cabinet. The lord chancellor (the minister of justice) could sit as a judge until the end of the twentieth century. Only with the Constitutional Reform Act 2005 did the lord chancellor cease to be head of the judiciary. The most senior judges as members of the House of Lords could participate in parliamentary debates. In the first part of the twentieth century a chief justice was removed to appoint in his place a senior politician. Until the mid twentieth century, when professional standing became the major factor in appointments to the bench, politicians were often made judges as a reward for political service or for the purpose of political management.

However, it had become accepted that judges should not be subject to pressure from government or politicians. As early as 1607 the King's Bench held that the King himself could not give judgment in any case; it was for the court to do that.[149] For Sir Matthew Hale, a noted jurist and chief justice of the King's Bench from 1671, independence was an unstated theme in his private rules for a judge, which were published in the eighteenth century.[150] Although the English courts did not have the power to strike down legislation, under the principles of judicial review they granted remedies against individual governmental acts regarded as unlawful—in the nineteenth century in claims against local government bodies, in the twentieth century against central government.[151] Beginning in the 1960s the pace of judicial review

[149] *Prohibitions del Roy* [1607] EWHC KB J23, 12 Co Rep 64, 77 ER 1342.

[150] Reproduced in Maija Jansson, 'Matthew Hale on Judges and Judging' (1988) 9 J Leg Hist 201.

[151] eg, *R v Local Government Board ex p Arlidge* [1915] AC 120; *Errington v Minister of Health* [1935] 1 KB 249.

quickened, and since the Human Rights Act 1998 the grounds on which government decisions can be challenged have expanded.

In short it took a significant period for the principle of judicial independence to imbed itself in the UK in legal, political, and social culture. It was as much a political as a legal achievement. Norms, customs, understandings, and conventions evolved to the point that it was regarded as anathema for ministers to attempt to influence the outcome of a decision in its favour, except through submissions in open court, a principle now embodied in statute.[152] The culture of judicial independence means that government complies with judicial orders, even though in many hundreds of judicial review and human rights challenges each year government decisions are declared unlawful or stuck down. Rarely will government seek to reverse a ruling. If it does it will be through accepted legal channels, including legislation. For the individual judge, ruling against the government is not a bad mark. Acceptance of judicial rulings and of judicial review are reflected in the relatively high levels of confidence which the public have in the judges. As in other jurisdictions judicial independence is reinforced by the support it receives from the bar. There is episodic criticism of judicial activism following specific rulings. Parliament occasionally legislates to limit judicial review and human rights challenges.[153] But on the whole political support for judicial independence is high, which is evident in the legislation placing on ministers the obligation to uphold it.[154]

As in the UK, the contours of judicial independence turn on the social and political context in which judges work. In some societies the public may accept attacks on judicial independence by populist politicians because they are indifferent to its value or are sympathetic to a narrative that the judiciary is biased and partisan, divorced from the popular will, or part of a state within a state. In other societies the judiciary may appear assertively independent, frequently overruling government decisions, but this might follow because judges have been corrupted by powerful commercial interests or even organized crime and are striking at government attempts to curb them through prosecutions and regulatory enforcement. Elsewhere the relative absence of rulings against the government may not be because the judiciary is supine but because a society is relatively homogenous and there is a high

[152] Constitutional Reform Act 2005, s 3(5).

[153] Judicial Review and Courts Act 2022, pt 1; Criminal Justice and Courts Act 2015, s 84(1)–(2).

[154] Constitutional Reform Act 2005, s 3(1).

degree of consensus around public policy. As well as the influence of these internal social factors, judicial independence may be strengthened by external advocacy or pressure, as where an independent judiciary is a precondition for a country to become a member of a regional organization such as the EU, or to receive financial support from an international financial institution such as the World Bank.

How context can shape judicial independence is illustrated by the appointment of Supreme and High Court judges in India. Article 123 of the Indian constitution provides that the president shall appoint Supreme Court judges after consultation with the chief justice of India. In *Supreme Court Advocates on Record Association v Union of India*[155] the Supreme Court held that only the chief justice and senior judges ("the collegium") could choose the judges. Judicial independence and the structure of the constitution were at the base of the court's reasoning. The background to the decision was that the judiciary had been scarred by prime minister Indira Gandhi's declaration of an Emergency (1975–1977) and the interference with the judiciary associated with her time in office.[156] Following criticism that the collegium system lacked transparency and facilitated favouritism, the government sought to establish a national judicial appointments commission. In what is known as the *Fourth Judges Case*[157] the Supreme Court held that this constituted a violation of judicial independence, the separation of powers, and the basic structure of the constitution. Following the case, criticism of the collegium system has continued but the legacy of the Emergency period is strongly embedded in judicial consciousness.

VI Judicial Accountability

Judicial independence is a foundational principle for the operation of the rule of law but runs together with judicial accountability. The two are mutually reinforcing. Accountability, transparency, and integrity in the judiciary, the UN has said, is 'an essential element of judicial independence and as a concept inherent to the rule of law'.[158] The exact mix of judicial

155 1993 (4) SCC 441, AIR 1994 SC 268.
156 P. 157 below.
157 *Supreme Court Advocates-on-record Association v Union of India* (2016) 5 SCC 1.
158 eg, UNGA 'Independence and impartiality of the judiciary, jurors and assessors, and the independence of lawyers' (16 July 2020) A/HRC/RES/44/9, preamble.

independence and accountability turns on a society's institutional architecture, specifically the role of the courts and their operation. Whatever form judicial accountability takes, it must be consistent with judicial independence and with judicial decision-making according to law. Its overall rationale is ensuring public confidence in the judges and the legitimacy of judicial power. It ensures that judicial decisions are checked by law, that judicial behaviour is consistent with the judicial role, and that judges recognize that public officials and the public have a justifiable interest in their performance.

In democratic societies institutions are regularly called on to account for their actions. Accountability functions to control power. The mechanisms for accountability have multiplied. Judges have not escaped the trend. Along with others entrusted with public power they are accountable to the community for its exercise. The traditional focus of accountability was internal, and centred on the judicial function, making decisions fairly and in accordance with law. Accountability through appellate review is an important aspect of this. Over time accountability has run more widely. Public justification is an essential aspect: exercises of judicial power must be supported by substantive reasons, not by simple recourse to legal, procedural, or constitutional values. Accountability extends as well to matters such as the composition, performance, and conduct of the judiciary and to the system of judging. Judicial accountability covers both the individual accountability of the judge and the institutional accountability of the judiciary.

Accountability of individual judges and of the judiciary as an institution runs through different topics discussed in the book. There is accountability to ensure impartiality and integrity in decision-making discussed in Chapters 2 and 3, for a judge's personal conduct and performance covered in Chapters 3 and 4, and for performance and better decision-making addressed in Chapter 5. After canvassing the different dimensions to judicial accountability, the discussion in this chapter focuses on crucial aspects of traditional accountability—reasoned decision-making and open justice—before concluding with a sketch of public accountability. Reasoned decision-making and open justice are fundamental principles in the common law as regards how judging is to be conducted. The first is a type of explanatory accountability, in that judges justify their decisions with reasons. Reasons are also conducive to good decision-making. Open justice goes to transparency and imparts information on the conduct of proceedings in court leading to judicial decisions. Along with the giving of reasons, it assists in legitimizing the exercise of judicial power.

(A) Dimensions of Accountability

Judicial accountability can be analysed in two broad categories. First is the subject matter of accountability. It is possible to identify three areas—decisions, judicial behaviour, and the judiciary as an institution. Next are what can be characterized as the mechanisms for accountability. Broadly conceived these mechanisms fall under the heads of legal, managerial, and public accountability. Finally, there is accountability through the parliamentary and public criticism of judges and the necessary restraints on this if judicial legitimacy is to be maintained.

Subject matter accountability: decisional, behavioural, and institutional

Decisional accountability turns primarily on the reasons judges give for their decisions. That requires that decisions be publicly available, specifically, that judgments be published. Public or commercial services do this for the higher courts on their websites, if not in hard copy. In a number of countries, non-governmental legal information institutes publish judgments online, at no charge, along with other legal material, to enable the public to access and understand the law.[159] Unless regulated the publication of judgments online opens the way to the extraction of information for the commercial purpose of attempting to forecast for the benefit of lawyers, litigation funders, insurers, and others the chances of success of certain types of claims with certain judges.

A further dimension to decisional accountability is the time taken to hear cases, delays in delivering decisions, disposal rates, and backlogs. Litigants and the public have a right to expect that judges will perform the task of decision-making efficiently and effectively.[160] Quantitative output data for judges, however, is only one measure of performance. It does not touch on process values such as fairness in hearing cases or qualitative values such as whether the content of a judge's decision is up to the mark. Moreover, it is affected by the adequacy of resources, over which judges have little, if any, control—for example, whether the parties have effective representation to present their case, and whether the judges themselves have support to do the job. Moreover, quantitative data fails to capture the importance of the lawmaking function of judges in a common law system. Senior judges are not only settling the parties' disputes but also establishing precedents. In

[159] eg, <www.bailii.org>; <www.commonlii.org>; <www.law.cornell.edu>.
[160] P. 121 below.

non-routine cases they may be applying legal principles to new situations or adapting those principles to changing conditions.

Secondly, there is behavioural accountability: judges may be called upon to account for their conduct as someone who occupies the role of judge. The most effective accountability for a person's conduct is to self. Judges are socialized into the norms of acceptable behaviour, whether this relates to how they conduct a hearing or to how they act as an individual. Self-reflection can improve a judge's performance and conduct. A judge acquires the reputation of being a 'good judge' since they have internalized the relevant norms. 'Good judging' becomes second nature. As well as accountability to self, judges are held responsible for their behaviour through informal, professional processes. Counsel who regularly appear before a judge and colleagues are crucial in this. A judge acquires the reputation of being a 'good judge' when they are fair, polite, impartial, and efficient in court, and their judgments deploy acceptable means of legal analysis and are delivered within a reasonable period. Judges can amend their behaviour in response to professional, collegial, and even public opinion.

Behavioural accountability for misconduct may occur informally as a leadership judge or colleagues point out a better way for a judge to act or to accomplish a goal, or that certain behaviour is unacceptable. Judges may be given a mentor for a period. If the judge reacts positively that can be the end of the matter. Judges may also be responsive to what any guidance or code of conduct suggests is the ethical course to be adopted as regards the type of issue the judge faces. Ultimately behavioural accountability may occur through the more formal disciplinary processes.[161] Dissatisfaction with the conduct of a judge may lead a litigant or lawyer to invoke the formal machinery for complaints. Moreover, at the initiative of a leadership judge or colleague a judge may be called to account and sanctioned under these processes.

In some jurisdictions, judges are subject to formal performance evaluation. The factors assessed may include legal knowledge, integrity, impartiality, communication skills, judicial temperament, and administrative ability. Measuring these features is not easy but may be attempted through use of surrogate factors. Feedback from an evaluation flows to the individual judge and might be more widely published. Evaluation may be undertaken by bodies comprised of judges, members of the legal profession, and laypeople,

[161] PP. 174–178 below.

who draw on the experience and views of those directly involved with the judiciary in the course of an evaluation. After evaluating individual judges, the next step would be to draw comparisons between them. Here the difficulties are enhanced. A full evaluation is not possible without knowing the details of matters such as the nature of the work the judge undertakes, the quality of the material typically presented by the parties, and the nature of the court. A judge with good metrics is not necessarily a good judge.

Institutional accountability has various aspects, but its main concern is how the judiciary as an institution is answerable for matters such as access to justice, the administration of the courts, the appointment, training, and disciplining of judges, and the efficient use of public resources. Decision-making in this regard is different from judicial decision-making, albeit that it varies depending on its legal base, rationale, subject matter, and methods. The principle of fairness which applies to court hearings would be a hinderance to administrative decision-making, although it is appropriate to determinations about judicial discipline. Scrutiny requires that data about matters needs to be collected. Moreover, not all aspects of judicial administration may be open to scrutiny. The assignment of cases to judges is regarded as an internal matter and an aspect of judicial independence.[162] Process accountability in this respect is lacking. Whatever administrative decision-making is involved, judges must act efficiently, impartially, competently, and with integrity in order to maintain public confidence in the judiciary as an institution. Public money is involved and the public are entitled to know that it is being appropriately and effectively spent.

Accountability for the institutional efficiency of judging is through a variety of mechanisms. As far as the contribution of individual judges is concerned, the accountability mechanisms are professional in character rather than bureaucratic or legal. As regards litigation, judges have an individual and collective responsibility to handle cases professionally and in an efficient manner. This is achieved in part through the way judges are allocated to the court's caseload and how individual cases themselves are listed and managed. Despatching judicial business efficiently, fairly, and professionally, and having procedures which are accessible, fair, and proportionate, are largely in the hands of the judges. Since these are essential to public confidence, leadership judges such as the chief justice may collect and publish information about such matters—through an annual report, a lecture, a press conference,

[162] PP. 28–29 above.

or an appearance before a parliamentary committee about the state of the judiciary.[163] In this way the judiciary explains its collective achievements and the issues it faces, as well as the steps taken to address them and what more needs to be done.

The tradition in common law countries has been against handing responsibility for key institutional features like budgets and the administration of the courts to the judges themselves, except with the highest (apex) courts.[164] This has been resisted because if the judges could set their own budget, they would have the power to determine priorities without the accountability which normally applies with the expenditure of public money. Accountability for the operation of the courts therefore lies with others: with the government in terms of resources and the overall structure (through legislation) of the justice system, and with public officials or an arm's length public body—a court service—as regards managing the courts. The judges may have limited responsibility, perhaps through the chief justice's involvement in negotiations for an acceptable budget, and through judicial participation on the board of the court service. Primary accountability, whether probity accountability for the use of resources, or performance accountability for the operation of the courts, lies with the responsible minister and the court service. They are accountable to parliament, auditors, and perhaps a court ombudsperson.

Mechanisms of accountability: legal, managerial, and public accountability

Legal accountability is the obvious starting point in any consideration of the mechanisms of judicial accountability. Judges are not subject to what has been called sacrificial accountability, in other words, they do not need to resign even if an appellate court finds them to be in serious error in their decision-making. Rather, judicial accountability is explanatory accountability: in performing the core judicial function of finding facts and considering the legal principles appropriate to those facts, judges must act in accordance with law and give reasons to the parties to explain the result. The obligation of judges in the exercise of the judicial function is to justify their decisions through these reasons. In turn those decisions must be made in accordance with the principle of open justice, which lends transparency to the process of judging. Accountability is thereby strengthened because the

[163] eg, Constitutional Reform Act 2005, ss 5, 7(2)(a).
[164] P. 31 above.

courts are open to the public and the media, and the reasons a judge gives are available for scrutiny by the profession and others.

Legal accountability also includes appellate review. A judge's decisions are subject to review for legal and other error (except for judges in apex courts), where other judges review a judge's decision. This could be characterized as a form of corrective accountability where the appellate court corrects the error of the lower court and allows the appeal or sends the matter back for correction or possibly a new trial. At common law a judge cannot be asked for any further explanation of the reasons given for a decision, a principle established by Holt CJ in the late seventeenth century.[165] The reasons stand alone as the judge's justification for the decision. Judicial independence and the judiciary's position as the third arm of the state are the background to this principle that judges do not have to explain their decision-making any further. If a judicial decision is unacceptable or the reasoning inadequate, no sanction may be imposed on the judge.

Nor has legal accountability anything to do with the formal mechanisms of political accountability to which public bodies (like the courts service) are subject. Senior judges may appear before legislative committees to give an account of the overall operation of the judiciary as an institution, and in some cases to assist understanding on the part of the legislators about areas of law and its administration. However, there can be no accountability as regards decision-making in particular cases. Nor can the judges be drawn on the merits of government policy or political matters more generally unless these relate to judicial administration. Accountability is confined to the remote possibility that senior judges can be removed by resolution of both houses of the legislature for aberrant decisions constituting misbehaviour or incapacity. There is also a tenuous form of parliamentary accountability in the rare case where the legislature decides to reverse the effect of a judicial decision.[166]

Managerial accountability flows from the administrative and managerial functions of judges. Individual judges will be accountable for their performance internally within the judiciary. Examples include the timelines of decisions, punctuality in court, and communicating with court staff about the progress of work such as the completion of written decisions without a hearing. Leadership judges such as a chief justice may have varying degrees

[165] *Knowles' Trial* (1692) 12 Howell's State Trials 1167, 1179. See also *MacKeigan v Hickman* (n 80) [90] (McLachlin J).

[166] *Vriend v Alberta* [1998] 1 SCR 493 [139] (Iacobucci J).

of accountability to the executive or parliament for the judiciary as an institution. This may include the use of resources, accountability for judicial appointments and discipline, and the efficient functioning of the courts covering matters such as court delays.

Public accountability takes various forms. One is the reputational accountability of judges about what they do through professional evaluation and public scrutiny of their decisions. Lawyers, academics, governments, members of parliament, the media, and members of the public comment on, and in some cases criticize, the decisions and reasoning of judges and the operation of the courts. Professional and academic accountability usually takes the form of a detailed critique of the basis of decision-making, focusing on the decisions of the apex courts. Academic writings now have greater salience in common law decision-making compared with the defunct convention that living authors could not be cited to a court.[167] Litigants, lawyers, and perhaps the public also assess judicial performance and behaviour. This includes matters such as the efficiency of decision-making (for example, whether judgments are delayed) and judicial conduct both in court and extrajudicially. In the main this is a form of soft accountability. In this regard the power-limiting function of accountability comes up against the principle of judicial independence. The advent of enhanced complaints and disciplinary procedures mean that this dimension of accountability can sometimes have a hard edge. Even if there is no formal requirement, a chief justice or other leadership judge may offer a limited public defence of a particular judgment (one of theirs or of another judge).

(B) Reasons

A legal duty for judges to give reasons for judicial decisions was long in the making in English common law. Senior judges gave reasons for their decisions by convention, and these were published in law reports. Until well into the twentieth century, however, there was no legal duty for the judges to state their reasons.[168] Until the advent of judge-alone civil trials in the mid nineteenth century, it was not the role of judges to find facts: the judge gave the jury directions, and the jury reached its conclusions without having to give

[167] P. 250 below.

[168] eg, *Cedeno v Logan* [2000] UKPC 48, [2001] 1 WLR 86 (PC, Trinidad and Tobago); *Hockey v Yelland* (1984) 157 CLR 124, 143.

reasons. A legal duty to give reasons was associated, in part, with the need for trial judges sitting without a jury to record their findings of fact so that there could be an appeal.[169] Appeals are against a judge's decision (the court's order), not the reasons behind it, so that the former may be upheld despite the appellate court considering that the reasons given are wrong. In the mid twentieth century it was still commonplace for judges in England to give judgments consisting of "We find the case proved", "This is not a case for an injunction", "Costs to the claimant", and "Leave to appeal refused". The position changed when the public mood was no longer one of deference to those exercising power, rather one of demanding the power-holder to account. In the UK the Human Rights Act 1998 underpinned this move, since the ECtHR had spelt out from the fair trial provisions of article 6 of the ECHR a duty on judges to give at least some reasons.[170]

It is now accepted in England and many Commonwealth jurisdictions that judges owe a duty to give public reasons in support of their decisions. This is the prime example of explanatory accountability. Reasons are part of the culture of justification for judges in most societies. Other public officials are called to account through different mechanisms, although there is a good argument that they, too, should generally have to explain why they have reached a decision affecting an individual. Judges, however, are not as public officials answerable for their decisions to the legislature, to the electorate, or in the other ways which operate in society for those exercising public power. Judges justify their exercise of public power through the reasons they publish to the parties and the community in specific cases. The legitimacy of their decisions derives from the published reasons. Public justification through reasons shows respect for the parties in a case. One consequence of a well-reasoned judgment is that public confidence in the judges should be enhanced. Another is that giving reasons promotes good decision-making. It acts as a restraint on arbitrary, irrational, peremptory, and lazy decision-making. Partly this operates at the level of the individual judge. The external dimension is the greater opportunity for scrutiny, supervision, and review by the parties and the public. Giving reasons is a part, perhaps the most important part, of open justice. It is now an accepted incident of the judicial process: reasons ensure that justice is not only done but seen to be done.[171] The extent and nature of the reasons differs, however, with the context.

[169] *Craven v Craven* (1957) 107 LJ 505, (1958) 21 MLR 80 (CA).
[170] eg, *Garcia Ruiz v Spain* (2001) 31 EHRR 22 [26].
[171] *R (CPRE Kent) v Dover District Council* [2017] UKSC 79, [2018] 1 WLR 108 [55].

The duty to give reasons varies with the nature of the decision, the circumstances of the case, and the complexity of the issues. Preparing reasons entails costs, including the opportunity costs of the judge spending time on other matters including hearing cases. These costs are highlighted when a judge has to be relieved from sitting in court to complete outstanding, reserved judgments, placing a burden on colleagues. Reasons in the judgments of an apex court are likely to be lengthy and must be publicly available. Cases involving the exercise of a discretion or where the resolution of an issue depends upon some intermediate conclusion of fact or law are likely to require at least some reasons.[172] What is in effect a final decision on a matter, since there is no realistic avenue of appeal, deserves adequate explanation. In high volume courts reasons may not need to be in the form of an elaborate judgment, so long as they indicate the basis of the decision. One way of addressing high volume, shorter matters is for judges to give concise *ex tempore* reasons. If matters are straightforward, short, simple reasons are all that is necessary. Rulings on evidential and procedural issues during the course of a trial can be relatively brief, as can a ruling on costs following judgment. Reasons may not generally be necessary with case management decisions provided that the basis of the decision is implicit from the circumstances in which it is made.

(C) Open Justice

The 'open examination of witnesses viva voce, in the presence of all mankind', as Blackstone put it, has long been a feature of English justice.[173] 'A closed court would be an anomaly in a free country', said *The Law Times* in 1860, 'the violation of one of the most valuable and revered principles of the political structure'.[174] The principle of open justice was reinforced in England by the reputation of the Court of the Star Chamber, which by reputation under Charles I was secretive, acted summarily, and used cruel punishments against opponents. Secret justice became anathema. The principle was bolstered with the use of juries in civil and criminal trials and members of the public having to attend court. In the nineteenth century writers like Jeremy Bentham underlined the case for the administration of justice to be held in public. Courts began to be built easily accessible to the public and

[172] See *Evans v The Queen* (2007) 235 CLR 521 [34], [77].
[173] *Commentaries on the Laws of England*, vol 3 (1783) 373–74.
[174] 'Closed Courts' *Law Times* (7 January 1860) vol 34, 177.

their judgments and orders were reported. The value of justice being conducted in public was recognized in the sixth amendment to the US constitution and later in other constitutions and human rights instruments such as article 6(1) of the ECHR.[175] In Commonwealth countries a common starting point for the principle of open justice is *Scott v Scott*,[176] a decision of the House of Lords over a century ago. The administration of justice, it held, had to be conducted in open court to which the public has access.

The principle that legal proceedings are to take place in public furthers judicial accountability. Society has an interest in how legal rights and obligations are affected by judicial decisions. 'An open court serves an educational purpose', said Dr DY Chandrachud, later chief justice of India, adding: 'The court becomes a platform for citizens to know how the practical application of the law impacts upon their rights.'[177] Secondly, public scrutiny acts as a guarantor of the quality of justice. Legal proceedings cannot be hidden. Through open justice the public can engage critically with how judges conduct legal proceedings and with their decisions. Echoing Bentham, Lord Diplock said that open justice 'provides a safeguard against judicial arbitrariness or idiosyncrasy and maintains the public confidence in the administration of justice'.[178] Thirdly, opening judicial processes to public scrutiny is a means of achieving the values of judicial independence, impartiality, and integrity since the public can observe and monitor them.

Open justice has various dimensions. At base the public must be admitted to courts to observe and hear legal proceedings, and the media must be free to report on them. Parts of trials may be broadcast, and proceedings in some courts are livestreamed. Members of the public and the media may also be able to apply to view a case remotely.[179] Secondly, listings of the cases which are being heard must be available in a timely manner, so that the public and the media can plan and then access the proceedings. Lists were traditionally pinned to notice boards at court buildings but are now accessible online. Thirdly, a corollary of the public hearing is the public decision: a court's decisions should be freely available to lawyers, the media, and the public. The reasons behind a decision in a court's judgment must also be publicly

[175] eg, Irish Constitution, art 34.1; Constitution of Jamaica, s 16(3); Constitution of the Republic of South Africa, s 34.

[176] [1913] AC 417 (a 'sacred part of the constitution', per Lord Shaw at 473).

[177] *Chief Election Commissioner of India v MR Vijayabhaskar* (2021) 6 SCC 233, AIR 2021 SC 2238 [22].

[178] *Attorney General v Leveller Magazine Ltd* [1979] AC 440, 450.

[179] eg, Courts Act 2003, s 85A (inserted 2022); Crime and Courts Act 2013, s 32.

available. An aspect of this is that generally those involved in legal proceedings are named, which is premised on the principle that what is known to the court should be known publicly. Judges are named even if proceedings are in private. That leads fourthly to the public's entitlement to access the documents placed before the judge which are referred to during proceedings. These include the pleadings, the witness statements, the expert reports, and the parties' written opening and closing submissions. In ordering access to these over a party's objections, a judge needs to balance the potential value of the information sought in advancing the purpose of the open justice principle against the risk of harm which disclosure might cause to the administration of justice and the legitimate interests of others.[180] Even if disclosed, the judge may order redactions for reasons such as commercial confidentiality. Finally, there is an argument that the openness of courts refers to the ability of individuals not only to observe and obtain information from courts but also to access the justice system they provide. Effective access to justice contributes to judicial accountability and legitimacy, although open justice in its primary sense concerns the rights of the public, rather than the rights of potential litigants to conduct legal proceedings.

An aspect of open justice in the common law system is that in the main parties and witnesses are named in legal proceedings. This differs from the civil law tradition where judgments are often anonymized. It also differs from the rights of privacy provided to data subjects under data protection laws.[181] There are exceptions to the general rule. First are those cases where anonymity usually applies as a matter of public policy, as with legislation protecting the identification of children in family proceedings and the victims of sexual offending, trafficking, or female genital mutilation.[182] Next, there are well-rehearsed practices to anonymize the names of those in certain types of proceedings. For example, claimants for asylum and international protection are usually given anonymity since publication of their names might create risks for them from their home countries especially if they are returned there.[183] Finally, a judge may make an anonymity order in the circumstances of a particular case.[184] In doing so the judge must balance

[180] *Cape Intermediate Holdings Ltd v Dring* [2019] UKSC 38, [2020] AC 629.
[181] Data Protection Act 2018, s 15(2)(b), Sch 2, Pt 2, paras 6, 14(2).
[182] eg, Children Act 1989, s 97(2); Sexual Offences (Amendment) Act 1992, ss 1–2; Female Genital Mutilation Act 2003, s 4A, Sch 1.
[183] Practice Guidance (CA: Anonymity in Asylum and Immigration Cases) [2022] 1 WLR 2103.
[184] eg, CPR 39.2(4).

against the principle of open justice whether non-disclosure is necessary to secure the proper administration of justice and to protect the interests of persons such as their privacy rights under article 8 of the ECHR. Factors justifying anonymity include a person's refusal to give evidence if they are named and the prospect that those involved in litigation may be subject to abuse or even violence if identified. Anonymity orders may be prospective in character where after legal proceedings a party is more likely to be reintegrated into the community if their identity is generally unknown.[185] Effective anonymization may involve not just using letters for a person's name but avoiding details which could permit their 'jigsaw' identification. Anonymity orders usually have two aspects: the party's name is replaced with a cipher, and the judge imposes reporting restrictions against identification of the anonymized party.

Scott v Scott[186] recognized that the open justice principle might need to give way to other interests. Over the years this has included the administration of justice and securing the interests of children, commercial secrets, and national security. In some cases the incursions on the open justice principle are contained in legislation. A striking example is that to address gun violence, Jamaica established special Gun Courts to sit in private ('in camera') so as to avoid witnesses being intimidated.[187] Secondly, in some contexts a judge may be able to make an order under the common law or procedural rules that a hearing (or part of it) is to be heard in private. Since there is a public interest in open justice, the parties cannot agree this themselves. In making an order a judge will need to have regard to the media's right under the open justice principle to attend court and report on proceedings.[188] Thirdly, in national security matters courts may be able to order a closed hearing. This may be coupled with the appointment of a 'special advocate', who represents the interests of the parties and who can see the closed material which the parties and their legal representatives cannot. The special advocate will represent the parties' interests in addition to the parties' own representatives. Consideration of the closed material will then take place in private session: the parties, their lawyers, and the public are excluded.[189]

[185] *C v Secretary of State for Justice* [2016] UKSC 2, [2016] 1 WLR 444.
[186] [1913] AC 417.
[187] *Hinds v The Queen* [1977] AC 195 (PC, Jamaica).
[188] *A v British Broadcasting Corporation* [2014] UKSC 25, [2015] AC 588; *Canadian Broadcasting Corporation v New Brunswick (Attorney General)* [1996] 3 SCR 480.
[189] eg, Justice and Security Act 2013, ss 6, 9.

(D) Public Accountability

Few people attend court as litigants, witnesses, or jury members, so that public awareness of what judges do in court depends largely on coverage by the media. The legacy media performs the valuable function of bringing to public attention the result and implications of specific decisions, the conduct of judges, and more general issues regarding the workings of the justice system. Economic pressures and the reduction of specialist court reporters have affected the extent and accuracy of coverage by the traditional media. Inaccuracies (and worse) are a regular feature of social media commentary. Courts have responded to the changing landscape of media coverage by appointing communication officers to arrange summaries of high-profile judgments, liaise with the media, and distribute information including by social media. Courts also sponsor outreach programmes and public education. These comprise attendance and speeches by judges at professional gatherings, universities, and schools; better public access to court buildings; and open days with mock trials and other matters for visitors. All this constitutes informal public accountability.

Meeting criticism

As with others exercising public power, judges cannot be shielded from politicians, the media, commentators, and civil society calling them to account for their decisions. The scrutiny typically focuses on specific cases and can lead to public criticism of the outcome and reasoning of judgments and sometimes of the specific judges. Criticism may extend more widely to issues such as the unfairness of particular laws, the perceived inefficiencies of court procedures, and the lack of access to justice. In some instances the pressure on judges can be considerable. Judges may be named and publicly disparaged by politicians, the traditional media, and anonymous commentators on social media even in cases without political connotations. It is not uncommon for newspapers to attack judges said to be too lenient to asylum seekers and immigrants. There have also been highly publicized cases of young children with terminal illnesses where the parents have conducted a vigorous campaign over months for a hospital to prolong their lives, maligning the judges who have upheld the medical decision not to do so. Public accountability of this nature presses on judicial independence.

Even when well entrenched, judicial independence can be especially tested in times of political and social stress. An example in the UK was the first Brexit case, when a Divisional Court held that the UK's withdrawal from the EU required legislation, contrary to the government's expectation that it could proceed expeditiously by executive decision.[190] The judges on the case were attacked in the media as 'enemies of the people'. Although obliged by the Constitutional Reform Act 2005 to uphold the independence of the judiciary, the lord chancellor did not issue an immediate refutation.[191] An example from Canada was that after the Supreme Court held that a federal court judge who the government had appointed to the court (and who had been sworn in) did not qualify for appointment, the prime minister accused the chief justice through the media of improperly attempting to control the court's membership.[192] There was a background of government disquiet about adverse rulings of the court, and the judge in question was portrayed (however wrongly) as more sympathetic to its position. In both cases the media campaign placed the judiciary under strain, albeit in different ways. Given the strength of cultural independence in the UK and Canada, there was no long-term damage as a result of these incidents to judicial independence and the judiciary's standing.

Attacks of this nature can potentially undermine public confidence in the judiciary, and therefore judicial independence. With the government and the legislature some steps are possible. Parliamentary procedures as in the UK exclude questions and debates on matters sub judice or reflecting on a judge's decision.[193] Provisions in the ministerial and MPs' codes of behaviour could oblige them to exercise restraint in criticizing judges and their decisions. Schemes where politicians are attached to courts for a limited period as observers mean that they are in a better position to appreciate how decisions are made and the pressures under which judges work. Informal seminars between judges and senior civil servants could further understanding of the problems each face. How to encourage greater restraint on the part of critics in the media, especially the purveyors of fake news on social media, is much harder. More education of the public about how courts operate is one step. When the first Brexit case went on appeal, the live-streaming of the proceedings probably had an educative effect, because it would have become clear to any viewer that while the matter might be politically simple it was legally complex. The attack on the judges fizzled. Furthering public understanding

[190] *R (on the application of Miller) v Secretary of State for Exiting the European Union* [2016] EWHC 2768. Upheld: [2017] UKSC 5; [2018] AC 61.
[191] ss 1(b), 3(1).
[192] *Reference re Supreme Court Act, ss 5 and 6* [2014] 1 SCR 433.
[193] *Erskine May Parliamentary Practice* (n 94) [22.21].

takes time and effort, as well as diverting judges from their function of deciding cases.

The contempt power

The UN Human Rights Committee has said that the principle of judicial independence requires that judges should be able to judge freely without being subjected to intimidation, obstruction, or interference.[194] In common law jurisdictions judges benefit from the protections conferred by the ordinary law relating to matters such as intimidation, harassment, threats of violence, and the vexatious use of court processes. Security measures may take practical form in arrangements for judges not only at court but as they go about their daily lives. Judges also benefit from the power to punish for contempt of court. This is a privilege accorded judges not for their own benefit but to enable them to decide cases independently on behalf of the community.[195] The rationale of the contempt power is to enable them to prevent or punish conduct which obstructs or interferes with the administration of justice either in relation to a specific case or more generally. The law's development in England has not been systematic. There have been many attempts to rationalize it.[196]

The following discussion concentrates on the part played by the contempt power in regulating the criticism of judges and their decisions. The context in which this occurs varies. Historically in England judges were accorded a high degree of deference. The power was only occasionally invoked, although there was the exceptional case where a newspaper editor was punished for the scurrilous abuse of a judge.[197] Lord Atkin summed up what seems to have been the prevailing view that judges 'can afford not [to] be too sensitive'.[198] In colonial societies, however, the contempt power was sometimes a means of suppressing criticism of a judge who actively supported the status quo. In India, Mahatma Gandhi was found guilty of contempt when criticizing a district judge's action as being in line with the spirit of suppressing civil resistance.[199] The same applied in apartheid South Africa, where the contempt power was used against critics of the judiciary's role in sustaining the

[194] UNHRC 'Views adopted by the Committee, under article 5 (4) of the Optional Protocol, concerning communication No 2844/2016' (13 July 2021) CCPR/C/132/D/2844/2016, para 5.5 (concerning Judge Baltasar Garzón).

[195] eg, *Pennekamp v Florida* 328 US 331, 366 (1946) (Frankfurter J).

[196] eg, Law Commission, *Contempt of Court* (Law Com CP No 262, 2024).

[197] eg, *R v Gray* [1900] 2 QB 36, 82 LT 534.

[198] *Sharma v The King-Emperor* [1943] UKPC 42 [4] (PC, Allahabad).

[199] *In re Mohandas Karamchand Gandhi* (1920) 22 Bom LR 368.

regime.[200] The context from the second part of the twentieth century has been of courts restricting the application of the contempt power to accord with the right to free speech set out in constitutional and human rights instruments.[201] As the *Latimer House Principles* make clear, contempt proceedings should not be used to restrict legitimate criticism of the performance of the judicial function.[202] However, the position has now become that judges must tolerate wrong-headed condemnation and, in some cases, outrageous attacks by disappointed litigants and the users of social media.

(a) Contempt in the face of the court

Attacks on judges during court proceedings can potentially be caught by the offence of contempt in the face of the court. As the name suggests contempt in the face of the court concerns conduct during legal proceedings in the court itself or directly connected with what is happening in court. The misconduct must denote wilful defiance of the court or disrespect towards it, or it must wilfully challenge or affront the court's authority and accordingly interfere with the administration of justice. The aim is to protect the administration of justice, not the dignity of the judge. The categories of contempt in the face of the court are not closed. Examples include disruptive or obstructive behaviour, insulting a judge in court, threatening or throwing something at them, shouting slogans and distributing leaflets in the public gallery, wearing offensive clothing, refusing to stand when directed, and taking photographs or filming proceedings.[203] This type of conduct may be punishable under other heads of the criminal law or there might be specific offences of disruptive or disrespectful behaviour. For example, taking a photograph in court has been an offence in England since 1925, although the potential penalty is a low fine.[204]

Lawyers have considerable scope for rudeness and discourtesy in court, since a judge will be reluctant to restrict them as they advance their client's case.[205] A judge will also treat litigants in person with considerable latitude, not only because they can lack knowledge and objectivity but also because

[200] eg, *S v Van Niekerk* 1970 (3) SA 655 (T); *S v Van Niekerk* 1972 3 SA 711(A).
[201] *Garrison v Louisiana* 379 US 64 (1964); *R v Kopyto* (1987) 24 OAC 81, (1987) 47 DLR (4th) 213 (Ontario CA); *S v Mamabolo* [2001] ZACC 17, 2001 (3) SA 409 (CC). India has not taken this path: eg, In *Re Arundhati Roy* (2002) AIR 2002 SC 1375, the Supreme Court found the well-known novelist and activist guilty of contempt for criticism of the judges.
[202] *Latimer House Principles* (n 6) (VII)(b).
[203] See Law Commission, *Contempt of Court* (Law Com CP No 209, 2012) [5.5].
[204] Criminal Justice Act 1925, s 41(1).
[205] See *Nikula v Finland* App no 31611/96 (2004) 38 EHRR 45.

bad behaviour on their part is unlikely to have an adverse impact on the court's authority or public confidence in its administration. Contempt in the face of the court can be dealt with by way of summary procedure, but this raises issues of fairness. There needs to be an adequate opportunity for reflection on all sides. It would defeat the very purpose of the contempt power if it were exercised arbitrarily or without affording procedural fairness to those charged. The precise nature of what they are alleged to have done needs to be identified so that they are able to excuse their conduct or to defend themselves against the charge.[206] The contemnor should have adequate time to prepare any defence and to obtain legal advice. If the judge who presses a charge for contempt also determines the matter there may be justified misgivings as to their impartiality.[207] Depending on the circumstances if there is no urgency the matter may be adjourned and dealt with by another judge. The open justice principle means that committal hearings should generally be heard in public and reasons for the decision given.

(b) 'Scandalizing' the judges

Statements attacking individual judges or the judiciary, not necessarily concerned with current proceedings, could be caught by the form of common law contempt known as scandalizing the judges (or scandalizing the court). As originally formulated its justification was 'to keep a blaze of glory around [the judges], and to deter people from attempting to render them contemptible in the eyes of the public'.[208] The test became whether there is a real risk that the statements are likely to undermine public confidence in the administration of justice. The offence is not concerned with the feelings of the judge. The courts have made clear that the offence cannot be used to stifle good faith, even wrong-headed criticism. Justice, said Lord Atkin in a leading case, is not a cloistered virtue.[209] The exposure and criticism of a judge's conduct and decisions, even in bad taste and containing factual inaccuracies, does not meet the threshold of the offence.

Following a report of the Law Commission, scandalizing the judges as an aspect of the contempt power has been abolished in England.[210] Among the reasons the Law Commission advanced in favour of abolition were the

[206] eg, CPR 81.6(3).

[207] *Kyprianou v Cyprus* App no 73797/01 (2005) 44 EHRR 27 (GC).

[208] *R v Almon* (1765) Wilm 243, 270; 97 ER 94, 105, per Wilmot J.

[209] *Ambard v Attorney General for Trinidad and Tobago* [1936] AC 322, 335 (PC).

[210] Crime and Courts Act 2013, s 33(1). See Law Commission, *Contempt of Court: Scandalising the Court* (Law Com No 335, 2012).

uncertainty surrounding the elements of the offence, that the offence was in principle contrary to the right of freedom of expression, its disuse was a sign that abolition was unlikely to have significant effects, and that prosecutions might provide a platform for the allegations and lead to a trial of the conduct of the judge concerned. For similar reasons the Law Commission recommended against a new offence of making false allegations of corruption or other serious misconduct about a judge. It argued that general offences addressed at public disorder and malicious communication could be invoked, and that judges could also take the initiative and sue for defamation. The upshot is that English judges endure patently false allegations of corruption, conspiracy, and gross misconduct, without a targeted offence against this type of behaviour.

Scandalizing the judges remains an offence in many jurisdictions. The ECtHR has concluded that although scrutiny and criticism are protected by article 10 of the ECHR (the right of freedom of expression), statements intended to insult a judge or the court could be made an offence consistently with that right. 'The work of the courts, which are the guarantors of justice and which have a fundamental role in a State governed by the rule of law, needs to enjoy public confidence. It should therefore be protected against unfounded attacks.'[211] In an appeal from Mauritius in 2014 the Privy Council held that to meet the constitutional protection on freedom of speech in that jurisdiction, a person to be guilty of scandalizing the judges had to intend to undermine public confidence in the administration of justice or be subjectively reckless as to this risk.[212] While eschewing any 'small jurisdiction' exception, it acknowledged that local conditions in some jurisdictions mean that the administration of justice was more vulnerable than in the UK and the need for the offence greater. The annex to the opinion listed at least twelve common law jurisdictions where scandalizing the judges remained an offence to which recent resort had been had—among them Australia, Canada, India, Singapore, and South Africa—even if a prosecution had not always been successful.

[211] *Zugic v Croatia* App no 3699/08 (ECtHR, 31 August 2011) [45], citing previous decisions from Germany, Austria, and Finland: [47].

[212] *Dhooharika v DPP (Commonwealth Lawyers' Association intervening)* [2014] UKPC 11, [2015] AC 875.

VII Conclusion

At its heart the principle of judicial independence is designed to ensure that judges have the ability to decide cases in accordance with law, free from pressures and inducements. These pressures and inducements can derive from government, business, or other external forces, or internally from within the judiciary, notably from judges more senior in the judicial hierarchy. They can bias a judge in favour of one of the parties to a dispute. Judicial independence is conceptually separate from impartiality, the subject matter of the following chapter. Judicial independence is concerned with external and internal forces which distort the decision-making process, whereas the focus of judicial impartiality is on the parties before the court and whether the judge is biased (or appears biased) in favour of one over another. In practice there can be an obvious relationship between the two, since judicial independence is aimed at ensuring that judges make decisions uninfluenced by extraneous factors not permitted by law.

Traditionally the structural protections of judicial independence have concentrated on the individual judge, rather than on the judiciary as an institution, and taken the form of tenure, financial, and similar protections. The structural protections of judicial independence may also operate at the institutional level in its recognition in a constitution or in specific statutory provisions. Many structural protections take *de jure* form. There have been various studies assessing judicial independence in different jurisdictions, seeking explanations for its success or failure. Assessments of what is categorized as *de facto* independence as in the UN Rule of Law Indicators and the annual EU Justice Scoreboard derive from the perceptions of judges and experts, public surveys, and official reports.[213] Empirical correlation of de facto and de jure judicial independence has produced generally positive, if slight, results.

A crucial aspect of judicial independence is what is categorized in this chapter as behavioural independence. Experience in various parts of the world demonstrate that a seemingly strong package of structural protections for judicial independence may be vulnerable through a determined effort on the part of an authoritarian and populist government to fix judicial appointments and deploy the disciplinary machinery (including dismissal) against members of the current bench, regarded as unsympathetic. Despite any

[213] United Nations Rule of Law Indicators (UN 2011) 10, 51, 70; Commission, 'The 2024 EU Justice Scoreboard' (Communication) COM (2024) 950.

formal rules espousing judicial independence, the reality can be of threats, pressures, inducements, and cues for judges to reach desired outcomes in specific cases. Even in jurisdictions where it is well entrenched, judicial independence can be tested in times of political and social crisis. So an aspect of behavioural independence is personal to the judge. It derives from an attitude of mind on the part of the judge, who 'must be free in thought and independent in judgment when acting judicially'.[214] The individual judge needs moral integrity, courage, and an independence of mind to resist pressures and blandishments.

The idea of judicial independence has considerable resonance. As well as its political and societal benefits, bodies like the World Bank have long contended that, as an aspect of the rule of law, judicial independence also has a positive impact on economic development. There is some evidence to support this.[215] The benefits of judicial independence have the potential for judicial hubris and overreach. It is common ground that judges cannot be completely independent—that would undermine the very aim which judicial independence is meant to serve. On occasions, however, judges have extended the core meaning of judicial independence and asserted judicial control over judges' pay and appointments to the bench as its corollaries.[216] While in particular contexts judicial control of these matters might be essential to judicial independence, the danger in overextending what is said to be the principle's application is that its meaning is diluted, and public cynicism or even political retaliation engendered. Excluding the executive completely from judicial appointments, for example, may not assist judicial independence since a political class less involved in the judiciary's future may become indifferent to, and ignorant of, its plight. Another possibility is that judicial orders under cover of judicial independence might in some contexts weaken yet further a democratic government under strain, leading eventually to inroads on judicial power.

Judicial accountability and judicial independence run together in their concern that judges decide cases in accordance with law. There can be a tension between the two, since strengthening judicial independence may lessen the force of judicial accountability. Moreover, in its practical application accountability depends on context: not all judges are subject to the same

[214] *Durity v Attorney General of Trinidad and Tobago* [2008] UKPC 59 [24] (PC, Trinidad and Tobago).

[215] *World Development Report 2017, Governance and the Law* (IRBD/World Bank 2017) ch 3.

[216] P. 45 above, p. 182 below.

mechanisms of accountability at any one time. In general terms, however, judges individually are answerable for their decisions and behaviour, and the judiciary as an institution must give an account of their part in judicial administration, and their involvement in matters such as judicial appointments and discipline. In addition to the legal accountability which occurs through judges giving reasons, and the principle of open justice, there are other accountability mechanisms, formal and informal, to which the judges are subject.

In the modern age, all those exercising power must expect criticism from politicians and in the media. Political criticism is moderated to an extent by various practices and conventions which disapprove of ministers and others commenting on specific judicial decisions. Criticism in the traditional and social media is less inhibited and especially acute when the subject matter is highly charged, or in times of political or social stress. Judges need fortitude, individually, and judiciaries need to act collectively, to uphold judicial independence. A crucial aspect of judicial independence is what is termed here as cultural independence. In short, the protection of judicial independence ultimately lies in a society's commitment to the principle, including the commitment of its political class, legal profession, opinion leaders, influencers, and civil society organizations. There is a clear interrelatedness between the judges, the judiciary as an institution, and the vitality of the rule of law in a society.

2
Impartiality

I Introduction

Impartiality and the appearance of impartiality in decision-making are, as Justice Mary Gaudron put it on one occasion, 'so fundamental to the judicial process that they are defining features of judicial power'.[1] Impartiality is the essence of the judicial oath, for English judges to 'do right to all manner of people after the laws and usages of this realm, without fear or favour, affection or ill will'.[2] In modern language, the judge undertakes to make decisions on their legal and factual merits, without being influenced by improper considerations (fear or favour, affection or ill will), and giving equal concern and respect to the parties whoever they are (doing right to all manner of people). The duty of impartiality requires both the reality and the appearance of impartiality, encapsulated in the well-known dictum that justice must not only be done but be seen to be done.[3]

It has long been the case that impartiality has been regarded as indispensable to proper judging. In his *On the Laws and Governance of England* in 1477, Sir John Fortescue, chief justice of the King's Bench, wrote that the judge was to swear that 'he will do justice without favour, to all men pleading before him, friends and foes alike . . . '.[4] Sir Matthew Hale, chief justice of the King's Bench 1671–1676, included impartiality among the rules he sketched for himself in 1668 for his conduct as a judge, although he sensibly took notice that judges could be sure to displease some and often all the parties in a case.[5] It seems reasonable to assume that these judicial views reflect society's preference that their judges should decide cases impartially. Impartiality

[1] *Ebner v Official Trustee in Bankruptcy* (2000) 205 CLR 337, 345.
[2] Promissory Oaths Act 1868, s 4.
[3] *R v Sussex Justices, ex parte McCarthy* [1924] 1 KB 256, 259.
[4] Shelley Lockwood (ed), *Sir John Fortescue: On the Laws and Governance of England* (CUP 1997) 74.
[5] Reproduced in Maija Jansson, 'Matthew Hale on Judges and Judging' (1988) 9 J Leg Hist 201.

Judging. Ross Cranston, Oxford University Press. © Ross Cranston 2025.
DOI: 10.1093/9780191890994.003.0002

seems essential to public confidence in the judges and the legitimacy of judicial power.

The chapter begins in section II with how judicial impartiality depends in large part on the individual judge, supported by institutional factors, including the focus in litigation on legally relevant matters. Section III of the chapter turns to the common law disqualification rules designed to further impartiality. There are well accepted categories where judges are disqualified because they may not be able to decide a case impartially or, more likely, it will appear to the objective observer that they are unable to do so. Examples include where the judge has a financial interest in the outcome or as a shareholder in one of the parties, a close association with a lawyer on one side, a strong opinion about who should win in this type of case, or a firm view about the credibility of one of the parties based on hearing their evidence on a previous occasion. How disqualification is furthered procedurally is the subject matter of section IV. The chapter focuses on impartiality in domestic courts, but impartiality is also a concern with international courts where national loyalty, geography, and the methods of selection can constitute powerful influences on the judges and the voting blocs with which they align themselves.

II Impartiality and Its Reach

As with judicial independence, impartiality rests on the individual judge and societal guarantees. These are the behavioural, institutional, and adjudicative dimensions examined in part (A). There is an obvious interrelatedness to them. There follows part (B), covering the difficulties in defining and giving force to impartiality when individual judges, as with all human beings, have backgrounds, experiences, values, and unconscious biases. The challenge addressed in part (C) is to identify biases and potential biases, in other words, the threats to impartiality. The viewpoint of the parties who appear in court has some force, but greater credence is given to the public's apprehension of bias, since ultimately at issue is the judiciary's legitimacy in the community.

(A) Behavioural, Institutional, and Adjudicative Dimensions

One way of analysing how impartiality plays out in judging is to consider what can be characterized as the behavioural, institutional, and adjudicative dimensions. The behavioural dimension concerns the obligations on the individual judge to act impartially; the institutional dimension refers to societal supports for the value of impartiality in judging; and the adjudicative dimension highlights how impartiality is furthered by procedural values in deciding matters, notably fairness, and the methodology of judicial decision-making with its concern with legally relevant matters, which limits the extent to which judges can bring biases to bear.

The behavioural dimension: the judge

The threats to impartiality, or at least its appearance, are various. Firstly, if a judge has an interest in the outcome of litigation, financial or otherwise, even relatively remote, that may be contrary to impartial judging, or at least to its appearance. So, too, may having a personal, social, financial, or other association with one of the parties before the court. More difficult, thirdly, are a judge's opinions about the parties or the matter in contention, either in specific or more general terms. Opinion is less tangible than interest and association. It encompasses a wide range of matters—personal values, social, religious, and political causes, intellectual positions, and previous experience of the litigants or the case which could potentially lead to prejudgement about a matter. There is a spectrum. At one end having a closed mind about a party or issue is illegitimate. Along the spectrum the judge may appear to be so strongly in favour, say, of a social cause that objectively this appears to predetermine the outcome. Further along the spectrum, however, the judge may have a preference, but may still have an open mind capable of considering fairly the arguments advanced by the parties. Fourthly, there are the unconscious biases to which judges may be prone when making quick decisions about people and situations, based on their background and experience, or derived from the social environment. Given their nature, identifying and addressing these unconscious biases can be especially challenging.

Against that backdrop one view, expressed by the Supreme Court of Canada, is that judicial impartiality is a state of mind or attitude in relation to the issues and parties in a case, by comparison with judicial independence, which connotes not only a state of mind but also a status or relationship with others resting on objective conditions and guarantees.[6] An impartial state of mind means that the judge decides a case with equal concern and respect

[6] *Valente v The Queen* [1985] 2 SCR 673 [15].

for both sides, and without partiality, apart from that which the judge will have towards the one with the better legal merits. This state of mind is not the same as a blank mind, which is impossible given a judge's background, training, and experience, but means not being influenced by extraneous matters or reaching a concluded view prematurely. As the Canadian Judicial Council's *Ethical Principles for Judges* provide, the obligation of impartiality does not presuppose that judges are free of life experiences, sympathies, or opinions but requires that they be sensitive to their own biases and consider different points of view with an open mind.[7] There is truth in the view that an open mind needs cultivating by self-reflection and inquisitiveness about other perspectives.

A state of mind goes only so far, and for the individual judge the duty to administer justice impartially is reinforced and given definition in several ways. First, there is the judicial oath, which as we have seen the judge takes on appointment. Most judges regard the judicial oath as serious business.[8] Secondly, the duty is given effect in the well-established rules at common law requiring that judges disqualify (or recuse) themselves if they will be biased (partial) in the legal sense when deciding a case as regards a party or issue, or more likely that there will be an appearance of such bias should they go ahead and decide it.[9] The common law also elaborated procedures for the efficacy of these rules in practice. These disqualification rules and procedures are backed by other norms, which govern how judges should conduct themselves to preserve public confidence in their impartiality and that of the judiciary as a whole. These conduct norms are covered in Chapter 3. Thirdly, impartiality is one of the essential values (or principles) set out in the guides and codes for judicial conduct.[10] These require the judge to avoid activities that are likely to cause them to refrain from sitting because of bias or a conflict of interest that would arise from such an activity, and to conduct themselves at and away from court in such a way as to enhance confidence in their personal impartiality and that of the judiciary.

[7] *Ethical Principles for Judges* (Canadian Judicial Council 2021) Commentary, 5A.4.

[8] *Starrs v Ruxton* 2000 JC 208, 253 (Lord Reed).

[9] The term 'recuse' is increasingly used to cover judges disqualifying themselves on application of a party, not just on their own initiative.

[10] eg, *Bangalore Principles of Judicial Conduct* (United Nations 2018) value 2; *Guide to Judicial Conduct* (revised edn, Courts and Tribunals Judiciary, July 2023) 8.

The institutional dimension: the judiciary

The disqualification and conduct rules are part of the institutional support for judicial impartiality. As well, there is the legal entitlement of persons to an impartial and independent judge, which is one aspect of the common law rules of natural justice. The common law in this regard is underpinned by the fair trial rights contained in human rights instruments such as article 6.1 of the European Convention on Human Rights (ECHR), and in constitutions such as article 165(2) of the Constitution of the Republic of South Africa. Impartiality is also part of the design and iconography of the courts, with the judge as the neutral person sitting between the parties, often at a raised level, and the figure of Justice, mainly blindfolded and depicted with scales, denoting even-handed, fair, and impartial treatment. Institutional means of bolstering impartiality also include the vetting which occurs when a judge is appointed, the socialization processes judges undergo once on the bench, and ongoing learning and experience concerning judicial ethics and practice.[11] The age of accountability and transparency demands not only that the judges be impartial but that there be rules and procedures in place to ensure this.

At the heart of the institutional dimension to impartiality, however, are societal values, the support for an impartial judiciary among the political class, opinion leaders, commercial interests, and civil society. To put it another way, judicial impartiality is an essential component of public confidence in the judges and the judiciary as a whole. The reputation of judges for impartiality is a building block in ensuring community compliance with the law and with the courts' orders. No longer, if it ever were the case, is Blackstone's view acceptable, that judicial impartiality cannot be challenged, '[f]or the law will not suppose a possibility of bias or favour in a judge, who is already sworn to administer impartial justice...'[12] In the modern age there is less deference to those in authority, including judges. It is part of the landscape that charges of bias, or potential bias, will be levelled against them.

Public confidence in impartiality must begin with the parties in each case, their belief that the judge deciding it is not prejudiced against them or partial to the other side for reasons not related to the legal and factual merits. It does not matter that a decision is legally correct if justice is not seen to be done. There is a common belief that parties in a case are more accepting of an adverse decision if they believe that decision-making has been fairly

[11] PP. 108–110, 159, 189 below.

[12] William Blackstone, *Commentaries on the Laws of England* (1768, Bk 3) (OUP 2016) 361.

conducted. In addition, respect for impartial and fair judging must be shared as well throughout society if the legitimacy of the judges and the judiciary as a whole is to be maintained. As a nineteenth-century English judge put it in considering that a small interest in a decision would disqualify a judge under the statutory scheme at issue, the object was to remove suspicion about the tribunal 'and so to promote the feeling of confidence in the administration of justice which is so essential to social order and security'.[13]

A belief that there is a system of 'telephone justice', where politicians and oligarchs can signal the desired outcome in a case, undermines the judiciary's reputation for applying basic tenets of the rule of law, including impartiality, and that all will be treated with equal concern and respect.[14] The understanding that citizens will need to pay a bribe if they go to court undermines impartiality and deters access to justice. There are those countries where corruption is so rife that bias in law enforcement and the judiciary contributes to a climate where human rights advocates can be targeted, physically harmed, or killed.[15] Knowledge of such matters—backstairs influence on judges, judicial bribery, and corruption—all lead to an erosion of trust by ordinary citizens, even if in run of the mill cases these forces have no purchase and judges act impartially. In all these situations restoration of the judiciary's reputation for impartiality and even-handedness requires fundamental political and social change. Appearances are, as ever, as important as the reality. As with judicial independence, impartiality is a social and political as well as a legal achievement.

Adjudication and impartiality

The adjudicative dimension to impartiality focuses on judicial decision-making and is summed up in the United Nations Basic Principles on the Independence of the Judiciary, that the judiciary 'shall decide matters before them impartially, on the basis of facts and in accordance with the law, without any restrictions, improper influences, inducements, pressures, threats or interferences, direct or indirect, from any quarter or for any reason'.[16] The adjudicative dimension to impartiality turns, first, on the application of accepted methods of decision-making. This has the effect of limiting the potential for partiality. The judge must address the arguments of the parties,

[13] Serjeant v Dale (1877) 2 QBD 558, 567 (Lush J).
[14] See p. 12 above.
[15] *Corruption Perceptions Index* (Transparency International 2021) 10.
[16] UNGA Res 40/32 (29 November 1985) and UNGA Res 40/146 (13 December 1985), para 2.

which has the effect of confining what will be considered in the justification of decision-making. For the court to decide a case on a matter which the parties have not agitated without offering them the opportunity to make further submissions could open the door to potential partiality (and inaccuracy) in decision-making, as well as conflicting with their sense of fairness.[17] Acting in conformity with accepted methods of judicial decision-making involves applying statute, following precedent, and reaching conclusions for legally legitimate reasons. As we see in Chapter 6, judicial decision-making is complex, and the exercise of judicial discretion is legitimately open to various influences. Inherent in the requirement of adjudicative impartiality, however, is that the judge should eschew improper influences such as financial interests, affinity with one side, or any personal or ideological commitment, and follow the recognized decision-making methodology of the common law.

The adjudicative dimension to impartiality depends, secondly, on judges following accepted procedural standards. This not simply, as the *Bangalore Principles of Judicial Conduct* put it, that the judge must perform their judicial duties without favour, bias, or prejudice.[18] Fair trial standards, consistency, and principles such as equality before the law, including hearing both sides, engaging with their respective cases, and being patient and even-handed, especially with litigants in person, further impartiality. Appellate review can also act as a curb on the prejudices and predilections of the individual judge as can sitting with other judges to decide a case. Because decisions are made in accordance with their factual and legal merits and both sides are accorded equal concern and respect, their status, wealth, or previous behaviour should generally not enter decision-making and therefore potentially infect it. (There are limited situations where the law may allow some of these factors to be considered, including the person deemed from their behaviour in previous litigation to be a vexatious litigant, whose right to bring legal proceedings may be curbed.)[19] Although there can be no compromise on the fundamentals of fair procedures, perfection regarding them is often unachievable in practice since account must be taken of the pressure on judges to deal with the caseload and to limit the resources allocated to any one case to maximize access to justice for others.[20]

[17] See *United States v Sineneng-Smith* 590 US 371, 379–80 (2020) (Ginsburg J for the court). Given its special position in Indian society, sua sponte decisions feature in its Supreme Court: eg, *In re Alleged Rape and Murder Incident of a Trainee Doctor in R G Kar Medical College and Hospital, Kolkata* 2024 INSC 613.

[18] *Bangalore Principles of Judicial Conduct* (n 10) value 2, para 2.1.

[19] See p. 209 below.

[20] See CPR 1.1(2)(e).

(B) Impartiality and the Judge's Background

It is unrealistic as well as undesirable to expect that judges will be like a clean sheet, divorced completely from all the commitments, experiences of life, and opinions which they had before appointment. Judges will inevitably have preconceived views about some parties and issues. There might also be a natural affinity, perhaps unconscious, with those who have similar life experiences or values to them. Professor JAG Griffith's famous critique was that with their common educational background, training, and pursuit of professional life as barristers, English judges shared characteristics and opinions, including a bias against groups such as demonstrators, trade unions, and squatters.[21] From a different perspective feminist judges have argued that women have different life experiences to men and can and do bring those experiences to judging, in the process making the law more responsive and inclusive.[22] There is a growing body of social science literature which explores how judges approach matters, albeit unconsciously, with certain predispositions.[23] Considerations such as these raise the issue of how judges can be impartial, or at least keep inappropriate biases in check.

One strand of argument is that adjudicative and procedural impartiality is threatened if the judiciary is drawn from too narrow a base. There is a benefit to impartiality, some contend, in appointing judges with more diverse backgrounds, experiences of life, and a greater knowledge of the persons and situations which come before the courts. The counter-argument is that the appointment of judges from a broader background may introduce identity-based decision-making, albeit in a different guise from that criticized by Professor Griffith. The misperception that judges cannot judge cases impartially, because of their background and experience, is illustrated by an oft-cited decision from the 1970s. There female law graduates brought a class action against a leading Wall Street law firm for systematically discriminating against women. Judge Constance Baker Motley was allocated the case. The law firm sought her disqualification. As an African-American and a woman, the firm argued, she was likely to have experienced workplace discrimination, and given her identity and knowledge she would strongly identify with other women who alleged discrimination. Motley refused to recuse herself: the law

[21] JAG Griffith, *The Politics of the Judiciary* (Fontana 1977).
[22] eg, Brenda Hale, *Spider Woman. A Life* (Bodley Head 2021) 190 (judge 1994–2020; president, UK Supreme Court 2017–20). See also pp. 260, 348 below.
[23] PP. 80–81, 244–245 below.

firm had not supported its allegation of bias with evidence. Further, since she had been on the bench, she explained, she had ruled against plaintiffs in civil rights cases, including women alleging sex discrimination in employment. If the background, sex, or race of each judge were, by definition, sufficient grounds for removal, she added, 'no judge on this court could hear this case, or many others, by virtue of the fact that all of them were attorneys, of a sex, often with distinguished law firm or public service backgrounds'.[24]

The reality is that although judges come to the job with a background of experiences, associations, and opinions, like Judge Motley their identity need play only an indirect and limited role in their conception as a judge. Judges must act in line with accepted methods of decision-making, whether these be those of the first instance or appellate court where they are sitting. These methods of decision-making mean that the judge is disposed to taking legally relevant factors into account, such as the facts of the case, precedent, and legal values, but militate against the consideration of improper or irrelevant matters. Acting in accordance with the principles of procedural fairness, the behavioural rules about disqualification for bias, and the guidance and codes for judicial conduct also lessen the role of untoward pressures and influences and any temptation to have regard to matters unconnected with the legal and factual merits of a case. Judges are better able to evaluate a matter impartially if they are aware of their prejudices and preferences, including the possibility of unconscious bias, and are sensitive to public perceptions relevant to impartiality.

Open-mindedness is sometimes advanced as the bridge between, on the one hand, judicial background and its influence and, on the other hand, the duty to act impartiality. Taking account of the different sides of a case with an open mind means that, despite any predilections regarding the issues in a case, the judge is capable of persuasion in light of the submissions of the parties. In a case in the Supreme Court of Canada a female black judge was unsuccessfully challenged for apprehended bias. She made a disparaging remark about the police and racism when she acquitted a black youth of assaulting a white police officer. The court held that there could be no reasonable apprehension of bias. While judges could not be neutral in the sense of being purely objective, they must strive for impartiality. Differing experiences appropriately assisted if these were not based on improper stereotypes

[24] *Blank v Sullivan & Cromwell* 418 F Supp 1, 4 (SDNY 1975).

or prevented a fair determination based on the evidence. The judge's oral reasons showed that she approached the case with an open mind.[25]

(C) Identifying Bias: Actual, Apprehended, Unconscious

Bias in English law—the common term for partiality—occurs where the judge without according equal concern and respect to both sides favours (or appears to favour) one side for reasons unrelated to the legal and factual merits of a case. How the law addresses bias has not followed a straightforward path. In the thirteenth century Bracton said that a judge was disqualified if there were suspicions of partiality arising from many causes—a relationship with the judge, friendship (or the opposite) with the party, if the judge was of subordinate status to the party, or if the judge had served as the party's lawyer.[26] Then in the *Earl of Derby's Case* the lord chancellor, sitting with the chief justice of England and master of the rolls, ruled that although the earl was the sole judge in equity in the area, he could not hear a case being brought against defendants of whom he was one.[27] As we have seen, Blackstone's opinion was that judges could not be challenged for bias. Despite this, the view in the *Earl of Derby's Case* was maintained, as Blackburn J put it in 1866, that 'any direct pecuniary interest, however small . . . does disqualify a person from acting as a judge in the matter'.[28] By the end of the nineteenth century suspicion of bias was emerging as an additional base for the disqualification of a judge from hearing a case.

Actual, presumed, and apparent bias

The position in modern English law is that judges can be disqualified for bias on three grounds, actual bias, presumed bias, and apparent bias. Actual bias occurs if the judge's capacity for objective judgement is swayed by partiality, if the judge exhibits hostility or partisanship towards one side, or if the judge has such a blinkered view as not being open to persuasion so that the matter is effectively prejudged. In England, cases where actual bias has been established are few and far between. That should not be surprising. A challenge of actual bias demands partiality, which is difficult to prove. There is

25 *R v S(RD)* [1997] 3 SCR 484 [29], [59].

26 *Bracton on the Laws and Customs of England* (Samuel E Thorn tr, Harvard University Press 1977) vol 4, 280–81.

27 (1613) 12 Co Rep 114, 77 ER 1390.

28 *R v Rand* (1866) LR 1 QB 230, 232.

a high threshold.[29] The rule is that judges cannot be questioned about extraneous influences affecting their state of mind—that would expose them to being harried by disgruntled litigants—although inferences can be drawn from their statements and conduct. A high threshold has been justified since a finding of actual bias could constitute a conclusion that there had been serious judicial misconduct justifying a judge's removal from office. In practice it has proved more convenient to address issues of partiality through the lens of apparent bias.

Presumed bias derives from *Dimes v Proprietors of Grand Junction Canal*.[30] There Cottenham LC affirmed decrees against a landowner in favour of a canal company in which he was a not insubstantial shareholder. These were set aside by the House of Lords on the grounds of his pecuniary interest in the decision, albeit that it affirmed the decrees after considering the matter on its merits. In England the decision was long taken as an authority to disqualify automatically a judge with a shareholding in a party to proceedings, however small the investment, subject to waiver by the other side or the doctrine of necessity which covers situations where there is no alternative judge who can sit. The reasoning was that the judge had an interest in the outcome of the proceedings. In England, presumed bias has been extended to other situations where a judge has a non-financial interest in the way a case is decided.[31] The ramifications of this approach have been mitigated by a *de minimis* exception with an inquiry into the potential effect of any decision on the judge's interest. In other Commonwealth jurisdictions, presumed bias has been subsumed under the head of apparent bias and for convenience this is the approach adopted here.

Apparent bias occurs where the circumstances would lead the fair-minded and informed observer—in other words, the objective observer—to conclude that there is a real possibility that a judge is biased.[32] The judge's perception is immaterial, although it may be relevant to understanding the facts and the nature of the challenge. Nor on appeal is there any inquiry into whether in fact the judge was influenced by particular considerations. Apparent bias includes an inclination or predisposition to decide the issue one way only, whatever the strength of any contrary arguments. English courts took a while to formulate this objective test for apparent bias. For a time there was

[29] See also *Reid v Commercial Club (Albury) Ltd* [2014] NSWCA 98 [68]–[74].
[30] (1852) 3 HL Cas 759, 794, 10 ER 301, 315.
[31] P. 88 below.
[32] *Porter v Magill* [2001] UKHL 67, [2002] 2 AC 357 [103] (Lord Hope).

confusion as to whether the test was whether there was a real danger as opposed to a reasonable apprehension of bias. The House of Lords sought to put the matter beyond dispute in 1993 by adopting a real danger of bias test, to be applied to all decision makers, not only judges.[33] The High Court of Australia identified how the real danger test emphasized the court's own view of the issue and underplayed the importance of public perceptions and thus of public confidence in the judiciary.[34] When applied by an appellate court, the real danger test came close to an inquiry into whether the judge was in reality affected by bias.

Within a decade the House of Lords changed course and the test became one of whether the fair-minded and informed observer, having considered the facts, would conclude that there was a real—not remote—possibility (not probability) of bias. That brought the test more into line with the jurisprudence of Commonwealth jurisdictions like Canada, Australia, South Africa, and New Zealand.[35] The new, objective test of a real possibility of bias is also the law in those jurisdictions with appeals to the Privy Council and in international arbitrations with an English seat.[36] Since the test is objective, not subjective, it is applied without reference to the views of any litigant raising the complaint. Litigants, it is realistically assumed, can lack objectivity.

Whether the challenge is of actual, presumed, or apparent bias the judge's state of mind can be irrelevant. Judges may be disqualified from hearing a matter although acting in good faith and believing that they are neutral and have the impartiality to hear it. In multi-member courts, if one member is disqualified for bias the whole court is potentially affected. The premise is that each judge will have played a full part in deliberations on the issues raised and that the judge disqualified to sit may have had an influence over the others.[37] If an issue arises at an early stage, however, the judge can withdraw from hearing the case without affecting the other judges. Moreover, it is always possible for the parties to waive bias. To be valid a waiver must be voluntary and clear, and made with full knowledge of the material facts. Those requirements will not be met if a party is pressed by the judge or counsel to

[33] *R v Gough* [1993] AC 646.

[34] *R v Webb* [1994] HCA 30, (1994) 181 CLR 41, 50.

[35] eg, *Wewaykum Indian Band v Canada*, 2003 SCC 45, [2003] 2 SCR 259; *Johnson v Johnson* [2000] HCA 48, 201 CLR 488; *President of the Republic of South Africa v South African Rugby Football Union*, 1999 (4) SA 147 [48]; *Saxmere Co Ltd v Wool Board Disestablishment Co Ltd* [2009] NZSC 72, [2010] 1 NZLR 35 [3].

[36] eg, *Prince Jefri Bolkiah v Brunei* [2007] UKPC 62 (PC, Brunei); *Halliburton Co v Chubb Bermuda Insurance Ltd* [2020] UKSC 48, [2021] AC 1083 respectively.

[37] *Stubbs v The Queen* [2018] UKPC 30, [2019] AC 868 [33] (PC, Bahamas).

consent to the judge sitting. A party failing to raise an objection in a timely manner may be held to have waived the right to do so later. Parties cannot reserve known points in order to attack what turns out to be an unpalatable judgment on grounds of bias.

Apparent bias and the fair-minded and informed observer test

Apparent bias is the most frequently encountered challenge to a judge's partiality in practice. Its yardstick in English law is that of the fair-minded and informed observer. The fair-minded and informed observer is a judicial fiction like the reasonable person in negligence. Over the years their qualities have expanded as new challenges have arisen. They now include a full understanding of the issues to be decided and of both sides of the argument. They know all the relevant circumstances including those not in the public domain. They read the text not just the headlines. They take a balanced approach. They are not complacent, unduly sensitive, or suspicious. They place whatever they have read or seen into its overall social, political, or geographic context. The fair-minded and informed observer is aware of court procedures, how cases are managed, the rules about admissible evidence, the legal traditions of the jurisdiction, and the close interaction between the judiciary and the profession. They are also taken to know that judges have sworn the judicial oath and are under strong professional duties to act impartially, are likely to express tentative views during a hearing, can change their minds during legal proceedings, and are trained to ignore the prejudicial and irrelevant.

The drawbacks to the fair-minded and informed observer test are patent. First, they are omniscient and of saintly temperament—somewhat removed from the average litigant and member of the public. The rules for disqualifying judges for apparent bias are supposedly founded on public perception, yet the application of the fair-minded and informed observer test produces results which the public must on occasion find difficult to grasp. Unwilling to accept the court's analysis, the public is, by definition, not being fair-minded and informed. The contradiction is evident in *Harb v Aziz*.[38] There the Court of Appeal was prepared to assume that the fair-minded and informed observer would conclude that there was a real possibility that the judge was biased against all members of a set of barristers' chambers and would therefore prefer to have their case heard by another judge if

[38] [2016] EWCA Civ 556.

represented by a barrister from those chambers. Nevertheless, the court went on to hold that on an examination of all the circumstances this would not, without more, lead the informed and fair-minded observer to conclude that there was a real possibility that this bias would affect the judge's determination of a case in which counsel came from those chambers.[39]

Secondly, the fair-minded and informed observer test distorts reality. As Lord Rodger put it, the whole point of inventing the fictional character is that they do not share the viewpoint of a judge, yet the court is itself deciding what the fair-minded and informed observer would think about any given situation.[40] The fact is that the fair-minded and informed observer has become an insider. This has led to the argument that the test for apparent bias should be the objective judgement of the court. The question would be whether the proceedings as a whole can be seen as fair and reasonable. It would be a matter of the court's judgement, considering as one factor the issue of public perception which lies behind the fair-minded and informed observer test. An acknowledgement that disqualification is, in fact, the judgement of the court would enable it to make explicit the range of matters presently disguised in the assessment of apparent bias under the fair-minded and informed observer test.

Unconscious bias

Unconscious bias is based on a person's background, experiences, and deep-seated thought patterns. It leads to preconceptions about the interests and behaviours of others and has special salience when decisions are made under pressure. Judges have long recognized that unconscious bias has a role in judicial decision-making. In an address to the Cambridge University Law Society in November 1920 a leading commercial judge, Scrutton LJ, spoke of the difficulty of obtaining impartiality, 'not . . .conscious impartiality; but the habits you are trained in, the people with whom you mix, lead to your having a certain class of idea [and] you do not give as sound and accurate judgments as you would wish'.[41] Around the same time, Cardozo CJ acknowledged that judges cannot escape unconscious bias any more than others and that, all their lives, 'forces which they do not recognize and cannot name, have been tugging at them—inherited instincts, traditional beliefs, acquired

[39] ibid [74]–[75].

[40] Lord Rodger, 'Bias and Conflicts of Interests—Challenges for Today's Decision-Makers' (24th Sultan Azlan Shah Law Lecture, Kuala Lumpur, 2010) 465.

[41] Lord Justice Scrutton, 'The Work of the Commercial Courts' (1921) 1 Cambridge LJ 6, 8 (judge 1910–34).

convictions . . . '[42] In 1942 Lord Wright expressed the sentiment in relation to decision-making that a judge does not approach a case with a blank mind but that 'subconsciously or consciously, trained mental processes. . . rules learned in the past function in his mind, his own past experience and his past reading of other cases all combine to lead to a judgment'.[43]

Knowledge about unconscious bias has deepened since then. A variety of cognitive biases have been identified to which judges could potentially fall victim.[44] Among them is confirmation bias, the tendency to seek or interpret information in a way that is consistent with an existing belief. It has long been known to lawyers. In his *Novum Organum* in 1620 Francis Bacon, at the time lord chancellor, explained that once a person's understanding has settled on something 'it draws everything else also to support and agree with it [and] if it encounters a larger number of more powerful countervailing examples, it either fails to notice them, or disregards them, or makes fine distinctions to dismiss and reject them . . . '[45] Another source of potential error is hindsight bias, where a person overestimates the probability of an event occurring because of their knowledge of what in fact happened. As Bramwell B put it: 'Nothing is so easy as to be wise after the event'.[46] An example would be to rank too highly a defendant's precautions post-accident to prevent the risk of harm as evidence that it was the defendant's negligence which caused it. The substantive law warns judges against succumbing to hindsight bias in this way. Motivated cognition occurs where without being consciously aware of it judges reason towards their preferred result by emphasizing law and facts supporting it. Thus they may decide in favour of the more likeable or sympathetic litigant on what seem to be objective and legitimate grounds.

There is also what has been called representativeness bias, where if one thing resembles another thing in a category the tendency is to regard the former as a member of that category. In this process statistical information can be discounted such as the frequency with which the first thing occurs ('base rate fallacy'). An example would be a formulation of the doctrine of *res ipsa loquitur*, that if the likely product of a defendant's negligence is an

[42] Benjamin N Cardozo, *The Nature of the Judicial Process* (Yale University Press 1921) 12. See also 167–68.

[43] Lord Wright, 'Precedents' (1942) 2 U Toronto LJ 247, 269–70 (reprinted (1943) 8 Cambridge LJ 118, 138) (judge 1925–47).

[44] See also pp. 244–246 below.

[45] Francis Bacon, *The New Organon* (1620, Bk 1, XLVI) (Lisa Jardine and Michael Silverthorne eds, CUP 2000) 43.

[46] *Cornman v Eastern Counties Railway Company* (1859) 4 Hurl & N 781, 786; 157 ER 1050, 1052.

accident, the fact of that accident taking place is assumed to be because the defendant was negligent. The defect in reaching that conclusion is that it ignores the overall rate of negligence which occurs. So-called anchoring bias refers to where an initial numeric value—the anchor—unconsciously influences later calculations. Most of the research concerns sentencing criminal defendants, but a simple example in the civil context would be a judge setting damages for personal injuries having a claimant's initial demand as an unconscious anchor in fixing the final amount. Sequential decision-making can also lead to what has been termed the 'gambler's fallacy', which is the misperception of chance. Runs of three or more of the same outcome are common in a random binary sequence in which the odds of either outcome are 50 per cent, but such runs seem unnatural. Consequently, judges may mistakenly think that deciding a sequence of unrelated cases in a way that favours one side is unnatural and that they must decide for the other side in the next case.

Implicit bias is an aspect of unconscious bias where a person demonstrates a negative attitude towards a specific social group without being aware of it. Concern typically focuses on racial and gender bias and how this is formed through a person's background and learned associations between particular qualities and a person's group membership. In the justice system there has long been concern with racial bias, the perceptions, attitudes, and stereotypes which give rise to it, and its consequences for litigants and others. In England a survey of several hundred lawyers, mainly advocates, practicing largely (but not wholly) in crime, reported incidents of racial discrimination by the bench, most notably against young black male defendants.[47] A US study involving over 100 trial judges found that they harboured the same kinds of implicit biases regarding race as others in the community, but that they largely managed to avoid the influence of these in the experimental cases when told a party's race.[48] In considering the relevance of such studies in the context of the treatment of Aboriginal and Torres Strait Islander peoples in Australian courts, the Australian Law Reform Commission accepted the presumption in the *Commentary on the Bangalore Principles* that personal impartiality on the part of the judge is to be presumed unless there is evidence to the contrary.[49] Given that the disqualification rules go only so far to address how cognitive and social bias may negatively impact judicial

[47] Keir Monteith and others, *Racial Bias and the Bench* (University of Manchester 2022).

[48] Jeffrey J Rachlinski and others, 'Does Unconscious Racial Bias Affect Trial Judges' (2009) 84 Notre Dame LR 1195.

[49] *Commentary on the Bangalore Principles of Judicial Conduct* (UNODC 2007) [53].

decision-making, however, the Commission went on to consider a range of institutional correctives involving judicial appointments, education, and complaints handling.[50]

In 2017 the president of the UK Supreme Court, Lord Neuberger, referred to unconscious bias as a major and universal problem, with many manifestations, and as almost an unknown unknown extraordinarily difficult to allow for or eliminate.[51] However, various measures are available to mitigate the effect of unconscious bias. The first is a familiarity with the forms which cognitive bias take, albeit this will not solve all the difficulties in identifying its reach in a specific case.[52] Certainly the judge must consider (as with the scientific method) material in the case before them which would falsify a conclusion, possibly the product of unconscious bias, instead of simply seeking evidence, arguments, and legal precedents which would support it. In particular, intuitive opinions and initial impressions must be tested against the evidence, the law, and the parties' submissions, doubly so if there is any doubt.[53]

Secondly, judicial practices and methods properly applied can ameliorate the impact of unconscious bias. Fundamental is that judges consider both sides of a matter in accordance with the requirements of fairness.[54] There are working practices which the judge will learn as they do the job, for example, to compensate for how they might interpret materials so as to favour the more likeable or sympathetic litigant. Generalist judges will gather from experience that they should not leap to conclusions in unfamiliar territory. Limitations on judicial discretion, through having to follow guidelines, can offset cognitive biases which occur through anchoring and other effects.[55] Proceeding to a conclusion along the steps laid down in the relevant law, procedural rules, practice directions, or guidance attenuates flaws like confirmation and hindsight bias. Measures such as these may be summarized in formal (or informal) checklists or contained in frameworks drawn up for judges to use in standard decisions in high volume jurisdictions. As well as ensuring accountability, the process of formulating reasons, even if brief and

[50] Australian Law Reform Commission, *Without Fear or Favour: Judicial Impartiality and the Law on Bias* (ALRC Report 138, 2021) ch 12 (hereafter ALRC, *Without Fear or Favour*).

[51] 'Fairness in the Courts. The Best We Can Do' (Address to the Criminal Justice Alliance, 10 April 2015) [18].

[52] *Halliburton Co v Chubb Bermuda Insurance Ltd* (n 36) [70] (Lord Hodge).

[53] P. 245 below.

[54] PP. 116–118 below.

[55] eg, Judicial College, *Guidelines for the Assessment of General Damages in Personal Injury Cases* (17th edn, OUP 2024).

orally delivered, can test a judge's intuitive conclusion and combat errors arising from unconscious bias.

Thirdly, although by definition unconscious bias may not lead to a judge deciding on recusal, there is the possibility that an appellate court might decide that their decision was infected by it. Two widely different examples suffice. In 1948 the Privy Council quashed the convictions and death sentences of appellants who had conducted a sectarian attack. Since no one had appeared at the trial to prosecute, the judge conducted his own examination of the prosecution witnesses. The Privy Council said that it was impossible to be sure 'that a judge, who himself examines the prosecution witnesses, escapes an unconscious bias in favour of accepting their evidence'.[56] In 2003 there was a successful challenge to the practice of appointing counsel to sit as part-time judges in the Employment Appeal Tribunal along with lay members.[57] The practice meant that counsel appearing before a tribunal as an advocate could have sat in the past as a part-time judge with the lay members hearing a case. The fair-minded and informed observer, the House of Lords held, was likely to think that the lay members would look more favourably on submissions by the advocate from whom they would have sought advice when sitting as a judge. 'Public perception of the possibility of unconscious bias', said Lord Steyn, 'is the key'.[58]

(D) Competing Values

The Civil Procedure Rules for England and Wales contain in the overriding objective a tension between dealing with cases justly and doing so at proportionate cost.[59] In the context of securing impartiality through the disqualification rules, a tension may emerge with values such as efficiency, cost, and necessity in their application in particular circumstances. An illustration is provided by case management, which is in the interests of efficiency and reduced cost in litigation. With case management a judge, who is allocated a case, manages it from the outset, conducts the trial, and determines any consequential matters such as costs and leave to appeal.[60] Deciding whether a judge should be disqualified because of a ruling made or conclusion reached

[56] *Adan Haji Jama v The King* [1948] AC 225, 233 (Somaliland, PC).
[57] *Lawal v Northern Spirit Ltd* [2003] UKHL 35, [2004] 1 All ER 187.
[58] ibid [14].
[59] CPR 1.1(1).
[60] P. 210 below.

at earlier stages of ongoing, perhaps lengthy, litigation must take account of factors such as the cost and disruption in bringing in a new judge. Whether there is apparent bias in these cases can turn on how sparing or generous a view is taken as to what the fair-minded and informed observer would think about a judge's earlier decisions.

As regards efficiency, there is a range of practical factors pertinent to the disqualification of a judge for bias. One is the point at which an allegation arises. If that is early in the process the chances of disruption and delay are less. It may even be possible to adopt a precautionary approach. Having a judge stand down at an early stage of proceedings, where bias is raised, may avoid the delays and wasted costs if it later becomes clear that the case must start again with another judge. A second factor is the reality of unmeritorious applications by oversensitive litigants, as well as illegitimate attempts to cause delay or engage in forum shopping. The fact is that litigants can lack objectivity and draw false conclusions about a judge's bias from earlier rulings in a case. Raising bias based on earlier rulings can also be part of a litigant's tactical game.[61] A third factor is that judicial resources are limited. No indulgence should be granted to a litigant to disqualify a judge from hearing a case unless the tests for bias are clearly met. Otherwise, there can be delay, and others will be deprived of access to justice by the resources wasted and the disruption caused.

In some cases it may be possible to address competing values through the doctrine of waiver, where a judge declares what might arguably be a disqualifying interest but the parties decide that any objection is not worth pursuing and that an early resolution of their dispute is preferable. In other words they consent, with full knowledge, to a judge hearing the case despite an arguable disqualifying interest. Necessity is another aspect, although it has a narrow remit. A judge may decide a case, notwithstanding that they would otherwise be disqualified, because otherwise the case would not be heard at all, or at least not heard without considerable delay and disruption. An example of necessity would be where all the sitting judges are subject to the same disqualifying interest; for example, all will be affected by a decision concerning taxation or judicial remuneration. If retired judges are affected by the same disqualifying feature, it may be possible to recruit judges from a comparable jurisdiction to decide the case. Another example would be the judge in an apex court which sits as a full bench: if the judge does not sit,

[61] A notorious example in England is *Bates v Post Office Ltd (No 4: Recusal Application)* [2019] EWHC 871 (QB), permission to appeal refused 9 April 2019, PTA A1/2019/0855.

the court may be evenly divided.[62] Necessity is not the same as convenience, as where there is only one judge sitting at a particular venue: while causing delay and disruption, the case can be postponed until another judge is available or the matter is transferred elsewhere.

III The Disqualification Rules

There are various heads under which cases of disqualification can be analysed. The four adopted here are interest, association, opinion, and prejudgement. Extraneous information has been posited as a separate head, but in this account it is coupled with prejudgement. These heads are categories of convenience and in the main not based on principle. A case falling under one might in some situations be treated as easily under another. Notably there is a considerable overlap of disqualification for interest and association. Except for presumed bias, which in English law determines the grounds upon which a judge will be disqualified for financial interest, the grounds of actual and apparent bias apply to cases falling under all four heads.

(A) Financial and Other Interests

English law on the disqualification of judges for interest is often traced to *Dr Bonham's Case*, where Lord Coke held that the College of Physicians could not receive any of the fines they imposed on physicians.[63] Coke's maxim in his *Institutes of the Laws of England*—that no person can be a judge in their own cause—is the foundation of the English rule of presumed disqualification where a judge has a financial or other interest in the outcome of litigation.[64] The corrupt judge, bought by a party to litigation, is the quintessential example of the judge with a pecuniary interest in the outcome. The elected judge in the United States deciding a case where one of the parties has made a large contribution to their campaign funds is in the same category.[65] In practice the issue often arises in more innocuous ways. *Dimes v Proprietors of Grand Junction Canal*[66] was the foundation of the common law rule that

[62] *Cheney v United States District Court for the District of Columbia* 541 US 913 (2004) (Scalia J memorandum).
[63] *Dr Bonham's Case* (1610) 8 Co Rep 113, 120–121; 77 ER 646, 652, 657.
[64] DEC Yale, 'Iudex in Propria Causa: An Historical Excursus' (1974) 33 CLJ 80, 80.
[65] *Caperton v A T Massey Coal Co* 556 US 868 (2009).
[66] (1852) 3 HL Cas 759, 10 ER 301.

judges are automatically disqualified from deciding a case if they have an interest in its outcome through a shareholding in one of the parties. The practice became for judges to convey to the parties beforehand that they had a relatively small shareholding and for the parties to waive the objection. For a century and a half it was assumed that the disqualification applied, however small the shareholding, but eventually English law followed Commonwealth jurisprudence and recognized a *de minimis* exception to the *Dimes* principle.[67]

The UK Supreme Court states expressly that its judges do not regard a small shareholding in companies involved in a case as a matter of recusal or disclosure.[68] In moving away from the *Dimes* principle the High Court of Australia said that a judge is only disqualified when having a shareholding in a party if there is a realistic possibility that the outcome of the litigation would affect the value of the shareholding. In those circumstances disqualification follows because, in the absence of some countervailing consideration of sufficient weight, a fair-minded lay observer might reasonably apprehend that the judge might not bring an impartial mind to the resolution of the case.[69] One reason the High Court gave for this approach was the illogicality of having different rules applying to disqualification for interest and for association when the two overlap. The High Court recognized disclosure as the proper practice for a judge who owns shares in a company to give the parties an opportunity to raise an objection. Consistently with constitutional principles, the Constitutional Court of South Africa has adopted the same approach regarding recusal of a judge for financial interest.[70]

The *de minimis* approach requires that the potential effect of any decision on the judge's interest be so small that the fair-minded and informed observer would not consider that there was a real possibility of the judge being biased. Any doubt is resolved in favour of disqualification. It seems inconceivable that a judge holding a small parcel of shares in a publicly listed company, where the parcel is only a part of their total assets, could possibly be influenced in its favour. Unless the financial health of the company is significantly at stake in the litigation, their financial interest would be little enhanced by a favourable decision and the resultant impact on the company's

[67] *Locabail (UK) Ltd v Bayfield Properties Ltd* [2000] QB 451 [10] (hereafter *Locabail v Bayfield*).

[68] 'Justices' Financial Interests' https://www.supremecourt.uk/corporate-information/justices-financial-interests accessed 4 June 2025.

[69] *Ebner v Official Trustee in Bankruptcy* [2000] HCA 63, (2000) 205 CLR 337 [37].

[70] *Bernert v Absa Bank Ltd* [2010] ZACC 28 [18], [54].

share price, even less so the dividends which would be payable. The problem may arise from shareholdings in private companies. Any inquiry into the potential implications for the judge of the litigation threatens the judge's privacy and might cause delay if the actual impact of a decision on the value of the shares is disputed. That is the advantage of the *Dimes* principle: disqualification is automatic so there is no need for an inquiry.

As well as a direct shareholding, a judge might have other financial interests, direct or indirect, in a party to legal proceedings. In the modern age these other interests are common. A judge might have a bank account, a mortgage, a payment instrument, or an insurance policy with a bank which is a party to a claim before them. The judge might be the beneficiary of a trust or have an interest in a fund which has investments in one of the parties. The judge might have interests in a company which, although not a party to the litigation, could benefit (or suffer) from the outcome. As with an ordinary shareholding, the issue is the potential impact of legal proceedings on these interests and whether the fair-minded and informed observer would consider that there was a real possibility that the judge is biased. The same applies when the financial interest is that of the judge's spouse, partner, or other family member. In *Locabail* the court suggested, firstly, that the link with the judge must be so close and direct as to render that other person's interest, for all practical purposes, indistinguishable from the judge's; and secondly, that the capacity of an interest to influence the judge's decision-making is dispelled if it is shown that the judge did not know about it (a point made in relation to the now discarded real danger test, but relevant here as well).[71]

The *Dimes* principle was extended to a limited category of non-financial interests in the *Pinochet* case. There the House of Lords had decided by a majority of three to two that the former head of state of Chile, General Augusto Pinochet, during a visit to London was not immune from arrest under extradition warrants issued by Spain for crimes of torture and hostage-taking committed while he was in office.[72] The human rights body, Amnesty International, had been given leave to intervene in the litigation to support the case against immunity. Lord Hoffmann, one of the majority, served as director and chair on a pro bono basis of a charity wholly controlled by Amnesty International. His wife was employed by Amnesty International.

[71] *Locabail v Bayfield* (n 67) [10], [18].

[72] *R v Bow Street Metropolitan Stipendiary Magistrate ex parte Pinochet Ugarte (No 1)* [2000] 1 AC 61.

When General Pinochet discovered the Amnesty connection, he applied to the House of Lords to set aside its earlier order on the grounds of bias. A newly constituted panel of five law lords held unanimously in *Pinochet (No 2)* that because of his relationship with Amnesty International, Lord Hoffmann had been automatically disqualified from hearing the case and the earlier judgment was set aside.[73] The interest of Amnesty International in the litigation was not financial but the cause of achieving the trial of Pinochet for crimes against humanity. It participated in the litigation to argue for that outcome. The charity Lord Hoffmann chaired shared, the court observed, that same object. His disqualification was automatic, without any investigation into whether there was a likelihood or suspicion of bias. The mere fact of the interest was sufficient unless there had been sufficient disclosure.

Pinochet (No 2) has been given a narrow application in later cases.[74] The courts have held that it must be possible to say, in effect, that a judge is acting in their own cause because of membership of a group identified with the case. There must be a substantial or meaningful connection with the issues that the judge has to decide. Active involvement in the institution of the proceedings would provide that connection, not mere membership of the group. All this is consistent with the *de minimis* exception to *Dimes*. Moreover, issues are now more likely to be resolved based on apparent, not presumed, bias. *Pinochet (No 2)* was decided at a time when the test for apparent bias was still the real danger test, rather than the fair-minded informed observer test. Lord Hoffmann's position would now be resolved by asking whether a fair-minded and informed observer, having considered the facts, would conclude that there was a real possibility that the judge might not bring an impartial mind to the resolution of the question to be decided.

(B) Association

In the seminal case on damages for breach of contract, *Hadley v Baxendale*,[75] two of the three judges had an association with the defendant; one had represented it as standing counsel and the other's brother had been managing director of the company. Neither judge felt obliged to disqualify themselves from

[73] *R v Bow Street Metropolitan Stipendiary Magistrate ex parte Pinochet Ugarte (No 2)* [2000] 1 AC 119.
[74] *Meerabux v Attorney General of Belize* [2005] UKPC 12, [2005] 2 AC 513 (PC, Belize).
[75] (1854) 9 Ex 341, 156 ER 145.

hearing the case. The world has moved on and standards have improved. So too have been the number of challenges under this head. Association and its opposite, antagonism, are now regular features of challenges for bias. Some types of association are fraught with danger. A family or personal association is one. Away from these, the bare allegation of an association because of a position the judge occupied or currently occupies, or their membership of a group, does not answer the relevant question. What is needed is a consideration of the nature and the intensity of the relationship and any passage of time between the association and the subject matter of the challenge. Associations between lawyers are especially tricky, sharpened through new patterns in the justice system such as the recruitment of judges from law firms (rather than the independent bar) and of more part-time judges.

Regarding a family or personal association, the *Guide to Judicial Conduct* for England and Wales offers the following guidelines, acknowledging the absence of hard and fast rules: first, judges should not sit on a case in which they have a close family relationship with a party or the spouse or domestic partner of a party; secondly, friendship with, or personal animosity towards, a party is also a compelling reason for disqualification, but friendship may be distinguished from acquaintanceship, depending on its nature and extent; thirdly, a current or recent business association with a party will usually mean recusal, as when a judge's solicitor, accountant, doctor, dentist, or other professional adviser is a party in the case; fourthly, past professional association with a party as a client need not of itself be a reason for disqualification although the judge must assess whether the particular circumstances could create an appearance of bias; fifthly, where a witness (including an expert witness) is personally well known to the judge all the circumstances should be considered, including whether the credibility of the witness is in issue, the nature of the issue to be decided, and the closeness of the friendship; and sixthly, judges should not sit on a case in which a member of their family appears as an advocate.[76]

The situations identified in the *Guide* are fleshed out in the case law. It demonstrates the difficulties in specific situations and how application of the guidance can be problematic. As regards witnesses, for example, cases fall on both sides of the line: in one the judge was disqualified because he knew as a long-standing family acquaintance a potential witness in what was to be a long commercial trial; in another, the passage of time had weakened

[76] *Guide to Judicial Conduct* (n 10) 22–23.

the association—an expert witness had been the judge's research supervisor, but that was thirty years previously.[77] Then there is association because of a judge's service with a body or past employment. In a case before the International Criminal Tribunal for the former Yugoslavia, a defendant appealed his conviction based on the presiding judge's prior membership of the UN Commission on the Status of Women. He unsuccessfully argued that a reasonable person could have an apprehension that now as a judge she was seeking to promote the Commission's legal and political agenda of punishing rape in armed conflict as a war crime.[78]

The judge currently serving, even pro bono, on an outside body like a university council must guard against apparent bias. The hazards are illustrated by the US Supreme Court decision that a federal district judge on the board of trustees of a university should have recused himself because his impartiality might reasonably be questioned. He was deciding a property dispute where, although not a party, the university had much to gain albeit that he did not know this at the time.[79] Depending on the context even a short association at the time of a decision may disqualify the judge for bias. That was the decision in the South Africa Supreme Court of Appeal when, during a hearing concerning a bitter labour dispute, the presiding judge spoke at a forum organized by the employer's closely aligned industrial relations advisers. Given the context where there was acrimony, hostility, and a fundamental conflict of interest between management and workers, the court unsurprisingly held that the average lay litigant would regard this as displaying too great an association with one side.[80]

Membership of a group may be suggestive of partiality towards its members or the cause it espouses or possibly of enmity towards non-members or those in other groups. The *Guide to Judicial Conduct* cautions judges to be careful about the extent and nature of their involvement and identifies the following factors to be taken into account: involvement must not compromise judicial independence or put at risk the status or integrity of judicial office; particular care is needed in becoming a public spokesperson for an organization; the time and the duties connected with it should not interfere with the performance of judicial work; there should be no active business

[77] Compare *AWG Group Ltd v Morrison* [2006] EWCA Civ 6, [2006] 1 WLR 1163 and *Resolution Chemicals Ltd v H Lundbeck A/S* [2013] EWCA Civ 1515, [2014] 1 WLR 1943.

[78] *Prosecutor v Anto Furundžija*, 21 July 2000, Case No IT-95-17/1A [195]–[215].

[79] *Liljeberg v Health Service Acquisition Corp* 486 US 847 (1988).

[80] *BTR Industries (Pty) Ltd v MAWU* 1992 (3) SA 673 [61]–[62].

management in the case of full-time judges; and the part played should not be for the purpose of lending status or respectability to the group.[81]

The facts of *Helow* are illustrative.[82] The petitioner, a Palestinian refugee living in Lebanon, claimed asylum in the UK because of a fear that, if returned there, she would be at risk from Israeli and other authorities on account of her Palestinian connections and activities. The judge dismissed her case. Subsequently, her representatives discovered that the judge was a member of the International Association of Jewish Lawyers and Jurists and sought to set aside the decision for apparent bias on the ground that the association was strongly opposed to the claimant's pro-Palestinian and anti-Israel views. The House of Lords dismissed her appeal. In doing so it examined the nature of the association and the significance of the judge's membership. The association's published aims were unobjectionable, and it could not be taken for granted that the membership shared the fervently pro-Israeli views of a selection of its published material. Moreover, it could be assumed that the judge could remain detached and reach an impartial decision according to law, and there was no evidence that this judge endorsed these extreme views (even if she had read them). Thus, the House of Lords concluded, the fair-minded and informed observer would not consider that there was a real possibility of bias. However, the case is a salutary warning that mere membership of some groups can give rise to challenges, even if unsuccessful.

What about past membership of a group? The reality is that judges are appointed to the bench having been members of different organizations. Like others they can be affected, perhaps unconsciously, by the friendship and institutional loyalty which flows from that. Such influences can survive through time despite resignation or the severance of any connection on appointment as a judge. The countervailing factor is that they now work in an environment whose ethos is to administer impartial justice. This can go a long way. In *President of the Republic of South Africa v South African Rugby Football Union*[83] the Constitutional Court of South Africa dismissed an application to disqualify four of the ten members of the court from hearing a case involving Nelson Mandela, the president of the country and president of the African National Congress, because of their membership before appointment of the ANC. As the court observed, judges are expected to put any party-political loyalties behind them on their appointment and given South

[81] *Guide to Judicial Conduct* (n 10) 12.
[82] *Helow v Advocate General for Scotland* [2008] UKHL 62, [2008] 1 WLR 2416.
[83] [1999] ZACC 9, 1999 (4) SA 147, 1999 (7) BCLR 725.

Africa's history 'it would be surprising if many candidates for appointment to the bench had not been active in or publicly sympathetic towards the liberation struggle'.[84]

Association between the judge and the lawyers and parties in a case may threaten impartiality. Judges must avoid direct association with individual lawyers who are engaged in current or pending cases before them. It required the High Court of Australia to reassert this 'most basic of judicial practice' when in a surprising decision an intermediate appellate court had held (by majority) that there was no apprehended bias when the trial judge socialized and exchanged numerous text messages with a barrister for one side even if this had nothing to do with the case.[85] Another dimension to this topic is the judge's close social relationship with a lawyer who is regularly involved in litigation before their court. In some jurisdictions there is a tradition of judges and members of the legal profession associating with each other for educational and social purposes. An example is the membership of judges and barristers of one of the four Inns of Court in England and Wales. Of itself this is not a sufficient reason for disqualification.

Nor is a judge disqualified because before appointment they were a member of a law firm representing one of the parties in the case the judge is deciding. Much will turn on factors such as the size of the law firm, the nature of the case, and the closeness of the relationship between the judge and the lawyer from the firm handling it. The judge will certainly be disqualified if they worked on the case currently being decided. Otherwise the passage of time attenuates any objection. Cooling off periods are used in some courts. There are the specific problems thrown up by lawyers serving as part-time judges, which is a feature of the judicial landscape in Britain.[86] English appellate courts have been robust in resisting challenges of apparent bias simply because the part-time judge and the advocate are members of the same barristers' chambers or have appeared or will appear together on the same side in unrelated litigation.[87] Barristers in chambers in England and Wales are in independent practice, and there are strong traditions of independence and ethical behaviour. That will not necessarily allay the fears of those unfamiliar with the history and nature of the barrister's position.

84 at [75].
85 *Charisteas v Charisteas* [2021] HCA 29, 273 CLR 289.
86 P. 169 below.
87 eg, *Watts v Watts* [2015] EWCA Civ 1297.

As to a judge's association with a former client, that does not automatically give rise to an apprehension of bias when the client appears in the judge's court. Much depends on the nature and length of the association, the time that has elapsed, and the information acquired. An intense or long association as counsel to one of the parties points to disqualification. In *Williams v Pennsylvania*[88] the judge had earlier had a significant, personal involvement as a prosecutor in a critical decision regarding the defendant's case. The US Supreme Court held that a serious question arose whether the judge could set aside his interest in the outcome, even with the most diligent effort; there was a risk that he could be psychologically wedded to his previous position as prosecutor. As well there was the judge's personal knowledge, which could well carry more weight than the parties' present arguments. An extreme case was the *Colorado Strikes case*[89] in the early part of the twentieth century, where certain miners were being tried for murder and other crimes alleged to have been committed during a long and bitter union recognition dispute. The trial judge refused to disqualify himself even though he had been counsel for the mining company on several occasions in similar cases, and according to the miners' affidavits had also condemned the mine-workers in vigorous language. As the *Harvard Law Review* at the time noted, the justice of the appellate court in disqualifying the judge was 'beyond question'.[90]

(C) Opinion

In 1952 the US Supreme Court upheld the constitutionality of streetcars (trams) in Washington DC broadcasting radio programmes to passengers.[91] Justice Frankfurter recused himself from hearing the case because in his opinion the practice was abhorrent. There was a good deal of shallow talk that the judicial robe did not change the person within it, he said, but it did. Overall, he continued, judges laid aside private views in discharging their judicial function, which was achieved through training, professional habits, self-discipline, and what he characterized as a fortunate alchemy by which judges are loyal to their duty. It was also true, he added, that reason could not control the subconscious influence of feelings of which it was unaware,

88 579 US 1 (2016).
89 *People v District Court* (1915) 60 Col 1, 152 Pac 149.
90 'Note' (1915) 29 Harv LR 430, 431–32.
91 *Public Utilities Commission v Pollak* 343 US 451 (1952).

and when there was ground for believing that such unconscious feelings may operate, or may lead others to believe this, judges should recuse themselves.

A greater challenge is posed by a judge's opinions on social and political issues than the annoyances of contemporary living. Prior to holding judicial office, a judge may have expressed social or political opinions or even held office in a civil society organization or a political party or NGO. That is generally no threat to impartiality so long as a judge is open to persuasion. Indeed, the judge's past life may assist impartiality by broadening their experience and receptivity to other perspectives. On appointment, however, a judge must generally refrain from expressions of opinion and detach themselves from such connections. A judge who publicly expresses an opinion relevant to an issue in a case is on a sure path to disqualification.[92] There is of course a certain irony in that opinions have to be expressed before a litigant can hope to challenge the judge for bias; the judge who holds the same opinion as a disqualified judge, but discreetly, may in theory hear a case.

The situation was clear-cut when Douglas J of the US Supreme Court recused himself in an environmental case, challenging the grant of oil drilling permits in the aftermath of the Santa Barbara oil spill, because he had publicly expressed himself on the very matter.[93] Similarly, in several extra-curial lectures Lord Steyn insisted that the powerful voices suggesting the abandonment of rights in the face of the terrorist threat had to be resisted, and he also expressed the view that the suspension of Article 5 of the ECHR—which prevents arbitrary detention—could not justify imprisonment without trial. In a lecture which attracted the attention of the international media he described the US detention of Taliban suspects at Guantánamo Bay as a 'legal black hole'. The result was that he had to disqualify himself from sitting as a law lord in the *Belmarsh* case, concerning the indefinite detention in the UK of foreign nationals suspected of terrorism.[94]

Generally, legal and related writing should not disqualify a judge, although the judge who has expressed trenchant views in favour of one side, albeit in general terms, may have to step aside.[95] The issue arose with the Special Court for Sierra Leone, which was established in 2002. It followed the brutal civil war perpetrated by a rebel force, the Revolutionary United Front (RUF), supported by the president of Liberia, Charles Taylor. Ultimately in

[92] eg, European Court of Human Rights, Rules of Court, r 28.2(d).

[93] Note, 'Disqualification of Judges and Justices in the Federal Courts' (1973) 86 Harv LR 736, 755n.

[94] *A v Secretary of State for the Home Department* [2004] UKHL 56, [2005] 2 AC 68.

[95] *Locabail v Bayfield* (n 67) 480, 496–97.

2013 the court's appeals chamber upheld the conviction and fifty-year sentence imposed on Taylor for war crimes and crimes against humanity. Early in the history of the court the appeals chamber heard a defence application that the president of the court, the eminent human rights lawyer Geoffrey Robertson KC, should be removed because of his severe criticism of the RUF in a book written before his appointment to the court. The court held that Justice Robertson could remain as a member of the court but should not participate in cases involving ex-RUF members since a reasonable person would apprehend bias, more so an accused person.[96]

Compared with the position in the nineteenth and first part of the twentieth centuries, very few English judges these days have a background as politicians. Judges must sever active political connections on appointment. (In some states in the United States, judges retain political affiliations after appointment since they are subject to periodic election.[97]) Judges who have served as members of the legislature or the executive may need to disqualify if as parliamentarians they were closely identified with the issue before them. Mere membership of the government or voting for the legislation at issue when in parliament is not enough.[98] However, there will be a sufficient nexus justifying recusal if the judge when a government minister or parliamentarian participated in the formulation and active promotion of the legislation and gave assurances about its application which are being contested in the litigation.[99] A judge who served as a senior civil servant would be in the same position, although a relatively small involvement in an issue when serving in government many years before should not give rise to apparent bias.[100]

Prejudice against a class of persons or a political cause can be a menace to the impartial administration of justice since it can be far-reaching in its effect. In an American case a judge began disbarment proceedings on his own motion against a lawyer who had been committed for contempt while defending members of the Communist Party. It would be difficult to deny that the judge was prejudiced against Communists and those associated with them; he had told another judge beforehand that it was questionable whether lawyers such as the defendant had a right to continue the practice of law because the Supreme Court had held that the Communist Party was dedicated

[96] *Prosecutor v Issa Hassan Sesay. Decision on Defence Motion Seeking the Disqualification of Justice Robertson from the Appeals Chamber* (SCSL-04-15-AR15) [2004] SCSL 1 [15].

[97] P. 154 below.

[98] *Panton v Minister of Finance* [2001] UKPC 33 (PC, Jamaica).

[99] *Davidson v Scottish Ministers No 2* [2004] UKHL 34, 2005 1 SC (HL) 7.

[100] *Wewaykum Indian Band v Canada* 2003 SCC 45, [2003] 2 SCR 259.

to the overthrow of the government. On appeal it was held that he should have disqualified himself from hearing any disbarment charge.[101]

(D) Prejudgement

Disqualification for interest, association, or opinion concerns, in a way, factors extraneous to legal proceedings. By contrast, an accusation of prejudgement is that a judge through a previous decision will not approach a matter with an open mind, giving rise to actual or apparent bias. In a sense there is considerable scope for such challenges since judges constantly make decisions across and during cases which may have a bearing on the decision immediately before them. The issue of prejudgement can arise in at least two contexts, one resulting from a judge's decisions in previous cases unconnected to the present case, the other from a judge's decisions in the same, ongoing litigation.

The first situation—bias in relation to a judge's previous decisions—is less troublesome. When making decisions on the law the judge will apply precedent, including their own previous decisions on a matter if these have not been disturbed on appeal. Even if a judge has been exposed to evidence in an earlier case, which touches on but would not otherwise be heard in the second, there should be no issue of disqualification since judges are trained to put out of their mind prejudicial but inadmissible evidence. There will be situations, however, where in a previous case a judge has made findings such that they should consider recusal. Lord Denning stood aside in a case involving the Church of Scientology when on some of the eight previous occasions it had been a party before him he had expressed critical views about it.[102] Trenchant findings on a person's credibility may cast doubt that the judge can approach the person's evidence with an open mind on later occasions. Similarly, the High Court of Australia found (by majority) that a judge should have disqualified himself when in an earlier case he had made an unqualified finding that under cover of a document retention policy a company had dishonestly concealed the destruction of evidence which might be prejudicial in claims against it for causing lung cancer like the present.[103]

[101] *Gladstein v McLaughlin* 230 F 2d 762 (9th Cir, 1955).
[102] *Ex parte Church of Scientology of California* The Times, 21 February 1978.
[103] *British American Tobacco Australia Services Limited v Laurie* [2011] HCA 2, 242 CLR 283.

As in other areas of disqualification for bias, however, much turns on context. In *O'Neill v HM Advocate*[104] the sexual offences and murder charges on which the defendants were indicted were severed, but the same judge presided at both trials although sitting with different juries. The judge described the defendants as evil, determined, manipulative, and predatory paedophiles of the worst sort after they had been convicted in the sexual offending trial. The Supreme Court held that the remarks were made in the context of the judge's judicial function of giving an indication as to the sentences to be imposed when sentencing occurred after the murder trial. The fair-minded and informed observer would also appreciate, it remarked, that this was a professional judge, with years of relevant training and experience. It did not assist the defendants' case that their counsel had not objected at any point until they were also convicted on the murder charges.

Statistical analysis has been brought to bear in Canada and Australia in specific cases to demonstrate that some immigration judges have a 100 per cent refusal rate compared with others and that because of this should be disqualified for bias in the applicant's case. So far appellate courts in these jurisdictions have taken the view that by themselves the bare statistics will not assist the hypothetical observer in making an informed assessment whether those judges will bring an impartial mind to the current proceedings in which they are being challenged for bias. As a Canadian federal court has put it: 'Such comparisons are meaningless unless they are compared with the approaches of other members, or unless the patterns and formulae do not adequately address the points at issue in any particular claim.'[105]

With respect to the second situation, a judge may make a series of decisions during ongoing litigation, typically on routine matters such as case management and the admissibility of evidence. None should ordinarily lead to the disqualification of the judge from further hearing the case. There are major benefits from case management in the efficiencies gained and the costs saved, doubly so in group litigation (a class action) or where the court operates a docket system with the one judge seeing a case through from the early stages to completion. It will only be the judge straying over the line from case management to adjudication on issues not yet properly decided where bias may arise. A judge will generally be expected to hear ancillary matters after judgment such as costs and any application for committal for contempt.[106]

[104] [2013] UKSC 36, [2013] 1 WLR 1992.

[105] eg, *IPP v Canada (Citizenship and Immigration)*, 2018 FC 123, [270]–[276]. See also *ALA15 v Minister for Immigration and Border Protection* [2016] FCAFC 30.

[106] *Otkritie International Investment Management Ltd v Urumov* [2014] EWCA Civ 1315.

More controversially, it has been held by the Court of Appeal for England and Wales that an appellate judge refusing permission to appeal is not barred from sitting on the substantive appeal after another judge has granted permission to appeal on hearing a review. The assumption is that the refusing judge will have the benefit of oral argument and be open to being persuaded that their initial view was wrong.[107]

Generally, there is no objection to a trial judge having previously made a decision about interim relief in a case, since that will have been based on the limited issue being raised at the time.[108] That during a hearing a judge comments adversely on a party or witness, opines that their evidence seems unreliable, or indicates a view about merits is also not sufficient of itself to give rise to apparent bias. The tradition of oral advocacy in the common law system does not discourage tentative expressions of a judge's thinking since the advocate is then able to address the issue. That is to be contrasted with the judge giving the inescapable impression of having a fixed view of one party's credibility or merits especially when not having heard the other side. As ever language is important. Opinions expressed in the course of a hearing in conclusive or vehement terms, or which are especially damming about one side, call into question whether the judge will take an impartial view in the final decision.

IV Procedure

Judges may recuse themselves on their own initiative or on an application for disqualification by one of the parties. Either way issues of potential bias need to be dealt with quickly and efficiently. First, matters may be dealt with informally. On receipt of a new case the judge considers whether there is a possibility of bias, albeit unconscious, or whether their involvement might give rise to a reasonable apprehension of bias in the eyes of the fair-minded and informed observer. They consider whether they have a relevant interest in the case, any association even if indirect with one side, any opinion they have expressed which may bear on its outcome, and the implications of any involvement in these or previous relevant proceedings. The court's administration should not allocate particular cases to a judge because of potential conflicts about which they have been notified or are aware. A newly appointed judge

[107] *Sengupta v Holmes* [2002] EWCACiv 1104.
[108] *Michael Wilson & Partners Ltd v Nicholls* [2011] HCA 48, 244 CLR 427.

may be a potential candidate for disqualification because of background factors or the litigation they have been involved in prior to appointment. These issues generally fade the longer a judge is in office. Background is less important when set against the judge's judicial output, and earlier professional involvement has less salience with the passage of time.

When an issue arises the judge assesses the strength of a potential issue. They may consult colleagues to obtain a second opinion. Recusal can cause a serious interference with the smooth listing of cases before a court. Even if the chances of a successful challenge are marginal, judges may be able to adopt a precautionary approach with applications to be dealt with 'on the papers' or at a short hearing by arranging for the matter to be reallocated to another judge without any disruption or delay in the court's work. The parties may remain ignorant of what has occurred. Judges have a duty to hear the cases allocated to them: recusal is not a cover to avoid sitting on a controversial or difficult case or because the judge may anticipate public opprobrium in doing so.

Secondly, where matters cannot be dealt with informally in this way the judge will disclose a potentially disqualifying factor to the parties. The *Guide to Judicial Conduct* for England and Wales encourages judges to make disclosure well before the hearing, if possible, since disclosure if followed by recusal close to the day of the hearing means costs for the parties and disruption if it needs to be postponed.[109] However, judges do not disclose matters which could not possibly give rise to apprehension on the part of the fair-minded and informed observer since this could cause significant disruption. When judges make disclosure, the expectation is that generally speaking the parties will waive any objection they could have. For example, the parties will generally consent to a judge sitting in an environmental challenge to a development after disclosure that the judge has a relatively small shareholding in the transnational company involved or is a member of an NGO such as the National Trust or a Wildlife Trust which has raised concerns about the development. It has been said that disclosure itself is a badge of impartiality: it is a factor which the fair-minded and informed observer will consider as relevant in evaluating whether there is a real possibility of bias.[110] The duty of disclosure continues throughout a case.

Thirdly, on an application for disqualification, or a party's failure to waive after disclosure, a judge may decide that the arguments for disqualification

[109] *Guide to Judicial Conduct* (n 10) 23.
[110] *Davidson v Scottish Ministers (No.2)* [2004] UKHL 34, 2005 1 SC (HL) 7 [54].

lack force and decide to hear the case, especially if the cost and delay for it to be heard before another judge is disproportionate given its nature. Reasons are desirable.[111] Difficulties arise if a party objects to a judge sitting—possibly after a potentially disqualifying feature is unearthed—once the case has begun. Not sitting will upset the court's work, place additional burdens on colleagues, and possibly foster opportunistic or tactical recusal applications in other cases. An aspect of this is forum shopping, where parties attempt to have their dispute determined by other judges who (without any suggestion of bias) might be more predisposed to their case. As in other contexts judges may face tough decisions since, if they refuse to recuse, an appellate court may set aside their judgment for bias even though in other respects it is sound. With multi-member courts it might be held on further appeal that all the judges were contaminated by the bias of one.[112] Much will turn on factors such as the nature of the judge's interest and the extent of interaction with the other judges leading to contamination. If appellate courts are to allow an appeal for bias they must in fairness have the judge's own account of the matter if there is no record. There is little merit to a challenge where a party has kept the issue of disqualification in reserve for use on an appeal should the party be unsuccessful on the substantive issues.

The current procedure in England and elsewhere is that the judge under challenge will generally decide the issue of recusal, unless there is an appeal. The presiding judge or the panel as a whole may make the decision as to whether one of its member should sit. At first blush the notion that the judge under challenge should decide the issue seems to breach the maxim that a person should not be a judge in their own cause. There is also the objection that a judge under challenge may not be in the best position to assess their bias, unconscious or otherwise, or how the fair-minded and informed observer would regard their conduct. Given the increased diversity of the bench it may also be that there is less agreement on how particular types of bias allegations should be handled. These factors have led to suggestions that bias challenges should be dealt with by a more sophisticated 'ethical infrastructure'. Most bias challenges are straightforward, and in such cases an elaborate machinery would be disproportionate, causing unnecessary delay, expense, and disruption to the court's business. There is also the danger that referring bias allegations for consideration elsewhere will encourage vexatious complaints by litigants in person who cannot accept that they have

[111] ALRC, *Without Fear or Favour* (n 50) 223–24.
[112] 78 above.

failed and tactical manoeuvring by a party's lawyers. The Australian Law Reform Commission considers that these concerns can be accommodated in a discretionary procedure for referring more difficult disqualification issues for decision by colleagues and a streamlined procedure for interlocutory appeals against disqualification decisions by single judges.[113]

V Conclusion

Impartiality is crucial to the administration of justice and public confidence in it. Impartiality is a commitment which judges must embrace and manifest through their decisions and everyday behaviour in court and outside. At base it is the state of mind of the judge, to act in accordance with the judicial oath. Judges need to cultivate impartiality as a habit of mind, sensitizing themselves to possible biases, including those which are unconscious. Impartiality must be on display to the general public. That is why the appearance of impartiality is as important as the reality, although without the reality the appearance would soon dissolve. Underpinning the judicial mind favouring impartiality are disqualification rules, as well as the behavioural standards for judges, often codified, at least to an extent, in guidance and codes of conduct. Ultimately judges are held to these standards through the disciplinary procedures considered in Chapter 4. One aspect of the institutional backing for impartiality is widespread public support in a community for an impartial and non-corrupt judiciary. Coupled with institutional factors and behavioural standards, the focus in the adjudicative process on legally relevant matters is important in limiting the extent to which judges can bring biases to bear.

Justice Oliver Wendell Holmes was perhaps the first judge to point out that judges come to judging with opinions, intuitions about public policy, 'avowed or unconscious', and prejudices.[114] None of this necessarily constitutes objectionable bias, subversive of impartiality. Impartiality is not the same thing as having no preconceptions, since a judge's background, education, legal practice, and experience on the bench will inevitably give rise to beliefs, commitments, and views of how the world works. There is no need for judges to divorce themselves completely from their beliefs and values, even if it were possible. Judges must be able to draw on their life experience

[113] ALRC, *Without Fear or Favour* (n 50) 241, 278.
[114] Oliver Wendell Holmes, *The Common Law* (Little, Brown & Co 1881) 1.

in judging, although they need also to be aware of any biases to which these or their interests and associations may give rise. In delivering the judgement of the Supreme Court of Canada in a case concerned with the civic engagement of judges, Abella J said that a judge's identity and experiences are an important part of who they are, and that judges should be encouraged to experience, learn, and understand 'life'—their own and those whose lives reflect different realities. She added that neither neutrality nor impartiality is inherently compromised by them.[115] In this regard it could be said that society has a right to expect that, within the limits of their role, judges will display common humanity and be responsive to societal needs and values. Empathy is not ruled out.[116]

In everyday judging the watchword is the possibility of apparent or unconscious bias. Conceptually, the test for determining apparent bias, at least in English law, is a fiction—that of a fair-minded, objective, and omniscient observer—although this does not adversely affect identifying apparent bias in practice. To avoid apparent (and actual) bias there is a developed set of common law behavioural rules regarding disqualification for interest, association, opinion, and prejudgement. Reinforced with relevant parts of the guides and codes of judicial behaviour, there are also the behavioural standards for judges in and away from court discussed in the next chapter, which minimize the occasions on which it is necessary for a judge to be disqualified from hearing or deciding cases. All these offer guidance on identifying improper influences and how they are to be mitigated. In addition, there are understandings and assumptions about the judge's path, some having a bearing on impartiality. Appointment as a judge may entail resigning from membership of organizations, disposing of financial assets, or curbing one's tongue both inside and outside court—to give just three examples.

When sitting, judges need to be proactive to avoid breaches of the disqualification rules. Listing officers need to be notified of possible conflicts a judge may have, and a case may be informally reallocated to another judge if a conflict is spotted when the judge receives it. An application by a party for disqualification needs to be dealt with expeditiously and reasons given. Just as it is the duty of judges to recuse themselves if a party's application is well-founded, there is also a duty to sit. Unnecessary recusal in a difficult

115 *Yukon Francophone School Board, Education Area #23 v Yukon (Attorney General)* [2015] 2 SCR 282 [34].

116 PP. 247–48 below.

case or one likely to attract public opprobrium not only transfers the burden to other judges but can also be costly and disruptive to the work of a court. Applications for recusal may be part of a litigation strategy, to remove a judge thought (perhaps on the basis of statistical analysis) to be unsympathetic to a party.

Litigants may appeal a judge's decision alleging bias. The reality is that litigants, particularly litigants in person, are apt to perceive actual bias when none exists. An objection about the bias of a judge may be coupled with a complaint lodged with the disciplinary body. Internet searches by litigants of what judges have done and said enables misguided, opportunistic, and tactical challenges to be mounted. However fanciful bias allegations may be, they need to be dealt with by procedures which preserve public confidence in the impartiality of the judge being challenged and that of the judiciary as a whole.

The disqualification rules have a narrow ambit. They do not address the less tangible unconscious biases, which Holmes and many other judges have long acknowledged. Compared with Holmes' time, however, there is wide recognition of the range of different cognitive biases which have a potential purchase on judicial decision-making. Judges need to be sensitized to the possibility of these and must consciously guard against them improperly influencing their behaviour and decisions. Addressing unconscious bias requires institutional action as well as action on the part of the individual judge. Judicial shortcuts, which are necessary for the efficient management of a judge's workload, are a fertile ground for unconscious bias. Not only must judges be aware of their disqualifying interests and unconscious biases, and take remedial steps to counter their effects, they need also to demonstrate impartiality through the fair way they conduct hearings and make decisions.

3
Integrity

I Introduction

Judicial integrity connotes adherence to the content of judicial virtue. Judicial virtue goes beyond 'first principles' like honesty and a commitment to the public interest to encompass the values of independence and impartiality, as well as the standards governing a judge's behaviour both in court and in the outside world. In-court standards include acting fairly, competently, and efficiently, exhibiting respect, patience, and decorum, and according equal concern and respect to all. Standards outside court extend beyond compliance with the law of the land to include the limitations which judges must accept on their rights as citizens. As with judicial independence and impartiality, judicial integrity has both individual and institutional dimensions. The individual judge must act with integrity, but public confidence also derives from the ethos of the judiciary as a whole and its standards of professional virtue. Given the privileged position which judges occupy in society, and the power the judiciary exercises, the public has a right to expect integrity in both the individual judge and the judiciary as an institution. To maintain the integrity of the institution, the judiciary needs to encourage and reinforce adherence to these values and the relevant behavioural standards by the judges, addressing shortcomings from the inadvertent and trivial through to the more serious.

The chapter begins in section II with the ways of securing judicial integrity. Critical is the judge's own character and conscience, what can be described as the internal aspect of judicial integrity. On top of that socialization in the judicial role should mean that the judge is attuned to a virtuous course when confronted with a challenging ethical issue. In difficult situations, or those which are not straightforward, guidance and codes may provide behavioural standards and pathways to an ethical choice. The chapter then turns in sections III and IV to some of the specific standards of behaviour upon which judicial integrity is founded. The subject matter is divided into first, integrity in the process of judicial decision-making and secondly, integrity in

Judging. Ross Cranston, Oxford University Press. © Ross Cranston 2025.
DOI: 10.1093/9780191890994.003.0003

the judge's behaviour away from court. In the eyes of litigants, the profession, and society, a perception that a judge's behaviour away from court breaches judicial values and behavioural standards can be just as inimical to reputation as breaches in the process of decision-making. Away from court not only must judges comply with rules against speeding and understating their taxable income, they must also accept restrictions in their private and family lives to which others are not subject, or at least not to the same extent, in relation to matters such as their right to freedom of expression and involvement in community activities.

II Safeguarding Integrity

Judicial integrity turns on many factors. The primary responsibility lies with the judges themselves, individually, but also collectively as new judges are socialized into the norms of virtuous behaviour by their colleagues and also provided explicit guidance and codes regarding accepted behaviour. The other branches of government have a role to play as well. The executive has the duty of ensuring the selection of judges with integrity if they have the power of appointment. The legislature must enact suitable laws for the appointment of virtuous judges, and for ensuring the investigation of complaints about judicial behaviour and the disciplining and, if necessary, removal of those not up to the mark.

(A) Integrity from Within

The judge may adopt a commitment to judicial integrity because it accords with judicial values and accepted standards of judicial behaviour. As well as these external factors in judicial virtue, judges need to have a disposition to integrity from within. No law, judicial guidance, code, or disciplinary process can guarantee judicial integrity unless the judge is committed to the norms of judicial virtue. These norms include first principles such as honesty, honourable conduct, and commitment to the public interest; judicial values such as independence and impartiality; and the implicit and explicit standards of behaviour laid down for judges. The best guarantee of judicial integrity is if a judge has internalized these first principles, values, and standards. The judge's moral compass as to what is required then ensures that they choose the right course as second nature.

The internal aspect of judicial integrity is that the person occupying the role of judge must be capable of acting with integrity and must do so in practice. Judges must place the obligations of judicial office above ego and personal interest and strive for judicial virtue. This turns in part on individual temperament, attitudes, and behavioural traits. It may be impaired by character defects or the consequence of mental (and perhaps physical) decline.[1] Issues of character should be attended to at the very outset in the appointment process: has a candidate for appointment as a judge exhibited tendencies in their professional or personal life which cast any shadow over their capacity to act with the integrity expected of a judge? After appointment there will be a socialization process which contributes to the internal integrity of the judge. A culture of integrity in a judiciary reinforces first principles and assists individual judges to comply with first principles, judicial values, and the expected standards of judicial behaviour.

Underpinnings to judicial integrity for the individual judge comprise the incentive to judicial virtue provided by the respect which it can earn them from others, not only judicial colleagues but the legal profession and the wider public. A reputation for judicial integrity in turn engenders public confidence not only in the individual judge but also in the judiciary of which they are part. Respect and public confidence are not empty concepts but are demonstrated in public opinion polling evaluating the standing of different institutions in a society. The legitimacy of judicial power turns on integrity, along with judicial independence and impartiality, especially when members of the public may not understand the legal rationale for a decision with which they disagree. The more intense focus on judges and their decisions in the digital age means that society no longer regards as acceptable features of judicial behaviour of an earlier age. Misconduct by a judge can now be amplified and is therefore potentially more corrosive of public trust and confidence. Judges in jurisdictions where integrity is highly prized should have an even greater incentive to live up to the standards it comprehends.

An underpinning to judicial integrity for the individual judge includes the behavioural standards, conventions, and understandings for judicial behaviour, some taking concrete form in law, ethical guidance, and codes of conduct. Judicial virtue should be part of the judge's fabric, the internal dimension, obviating the need most of the time for reliance on these external norms of appropriate behaviour. When facing a difficult issue, for which

[1] See *Stewart v Secretary of State for Scotland*, 1998 SC (HL) 81, 83, 87; *Re Chief Justice of Gibraltar* [2009] UKPC 43, [222]–[223] (PC, Gibraltar).

there seems to be no immediate answer, judges may also seek informal, ethical advice from other judges respected for their integrity and judgement. Many jurisdictions now take the view that in an age of accountability more is needed than reliance on the individual judge's sense of virtuous conduct, coupled with informal advice from colleagues.

Making certain that those chosen as judges are of 'good character' is more demanding with candidates coming from more diverse backgrounds and areas of legal practice. In a previous age the selection of judges from a relatively small pool of senior advocates appearing before the courts meant that there was already a considerable fund of knowledge about the character of those eligible for appointment. Pre-appointment vetting must involve self-declaration about a range of matters. As well, proactive inquiry of criminal records, the tax and insolvency services, and relevant professional regulatory bodies is necessary. A candidate's business partners, participation in social activities, and use of social media and online networking sites need also to be explored to uncover associations or views which would undermine public confidence if widely known. The American Bar Association has a detailed system of vetting, not only for competence but also for character.[2] None of this is to underestimate the difficulties of deciding whether good character is established.

(B) Socialization

Another aspect to ensuring integrity from within is socialization. A new judge will arrive with prior values, often moulded by the ethical standards of the legal profession. Socialization is the process by which a new judge acquires the knowledge and attitudes required to adapt and integrate into the role as judge. There are two sides to this: a judge adapts their conduct to the new role, and the court itself has mechanisms to encourage this. The judge learns about both behavioural norms and institutional values. These may conflict, to a varying extent, with the judge's existing attitudes and behaviour. As well as ensuring satisfaction on the new judge's part with their new career, and their effective performance of it, positive socialization into the role contributes to better compliance with the norms of judicial virtue. Judicial integrity becomes embedded in the sense of both the individual and collective

[2] P. 152 below.

understanding of appropriate conduct. This can lead to changes in a judge's behaviour both in court and in everyday life.

Socialization is sometimes divided into anticipatory and organizational socialization. What has been called anticipatory socialization occurs during preparation for a role. Judges who as lawyers had a litigation practice will have observed judges and have a view of what they and other lawyers regard as virtuous judging. The aspiring judge may have had shadowing or mentoring possibilities. In England and Wales, a new judge will typically have sat as a deputy judge or in some other judicial capacity before appointment to a full-time position. In the process they will have experienced informal (and implicit) patterns of communication as to how to behave—from observations as a judicial pupil, from listening to conversations between existing judges, and from informal discussions with full-time judges. Along with that they will have participated in formal training and acquired access to the bench books and other documents which contribute to their training for judging. On full-time appointment, however, judges are not fully minted; the socialization process continues.

Organizational socialization pertains to the socialization of the judge at the beginning of their career and after appointment in learning on the job. Initially, the new judge may receive informal advice from a senior judge, or in the shape of a manual of some sort, or both, as to issues relevant to behavioural standards such as dealing with litigants in person and expected completion times for reserved judgments. Socialization continues informally as judges observe other judges and adapt their own behaviour to the norms of judging. Judges may have role models. Socialization also takes place more systematically through sitting with other judges, mentoring, guidance, and training. It may happen on a one-to-one basis as judges exchange knowledge on how to handle specific situations which raise ethical issues. It can also occur collectively with before- and after-court discussion between judges who have sat on panels hearing cases.

Socialization is not confined directly to behavioural standards. It can still have indirect force on behaviour, however, as the judge learns to accommodate to what might be the greater isolation compared with their previous work and to the restrictions which are a concomitant of the role. Nor is socialization necessarily sophisticated. 'How would that look in the media' is a powerful caution regarding judicial conduct. Socialization is not always linear but may take place episodically. It can comprise both rewards and punishments. During training, for example, judges may be praised for their answers if confronted with hypothetical ethical problems, or how they behave in role play in mock hearings, but can equally be embarrassed when in doing so they diverge from the accepted course. Socialization is a pressure to conformity. In as much as there is conformity in behavioural standards that can contribute to judicial integrity; in as much as there is conformity in decision-making (the subject matter of Chapter 6) it can be stultifying to the individual and a dead hand on legal development.

A court's mechanisms for the positive socialization of judges include what have been termed the 'agents of socialisation'. These operate in various ways. First, there is social influence or peer pressure, which promotes conformity with behavioural norms. At the outset a new judge may be listed to sit with experienced judges to observe how they conduct themselves. Even for the experienced advocate, the part-time judge, or the judge appointed from a lower court, judging in the new role can be a learning experience. Secondly, conformity with behavioural norms may be encouraged through the benefits which senior judges can confer. Judges may be nominated early to valued administrative committees or to leadership positions if they adapt readily to the role including the behavioural expectations. On the other hand those, say, with outstanding judgments may feature in a formal or informal list of defaulters with which colleagues become acquainted. Serious misconduct may deny a judge promotion or earn transfer to a less attractive post. Thirdly, there is formal training. Typically this is judge-led, since the peer group model of judicial training is regarded as the most effective. Training can encompass the ethical and other standards which are embedded as collective understandings of appropriate conduct, as well as the content of ethical guidance and codes of conduct.

(C) Guidance v Codes

Conformity with judicial values and behavioural standards does not require written guidance or a code or, indeed, the heavy hand of disciplinary processes. However, these perform valuable functions. First, they act in an educative or prescriptive manner, offering suggestions to the judge faced with an unfamiliar or ambiguous situation where the appropriate course is unclear. Secondly, they may assist the judge internalize the norms of judicial virtue by making them explicit. Thirdly, guidance or a code may act in a proscriptive way, indicating that a particular course of behaviour was unacceptable and that some sanction—even if only formal advice as to future conduct—is justified by its breach. Finally, express behavioural standards notify the public about how judges should act, which should facilitate greater community confidence in judges and the judiciary.

Until the late twentieth century the standards of conduct expected of judges in many common law and European jurisdictions were contained largely in informal conventions and practices. The United States was an exception, where in 1924 the American Bar Association (ABA) first adopted a *Canons of Judicial Ethics*. Elsewhere there might be limited direction. In England there was guidance for relations with the media. For a short time there was also an obligation on judges to declare whether they were Masons on the basis that one of its aims is mutual self-advancement, which might threaten impartiality.[3] But generally speaking it was assumed in major common law jurisdictions that with the relatively small pool from which the senior judges were typically chosen—leading advocates or lower court judges—much could be taken for granted as regards proper behaviour.

Anticipatory and organizational socialization of a judge was backed with informal mechanisms. A tendency to step out of line might be dealt with by a 'quiet word' to an aspirant judge or a serving judge. In extreme cases of unacceptable behaviour the judge would be nudged into retirement, or dismissed or threatened with dismissal if without the tenure protection of a senior judge. There was some variation in the behavioural standards depending on the level of court or the jurisdiction. For example, where judges were posted to sit in courts in smaller communities they might be expected to drastically limit their friendships with the legal community there, since otherwise members of the local bar would be unable to appear before them and there would be disruptions since cases would have to be transferred to another area to avoid a conflict of interest. In an age of enhanced accountability for public figures, however, it was difficult for the judiciary to avoid what the legal profession had already undertaken by way of articulating standards of expected behaviour in a code or guidance. An early model was provided by the Canadian Judicial Council, constituted by statute in 1991, which published its *Commentaries on Judicial Conduct* the same year, followed by *Ethical Principles for Judges* in 1998.[4]

[3] On the media guidance, see Media Guidance for the Judiciary (London, Judiciary of England and Wales, 2024). The obligation to declare Masonic affiliation followed the report of the Home Affairs Select Committee, *Freemasonry in the Police and the Judiciary* (HC 1996–97, 192) but was abandoned after *Grande Oriente d'Italia di Palazzo Giustiniani v Italy*, No 1, App no 35972/97 (ECtHR, 2 August 2021); No 2, App no 26740/02 (ECtHR, 31 May 2007). See HC Deb 5 November 2009, vol 498, col 57WS.

[4] Canada Judicial Council, *Ethical Principles for Judges* (rev edn, CJC 2021) (hereafter *Canadian Ethical Principles*).

The *Bangalore Principles of Judicial Conduct* were a catalyst for change in many countries.[5] Adopted in 2002 they were drafted under the auspices of the United Nations Judicial Group on Strengthening Judicial Integrity, composed of chief justices and judges from around the world. The Economic and Social Council of the United Nations endorsed the *Bangalore Principles* in a Resolution in 2006 as building on the UN Basic Principles on the Independence of the Judiciary of 1985.[6] The United Nations Office on Drugs and Crime (UNODC) convened an inter-governmental expert group and subsequently published a detailed *Commentary on the Bangalore Principles of Judicial Conduct*.[7] Countries have either adopted the *Bangalore Principles* or used them as a basis for their own judicial guidance or code of judicial behaviour. They continue to offer signposts for judicial consideration of difficult ethical issues.[8] Enforcement is contemplated, since the principles presuppose that judges are accountable for their conduct. The *Commentary on the Bangalore Principles* states that under them disciplinary action will depend on factors such as the seriousness of the transgression, whether there is a pattern of improper activity, and its effect on others and on the judicial system as a whole.[9]

In England and Wales the process proceeded by steps. In the early 1990s Lord Bingham gave a widely distributed lecture on judicial ethics, his thinking stimulated by an Australian judge's book on the subject.[10] The *Guide to Judicial Conduct* for judges in England and Wales was first adopted in 2004 as one of the early products of the newly constituted Judges' Council.[11] It drew on the *Bangalore Principles of Judicial Conduct* and guidance and codes elsewhere, specifically the *Guide to Judicial Conduct* published for the Council of Chief Justices of Australia.[12] The *Guide to Judicial Conduct* for the English judiciary has been amended from time to time, partly in the light of changed circumstances such as the advent of social media. More recent versions of the *Guide* have brief discussions of the three general values—independence,

[5] *Bangalore Principles of Judicial Conduct* (United Nations 2018).

[6] ECOSOC Resolution 2006/23 of 27 July 2006. On the UN Basic Principles see pp. 4–5 above.

[7] *Commentary on the Bangalore Principles of Judicial Conduct* (UNODC 2007) (hereafter *Commentary on the Bangalore Principles*).

[8] eg, *Ayers-Caesar v Judicial and Legal Service Commission* [2025] UKPC 15 [32] (Lord Reed) (PC, Trinidad and Tobago).

[9] *Commentary on the Bangalore Principles* (n 7) para 19.

[10] Thomas Bingham, 'Judicial Ethics' in Ross Cranston (ed), *Legal Ethics and Professional Responsibility* (OUP 1996); James Thomas, *Judicial Ethics in Australia* (Law Book 1988).

[11] Now *Guide to Judicial Conduct* (revised edn, Courts and Tribunals Judiciary, July 2023).

[12] Council of Chief Justices of Australia, *Guide to Judicial Conduct* (Australian Institute of Judicial Administration 2002).

impartiality, and integrity—followed by guidance on specific issues. In addition to the *Guide* there is a broader statement about the behaviour expected of judges, stimulated in part by concern within the judiciary and more generally in society about bullying, harassment, and discrimination. In outline it urges judges to treat people with respect, not to abuse their authority, to remain patient when encountering difficulties, to support judicial colleagues and staff, and to be open to feedback.[13] There are also policies on matters like whistleblowing, which enable complaints about harassment, discrimination, and bullying by other judges.

From the outset the *Guide to Judicial Conduct* has made clear that it is intended to assist judges on issues and so sets out core principles to assist them reach their own decisions. Judges are encouraged to consult a senior judge if a problem arises. The *Guide* now makes explicit that it is not a code and that responsibility for deciding whether a particular activity or course of conduct is appropriate rests with the individual judge.[14] That reflects the position explained in greater detail in the *Canadian Ethical Principles*: the principles are aspirational, are not intended to be a code of conduct setting minimum standards, are advisory in nature, do not preclude reasonable disagreements about their application in particular cases or imply that any departure from them necessarily warrants disapproval, and are intended to be applied in light of all of the relevant circumstances and consistently with the requirements of judicial independence and the law.[15] Constantly reiterated in versions of the English *Guide to Judicial Conduct* is that they are to be read against the background of the conditions of appointment and terms of service the judge accepted when assuming office.

In England, following the adoption of formal disciplinary machinery under the Constitutional Reform Act 2005, the *Guide to Judicial Conduct* states that it may be considered in disciplinary proceedings but that there is no obligation that it be followed. The choice of guidance over a code seems motivated by a number of factors. First, there is a concern with judicial independence. As the 2013 version of the *Guide* put it, judges in performing judicial duties should be independent of judicial colleagues and solely responsible for their decisions in ethical as well as other matters. That concern is also evident in other ethical codes like the Canadian. Secondly, there has

[13] eg, 'Statement of Expected Behaviour', issued by Burnett LCJ in 2023, now *Guide to Judicial Conduct* (n 11) Annex A.

[14] *Guide to Judicial Conduct* (n 11) Introduction.

[15] *Canadian Ethical Principles* (n 4) Introduction, para 4.

been a recognition that a black-letter law approach is not appropriate when there is a range of reasonably held opinions about some of the behavioural restraints expected of a judge. Thirdly, there is the belief that even with an expanded and more diverse judiciary it remains possible to rely on judges, whose core function is to uphold standards for the community, to conduct themselves appropriately.

Contrast the judicial codes in the United States. When in 1924 the ABA first adopted its *Canons of Judicial Ethics* these were in the nature of guidance. However, in 1972 the ABA introduced its *Model Code of Judicial Conduct*, which has been adopted in most states, sometimes in modified form.[16] The *Model Code* contains mandatory rules. On occasions it has been subject to constitutional challenge.[17] The 2007 edition is structured into four canons stating overarching principles, often followed by distinct rules with enforceable duties. In addition to the ABA *Code*, in 1972 the Judicial Conference of the United States adopted a *Code of Conduct for United States Judges*, which applies to federal judges except those in the Supreme Court.[18] In 2023 the US Supreme Court finally adopted its own code after several scandals.

The adoption of mandatory codes in the United States seems firstly to reflect the more rule-based approach to regulation in American political culture. Secondly, compared with Britain there may be a greater concern in the United States about judicial behaviour, partly because judges come from very diverse backgrounds including state judges who are elected, and partly because judges wield greater potential power because of federal and state constitutional provisions. Thirdly, at the time the ABA *Model Code* was adopted there was concern that the original ABA *Canons* were hortatory when what was needed in light of recent experience were firmer norms for judicial behaviour. The response in the ABA *Model Code of Judicial Conduct* as well as the *Code of Conduct for United States Judges* is to inform judges, as well as the public, that there are bright lines for judicial conduct.

Coupled with their greater specificity and statutory backing, the codes of judicial behaviour in the United States might seem better able to facilitate enforcement and the imposition of penalties for serious breaches. Express

[16] *Model Code of Judicial Conduct* (American Bar Association 2020) (hereafter ABA *Model Code*).

[17] eg, *Republican Party of Minnesota v White* 536 US 765 (2002) (canon prohibiting judges seeking election from expressing views held to violate first amendment of US Constitution); *Williams-Yulee v Florida Bar* 575 US 433 (2015) (canon upheld prohibiting elected judges from personally soliciting campaign funds).

[18] *Code of Conduct for United States Judges*, Guide to Judiciary Policy, vol 2, A, ch 2 (hereafter *Code of Conduct for US Judges*).

statements in the *Guide to Judicial Conduct* for England and Wales that it is not a code and does not contain rules (other than when stated) suggest that it is not equally enforceable. Vague standards in the *Guide* such as 'undermining trust and confidence in the judiciary' and 'bring[ing] the judiciary into disrepute' are potentially open to wide, inconsistent, and possibly abusive interpretations. On the other hand, some provisions represent what is the position in law, as with those bearing on disqualification for bias, and others might be said to be founded on the judicial oath. In practice the *Guide to Judicial Conduct* is a starting point for decisions taken according to the disciplinary procedures under the Constitutional Reform Act 2005, and its provisions are often cited in support of decisions about judicial misconduct and the imposition of sanctions.[19] The individual judge may have decided that on consideration of the *Guide* a course of conduct is appropriate, but the disciplinary machinery may reach the opposite conclusion.

III Integrity in the Decision-Making Process

Various aspects of the integrity of the decision-making process are examined in this part of the chapter. The focus is on the process of decision-making, not the substance of decisions. What could be termed fidelity to law (or more broadly, integrity in adjudication)—complying with the substantive standards for judicial decision-making of applying legislation and following precedent—is discussed in Chapter 6(III). The integrity of the process of decision-making, discussed in this chapter, is threatened by the judge acting unfairly, ineptly, abusively, or corruptly. If the judge acts in these ways, there may be consequences for both the judge's decision and the judge. The decision itself might be vitiated, and the judge may be sanctioned for misconduct in accordance with the judiciary's disciplinary procedures. Errors honestly made in the process of judicial decision-making do not constitute misconduct.[20] These do not threaten the integrity of the decision-making process, although they may lead to a successful appeal, and cause embarrassment to the judge and perhaps the judiciary as a whole.

[19] See Judicial Conduct Investigations Office, *Judicial Discipline. Misconduct and Recommending Sanctions* (JCIO 2024) [25].

[20] *Durity v Attorney General of Trinidad and Tobago* [2008] UKPC 59 [24] (PC, Trinidad and Tobago).

(A) Fairness, Competence, Efficiency

The integrity of judicial decision-making turns, firstly, on the adherence by the judge to legal standards in the performance of their duties. Three standards are singled out for attention, procedural fairness, competence, and efficiency—fairness in the treatment of the parties in legal proceedings and in considering their case, and competence and efficiency (including timeliness) in the discharge of these duties. Individual judges acquire reputations in relation to these standards with their colleagues, the legal community, and perhaps more widely with the public. Mediated through a jurisdiction's legal culture and traditions, the esteem for individual judges feeds into the reputation of a judiciary collectively in dispensing justice. That reputation affects a judiciary's ability to secure resources as well as its social standing. It in turn reflects back on individual judges, shaping a jurisdiction's attractiveness as a forum for dispute settlement, including with parties abroad. Clearly reputation is not built on procedural fairness, competence, and efficiency alone. The substance of judicial decisions is also an important component. Coupled with respect for a judiciary's jurisprudence, its reputation for fairness, competence, and efficiency carry weight internationally.

Procedural fairness

Fairness colours the public perception of the judge: being treated with equal concern and respect, having the opportunity to participate, a perception that the judge cares, and judicial impartiality—all these feed into a positive evaluation of the judge and the judicial system.[21] Procedural fairness in the conduct of legal proceedings is embedded in the common law, procedure rules, and human rights instruments such as article 6 of the European Convention on Human Rights (ECHR). At base it involves notice and the opportunity to be heard. A fundamental principle is that the judge should 'hear the other side' (*audi alteram partem*). Related to procedural fairness is that everyone has the right to be treated on an equal footing and with equal concern and respect.[22] There are various aspects to procedural fairness.

First, the parties must have a reasonable opportunity to advance their case and to be notified of and be able to respond to the case against them. If the judge has not heard the one side that party will not have been on an

[21] Australian Law Reform Commission, *Without Fear or Favour: Judicial Impartiality and the Law on Bias* (ALRC Report 138, 2021) paras 7.22–7.24 summarizes the evidence on this.

[22] eg, CPR 1.1(2)(a).

equal footing. The other side of the coin is that the parties must identify the issues and evidence so that each can respond to the other side's case. The judge can then adjudicate on those issues and that evidence. The judge's task is bounded by the way in which the parties frame and advance their case. In the common law there is generally no additional duty on a judge to carry out some type of inquisitorial function or to ascertain some independent truth.[23]

The requirement that judges guarantee the parties the opportunity to advance their case and to address the other side's case takes various forms. If an issue is first raised at a late stage in legal proceedings such as a party's closing speech, unfairness arises if the evidence of witnesses was given on a different basis but the new issue is used by the judge to decide the case.

Another aspect of being able to advance one's case is the long-established rule in England that in general A must challenge by cross-examination a material point in the evidence of a witness of the opposing party, B (including an expert witness for B), if A submits that the judge should not accept that point. The rule ensures fairness by giving the witness the opportunity to explain their evidence and, if an expert, to defend their professional reputation if it is challenged. It also allows the trial judge to make a proper assessment of all the evidence in the case. The rule is not rigid and its application depends upon the circumstances, the fundamental question being whether, taken as a whole, the trial is fair.[24]

Secondly, in the common law system judges should generally decide the case on the evidence, arguments, and points of law advanced before them. If a judge makes findings on a matter (say, bad faith against a claimant) when that has never been suggested or pleaded, that would be procedurally unfair. There is unfairness not only because the judge has not given the claimant an opportunity of answering a case never put, but also because without broaching the matter with the parties the judge may fall into error as regards its ramifications for other aspects of the case. A corollary is that if a judge is to make a significant adverse finding against a person who is not a party to the proceedings such as a witness, fairness may require that the issue be put to that person (if necessary, by recalling them), giving them the opportunity to refute it if they are able. The issue arose in *SW v United Kingdom*,[25] where 'out of the blue' in his judgment a judge made damming findings against a social

[23] *Sainsbury's Supermarkets Ltd v Visa Europe Services LLC (European Commission intervening)* [2020] UKSC 24, [2020] Bus LR 1196 [241]–[242].
[24] *Griffiths v TUI UK Ltd* [2023] UKSC 48, [2025] AC 374 [70].
[25] (2021) 73 EHRR 18.

worker who had given evidence in a fact-finding hearing about whether children should be taken into care. As a result, she was unable to obtain further employment and suffered stress-induced fibromyalgia. The Court of Appeal set aside the judge's findings as being in breach, by a wide margin, of the duties of fairness, as well as of SW's rights to respect for her private and family life under article 8 of the ECHR[26]. It could not award compensation under domestic law, but SW obtained a monetary award from the European Court of Human Rights (ECtHR).

Related to this is if a judge is to rely in their judgment on a legal source not cited by the parties, they should generally invite submissions about its application to the case or relist the case for further argument if the outcome may turn on it. Otherwise, a party will not have been heard on the ground which the judge uses to decide the case against it. If this new legal source casts an entirely new light on the case, the preliminary issue to be considered is whether it is proper to enter upon the new material at all.[27] For similar reasons judges should not generally use any special knowledge or expertise they may happen to have without informing the parties so they can comment on it if necessary. However, there is no need for a judge to canvass with the parties every nuance or inference they draw. Justice is fairly done between the parties if the judge's decision is in accordance with the available evidence and the law.

Thirdly, during legal proceedings a judge must not receive communications from one side only about which the other side is ignorant. Procedural fairness demands that judges base their decisions on matters known to both sides. *Ex parte* communications as they are sometimes called have long been deplored in the common law for the purpose of influencing the decision since it would 'divert the course of justice'.[28] Later, the rule became that a judge must not receive a private communication from a party without the consent of the other, irrespective of whether it would work to the latter's prejudice: the risk that it might do so was enough.[29] Along similar lines it also became the rule that a judge must not be with one side during legal proceedings, without the other side also being present, even if on that occasion there is no discussion of the case.[30] *Ex parte* communications might result in an

[26] *Re W (A Child)* [2016] EWCA Civ 1140, [2017] 1 WLR 2415.

[27] *Hoecheong Products Co Ltd v Cargill Hong Kong Ltd* [1995] 1 WLR 404, 409 (PC, Hong Kong).

[28] *Re Sombre* (1849) 1 Mac & G 116, 122; 41 ER 1207, 1209 (Lord Cottenham LC).

[29] *Kanda v Malaya* [1962] AC 322, 337 (PC, Malaya).

[30] *Charisteas v Charisteas* [2021] HCA 29, 273 CLR 289 [13].

application for the judge's disqualification on the ground that in the circumstance in which it occurred a fair-minded and informed observer would conclude that there was a real possibility that the judge was biased. Apart from the possibility of apparent bias, these practices create a situation in which concerns can reasonably be raised about the judge's impartiality, however innocent the *ex parte* contact may have been. Judges risk fostering an impression of favouritism towards one side and encourage suspicion in the other by leaving them in the dark about exactly what was or might have been said in their absence.[31] Judges must disclose significant communications or contacts involving one side only, even if inadvertent or innocent.

There are public interest exceptions to the principles of procedural fairness. For example, the commercially sensitive information of one side may be kept from the other and confined to a 'confidentiality ring' of the latter's lawyers and experts. Another example is the judge making a without notice (*ex parte*) order in situations of urgency such as freezing the assets of a party where there is a genuine fear that they will be dissipated abroad. If an interim order is made there will be a return date for a full hearing with both parties present to decide if the freezing order is to be continued. A third example is that a judge may limit the application of the principles of procedural fairness for a legitimate purpose such as protecting the court's own processes, so long as any limitation is reasonably proportionate to that aim. Thus a party may be refused permission to amend their case because it is too late in the proceedings, or have their case struck out completely for non-compliance with the rules or with a court order.

Competence

'Competence and diligence are prerequisites to the due performance of judicial office', says value 6 of the *Bangalore Principles of Judicial Conduct*. The *Commentary on the Bangalore Principles* adds that competence in the performance of judicial duties requires legal knowledge, skill, thoroughness, and preparation. It explains the duty on judges to maintain their knowledge and skills to keep themselves informed. Judges cannot know all the relevant law they will administer, and often the submissions of the parties explaining it will be crucial. However, diligence in preparing each case is essential. As Lord Mansfield once remarked, he was not ashamed to say that at the outset of a case he might know little about it, but 'I never give a judicial opinion

[31] *Bubbles & Wine Limited v Lusha* [2018] EWCA Civ 468 [23]–[24] (Leggatt LJ).

upon any point, until I think I am master of every material argument and authority relative to it.'[32] These days the requisite knowledge and skills for judges extend beyond the law and its application to include the proper management of litigation. Judicial time is a limited resource. Judges cannot be expected to spend endless time on any one of their cases. So long as a party has been treated fairly and has had a reasonable opportunity to advance their case, a judge must progress to the next case. There is a resultant tension between correctness and efficiency.

Appointments can sometimes be made of those who for a number of reasons prove unsuitable to the role of a judge. The risk of this occurring does not necessarily reduce with more elaborate methods of appointing judges.[33] At this stage it is sufficient to note that it is sometimes a mystery that certain judges were selected in the first place given the lack of suitable skills or inability to write timely and adequately reasoned judgments. In other cases a judge may be appointed for political reasons despite being short of the mark through incompetence, an absence of adequate experience, a lack of diligence, or character defects. Judicial competence may also be impaired because of physical or mental decline, or because the judge's performance is affected by substance abuse. Illness, stress, and the pressure of work may mean that the judge is not able to function properly, for example, they build up a large backlog of reserved judgments. The judge is not acting unethically. With release from sitting in court, reasonable adjustments, or treatment they may function normally again. But at a certain point a judge will become unfit for judicial office if their disability manifests itself in misconduct in court or if there is no improvement in sight as with the completion of outstanding judgments despite time off from sitting for this purpose.

Removal of judges in these circumstances can be time consuming and difficult if the judge insists that a return to work is possible or that they are not suffering from a mental disability. To require a judge to undergo a psychiatric examination requires sensitivity because of the implications for judicial independence, even if there is a legal power to do this.[34] Handling cases of physical disability may be no easier. A judge suffering a severe stroke may hope to return but is ultimately removable if they are unable to perform judicial functions.[35] In some cases the view may be taken, in line with general

32 *R v Wilkes* (1770) 4 Burrow 2527, 98 ER 327 at 2549, 339 respectively.
33 See pp. 159–164 below.
34 Judicial Officers Act 1986, s 34 (New South Wales).
35 *Gratton v Canadian Judicial Council and Attorney-General of Canada* [1994] 2 FC 769.

employment law, that reasonable adjustments can be made to accommodate the physically disabled judge. However, there comes a point when the incapable judge must be removed or eased out if dismissal is not possible. The experience of Sir Kenneth Jacobs is, however, salutary. A person of integrity, he quickly retired from the High Court of Australia in 1979 when he was diagnosed with an illness which meant he could not resume sitting for some time. He did not wish to place a burden on the other six judges of the court in the meanwhile. However, he had been misdiagnosed and lived for another thirty-eight years.

Efficiency and delay with reserved judgments

The *Commentary on the Bangalore Principles* states that judges must manage as well as decide cases. A judge is responsible, it explains, for the efficient administration of justice in their court. That involves case management, including the prompt disposition of cases. 'If the judge is not diligent in monitoring and disposing of cases', it says, 'the resulting inefficiency will increase costs and undermine the administration of justice'.[36] The overriding objective in the Civil Procedure Rules of England and Wales of dealing with cases justly and at proportionate cost includes, so far as practicable, ensuring expedition and fairness, and proceeding in ways proportionate to the nature, importance, and complexity of the issues.[37] The potential clash between the principles of justice and efficiency needs to be managed. Within limits parties must have the time to prepare and advance their case. Moreover, judges must maintain an open mind and not give the impression of prejudgment, albeit that they may have an intuitive view of the outcome as well as being under pressure to deal with their cases expeditiously.

An important aspect of efficiency is the timely delivery of reserved judgments, a component, the *Bangalore Principles* suggest, of a judge's competence.[38] Delay with some judges is attributable to indecisiveness, writer's block, inefficiency, inability, or the failure to write a reserved judgment bit by bit when time is available. At some point delay in the delivery of reserved judgments becomes a factor in an appellate court's conclusion that a judgment is unsafe and that a new trial must be ordered. An appellant may be able to establish a causal link between the delay and the alleged errors or failings

[36] *Commentary on the Bangalore Principles* (n 7) para 196. See also *ELI-Mount Scopus European Standards of Judicial Independence* (European Law Institute 2024) Standard 22.
[37] CPR 1.1(2)(c)(d).
[38] *Bangalore Principles of Judicial Conduct* (n 5) 6.5.

in the judgment. The appellate court may conclude that, because of delay, a judge's recollection of the evidence is at fault (especially where there is no recording or transcript). Another possibility is that delay means that a judge has to spend so much time and effort in reintegrating themselves into the case that they miss vital points.[39] Delay may be so lengthy that the parties' fair trial rights as in article 6 of the ECHR are engaged, although this will depend on circumstances including the complexity of the matter, the conduct of the parties, and what is in dispute.[40]

None of this will assist the parties faced with a delayed judgment since by definition any appeal follows the delayed judgment and itself takes additional time, although it may send a signal to other judges about the adverse consequences of delay in completing their own reserved judgments. In extreme cases delay in giving judgment may become such a problem that steps have to be taken to remove the judge from the bench on the basis that they are, in effect, not competent to perform their judicial duties. The process may be managed informally, so that the errant judge retires without fanfare. In other cases, the disciplinary machinery will be invoked, with the attendant publicity, which may lead to the judge's resignation to avoid forceable removal and further embarrassment.[41]

Delay exceeding three months after the conclusion of the hearing in handing down a judgment is a potential basis for a finding of misconduct in England and Wales. Factors such as the length and nature of the trial, the number of a judge's outstanding judgments, the extent of the delay, and factors such as illness have a bearing on any finding.[42] If judges are having difficulty in completing written judgments, they may be accommodated by the reallocation of cases so that they have additional writing time. That, however, can put pressure on the other judges who must take on additional work.[43] Delay may be explicable if a judge has been assigned to other heavy duties before completing outstanding judgments. However, a judge may be unable to complete judgments through a disposition to procrastinate.[44]

[39] *Tex Services Ltd v Shibani Knitting Co Ltd (In Receivership)* [2016] UKPC 31 [49] (PC, Mauritius); *Bank St Petersburg PJSC v Arkhangelsky* [2020] EWCA Civ 408, [2020] 4 WLR 55 [77]–[84]. cf *Pickle Properties Ltd v Plant* [2021] UKPC 6 (PC, British Virgin Islands).

[40] *Doran v Ireland* (2006) 42 EHRR 13; *Olujic v Croatia* (2011) 52 EHRR 26 [86]–[91].

[41] *Application Pursuant to Constitution, section 18(1) by Justice Sir Bernard Sakora* (2020) SC1980 (SC, Papua New Guinea).

[42] *Judicial Discipline. Misconduct and Recommending Sanctions* (n 19) Annex A [23].

[43] See *Smart Education Program Pty Ltd (in liquidation) v CLGC Australia Pty Ltd* [2023] FCA 826 [1]–[8].

[44] See *Bruce v Cole* (1998) 45 NSWLR 163.

The unfortunate truth is that some judges are simply not up to the mark in making decisions or completing written tasks which the appointing body did not consider or uncover.

Whatever the cause of delay in its completion, the parties are deprived of the court's judgment. That prolongs or may increase their anxiety, incurs financial loss through opportunity costs, and weakens public confidence in the integrity of the justice system. 'Left unchecked', it was said in one case, 'it would be ultimately subversive of the rule of law'.[45] Some jurisdictions have refined their procedures for handling inquiries about outstanding judgments, including funnelling them in such a way that a party's identity is not revealed to obviate any fear that the judge will take against an inquirer. There should be no inhibition about inquiring about a delayed judgment. Ireland has a register of outstanding judgments, which are listed before the responsible judge at prescribed intervals for them to explain when the judgment(s) will become available.[46] As an incentive to diligence, jurisdictions such as the US (for federal district judges) and South Africa have gone one step further and in different forms publish the names of judges with the cases which have been outstanding for longer than six months.[47]

(B) Behaviour at Court

At the heart of the judge's behaviour at court is to maintain public confidence in the integrity of the judiciary and the justice system. That extends not only to conduct in court but more generally to the performance of judicial duties. Higher standards are expected of judges than others. Under the heading 'Integrity', the *Guide to Judicial Conduct* for England and Wales states that judges must be courteous, patient, tolerant, and punctual; respect the dignity of all; and ensure that no one in court is exposed to any display of bias or prejudice from any source.[48] The *Guide* adds that arrangements will need to be made so that those with a disability are not at a disadvantage.

Especially in court judges must conduct themselves so as not to jeopardize fairness or undermine impartiality or its appearance. Judges must uphold the status of judicial office and maintain authority. They do this by acting with

[45] *Bank St Petersburg PJSC v Arkhangelsky* [2020] EWCA Civ 408, [2020] 4 WLR 55 [79].
[46] Courts and Court Officers Act 2002, s 46.
[47] 28 USC § 476 (2018); Republic of South Africa, Judiciary, Reserved Judgment Reports for the Chief Justice, Reserved Judgments at 31 December 2022.
[48] *Guide to Judicial Conduct* (n 11) 9.

dignity and decorum. Conventionally judicial authority is conveyed through a detached and formal demeanour. However, judging is a social as well as a legal activity. The judge interacts with the parties or their legal representatives. A judge may need to depart from the conventional demeanour to ensure effective communication with, and the participation of, a party. With a litigant in person, for example, the judge may need to proceed at a slower pace, assume a more familiar manner, and explain legal terms and processes in conversational language.[49] Involvement in a case of a child or vulnerable adult may require the judge to adopt a welcoming attitude.[50]

A judge's failure to observe the standards of in-court behaviour can have various consequences. First, it may be sufficiently serious to justify an appeal and possibly a new trial. The judge may have denied a party the opportunity of a fair hearing for their case or acted in such a way that there is, at the least, apprehended bias on their part. Thus an appeal was allowed where the trial judge had used what the court described as unrestrained and immoderate language in dismissing what would ordinarily have been an uncontroversial application.[51] Amongst other things the judge told the lawyers that the 'lunatics' had taken over the asylum, that he bitterly resented spending his weekend reading 'this codswallop', and that he was nothing short of appalled that public funds could be expended upon 'such nonsense'. The Court of Appeal remarked: 'Appointment as a judge, at whatever level, is not a license for intemperate language or for being gratuitously rude to advocates and others appearing before you.'[52] In addition to there being an appeal, the judge may be censured by the relevant disciplinary body. A sanction may be justified even where the misconduct seems minor because of its impact on a litigant or a community. Thirdly, the most egregious behaviour could lead to a judge's removal as where they repeatedly make inappropriate comments in court, issue unjustified orders against parties, favour one side, and openly criticize colleagues.[53]

As well as inappropriate language and rudeness, there can be trouble for the judge if expressing views inconsistent with the judicial role. Treating the bench as a pulpit about a judge's social views could undermine the notion of the rational and impartial consideration of a case. In a Canadian decision

[49] PP. 208–209 below.
[50] See 1A PD (vulnerable parties and witnesses).
[51] *In the Matter of A (Children)* [2015] EWCA Civ 133.
[52] ibid [13].
[53] eg, *Re Levers (Judge of Grand Court of the Cayman Islands)* [2010] UKPC 24 (PC, Cayman Islands); *In re Simon*, 41 NYS 3d 192, 63 NE 3d 1136 (2016).

a judge while sentencing a defendant commented that her impression was that in that region of New Brunswick the honest were outnumbered by the dishonest. She went on to wonder aloud whether she was not 'surrounded by crooks' where she lived. A few days later she apologized in open court. The province's judicial council found that she should be removed from office because she had undermined public confidence in the judiciary and created a reasonable apprehension that she would not be impartial. The Supreme Court of Canada upheld the council's decision. Giving the judgment of the court, Arbour J stressed that while judges must be free to speak in their judicial capacity, the council as the regulatory body for judges 'must also be equally sensitive to the reasonable expectations of an informed dispassionate public that holders of judicial office will remain at all times worthy of trust, confidence and respect'.[54]

Short and atypical outbursts will not necessarily demonstrate a lack of impartiality, result in unfairness, or cause an erosion of public confidence. Conducting a hearing can be as stressful for a judge as for the parties. It has long been recognized that judges can lose patience or become irritated when an advocate or a litigant in person is bad-mannered, fails to address the issues, or takes an inordinate amount of time to advance their case. In the mid nineteenth century it was said: 'Patience is, questionless, one of the first of judicial virtues; but . . . the unendurable tedium of some Chancery barristers certainly passes all sufferance and longanimity'.[55] Judges are entitled to call advocates to account in these circumstances. One of the traits of good advocacy is to accommodate to the judge's indications as to relevant issues and need for concision—as well as other traits such as judicial irritation—while not compromising their client's case.

At the point where the judge insults or unreasonably threatens the parties, however, or attempts to intimidate, degrade, humiliate, or coerce them, judicial behaviour trespasses onto the forbidden territory of harassment or bullying. That conduct may thwart the parties from putting their case, foster a sense of injustice, and diminish the reputation of both the judge and the judiciary of which they are part. Occasionally cases surface where judges are alleged to have behaved badly towards their colleagues.[56] Where this becomes public it may undermine confidence in the judicial system.

[54] *Moreau-Berube v New Brunswick (Judicial Council)* [2002] 1 SCR 249 [72].
[55] 'Law Reform: Its Progress and Prospects' (1853) 47 Fraser's Magazine 355, 362.
[56] See *Fingleton v The Queen* (2005) 227 CLR 166.

Judicial humour treads a fine line between the acceptable and the impermissible. The conventional view is that humour should be avoided since it can undermine the dignity of the judge's office and cast doubt on whether the parties' case is being taken seriously. For them legal proceedings are usually a serious business. Another difficulty with humour is that some (including judicial colleagues) may not appreciate its funny side. It may give offence, cause embarrassment, or display a lack of sensitivity to the feelings of others. In extreme cases the fair-minded and informed observer might conclude that there was a real possibility that it conveyed scorn and contempt for a party or their case such that the judge should be disqualified for bias. Used sensitively, however, humour may on occasion ease tensions during a hearing, or perhaps express a point simply and clearly.

"[A]n overspeaking judge is no well-tuned cymbal", wrote Sir Francis Bacon, lord chancellor 1617–1621.[57] As we have seen, a fundamental value for the judge is judicial impartiality. Judges must be, and appear to be, independent and impartial in their conduct of litigation. Interruptions can potentially undermine that. Under the adversarial system the core principle in both civil and criminal litigation is that the judge remains aloof from the fray and neutral between the parties.[58] That does not mean that a judge should remain silent. It assists the parties to know what is troubling the judge so the point can be addressed. The convention is that as soon as a judge speaks, an advocate pauses, even if in mid-sentence. There is a distinction, however, between interruptions during a party's evidence and interruptions during submissions where greater latitude is permitted. During submissions the judge needs to understand and test a party's case. They may already have a view of a case from the parties' written submissions but they must retain an open mind and not give the impression that they are not prepared to listen. As to a party's evidence, a judge is entitled to intervene to clarify answers which are unclear, although it may be preferable to do this at a break in the evidence or at the end since matters may become clearer as the evidence proceeds. Intervention may also be necessary where an advocate asks a question which is too complex or cross-examination strays into being intimidatory.

However, it is not for the judge to take over the cross-examination of a witness in adversarial proceedings. That is the task of the other side. In some cases issues will have been avoided by the parties for good reason, substantive

[57] James Spedding, Robert L Ellis, and Douglas D Heath (eds), *The Works of Francis Bacon* (new edn, Longmans & Co 1870) vol 6, 508.

[58] The seminal authority is Denning LJ in *Jones v National Coal Board* [1957] 2 QB 55, 64.

or tactical, and it is not for the judge to upset this with an inappropriate line of questioning. As a matter of law interventions may found an appeal either because of their number or character. First, interventions may undermine the judge's ability properly to evaluate and weigh the evidence or otherwise to assess the case by calm and dispassionate consideration.[59] Secondly, interventions may give rise to apparent bias through prejudgment of the case. Thirdly, the judge's interruptions may cause unfairness in deflecting a party from fully presenting their case.[60] An unfair hearing cannot be saved by a considered judgment. The problem can be especially acute with the litigant in person who is usually less able to advance their case or to withstand interventions compared with the professional advocate. Litigants in person are also liable to perceive partiality if the judge takes too active a role. Asking questions on issues central to the case, which the litigant in person has not posed, may be necessary.[61] In making allowances in favour of the litigant in person, however, judges must avoid tipping the scales too far.

(C) Abuse of Position

Fundamental is that judges must not abuse their position to gain preferential treatment for themselves or anyone else in the course of legal proceedings. The official commentary on principle 4.9 of the *Bangalore Principles of Judicial Conduct* gives the simple example of the judge stopped for a traffic violation.[62] The judge should not volunteer their judicial status to the police nor contact any official to inquire 'whether anything could be done' about a penalty notice issued for the violation. The latter, it comments, gives the appearance of impropriety even if no attempt is made to use the judge's position to influence the outcome of their case. Principle 4.9 itself adds that a judge should not convey or permit others to convey the impression that anyone is in a special position to influence the judge improperly in the performance of judicial duties. This type of impropriety shades into corruption.

A grave vice is for a judge to interfere, or to attempt to interfere, with a case before another judge. Behaviour of this nature might constitute perverting or interfering with the course of justice. Even if no criminal offence is involved,

59 *Yuill v Yuill* [1945] P 15, 20.
60 *Serafin v Malkiewicz* [2020] UKSC 23, [2020] 1 WLR 2455.
61 On litigants in person pp. 208–209 below.
62 *Commentary on the Bangalore Principles* (n 7) para 145.

it could constitute behaviour trenching on the independence of the other judge. The principle is designed to insulate judges, not only from outside pressure but also from pressure from within the judiciary. A simple inquiry of another judge as to the possible outcome of ongoing proceedings in which they are not directly involved could be misinterpreted and place the other judge in an invidious position. If it were known, it could undermine public confidence in the inquiring judge and perhaps in the wider judiciary. None of this precludes a judge when facing a practical or substantive problem in a case from actively seeking the assistance of other judges, although acknowledging this the *Commentary on the Bangalore Principles* notes that judicial decision-making is always the responsibility of the individual judge charged with the matter.[63]

The Hlophe case in South Africa illustrates the vice. Hlophe was Judge President of the Western Cape. In 2021 the Judicial Conduct Tribunal of South Africa concluded that he had breached section 165 of the Constitution (which provides, inter alia, that no one 'may interfere with the functioning of the courts'); that his conduct seriously threatened and interfered with the independence, impartiality, dignity, and effectiveness of the Constitutional Court; that it threatened public confidence in the judicial system; and that he was guilty of gross misconduct under section 177 of the Constitution justifying his removal from office. The basis of this conclusion was that in 2008 he had visited Justices Nkabinde and Jafta in their chambers at the Constitutional Court and improperly attempted to influence them to decide a case in a manner which would favour Mr Jacob Zuma, soon to be president of South Africa. The case had been heard but judgment was reserved.[64] Following the tribunal's decision, the Judicial Service Commission endorsed the tribunal's conclusion and referred the matter to the National Assembly, which voted to remove the judge from office. In March 2004, President Cyril Ramaphosa made a formal order to that effect.

There was a broadly similar allegation against Murphy J, a judge of the High Court of Australia. In July 1985 he was convicted by a jury in the Supreme Court of New South Wales of attempting to pervert the course of justice. The Court of Criminal Appeal of New South Wales quashed the conviction because of the judge's summing up, but ordered a new trial since there was evidence upon which a jury properly directed could convict.[65] At his second

[63] ibid para 39.

[64] *Justices of the Constitutional Court v Judge President M J Hlophe*, Judicial Conduct Tribunal, Judiciary of South Africa, 9 April 2021, [111]–[112], [123]–[124].

[65] *R v Murphy* (1985) 4 NSWLR 42. See also (1985) 158 CLR 596, (1986) 5 NSWLR 18.

trial Murphy was acquitted. The accusation against Murphy was that he had sought to influence Clarence Briese, the chair of stipendiary magistrates in New South Wales, in relation to committal proceedings being heard by another stipendiary magistrate regarding Morgan Ryan, a Sydney solicitor, who was charged with forgery and conspiracy. Ryan was said to be associated with organized crime. The prosecution case was that Briese wanted more judicial independence for stipendiary magistrates, and in return for assisting with this Murphy had asked in a telephone conversation with Briese about 'my little mate', in other words Ryan. A Parliamentary Commission of Inquiry was established following the second trial but abandoned when Murphy unexpectedly died of cancer.

Abuse of position took a different turn in Ireland in the 'Sheedy affair', where a judge improperly amended the order of another judge. Mr Philip Sheedy had pleaded guilty to causing death by dangerous driving and HH Judge Matthews ordered him to serve a sentence of imprisonment. Following the intervention of a judge of the Supreme Court, Mr Justice Hugh O'Flaherty, the case was relisted before HHJ (later Mr Justice) Cyril Kelly, without the police or director of public prosecutions being notified. At the hearing Kelly suspended the remainder of Sheedy's sentence. The chief justice conducted an inquiry and concluded that the behaviour of both O'Flaherty and Kelly had damaged the administration of justice. Following an indication by the government that it would consider seeking their removal by the Oireachtas (Parliament) under article 35.4.1 of the Irish Constitution, both O'Flaherty and Kelly resigned.

(D) Corruption

Abuse of position shades into corruption, the pre-eminent judicial vice. It can take various forms: bribery, intended to influence a judge in decision-making; extortion, designed to have a judge act corruptly through physical violence or threatening to release damaging information; nepotism, enabling a family member or friend to benefit from a court appointment or funds under court control; and misuse of public resources under the judge's control, such as the sale of court offices. Corruption can occur in the determination of judicial issues (eg, bribery of a judge to deliver a false judgment); in court processes (eg, bribery so a court document is 'lost' or fabricated); in the appointment, promotion, transfer, or dismissal of a judge; or in administrative matters (eg, the embezzlement of court funds).[66] Facilitating judicial corruption are a lack of transparency and complex procedures, where the results of bribery can be masked. Judicial corruption may reflect broader patterns in society, where corruption is endemic in other walks of life, or where groups such as organized crime extend their influence into the workings of the state.

Judicial corruption can have profoundly deleterious effects for individuals, businesses, and public confidence in the judiciary. First, for litigants, corruption can deprive them of their rights if they do not receive a fair hearing or if their case is not decided according to law and its legal merits. The basic principle of equality before the law is undermined. Secondly, judicial corruption undermines trust in the administration of justice and weakens the capacity of the judicial system to act as the backstop guarantee of human rights. Public confidence in the impartial administration of justice is undermined and the capacity of the judicial system to guarantee the protection of human rights weakened. Thirdly, as far as the economy is concerned, rights conferred in areas like contract, property, and statutory law are subverted. Businesses can no longer expect the courts to resolve their disputes objectively. Conversely, a judiciary with a reputation for integrity may have a beneficial impact in other parts of society and the economy. An important element of the success of the 'clean hands' movement in Italy in the 1990s was that investigations by the judiciary led to the removal of a whole class of corrupt politicians who were exposed as receiving bribes and kickbacks from business seeking public contracts.

Sir Jonah Barrington has a place in history as the only judge in the UK to be removed from office by parliamentary resolution under the Act of Settlement 1701. The cause was corruption. Barrington had been appointed to the Irish Court of Admiralty in 1798. There was little work, and the court had a limited jurisdiction. In 1805 and 1806, and again in 1810, he received into his own bank account the proceeds of the court-ordered sale of two derelict vessels. In 1810 a ship salvager asked the court to pay £40 over to him but Barrington delayed the order. He used the time to leave Ireland. Barrington eventually settled in France, where he spent his time writing. However, he continued to receive his judicial salary of £1,000 per annum, his duties being performed by deputies. All this came to light in the late 1820s during an inquiry by commissioners into court officers in Ireland. Although Barrington

[66] *Commonwealth Anti-Corruption Benchmarks* (Commonwealth Secretariat 2021) Guidance to Benchmark 4, BM 4(C).

may have had a defence, he remained in France, protesting his innocence. Finally, the House of Commons passed a motion, addressed to the King, requesting his removal. Barrington made submissions during the debates in the House of Lords, but they agreed with the House of Commons that he should be removed.[67] Barrington was dismissed from office in 1830.

In previous centuries many commentators had painted an unhappy picture of venal judges. One among many was the satirist Edward Ward, who wrote in his 1692 poem, *The Miracles Performed by Money*: 'Votes of scarlet judges bought and sold, If purchased by the mighty power of gold'. It is difficult to know whether this was an accurate portrayal of judicial behaviour. From the fourteenth century the Kings' judges swore an oath not to take a fee, gift, or reward from anyone but the Sovereign, except food and drink, and then only of small value. That exception had an elastic meaning; in 1534 the chief justice of Common Pleas received a present of a barrel of sturgeon. In a period when gift-giving routinely accompanied social interactions, gifts were offered and taken by judges, although historians have discounted their influence on judicial decision-making. That was the line Francis Bacon, the lord chancellor, took in 1620, when allegations were brought before a parliamentary committee that he had taken bribes. He acknowledged that he had accepted gifts from two claimants, whose trial was pending, but that this did not affect his decision, which was for the other side. However, at his impeachment Bacon pleaded guilty to improperly taking gifts and loans in many cases, and conceded: 'I am guilty of corruption'.[68] Underlying the whole episode was the King's abuse of royal monopolies, to which Parliament took strong exception. The King's favourite, Buckingham, was trying, with the help of Edward Coke, to make Bacon the scapegoat.

Bribery fell away in the following centuries. The problem became the sale of offices. Lord Macclesfield LC was impeached in 1720 under twenty-one articles for taking money for appointing Chancery masters, taking suitors' funds in breach of trust, and concealing irregularities in Chancery where masters had dissipated suitors' funds to speculate (unsuccessfully) on the stock exchange. Parliament was unimpressed by his defence that he did not take bribes in relation to the outcome of cases, and that the sale of these judicial offices was a long-standing and well-known practice, especially when statute was against it.[69] There were regular attempts in the nineteenth century

[67] House of Lords Journal, vol 62, 20 July 1830.

[68] *Proceedings in Parliament against Francis Bacon Lord Verulam* (1620) 2 St Tr 1087, 1105.

[69] *Trial of the Earl of Macclesfield* (1725) 16 State Trials 767.

to suppress abuses around judicial offices and fees. Royal Commissions and the occasional parliamentary intervention exposed unsavoury practices. In 1865 a parliamentary committee examined whether Lord Westbury LC had corruptly engineered the retirement of judicial officers so as to appoint his sons and another relative to the positions. Although they exonerated him, they found that with respect to one office he had failed to make proper disclosure, and with the respect to another he had acted 'with haste and want of caution'. Following condemnation by the House of Commons for his disregard of the public interest, Westbury resigned as lord chancellor—albeit he continued to sit as an appellate judge.

Judicial corruption is a reality around the world. One indication is Transparency International's global corruption barometer, which includes the public's perception and experience of corruption in using the courts.[70] The Council of Europe's Consultative Council of European Judges said in 2018 that judicial corruption was a reality in several member states, which affected public trust in the administration of justice.[71] In 2017 UNODC, with the support of the statistician-general of Nigeria, published the results of a nationwide household survey on corruption, in which many Nigerians reported judges taking bribes.[72] Elite and public opinion surveys in other countries conclude that judges are corrupt. Public perceptions are not necessarily an accurate reflection of the degree to which a country's judiciary is corrupt. Given its nature, which will be concealed by the participants, it is difficult to know the full extent of judicial corruption. One problem is that a government may use a false accusation of corruption as a cover to remove a judge whose decisions cause it trouble. However, specific instances of judicial corruption surface when judges are dismissed for taking bribes from litigants and lawyers to fast-track a case, slow it down, or find in their favour. Sometimes courts need to assess whether there is corruption in the judiciary of another country, for example in the context of an application for the extradition of a person who objects on the basis that their fair trial rights were jeopardized because of corruption in the judiciary of the requesting state.[73]

Judicial integrity is best assured by the judiciary itself taking internal measures to monitor and sanction misconduct, and individual judges disavowing bribes, nepotism, and the misappropriation of public resources. Judges may

[70] <https://www.transparency.org/en/gcb> accessed 12 June 2025.

[71] CCJE, Opinion no 21, *Preventing Corruption Among Judges* (9 November 2018).

[72] United Nations Office on Drugs and Crime, *Corruption in Nigeria. Bribery: Public Experience and Response* (UNODC 2017) 7–8, 43, 75.

[73] eg, *Popoviciu v Romania* [2023] UKSC 39, [2023] 1 WLR 4256.

need support to withstand improper pressures and inducements. Of prime importance is that the state must ensure that judicial salaries, pensions, and other conditions of service are reasonably generous to reduce any felt need to take bribes. Ensuring a non-corrupt judiciary depends as well on institution building such as open justice, transparency in judicial administration, and the introduction of ethical guidance and codes with, if necessary, the removal from office of corrupt judges. The Council of Europe's Venice Commission has approved vetting post-appointment of judges in Albania, coupled with the establishment of an independent commission to investigate judicial assets, links with organized crime, and professional competence.[74] As a result more than one hundred judges were dismissed, including most members of the Constitutional Court. One of these was dismissed for insufficient disclosure of her assets and failing to recuse herself in a case. The ECtHR held that this did not constitute a breach of her fair trial rights and her private life under articles 6 and 8 of the ECHR.[75]

There is a relationship between judicial corruption and corruption within the wider society. General laws and specific laws for judges must criminalize corruption. Where corruption in the judiciary is endemic there will need to be proactive enforcement from an outside anti-corruption agency. Action by the judiciary itself may be compromised and complaint-based enforcement inadequate. Because of judicial independence, however, the measures will need careful drafting. The Venice Commission had concerns with a Moldovan law enabling their anti-corruption agency to have undercover agents pretending to be ordinary citizens making applications to court.[76] There is also a need to foster a political and societal culture which nurtures judicial integrity and discourages judicial corruption. Reform of the court structures may reduce the opportunities for patronage and fiscal improprieties. The experience of the UK is instructive in that it took a considerable time for the judiciary to become free of corruption in its various forms. To an extent the introduction in the nineteenth century of more efficient court machinery, less open to discretionary abuse, moved in parallel with reform in other parts of the state such as the changes following the Northcote-Trevelyan report in 1854, which paved the way for appointments to the British civil service to be on merit rather than as a result of influence or nepotism.

[74] 'Compilation of Venice Commission Opinions and Reports Concerning Vetting of Judges and Prosecutors' CDL-PI(2022)051.

[75] *Xhoxhaj v Albania* (2021) 73 EHRR 14.

[76] Venice Commission, Opinion no 789/2014, CDL-AD(2014)039.

Requiring judges to declare financial interests and those of their relatives is advanced as a means for controlling corruption. The United Nations Convention against Corruption requires states to consider systems for public officials—which includes judges—to register outside activities, employment, investments, assets, and substantial gifts and benefits from which a conflict of interest may result.[77] Asset declarations by judges are mandatory in a number of countries. An example is South Africa, where judges must disclose details of their registerable interests and those of immediate family members.[78] However, registration of financial interests must be necessary and proportionate to the specific situation in a jurisdiction. In its evaluation reports for the UK, GRECO, the Council of Europe's anti-corruption body, concluded that there was no need for registration since nothing indicated that there was any element of corruption in relation to judges.[79] With registration of judicial interests much depends on ensuring that the declarations are accurate. In some jurisdictions the register is confidential. Consequently, there must be internal procedures to ensure compliance. There must also be gateways for cross-checking a judge's declaration with, for example, the tax authorities. Where judicial declarations are public, the system can be self-enforcing to the extent that the media, NGOs, and others have an incentive to uncover false declarations.

IV Extrajudicial Conduct

Judges need extra care to comply with the ordinary law of the land, when driving, filing tax returns, renting a property, or paying child maintenance. On becoming a judge a person also accepts additional restrictions in their public and private lives—on their freedom to act and to speak. Because of their special position in society, judges cannot exercise their rights in the same way as others. To uphold the stature of judicial office, and to maintain public confidence in the judiciary, judges are constrained in what they can do in their everyday lives, whether this be commenting on social and political issues, having active social media accounts, or being involved in businesses and charities. These restrictions may be different depending upon the nature

[77] UNTS v 2349, arts 2(a)(i), 8(5), 11; *Implementation Guide and Evaluative Framework for Article 11* (United Nations 2015) 21.
[78] Judicial Service Commission Amendment Act 2008, s 13.
[79] *Fourth Round Evaluation Report on the UK*, Greco Eval IV Rep (2012) 2E, para 133.

of the judge's role and jurisdiction. Aspects of these restrictions live on, in modified form, after a judge has retired. There has been some relaxation in recent decades. It is now better appreciated that there is a public interest in judges participating, insofar as their office permits, in the life and affairs of their community.

(A) 'Free Speech'

The UN's Basic Principles on the Independence of the Judiciary affirm what has come to be called the right of 'free speech' of judges, cautioning, however, that in exercising this right judges should always conduct themselves in a manner which will preserve the dignity of their office and the judiciary's reputation.[80] Related to these restrictions on free speech are the specific provisions introduced by some judiciaries relating to contact with the media and the use of social media.[81] The justification for restrictions on a judge's right of free speech is not only because its exercise may give rise to allegations of partiality, but also because its content may undermine public confidence in the judiciary. Judicial independence as a rationale for restrictions on judicial speech is obvious in matters of public controversy, which are the responsibility of government and the legislature. The specific prohibition on commenting on impending litigation is because it might impair the fairness of the proceedings and affect the outcome.[82]

In some contexts the right of free speech for judges has to be read against a backdrop of the rights contained in a constitutional or human rights instrument. The right to free speech contained in the first amendment to the US Constitution was the reason given by the US Supreme Court in deciding that a rule from the ABA *Model Code of Judicial Conduct* was unconstitutional in restricting what judges could say about controversial issues during their campaign for election to the bench.[83] Unseemly advertising is consequently protected with some candidates for election to judicial office announcing their approach to matters which will come before them once they are sitting,

[80] Principle 8.
[81] eg, *Guide to Judicial Conduct* (n 11) 16–17, 21–22; *Media Guidance for the Judiciary* (n 3) preface; *Social Media Guidance for the Judiciary* (Judiciary of England and Wales 2024); *Canadian Ethical Principles* (n 4) paras 5.B.15–5.B.17, 5.B.20.
[82] cf ABA *Model Code* (n 16) r 2.10(A).
[83] *Republican Party of Minnesota v White* 536 US 765 (2002). On elected judges in the US see pp. 153–154 below.

and groups attacking (or defending) the decisions of incumbent judges with gusto. Conversely, the ECtHR has recognized the limits to judicial free speech in considering the application of article 10 of the ECHR (the right to freedom of expression) when a Russian judge was removed from office for making critical statements about the judiciary.[84] The court held that in the circumstances of that case the judge's statements had to be regarded as fair comment on a matter of great public importance, and her dismissal could have a chilling effect on other judges wishing to participate in public debate about the effectiveness of judicial institutions in Russia. It noted, however, that the duty of loyalty and discretion owed by judges required that the dissemination of even accurate information was carried out with moderation and propriety.[85]

Judges speaking out on controversial public issues or engaging with the media will, at the very least, attract criticism. In a leading US antitrust claim against Microsoft, the Court of Appeals for the District of Columbia allowed part of an appeal because during the trial the judge had discussed the case at length with reporters from the media. Although occurring in secret, that was in breach of the *Code of Conduct* for US judges in that the judge's conduct harmed judicial neutrality. The Court of Appeals added that judges appearing to covet publicity may 'lead any objective observer to wonder whether their judgments are being influenced by the prospect of favourable coverage in the media'.[86] Matters may go further, and judges may be subject to disciplinary action for their public statements. In line with the position elsewhere, South Africa's *Code of Judicial Conduct* provides in article 12(1)(b) that unless it is necessary for the discharge of judicial office a judge should not become involved in any political controversy or activity. At a webinar Chief Justice Mogoeng expressed a view taken to be contrary to the government's official policy on the Israel–Palestine conflict. The Judicial Conduct Committee upheld a decision that the judge had breached the code and infringed the constitutional separation of powers by involving himself in a matter which was the responsibility of the executive government.[87] He was ordered to apologize. In his judgment Zondi JA held that article 12(1)(b) seeks to protect and preserve the integrity and independence of the judiciary, which would otherwise be compromised if judges were involved in such

[84] *Kudeshkina v Russia* (2011) 52 EHRR 37. See also *Baka v Hungary* (2017) 64 EHRR 6.
[85] *Kudeshkina v Russia* (n 84) [93].
[86] *United States v Microsoft Corp* 253 F 3d 34, 115 (DC Cir 2001).
[87] *Chief Justice Mogoeng v Africa4Palestine* [2021] JSC/819/20; JSC/825/20; and JSC/826/20, [52].

controversies. Dambuza JA agreed. She added that accepting appointment as a judge 'comes with certain restrictions which would not be acceptable to ordinary citizens. They accede to limitations to their own freedoms in order to promote the rights of other citizens for the public good'.[88]

English judges generally avoid public comment on controversial issues. At one time the position was governed by what was known as the Kilmuir rules, enunciated in 1955. Their origin was a request by the BBC for judges to participate in a series on 'great judges of the past'. Lord Kilmuir LC refused his approval: so long as judges remained silent, he reasoned, their reputation for wisdom and impartiality remained unassailable, but every utterance made in public, except in the actual performance of their judicial duties, necessarily brought potential criticism. In 1987 Lord Mackay LC abolished the Kilmuir rules because they were inconsistent with judicial independence. However, by long-standing convention, the *Guide to Judicial Conduct* explains, judges do not comment publicly on government policy or proposals, public appointments, and individual cases.[89] The conventions are said to promote the dignity of judicial office, the finality of judgments, impartiality, and judicial independence. The *Guide* adds that judges should avoid any appearance of political ties, for example, by speaking within political forums.[90] There are also the conventions against commenting on their own cases or those of colleagues and in expressing views which would expose them to challenges about sitting on future decisions because of apparent bias.

(B) Behaviour Away from Court

Judges must accept restrictions on their private lives more burdensome than for those in other professions. At base this is to uphold the status of judicial office and public confidence in the administration of justice and the judiciary. While judges are entitled to a private life, as the *Guide to Judicial Conduct* for English judges puts it, they 'should not act in a way, even in their private or family life, which could reduce respect for judicial office or cast doubt on their independence, impartiality, or integrity. They should avoid situations in which risks of this kind are likely to arise'.[91] Involvement in

88 at [99].
89 *Guide to Judicial Conduct* (n 11) 16.
90 ibid 15.
91 ibid 10.

political activities would bring into question judicial independence, as well as risk involvement in controversial issues. Regular association with a litigant (or potential litigant) would threaten impartiality and open a judge to challenge for apparent bias.

There is a long list of single instances as to what judges are advised they can or cannot do away from court. These may be in the guidance and codes on judicial ethics, and the rulings of disciplinary bodies and courts. The most important can be categorized under five broad heads. First are those situations where the judge's behaviour falls below community standards and could give rise to legal liability but may not constitute a criminal offence. Judges fiddling travel expenses, avoiding tax liabilities, misusing their position for personal benefit, ignoring the spirit of public health measures, misemploying public moneys under their control, or engaging in discrimination, harassment, or bullying of staff—all fall into this category.[92] Allegations of this nature need to be tested against the evidence and understood in light of all the circumstances. That is because in some jurisdictions a government may attempt to discredit a judge with accusations along these lines in retaliation for the judge having ruled against it. Secondly, there is conduct which detracts from the judge's performance as a judge. This is one of the reasons that judges should not engage in commercial activities or act as a director, trustee, or legal adviser to a company. Holding and managing assets acquired before appointment as a judge or through inheritance must not involve frequent financial and business transactions.[93]

That leads, thirdly, to a judge's association with an outside cause or institution. An issue could arise, for example, with membership of a group with a specific agenda, especially one concerned with social or political change. The public perception might be that the judge shares the organization's agenda, which could threaten judicial impartiality. One example is the *Pinochet* case, where a judge's links with Amnesty International, an intervener in the case, led the House of Lords to set aside its earlier decision.[94] Consequently, judges should steer clear of those whose cause might be at issue in legal proceedings. Membership of a club which does not admit women members is an example of a questionable institutional association. Among members of the public the judge's membership has the potential to call into question their commitment

[92] An example of financial impropriety is *Sarojini Ramaswami v Union of India*, 1992 AIR SC 2219, (1992) 4 SCC 506.

[93] See *Code of Conduct for US Judges* (n 18) Canon 4, (D)(1).

[94] PP. 88–89 above.

to equality before the law and thereby erode public confidence in the judiciary. As to religion, judges may join any religious group, but if as a result they have beliefs in conflict with contemporary social attitudes they may be unable to sit in cases where these are at issue.[95]

Not every association of a judge with an outside cause or institution is fatal. The association must lead to concern about a judge's impartiality or compromise public confidence in the judiciary. In a cause célèbre in Canada, a judge became the unpaid acting dean of a new law school in difficulties. It focused on aboriginal, environmental, and natural resources law. The chief justice, after approval from the minister of justice, granted the judge special leave under the Judges Act to undertake the task.[96] The Canadian Judicial Council, constituted under the Judges Act, ruled that the judge was in breach of that Act which prohibits a judge engaging in an occupation or business other than their judicial duties.[97] The judge sought judicial review and the court held that the Council had misinterpreted the Act. The prohibition was against remunerative commercial engagements, not this type of appointment.[98] As to the ethical issue of misusing the judge's judicial status, the court said that the test was not whether the judge's association with the outside institution bolstered its reputation. It was precisely for that reason that law schools sought to have judges teach and universities made them chancellors. If that were the test, then no judge could ever join or participate in any extra-judicial civic, religious, or charitable organization.[99]

Concern over gifts and the like from outside interests, the fourth category, led the US Supreme Court to adopt its first code of ethics in 2023.[100] There had been public controversy around justices who had accepted lavish gifts from wealthy donors. As regards gifts, the code cross-refers to the Judicial Conference Regulations on Gifts, made under federal law and applying to other federal judges.[101] All federal judges, including US Supreme justices, also file financial disclosure reports covering details of gifts, nongovernmental income, investments, and significant debts. As with the US Supreme Court code, the UK Supreme Court in its *Guide to Judicial Conduct* states the obvious, that no justice or family member should ask for or accept any gift,

[95] cf *Page v Lord Chancellor* [2021] EWCA Civ 254, [2021] ICR 912.
[96] Judges Act, RSC 1985, c J-1, s 54.
[97] ibid s 55.
[98] *Smith v Attorney General of Canada*, 2020 FC 629, [2020] 4 FCR 3.
[99] ibid [130].
[100] *Code of Conduct for Justices of the Supreme Court of the United States*, 13 November 2023.
[101] *Judicial Conference Regulations on Gifts*, Guide to Judiciary Policy, vol 2, pt C, ch 6.

loan, or favour in connection with their judicial duties.[102] The *Guide* later cautions about accepting a gift or hospitality which might appear to relate in some way to a justice's judicial office and might be construed as an attempt to attract judicial goodwill or favour. Gifts or hospitality of modest value may be unobjectionable if given, the *Guide* suggests, as a token of appreciation for a speech, lecture, or participation at an event.[103]

Fifthly, there are the general constraints on a judge's private life which appointment as a judge brings and which do not apply to others. As the *Guide to Judicial Conduct* puts it, judges must accept that the nature of their office exposes them to considerable scrutiny and puts constraints on their behaviour: although they are entitled to a private life, they 'should not act in a way, even in their private or family life, which could reduce respect for judicial office or cast doubt on their independence, impartiality or integrity . . . [and] should avoid situations in which risks of this kind are likely to arise'.[104] Indiscretion in sexual matters may fall within this description, although mores change and what would have been regarded as incompatible with judicial office at one time might not be regarded in the same light today. The *Guide* warns that judges must be prudent in managing their financial affairs and in their personal relationships, social contacts, and activities.[105] As previously indicated, because of the risks to the safety of themselves and their families, and to the reputation of the judiciary by expressing or appearing to endorse views which could cast doubt on their objectivity, a judge's use of social media is curtailed.

(C) Judicial Confidentiality

Judicial confidentiality has two aspects. The first derives from the principle of judicial independence; the second, the need to maintain public confidence in the judiciary. The first aspect is the long-established common law rule that judges cannot be compelled to give evidence relating to the performance of their judicial functions.[106] The immunity covers evidence about their deliberations when reaching a decision. It has been called deliberative secrecy, but potentially has a wider ambit. It would not extend to the evidence of a judge

[102] *Guide to Judicial Conduct* (UK Supreme Court 2019) [4.4].
[103] ibid [5.14]–[5.16].
[104] *Guide to Judicial Conduct* (n 11) 10.
[105] ibid 9.
[106] *Duke of Buccleuch v Metropolitan Board of Works* (1872) LR 5 HL 418, 433.

about a murder committed in front of them in court. The murder would not relate to their functions as a judge. The position would be no different from if the murder had taken place in the judge's presence in the street outside the courtroom. The immunity rule does not affect the competence of judges to give evidence. The Court of Appeal of England and Wales has said that if a situation arises where their evidence is vital, judges should not allow the rule to stand in the way of their giving evidence.[107] An example might be evidence of the precise undertaking a party gave to the court, but it is difficult to imagine this being necessary when there should be a court order containing its terms, a transcript, an electronic recording of the proceedings, or a note by counsel.

The immunity of judges from being compelled to give evidence about their judicial functions came into sharp focus when a Royal Commission in Canada into a miscarriage of justice ordered superior court judges who had heard a reference about the conviction to testify before it. The Supreme Court of Canada held that, like judges in a civil court, the Commission under its statutory powers could not compel the judges to give evidence as to how and why they reached their decision.[108] That followed from the principle of judicial independence, which required that other branches of government not impinge on the essential authority and function of the court. Nor could the Royal Commission compel evidence about the composition of the bench that heard the case. That went to the institutional aspect of judicial independence, since courts had to control administrative matters relating to adjudication without interference from the legislature or executive. The Supreme Court accepted, however, that circumstances could exist where the Parliament could enact laws to inquire into the integrity of particular judges and relating to the functioning of the courts.

The second aspect of judicial confidentiality is stated in the *Bangalore Principles of Judicial Conduct*, that confidential information acquired by judges in their judicial capacity must not be used or disclosed for purposes unrelated to their judicial duties.[109] The *Commentary on the Bangalore Principles* emphasizes the use for personal gain of confidential information which comes a judge's way through, say, the conduct of commercial litigation.[110] The provision parallels the restrictions on others such as lawyers

[107] *Warren v Warren* [1997] QB 488, 497 (Lord Woolf MR).
[108] *Mackeigan v Hickman* [1989] 2 SCR 796.
[109] *Bangalore Principles of Judicial Conduct* (n 5) [4.10].
[110] *Commentary on the Bangalore Principles* (n 7) [154]–[155].

and bankers who are entrusted with confidential, price-sensitive information. Impropriety of this character undermines the standing of the judiciary as a whole and public confidence in it. As well as its ethical dimension, the *Bangalore Principles of Judicial Conduct* cast a wider net. One aspect is the disclosure by a judge, say to a friend, about a decision reached by their court before it is made public. That is an ethical breach, and in some circumstances the information could be used to commercial advantage.

Another breach of judicial confidentiality is the disclosure of matters relating to the making of a judicial decision and of internal judicial discussions referring to persons. The traditional view was that a judgment was the final word on a matter and that a judge could not be asked for, and should not disclose, any further explanation. The justification was that public confidence in the official judgment would be undermined if judges disclosed uncertainties and changes in their views or those of colleagues before a judgment was delivered, or the nature of discussions and disagreements with colleagues over the result and its reasoning. As with the justification for the confidentiality of discussions in cabinet and between ministers and public officials, judicial confidentiality could also be said to promote candid and rigorous consideration of a matter, untouched by concerns about public or political opinion. On the other hand, it might be that public understanding would be enhanced if judges disclosed in careful fashion the challenges and difficulties in reaching their decisions. In this regard the public interest could trump the duty of confidentiality as it can with any issue of confidentiality.

(D) Former Judges

Former judges who are still active may engage in private dispute resolution as arbitrators or mediators, serve as judges in the courts of other jurisdictions, or be appointed to public bodies or conduct public inquiries for government or private reviews for commercial and financial organizations. Occasionally a former judge's arbitration award may raise eyebrows when it is challenged in court. Sitting in other jurisdictions may attract controversy when the government there is not democratic or has a bad record on human rights. In India public appointments for former judges are said to benefit those who favoured the government when on the bench. None of these activities is a huge break from judging. Nor, in general, is any of them likely in itself to dent severely the reputation of the judiciary of which the judge was part. At some point, however, the position may become such that the judge decides to draw a line because of the individual and institutional costs.

Until its revision in 2020, the *Guide to Judicial Conduct* for England and Wales restated what had long been regarded as the convention, that on termination of their appointment judges should not return to private practice as an advocate for remuneration or offer to provide legal advice.[111] The justification the *Guide* gave for continuing the convention was that a former judge might still be regarded by the public as a representative of the judiciary and any activity which might tarnish its reputation should be avoided.[112] It seems that the prohibition was also because the former judge might appear to have an unfair advantage over other lawyers as a result of deference, preferential treatment, or inside knowledge if appearing in the court where they had been a judge. Since the 2020 version of the *Guide*, retired judges have simply been advised that because the public might perceive that they are still associated with the judiciary, they should exercise caution and that, by reference to the *Guide*'s provisions, should avoid activity that may tarnish its reputation.[113] In addition to the *Guide*, the terms and conditions of service for judges have stated that candidates accept appointment upon the understanding that it is 'intended for the remainder of a person's professional life' and that 'following termination of their appointment they will not return to private practice as a barrister or a solicitor'. It is doubtful whether the convention or the terms and conditions of service are enforceable.[114]

The convention had been abandoned in Australia, where conduct rules permit retired judges to return to practice after specified periods. For example in New South Wales, after a period of five years from when they ceased to be a judge, former judges are able to appear as a barrister before the court where they were a judge, or before a court from which appeals lie to their former court.[115] However, the Australian *Guide to Judicial Conduct* states that former judges should be careful not to conduct themselves in a manner which may reasonably be perceived as incompatible with the overriding objective that justice must be done and seen to be done, and that public confidence in the independence, impartiality, and integrity of the judiciary is maintained. Consequently, the *Guide* adds, it may reasonably be perceived

111 *Guide to Judicial Conduct* (Judiciary of England and Wales 2013) [9.1].
112 ibid [9.2].
113 eg, *Guide to Judicial Conduct* (n 11) 6.
114 cf *White v Bar Council of Ireland* [2016] IEHC 283, [2018] IECA 48.
115 eg, New South Wales, Legal Profession Uniform Conduct (Barristers) Rules 2015, r 101A(2)(a).

to be incompatible with the overriding objective for a former judge to appear, even if permitted by the conduct rules, particularly when the former judge's judicial colleagues remain as judges or a judgment of the former judge will be considered in the case.[116]

The relaxation of rules against a return to practice reflects changing demographics. Judges are living longer and continue working after compulsory retirement from the bench. Others retire early because they find that judging is no longer attractive and want to return to practice or to more remunerative or challenging opportunities. Depending on the jurisdiction a former judge returning to practice and giving legal advice or appearing in court may need to obtain a certificate or licence from the regulatory body for practicing lawyers. Otherwise, there is a regulatory gap in that the former judge is not accountable to any professional body or to the judiciary of which they were a member. Professional regulation will not prevent any damage to the integrity of the judiciary if a former judge becomes embroiled in public controversy, even if unintentionally. Apart from professional regulation, a second approach is to prohibit former judges from certain types of activity and practice. Judges while still on the bench might be prohibited, for example, from negotiating with law firms about post-retirement employment. Promoting themselves by reference to their former status as a judge might be proscribed. There might be a time bar on practicing before their former court, or before courts with appeals to that court. There might be additional restrictions such as appearing in any court in areas of the law which they adjudicated upon while on the bench, or appearing in court at all so that only an advisory practice is permitted.

V Conclusion

Judicial integrity does not require that judges be paragons of virtue. First principles of behaviour are, however, fundamental. As the *Commentary on the Bangalore Principles of Judicial Conduct* describes them, integrity is the attribute of rectitude and righteousness; its components are honesty and judicial morality; and the judge should always, not only in the discharge of official duties, 'act honourably and in a manner befitting the judicial office; be free from fraud, deceit and falsehood; and be good and virtuous in behaviour

[116] Council of Chief Justices of Australia and New Zealand, *Guide to Judicial Conduct, Third Edition (Revised)* (Australian Institute of Judicial Administration 2023) paras 7.1, 7.3.

and in character'.[117] In addition to these first principles are the judicial values of independence, impartiality, and fidelity to law, as well as the behavioural standards of judicial virtue, some contained in unwritten conventions, others in a judiciary's guide or code of judicial conduct. These behavioural standards can vary with the context in which the judge acts. They typically cover behaviour in court and a judge's extrajudicial activities. Socialization into the standards of judicial virtue occurs in anticipation of appointment as a judge, and continues once the judge begins judging. Compliance with them should be reinforced over time as a judge performs the role in accordance with expected standards of behaviour. Adherence to these standards should become second nature for the individual judge. Ultimately judicial integrity must be self-enforcing and internalized.

At an elementary level judges must not be corrupt or abuse their power. They must also be competent. Competence is not confined to legal knowledge alone, but it also encompasses principles and standards such as intellectual honesty, as well as efficiency in managing a case and delivering timely decisions. Judges need to be able to make difficult and unpopular decisions. That requires judicial courage. They must be able to withstand pressures and influences. Judicial courage must be coupled with fidelity to law—decisions must be based on the law and the facts without regard to the identity of the parties—and a commitment to fairness and integrity in the processes of decision-making. Integrity in decision-making processes demands that each party's case be considered with an open mind. Alongside this is that the judge must accord everyone equal concern and respect, which may require taking account of cultural and social differences. In court bad temper, rudeness, constant interruptions, and insensitive remarks will not inspire the confidence of the parties or the profession. Courtesy, patience, punctuality, individual consideration, equal treatment, and a respect for the dignity of all involved in judicial processes are demanded. The judge must also ensure that no one in court is exposed to bias, prejudice, discrimination, or harassment. A simple example is the fine line which can occasionally materialize between tough cross-examination on the one hand, and disrespectful and unfair treatment of a litigant or witness on the other. None of this is easy.

All these qualities go to the fairness of the proceedings and the satisfaction of litigants, albeit that one side must lose and be disappointed by the outcome. While in different form, values and standards apply to a judge's

[117] *Commentary on the Bangalore Principles* (n 7) para 101.

behaviour outside the courtroom. These relate firstly to a judge's behaviour with colleagues, with those directly working with them, and with court staff generally. Judicial integrity mandates respectful behaviour, without any hint of bias, prejudice, bullying, or harassment. Away from court, judges must conduct themselves in a manner so that public confidence in the judiciary as an institution is maintained. This requires them to comply with the law of the land in matters as simple as driving, but also to accept restrictions on their lives to which others are not subject. Free speech is one casualty, where in the interests of the judiciary as a whole the judge is limited in what can be said in speeches and lectures, in contacts with the legacy media, and in their social media activity. Former judges are also bound to behavioural standards, generally informal and unenforceable, so as not to tarnish the judiciary's reputation in the eyes of the public. Specifically, that includes confining the range of their work when resuming legal practice, as well as keeping within bounds their contributions to public debate in areas which are highly politically or socially contentious.

PART II
PRACTICE

4
Legal and Policy Framework

I Introduction

In giving the advice of the Privy Council in 1938, Lord Atkin said that the independence of judges was protected by provisions for their appointment by the Crown, that they held office during good behaviour, and that their salaries were fixed in legislation. He added: 'These are three principal pillars in the temple of justice, and they are not to be undermined.'[1] This chapter explores the practical implications of Lord Atkin's 'pillars in the temple of justice', what is described in less high-flown terms here as the legal and policy framework for judging. Examination of this framework is partial, and other aspects are covered elsewhere in the book. Appointment and length of service are dealt with in section II of the chapter, but taking account of the reality that, by contrast with Lord Atkin's day, the selection of judges does not always lie with the executive, nor is the appointment of senior judges for life. Section III returns to the point made in Chapter 1, that the other side of the coin to judicial independence is accountability. An aspect of judicial accountability is that while senior judges still hold office during good behaviour, they along with other judges are subject to disciplinary procedures if they misconduct themselves. Section IV of the chapter examines judicial salaries, along with other conditions of service, including those relating to community engagement.

The framework for judging is contained in both the law and policy. Its different aspects—appointment and length of service, removal and discipline, and conditions of service—have a bearing not only on judicial independence, as Lord Atkin suggested, but also on the other fundamental values of judging considered in Part I of the book, namely, impartiality and integrity. Thus partisan judicial appointments are facilitative of decision-making affected by bias; limited tenure and a power of arbitrary removal are a potential threat to independent judging; and poor remuneration and conditions of service are conducive to bribery, corruption, and the erosion of judicial

[1] *Toronto Corporation v York Corporation* [1938] AC 415, 426 (PC, Canada).

Judging. Ross Cranston, Oxford University Press. © Ross Cranston 2025.
DOI: 10.1093/9780191890994.003.0004

integrity. There is no template for perfection. Measures which in one jurisdiction are neutral as regards independence, impartiality, and integrity would in other jurisdictions be essential (or inimical) to their maintenance. Moreover, it is well to recognize that independence, impartiality, and integrity are sometimes proffered as the justification for specific measures of law and policy regarding judging, whereas the relationship is tenuous and other motivating factors are at work.

II Appointment and Length of Service

The UN Basic Principles on the Independence of the Judiciary provide that judges of integrity and ability have to be selected through a process which is non-discriminatory, and which is effective in safeguarding against appointments for improper motives.[2] Concern about the politicization of the process in parts of continental Europe has led to placing the responsibility for judicial careers in the hands of judicial councils, independent of the executive and legislative branches.[3] This and other methods of selecting judges are explored in this section of the chapter, before it turns to a judge's term of office. Strong tenure contributes to judicial independence but also enables a judge to remain in office when their faculties are impaired or their behaviour is under a cloud. Depending on the context, judges with weaker tenure may or may not be as insulated from outside pressure according to whether in practice they are subject to dismissal, demotion, or transfer.

(A) Models of Selection

There are various models for selecting judges—by the executive government, by popular election, by a body of judges and others (referred to as a 'selection commission'), or by the judges themselves. Each has variations in practice; each is contested. Historically, selection by the executive government was the norm and it remains in place in many jurisdictions. Selection by popular election was adopted at state level in the United States in the nineteenth

[2] UNGA Res 40/ 32 (29 November 1985) and UNGA Res 40/ 146 (13 December 1985) (hereafter UN Basic Principles).

[3] Council of Europe, *European Charter on the Statute for Judges* (1998) DAJ/DOC(98)23, principle 1.3.

century. State courts handle some ninety-five per cent of the caseload of American courts, and most states now use elections as some part of their selection process. Establishing a commission for the selection of judges is a twentieth century phenomenon. It has been adopted for a variety of reasons, including furthering judicial independence and promoting judicial diversity.

In relation to each of these models there are four points to note. First, the manner of selecting and appointing judges may have a bearing on whether a judiciary is independent and impartial. Secondly, it is impossible to select as judges those without opinions or commitments; that is part of their humanity.[4] Increasing diversity is justified as bringing to the judiciary a wider range of experience and expertise. Thirdly, a failure to appoint an eminently qualified person for appointment may be as corrosive of institutional legitimacy as an overly partisan appointment. Finally, there is a distinction between the selection of a judge and their formal appointment. Judges can be selected in various ways, but their formal appointment will not take place until they have sworn the judicial oath. The appointment of senior judges will likely be under the hand of the head of state.

Executive government

The tradition in Britain was for judges to be selected by the executive government. Originally the monarch chose and appointed them, but with the emergence of constitutional government the lord chancellor assumed the role of identifying those to be appointed. In the case of the most senior appointments, the prime minister would propose the name to the monarch for formal appointment. There was a strong political element in judicial selection. Lord Halsbury LC, in office at various time between 1885 and 1905, was notorious for rewarding members of his own party, the Conservatives, with judicial preferment, doubly so because some were by common consent bad judges. In the twentieth century the situation began to change, and although judges continued to be political appointees, lord chancellors did not act in an overly partisan manner in their selection. The criticism became that the system relied too much on being known by the senior judiciary, since the lord chancellor and his key civil servants would take 'soundings' from them about possible appointees. The quest for greater diversity drove the adoption in Britain of a selection commission, and there is now virtually no political input into the selection of judges.

[4] PP. 74–75 above.

In the common law world the selection of judges by the executive government still predominates. As Lord Bingham remarked, 'there is nothing inherently objectionable in the appointment of judges by the executive . . . it makes practical sense that judges should be appointed by the body, which is thereafter responsible for paying them, accommodating them and servicing their professional requirements'.[5] Context is everything. There is a distinction between executive appointments in democracies on the one hand, and in authoritarian states on the other where judges are appointed who will support the incumbent ruler. Depending on the institutional and political context, there is a democratic argument against transferring the power of selection from the executive to a commission of unelected (or mainly unelected) persons.[6] On the other hand, executive selection can lack transparency. Judicial appointments to the US federal courts are now made on party political lines. Undertaken without consultation or taking account of what consultees say, it can result in the appointment of the less able or the biddable. Private communications by the executive with potential appointees to gauge their views on the justiciable issues of the day subverts judicial independence.

In some cases, as with US federal judges, the approval of the legislature might be an additional step in appointments after the executive has nominated a judge. In the context of appointments there, especially to the US Supreme Court, legislative confirmation can degenerate into an unseemly spectacle because presidential nominations are intensely partisan. In other contexts legislative involvement in the selection of judges can offer a helpful democratic input, so long as there are tight procedures and a respectful and constructive attitude on both sides. Since the early 1950s the American Bar Association (ABA) has provided assistance to all involved in judicial appointments through its ranking of those nominated to the US Supreme Court and the federal district and appellate courts as 'well qualified', 'qualified', or 'not qualified'. Evaluation aspires to be a politically neutral peer assessment of each nominee's professional competence, integrity, and judicial temperament, based on extensive, confidential interviews with judges, lawyers, and professional colleagues. That will be coupled with a survey of a nominee's writings and a detailed interview with them. In the intensely divided political climate in the US, ABA evaluations have been contested.

[5] *Kearney v Her Majesty's Advocate* [2006] UKPC D1, [2006] HRLR 15 [5].
[6] See former Chief Justice Mason, 'The Appointment and Removal of Judges' in Helen Cunningham (ed), *Fragile Bastions: Judicial Independence in the Nineties and Beyond* (Judicial Commission of New South Wales 2000) 16–17.

In response to the pressure to widen the pool of possible appointees, the arrangements for the executive appointment of judges have been modified in many jurisdictions to provide greater transparency as to the criteria for candidates and the procedures followed. There are different systems and these may be enshrined in policy rather than statute. Generally, there will be an advertisement inviting applications or expressions of interest to fill vacancies. The resultant long list will be whittled down after consultation, perhaps with the chief justice, who may in turn consult other judges, and with the bar and, in a federal system or one with devolved governments, with those other governments as well (at least for appointments to the apex court).[7] Candidates on the shortlist may be interviewed, and there will be criminal and reputational checks on those whose name or names go forward. The final choice then lies with the Attorney General, the minister for justice, the prime minister (or the premier or elected governor of a state), or perhaps the whole cabinet.

Elections

Apart from the United States, very few countries have adopted the system whereby voters elect judges. While US Supreme Court and federal judges are selected by the executive, many judges at the state level are elected by the general population. The move to make judges responsible to the people in periodical elections obtained impetus with Jacksonian populism, but when in the middle of the nineteenth century the notion of electing judges really took hold it was to limit party patronage and cronyism in their appointment and to strengthen judicial independence. By the early twentieth century nearly three-quarters of the states elected their judges. However, a concern from that time was that party bosses controlled the list of candidates for judicial election, as James Bryce put it, throwing the choice into the hands of 'knots of wirepullers inclined to use every office as a means of rewarding political services'[8] That led some states to adopt nonpartisan elections where party affiliations did not appear. This did not go far enough for judicial reformers, who took the view that even with nonpartisan elections voters were not sufficiently knowledgeable to select the best qualified candidates. Some states introduced so-called merit selection (or the Missouri plan, after an early state to adopt it), where a commission of judges, lawyers, and perhaps others choose a pool of qualified candidates from whom the state governor makes

[7] eg, High Court of Australia Act 1979, s 6.
[8] James Bryce, *The American Commonwealth* (new edn, Macmillan 1914) vol 1, 507, 512.

appointments as judicial vacancies occur. Judges appointed in this way are subject to election after a term in office (retention elections), where they do not face opponents and the only issue for voters is whether they should continue in post.

From the last part of the twentieth century judicial elections have been transformed with higher profile campaigns. Money spent to support the election or defeat of candidates for judicial office has increased considerably. In early 2025 some $100 million was spent on the election campaign for a position on the Wisconsin Supreme Court. Qualified candidates who lack connections to wealthy contributors may be impaired in their ability to compete effectively. Finance from commercial and other interests creates conflicts of interest when these interests litigate before a judge whose candidature they supported.[9] Judges making decisions favouring campaign contributors may be accused of favouritism irrespective of the merits of a decision. The problem has been accentuated by the decision in *Citizens United v Federal Election Commission*,[10] where the US Supreme Court held that the First (free speech) Amendment of the US Constitution prevented restrictions on corporate interests funding advertisements and other political campaigning. That has led to spending on advertising in judicial elections by outside interests, whose donors need not be identified, independent of a judge's own campaign and any ethical or other restraints on the messages it can convey.

Campaigns for judges' elections reflect the polarized nature of American society and culture. Attack advertising is not uncommon. Incumbent judges have been challenged and, in some instances, removed for decisions on controversial, especially criminal justice, issues. The tone was set in 1986 when Bird CJ and two other judges of the Californian Supreme Court were defeated in a campaign which highlighted their unwavering decisions overturning the imposition by trial courts of the death penalty. In 2010 voters in Iowa denied retention to three judges of the state Supreme Court when the previous year the court had legalized same-sex marriage on constitutional equal protection grounds. These trends have not been uniform, either across the country or from one election to the next in any one state. The ABA has been concerned about the adverse consequences for the reputation of American judges for

[9] *Caperton v A T Massey Coal Company* 556 US 868 (2009).

[10] 558 US 310 (2010). States may limit judicial candidates soliciting election funds on grounds of judicial integrity: see *Williams-Yulee v The Florida Bar* 575 US 433 (2015).

impartiality and for public confidence in the justice system more generally, and as a result has considered rethinking judicial elections.[11]

Selection commissions

Major motivations for the establishment of selection commissions for judges have been, first, to secure judicial independence and, secondly, to further judicial diversity. Selection commissions appointing judges vary in their constitution, membership, and scope. Some are firmly established in law and have a high degree of independence from the executive government; others can be abolished overnight. Some have conferred on them additional functions such as judicial discipline. Selection commissions may be more limited as with the bodies operating in many US states, including those with retention elections, which vet candidates for judicial vacancies and provide a list to the appointing authority, typically the state governor.[12] Whether the executive has a role in a selection commission turns partly on the machinery's design. One aspect is if politicians or political nominees are commission members. Another is if the commission has to present only one or several names for any one vacancy. If a commission has to provide a list of three names, say, for every vacancy there is obviously an element of choice for the executive from within the list. Where only one name is advanced for each vacancy, the executive may be limited to rejecting the name and requesting the commission to reconsider. The commission may stand its ground and effectively the executive may have no choice. The executive's role also depends partly on the social and political context. In a society with a strong executive, a selection commission may be suborned whatever its de jure independence.

South Africa provides an example of a commission established to further both judicial independence and diversity. The need to bolster judicial independence and to restore the legitimacy of the courts was apparent after the apartheid period. Under apartheid judges were appointed by the executive. There was the perception that with honourable exceptions the white judges appointed had been complicit in the system. To enshrine the changes, the 1996 South African Constitution established an independent Judicial Service Commission, which is responsible for judicial appointments and discipline. The commission comprises judges (the chief justice presides at meetings),

[11] *Justice in Jeopardy. Report of the American Bar Association Commission on the 21st Century Judiciary* (American Bar Association 2003) 92–97.

[12] eg, Constitution of the State of New York, art VI, s 2 (c)–(e) (Court of Appeals); Constitution of the State of Florida, art V, s 11.

legal representatives, political appointees, and politicians.[13] Commission interviews for those short-listed are held in public, which enables civil society groups to raise concerns. Over time there has been criticism that partisan political behaviour was eroding the commission's standing.

Judicial independence was the prime motivation for the establishment in many civil law countries of judicial councils. These are independent of both the legislative and executive branches. Judicial councils existed in France and Italy from the years immediately after the Second World War, spread to Spain, Portugal, and Greece after the collapse in those countries of authoritarian regimes, and were then on the collapse of communism adopted in central and east European countries, in part following recommendations of the European Union and the Council of Europe. Latin American countries also adopted judicial councils. The typical judicial council is responsible for the appointment, training, promotion, and disciplining of judges.[14] Usually not less than one-half its members will be judges elected on a representative basis by other judges, with other members appointed from civil society and elsewhere. Consequently, judicial councils are under the control of the judiciary, or elements of it. In some jurisdictions judicial councils have been captured by judicial oligarchs who reward their allies and suppress criticism. This produces the paradox of dependent judges within an independent judiciary.

Ensuring a more diverse judiciary—the second reason for establishing a selection commission to undertake judicial appointments—was very much the basis in England and Wales for establishing the Judicial Appointments Commission under the Constitutional Reform Act 2005. The selection of judges by the lord chancellor under the previous system was criticized. His process of consulting senior judges led to recommendations for appointments from the narrow pool of leading, mainly male barristers. While on the whole selections were made on merit, women, minorities, and solicitors were unsurprisingly overlooked. The Commission is chaired by a layperson, and the number of commissioners who are judges must be less than the number of those (including the chair) who are not.[15] The Commission advertises vacancies, receives applications, and conducts assessments and interviews.

[13] Constitution of the Republic of South Africa, 1996, s 178 (hereafter South African Constitution). See also Judicial Service Commission Act, 9 of 1994, as amended.

[14] eg, *European Charter on the Statute for Judges* (n 3), principle 1.3; Council of Europe, 'Judges: Independence, Efficiency and Responsibilities', Recommendation CM/Rec(2010)12, paras 26–29 and Explanatory Memorandum, paras 34–36.

[15] Constitutional Reform Act 2005, s 61, Sch 12, para 3A; Judicial Appointments Commission Regulations 2013, SI 2013/2191.

Selection panels contain a judicial member and two lay persons. The selection of UK Supreme Court judges is by ad hoc selection commission, and in England and Wales the Judicial Appointments Commission's procedures are modified for the selection of leadership judges like the chief justice and members of the Court of Appeal. There are separate commissions for Scotland and Northern Ireland. Critics contend that this machinery has not had the impact on diversity it was supposed to have had.

Judicialized selection

There will generally be some judicial involvement in selecting judges, even if only indirectly. Executive selection will often follow consultation with the chief justice or the judiciary more widely about the names of potential appointees. That may also occur with elected judges in systems which work on the basis of 'appoint first, elect later'. Where there is a judicial commission or council, judicial input occurs since judges are members, membership often comprising a majority of judges. There is also the role of judges in the selection process itself, through their membership of selection panels or as consultees or referees. Even where lay people and representatives of civil society are involved, perhaps in the majority, they may defer to the judgement of judicial members, or perceive their role as corroborating the judicial evaluation of candidates. Especially with senior level appointments, judges may leave these bodies in little doubt as to who should be selected. Whatever the de jure position, de facto the judges have the upper hand.

Judicialization of selection operates de jure in India. The Supreme Court has decided that under the Constitution they and they alone must control the selection of judges for the Supreme and High courts. Articles 124 and 217 of the Indian Constitution provide that Supreme Court judges shall be appointed after consultation with the chief justice of India, and High Court judges after consultation with the chief justice of India, the governor of the state, and the chief justice of the relevant High Court. In *Supreme Court Advocates-on-Record Association v Union of India (the Second Judges Case)*[16] the Supreme Court held that only the chief justice and the senior judges of the court ('the collegium') could select the judges. Judicial independence and the structure of the Constitution were the justifications for the court's conclusion. The background to the decision was that the judiciary had been

[16] (1993) 4 SCC 441, AIR 1994 SC 268, overruling *S P Gupta v President of India (the First Judges Case)* (1981) Supp SCC 87, AIR 1982 SC 149. It was affirmed in *Re Special Reference 1 of 1998 (the Third Judges Case)* (1998) 7 SCC 739, AIR 1999 SC 1.

scarred by Prime Minister Indira Gandhi's Emergency (1975–77) and the interference with judicial independence associated with her time in office, typified by the forced transfer of judges unsympathetic to her government.[17]

Following criticism that the collegium system lacked transparency and facilitated favouritism, the Union government sought to establish a national judicial appointments commission. The National Judicial Appointments Commission Act 2014 and the Constitution (99th Amendment) Act 2014 established the Commission and amended articles 124 and 217 of the Constitution. In what is known as the *Fourth Judges Case*, the Supreme Court held that these measures were a violation of judicial independence, the separation of powers, and the basic structure of the Constitution, as well as constituting a threat to the privacy of the candidates being considered.[18] In the opinion of Jagdish Singh Khehar J, civil society had not yet sufficiently evolved in India to have a hand in selecting judges, and safeguarding the rights of citizens could only be ensured by keeping the judiciary absolutely insulated and independent from the other organs of government.[19] In his dissent Chelameswar J remarked that the primacy of the judges in judicial appointments 'is not the only means for the establishment of an independent and efficient judiciary'.[20] Criticism of the collegium system in India raises in stark form the flaws in a system of wholly judicialized selection.

The selection of judges by judges must confront the issue of affinity bias, the well-known tendency when choosing candidates to favour those closest to the selectors in their interests, beliefs, and background. Although rational factors may be important in selecting judges, the final choice may result because of the feeling on the part of leadership judges in the case of senior appointments, or the judicial member of a panel in other cases, that someone is uniquely qualified because even if they are not well known they are of a similar professional background. This has nothing to do with overt prejudice. Rather, judicial selectors are human and unconscious bias is a tendency which all have. Nor is it to deny the necessity for judicial input when judges are selected, since laypeople can never fully appreciate the nature and context of judging and all the qualities essential for the job. The prime danger when judges have the determining voice in selecting judges is self-replication.

[17] See pp. 22, 45 above.
[18] *Supreme Court Advocates-on-record Association v Union of India* (2016) 5 SCC 1.
[19] ibid [205].
[20] ibid [98].

(B) Selection Processes

The process of selecting judges involves matching an applicant to a notion of what constitutes a good judge. The good judge will have the values of independence, impartiality, and integrity. These values encompass fairness and a sense of justice. Then there are first principles qualities like honesty, courtesy, and patience. The skills and abilities required of a good judge vary depending on the role and responsibilities involved. Although there will be some overlap, those required of a judge in an apex court do not match completely those needed by the judge appointed to try small claims. Appointees must be able to exhibit judicial values, qualities, and skills in their everyday conduct. Considerable care is required since, once appointed, judges, especially senior judges, have a protection against removal through tenure protection. The overriding need is to maintain public confidence in both the individual judge and the judiciary as an institution. One dimension to public confidence is the extent to which the judiciary reflects the diversity in society.

Eligibility, good character, and merit

Eligibility criteria for selection as a judge are usually straightforward if they are objective in character—citizenship, age, being in practice a minimum number of years are examples. There can be the occasional difficulty, as there was with the requirement for provincial representation on Canada's Supreme Court when in 2013 the prime minister announced the appointment to the court of a federal court judge to one of the three seats reserved for Quebec. The chief justice had warned that as a federal court judge the nominee might not be eligible. The appointment was challenged and the matter referred to the Supreme Court. It concluded by a six to one majority that the relevant sections of the Supreme Court Act when interpreted in their historical and constitutional context meant that appointments for the Quebec positions had to be from current senior judges in Quebec or current advocates of ten years' standing in that province. Although the nominee had been sworn in, his appointment was therefore void. The court held also that legislation which had been introduced to overcome the problem was invalid.[21]

Good character is a common requirement in selecting a judge.[22] There is a sliding scale with the criteria for assessing good character moving from the relatively objective to the more subjective. Reliance on general reputation

[21] *Reference re Supreme Court Act, ss 5 and 6* [2014] 1 SCR 433.
[22] eg, Constitutional Reform Act 2005, s 63(3).

is relatively subjective. Self-declaration by an applicant of potentially relevant matters only goes so far, even if backed by making the failure to provide full, accurate, and continuing disclosure evidence of unsuitability. Obtaining information from official sources assists objectivity—criminal records, the tax authorities, insolvency and company records, and professional regulatory bodies. A statutory pathway may enable the selection body to access this information despite any legal duty which these bodies would otherwise have to maintain confidentiality.[23] The selecting authority must still interpret the information. Motoring offences are a hardy perennial, minor speeding offences on the one hand, serious driving offences on the other.[24] Disputes with the tax authorities raise similar problems. A candidate's business partners, participation in public controversies, and use of social media and online networking sites need exploring to uncover associations or views which would undermine public confidence if more widely known. Are social, political, and religious views forcefully conveyed to be treated as indicating unsuitability along with those which indicate discrimination, harassment, and victimization? Extending good character to whether potential appointees have consistently demonstrated professional respect and courtesy for their colleagues, clients, and others involved in the legal process presents a practical, albeit not insuperable, challenge.[25]

Merit is another common requirement in judicial selection.[26] There are a number of relevant aspects. The first is to identify a standard for merit. The president selecting a chief justice or the judge of an apex court may regard the most meritorious as the one who will give support in a disputed election or when their policies are challenged in the courts. A minister of justice may see considerable merit in someone they knew from school or at the bar. A chief justice may exclude considering for an appellate appointment anyone who has not come through the ranks, whereas the outstanding candidate may be a lateral appointment from outside. A selecting body with a limited field of candidates may regard as meritorious one marked as 'appointable' for selection when no one is regarded as 'well qualified'. Merit in judicial appointments is usually measured, however, against the standard of professionalism. That combines personal and professional characteristics. For any one vacancy this needs to be assessed at an individual level but also comparatively.

[23] eg, ibid s 107(2).

[24] eg, *R (Jones) v Judicial Appointments Commission* [2014] EWHC 1680 (Admin) (Div Ct).

[25] Australian Law Reform Commission, *Without Fear or Favour: Judicial Impartiality and the Law on Bias* (ALRC Report 138, 2021) para 12.33.

[26] eg, Constitutional Reform Act 2005, s 63(2) ('Selection must be solely on merit').

No candidate may be appointable since the best of the applicants may still not meet the standard. There is also the difficulty, especially with an initial appointment, that the selector needs to estimate a candidate's potential to perform judicial functions. These are not equivalent to those performed in legal practice.

If professionalism is the standard for merit, the second aspect is spelling out valid criteria for identifying it. The European Court of Human Rights (ECtHR) has said that judges with merit are those possessing moral integrity and technical competence to perform the judicial function in a state governed by the rule of law.[27] The moral integrity the court requires would extend beyond good character to include other personal characteristics—a commitment to judicial independence and impartiality, and a capacity to act with fairness, tolerance, and sensitivity to difference and particular needs. The technical competence the ECtHR identifies would encompass what is necessary in everyday legal work—the ability to access legal knowledge; a talent to write well-reasoned and timely decisions; a capacity to weigh evidence to decide facts; an ability make decisions under pressure and at speed; a capacity to manage a large list efficiently, to organize one's time, and to meet priorities; and an understanding as to what it is to act fairly, with sound judgement, and a sense of justice.[28] These different aspects will weigh differently depending on the nature of the appointment, from the aspirant to membership of an apex court to the one seeking to be a judge in a small claims court.

Technical competence and moral integrity do not exhaust professionalism.[29] In light of modern day judging, non-technical skills such as interacting with others are essential. Aspects of this are the ability to conduct legal proceedings calmly, courteously, and patiently; to maintain an appropriate demeanour; to treat others with equal concern and respect; and to be considerate, tactful, and empathetic. Along with these interpersonal skills is the ability to communicate effectively, which can be broken down into establishing authority; inspiring respect and confidence; listening with patience and courtesy; explaining relevant legal and procedural matters; and asking questions in clear and readily understood language. An awareness of the diverse community in which judging takes place is also an essential

[27] *Astraosson v Iceland* App no 26374/18 (ECtHR, 1 December 2020) [220] (GC).
[28] eg, *Judicial Skills and Abilities Framework* (Courts and Tribunals Judiciary 2025); *Suggested Criteria for Judicial Appointment* (revised by Kathy Mack, Australasian Institute of Judicial Administration 2024).
[29] ibid.

aspect of professionalism. For some appointments leadership skills will be part of merit.

A third aspect with merit is how to evaluate the knowledge, skills, and abilities that it comprises so that meritorious candidates do not miss selection. One problem is category error. At one point in England, merit was identified with being a leading advocate. Although there is a considerable overlap, there is no necessary equivalence between success as an advocate and success as a judge. Another problem is if evaluation becomes divorced from the needs of everyday judging. Legal, communication, and effective working skills have a gap if they omit the ability to produce timely, reasoned decisions and judgments. Self-assessment exercises, where candidates are marked on the examples they give of how they demonstrate a skill, have significant drawbacks. First, the skills identified may be prolific and not concentrated on those essential to good judging. Secondly, there may be a failure to take a holistic view. Thirdly, there will be those able to construct examples of a skill (possibly with paid, professional assistance) that score highly, whereas the reality is that they are not be up to that mark of everyday judicial work compared with others who do not score as well. While resource intensive, the peer assessment of an applicant's professionalism through detailed interviews along the lines of the ABA's evaluation of nominated Supreme Court and federal judges potentially produces a more accurate assessment of merit, at the same time contributing to the evaluation of character.

Diversity and merit

A preliminary issue is what is meant by diversity. The focus has been on the under-representation (or absence) in the judiciary of women and members of particular racial and similar groups. Historically in England judges were overwhelmingly white, male, former barristers, and from a relatively narrow social and educational background. From the very early years of the twenty-first century there has been a concerted effort to redress the gender and ethnic imbalance. In South Africa, where historically the bench had a similar background—white, male, and former senior advocates—the constitutional imperative post-apartheid has been that judicial appointments address the 'need for the judiciary to reflect broadly the racial and gender composition of South Africa'.[30] In India there is a significant gender gap in the Supreme Court and High Courts and concern as well with religious and

[30] South African Constitution, s 174(2).

caste disparities. The concern with diversity now goes beyond gender and ethnic or similar imbalances. Its full reach for some lies in discrimination law, which extends to a wide range of protected characteristics.[31] It might also stretch to socio-economic background and professional difference. A future Master of the Rolls of England and Wales suggested that in the context of the quality of decision-making, diversity was best viewed as diversity in the experience of life.[32]

Against that definitional complexity, the arguments for diversity in judicial appointments are fourfold. First is the equity argument, that all meeting the criteria to be a judge should have an equal opportunity for appointment or promotion. More broadly, this could be seen as part of movement for equal citizenship and justice. Related is the second, a benefit argument, that the judiciary as a whole will profit from expanding the pool of candidates available for selection as judges. Put negatively, the argument is that the judiciary is missing out on the talent in certain groups in society which more diverse appointments would bring. Thirdly, there is a legitimacy argument, that public confidence in the judiciary as an institution is enhanced when the judiciary is more reflective of the society in which it operates. In this context, whether a particular group should be represented turns on whether its characteristics bear on the judiciary's legitimacy. Gender and racial diversity meet this test, if a society is committed to remedying historic inequalities and winning the confidence of groups who have traditionally been excluded from or distrustful of state institutions. Finally, there is a difference argument (sometimes expressed as a quality argument), that a more diverse judiciary will produce different, even better decision-making, since it will draw on the experience and knowledge of a broader section of society.

These arguments have not passed unchallenged. Perhaps the most problematic is that diversity in judicial appointments will make a difference to, even enhance the quality of, the processes and the outcomes of decision-making.[33] The argument is that judges, particularly with lawmaking in the apex courts, will draw on their own values and experiences in hard cases. In these circumstances a diversity of values and experiences is likely to produce better outcomes. None of this is an argument for the appointment of those not meeting the merit requirements, even less for a representative judiciary.

[31] eg, Equality Act 2010, s 4.

[32] Terence Etherton, 'Liberty, the Archetype and Diversity: A Philosophy of Judging' [2010] PL 727, 745–46.

[33] P. 260 below.

Irrespective of background, judges still need the legal and other skills essential for judging, as well as judicial virtue. With those points in mind, greater diversity has the advantage of introducing into the judiciary insights and arguments which might otherwise be overlooked, and of facilitating by new appointments challenges to long held assumptions.

The methods to achieve greater diversity in the judiciary are various. First is the use of typical management tools. An example is a policy to widen the pool of potential applicants by encouraging lawyers from under-represented groups to apply to be a judge and once appointed to support their career development. Administrative arrangements are part of this. These include mentoring programmes for those from under-represented groups and the appointment of diversity and community relations judges. Responsibility may be placed on leadership judges obliging them to report progress. Part of these arrangements might be building a more inclusive culture within a judiciary through training, best practice, and flexible working.[34]

A second avenue to a more diverse judiciary is to sanction an equal merit (or tipping) provision in appointments. The UK's Constitutional Reform Act 2005 imposes a duty to select judges solely on merit although, subject to that, to have regard to encouraging diversity in the range of persons available to be selected.[35] An amendment to the Act in 2013 added that it is permissible to prefer one person over the other for the purpose of increasing diversity where the two are of equal merit, notwithstanding the merit requirement or the anti-discrimination provisions in the Equality Act 2010.[36] The equal merit test has been applied to under-representation on the grounds of ethnicity and gender, its measure a comparison of figures from the national census regarding diversity with the composition of the bench.

Frustration with the failure of these first two methods of addressing the diversity deficit leads to the third, the adoption of affirmative action. One approach to this is that adopted at different times in Canada, Australia, and South Africa, where members of under-represented groups were appointed in pragmatic fashion to many of the vacancies becoming available. Another approach is the adoption of quotas for under-represented groups. The European Commission for the Efficiency of Justice (CEPEJ), part of the Council of Europe, has proposed guidelines under which member states

[34] eg, *Judicial Diversity and Inclusion Strategy 2020–2025* (Courts and Tribunals Judiciary 2020).

[35] Constitutional Reform Act 2005, ss 63(2), 64. See s 27(5) (Supreme Court).

[36] ibid, s 63(4). See also s 27(5A) (Supreme Court).

should consider temporary gender quotas for judicial promotions if the gender gap persists among leadership judges.[37] Confusingly, the guidelines seem to suggest that a policy of gender quotas is equivalent to the adoption of an equal merit approach. A commonplace criticism of quotas is that they may disadvantage their beneficiaries if they are regarded as not winning appointment on merit. On the other hand, if one accepts the quality argument for diversity, quotas have a utilitarian value. A more radical variant of quotas is to have them as a cap on dominant groups. Ceiling quotas shift the burden from under-represented groups having to demonstrate that merit is not threatened onto over-represented groups who need to show that their continuing dominance is justified.

(C) Length of Service

A judge's length of service may be for life, until a fixed retirement age, for a fixed period, or until completion of a specific task. The type of tenure may be enshrined in a constitution, fixed by legislation, or contained in a more informal arrangement. Each type of arrangement has practical implications for judges and judging.

Life tenure

Life tenure for English judges was not explicit in the Act of Settlement 1701 but followed from its good behaviour clause: if judges could only be removed for breach of that standard that presumed that they were appointed for life. Life tenure continued for the senior judiciary until a compulsory retirement age of seventy-five was introduced by the Judicial Pensions Act 1959.[38] The government justified the change for the reason that life tenure has the drawback that at some point the capacity to do the job declines but judges are slow to recognize when they are past their prime. Public confidence was also a reason for the change, not least in Commonwealth countries which were still sending appeals to the Privy Council and which had lower retirement ages for their own judges. Although there would be some loss of judicial talent with a mandatory retiring age, Lord Kilmuir LC reasoned, there was a need to ensure justice was seen to be administered by those mentally and

[37] *Guidelines on Gender Equality in the Recruitment and Promotion of Judges* (adopted 6–7 December 2022) CEPEJ(2022)10, [12].

[38] s 2(1).

physically competent.[39] The change did not affect the life tenure of existing judges if they chose to remain in office.[40]

Supreme Court judges in the United States enjoy life tenure, as do other federal judges. That maximizes their independence but shields judges when their faculties decline. Supreme Court judges are generally appointed relatively young, stay longer, and tend to die in office or remain in post until a president is in office who can name a like-minded successor. Incentives are provided to other federal judges to retire under the 'rule of eighty', whereby they can receive the equivalent of their salary regardless of whether they work full-time. To meet the requirements of the rule a judge must be at least sixty-five and their age and their years of service combined must equal eighty. Thus the seventy-year-old judge with ten years' service qualifies, as does the sixty-five-year-old judge with fifteen years' experience.[41] Instead of retiring completely the judge who qualifies under the rule can also take 'senior status', remaining as a serving judge with salary, chambers, and a law clerk, but assuming a reduced workload.[42] A judge taking senior status, as well as a judge who retires, creates a vacancy, which frees up a position to be filled by a new appointee.[43]

Fixed retirement age

Apart from life tenure there will usually be a fixed retirement age beyond which judges are no longer able to sit. That is an inevitable feature if judges are appointed until a mandatory retirement age, although in some circumstance they may be able to sit beyond that age (perhaps on a part-time basis) until they reach a further, final age. Until the legislation was amended in 2022, judges in England and Wales had to retire when aged seventy, but the legislation enabled the chief justice to authorize them to continue to sit part-time if needed until they were finally disqualified at age seventy-five.[44] A variation is that the judge appointed for a fixed term may be required to retire at a specified age such as seventy, even if they have not served their full term.

The key public policy issue in this regard has been to fix the retirement age. The practice in Britain has oscillated, but the policy considerations

39 HL Deb 8 December 1959, vol 220, col 124.

40 Judicial Pensions Act 1959, s 3(1).

41 28 United States Code 371(c).

42 ibid 371(e).

43 ibid 371(d).

44 Judicial Pensions and Retirement Act 1993, s 26(1), (5), Senior Courts Act 1981, s 9(1), (1A).

have remained remarkably constant. In 1914 a Royal Commission had recommended that the retirement age for judges in the King's Bench division should be seventy-two. This was an age considerably higher than for civil servants, the Commission said, but judges were appointed later in their career, it took time to learn the job, and seventy-two was not an age so advanced as to make it probable that judicial duties would not be adequately performed owing to the deterioration of mental or physical powers. It was necessary to bear in mind, the Commission added, 'that knowledge, experience and ripe judgment are more valuable in judicial work than energy or power of initiative . . . and that it would be unwise to adopt a rule which . . . might often deprive the State of the services of one who was at the zenith of his powers as a Judge'.[45] A subsequent Royal Commission also took the view (with two members dissenting) that a mandatory age of retirement for King's Bench judges at seventy-two was 'sufficiently high to meet all the reasonable demands of those who stress the paramount importance of experience of the Bench'.[46] This notion that the capacity to judge continues beyond the normal retirement age for other professions is a recurrent theme.

When life tenure for the senior judiciary was finally abolished in 1959 the mandatory retirement age chosen was seventy-five. To meet the contrast drawn in debate with the lower retirement ages for civil servants (sixty or so), company directors (seventy), and county court judges (seventy-two), Lord Kilmuir LC returned to the point made by the 1936 Royal Commission, that 'broadly, there is a more reflective and deliberative quality required in the Judiciary, and especially in the Appellate Judiciary, which is a reason for having a higher age limit'.[47] Some thirty-five years later the Judicial Pensions and Retirement Act 1993 introduced for the senior judiciary a retirement age of seventy, extendable on a part-time basis until seventy-five. The justification for the reduction was consistency between retirement ages for all judges, since lower court judges had had a lower retirement age. When the retirement age for English judges was increased again to seventy-five in 2022, the justification was to attract and retain sufficient judges, coupled with the demographic reality of enhanced health and longevity in society.[48]

[45] *Royal Commission on Delay in the King's Bench Division. Second and Final Report of the Commissioners* (Cd 7177, 1914) 40 (the St Alwyn Commission).
[46] *Report of the Royal Commission on the Despatch of Business at Common Law 1934–6*, (Cmd 5065, 1936) 91 (the Peel Commission).
[47] HL Deb 8 December 1959, vol 220, col 124.
[48] *Judicial Mandatory Retirement Age. Response to Consultation* (Ministry of Justice 2021) 9–10, 31. See Public Service Pensions and Judicial Offices Act 2022, s 121, Sch 1.

There is no ideal retirement age for judges. In some jurisdictions it is comparable to the retirement age for the general population. In India, for example, the Constitution sets the retirement age for judges in Supreme Court at sixty-five and in the High Courts at sixty-two.[49] That is relatively young in the modern age. Elsewhere it is higher. In New South Wales it is seventy-five, but retired judges may sit as acting judges until they are seventy-eight.[50] Apart from the issue of judicial senescence, factors pointing to an earlier age for retirement are the opportunities it provides for new and more diverse appointments. Factors indicating a later age are the cost of paying full judicial pensions when judges retire young, the loss of experience and skills from early retirement, the need to provide a reasonable period of service in jurisdictions where judges are appointed after a career in practice, the ethical issues raised if judges retire young and wish to return to practice, and age discrimination laws making a mandatory retirement age unacceptable without justification (which might be easier to demonstrate if it is on the high side). Whatever the retirement age, it is convenient to have statutory authorization for a judge to complete outstanding work beyond their date of retirement.

Appointment for a period

Appointment of judges for a specific period can take various forms. First, there are fixed term, full-time appointments. These are common in constitutional courts such as the South African Constitutional Court, where judges serve non-renewable terms of twelve years or until they attain the age of seventy, whichever occurs first, unless Parliament extends the judge's term.[51] Fixed term appointments can result in a regular replenishment of the bench, which may mean that the court is more attuned to the contemporary values and aspirations of the society. It has the disadvantage that a judge, widely acknowledged as outstanding, is lost to the court at the end of their term. An important cohort of US federal judges—its bankruptcy judges—are appointed for renewable fourteen-year terms.

Except for appointments to constitutional courts, the European Commission for Democracy through Law (the Venice Commission) advises against fixed term appointments for ordinary judges because of concerns about judicial independence.[52] This cannot be a universal recipe. In the

[49] Constitution of India, arts 124(2), 217(1).
[50] Supreme Court Act 1970, s 37(4).
[51] South African Constitution, art 176.1.
[52] 'Report on the Independence of the Judicial System Part I: The Independence of Judges' adopted by the Venice Commission at its 82nd Plenary Session (Venice, 12–13 March 2010) CDL-AD(2010)004, para 35.

Commonwealth, the *Latimer House Principles* recognize that there are some smaller jurisdictions which have no alternative but to appoint judges to serve in their higher courts for a fixed term of years, often on a part-time basis.[53] These may be non-nationals, needed to plug a gap in a specialist area such as commercial law, or to serve on an appellate court whose caseload does not warrant full-time judges.[54] Appointments in smaller jurisdictions for a fixed term may also be justified to assist in capacity building, to insulate the bench from local pressures, and if needed only part-time to avoid the expense of a permanent establishment.

The second form which specific term appointments can take is the part-time judge (the 'acting' or 'deputy' judge). Their term may be extendable. Provision is made in section 175 of the South African Constitution for the appointment of acting judges, and they feature in some other Commonwealth jurisdictions. In England and Wales such judges are a prominent feature of the landscape—part-time deputy district judges, part-time recorders (to sit in the Crown and county courts), and deputy High Court judges. As well as adding to judicial resources, these positions offer those contemplating a judicial career an insight into full-time judging, at the same time enabling some assessment of their suitability. The period cannot be too short. In *Starrs v Ruxton*[55] part-time sheriffs were appointed by the executive for one year at a time. Although renewable, there was no guarantee that it would be, and there was the possibility of an appointee not being allocated work. The court held that these arrangements were incompatible with article 6.1 of the European Convention on Human Rights (ECHR): judicial independence could be threatened not only through interference by the executive, but also by the judges being influenced, consciously or unconsciously, by their hopes and fears about reappointment or a permanent appointment if they desired one. The lack of security of tenure gave rise to a real risk on the part of a well-informed observer of judicial dependence upon the executive.[56]

As a result of this decision, the terms of appointment of temporary judges in Scotland and elsewhere in Britain were changed. In England and Wales the position of assistant recorder was abolished, and recorders were given

[53] *Commonwealth (Latimer House) Principles on the Three Branches of Government* (Commonwealth Secretariat 2009) Guidelines para II (1) (hereafter *Latimer House Principles*).

[54] eg, Gibraltar Constitution Order 2006, s 63(5); Cayman Islands Constitution Order 2009, Sch 2, SI no 1379, 101(1).

[55] 2000 JC 208, [2000] HRLR 191. See also *Millar v Dickson* [2001] UKPC D4, [2002] 1 WLR 1615 (PC, Scotland).

[56] *Starrs v Ruxton* (n 56) 248, 252.

enhanced security of tenure. The result is that at the end of a term of appointment (in practice, five years), they are reappointed, although the lord chancellor, with the agreement of the chief justice, may decline to extend an appointment on the grounds of incapacity, misbehaviour, or the failure to comply with the terms of appointment.[57] This approach was upheld in a Scottish appeal involving the appointment of a temporary judge for a three-year period to the Court of Session. The Privy Council held that the judge enjoyed security of tenure since it was not open to the Scottish Ministers to withdraw the commission at any time during that period. This was compatible with the common law and article 6.1 of the ECHR.[58] In the course of his judgment, Lord Hope also commented on the judge sitting in retirement: that was compatible with article 6.1 since they had established their independence by sitting as permanent judges and had no prospect of further advancement.[59]

Ad hoc appointments

Ad hoc appointments as Commissioners of Assize were made at one time in England to assist with the work usually undertaken by High Court judges on circuit and in family matters.[60] These were temporary appointments, made for no specified period. Their replacement is the deputy High Court judge. This role may be filled by those appointed for a single six-year term who are possibly interested in full-time appointment to the High Court.[61] Ad hoc appointments may be necessary to hear specific cases. An example is where all the local judges appear to be conflicted. Take the facts of *Misick v The Queen*,[62] where the former president of the Jamaican Court of Appeal was appointed on the recommendation of the independent Judicial Service Commission to conduct a high-profile trial in the Turks & Caicos islands. The former premier, his ministers, and associates were accused of corruption and money laundering. They objected that the judge's appointment was unconstitutional because his security of tenure as an ad hoc judge was insufficient to guarantee the judicial independence required

[57] Courts Act 1971, s 21 (4A)–(4C) (as amended by the Constitutional Reform Act 2005).
[58] *Kearney v Her Majesty's Advocate* [2006] UKPC D1, [2006] HRLR 15.
[59] ibid [27].
[60] *Royal Commission on Assizes and Quarter Sessions 1966–69* (Cmnd 4153, 1969) paras 15, 26 (Beeching Report).
[61] Senior Courts Act 1981, s 9(4).
[62] [2015] UKPC 31, [2015] 1 WLR 3215.

and that therefore they were being denied their fair trial rights before an independent and impartial court. The Court of Appeal and the Privy Council dismissed their appeals. The Privy Council said that there needed to be both a reality and appearance of judicial independence. Although security of tenure was important as demonstrating independence from executive control, and although a short-term appointment might indicate a lack of independence, the risk to independence was far less where control was with an independent commission. Given the judge's long and distinguished judicial career, and the specific invitation to undertake the trial outside his home territory and in retirement, the reasonable objective observer would see no danger of a lack of independence. The position was the reverse, particularly since there was no expectation of a renewal or further appointment.[63]

III Removal and Discipline

The standards of conduct expected of a judge are drawn from first principles like honesty, courtesy, and patience, fundamental values like independence, impartiality, and integrity, guides and codes of judicial conduct, statutory and case law, conventions and accepted practices, and terms and conditions of appointment.[64] The legal and policy framework if judges transgress standards has a long history, but only relatively recently has it been become more significant for judicial practice. The most serious sanction is dismissal but since 1701 and the Act of Settlement removal of senior judges in common law countries has generally required legislative approval—an almost insurmountable hurdle. For many years there was no disciplinary procedure for less egregious conduct than that justifying removal. What was called for was a simpler process, with a range of sanctions, geared to the seriousness of any breach of standards. Three centuries after the Act of Settlement disciplinary machinery along these lines has been adopted in a number of common law jurisdictions. In its absence resort must be had to informal measures or to procedures ill-suited to the purpose.[65]

[63] ibid [21], [26]–[28].
[64] See Chapter 3.
[65] eg, *Suo-Motu Contempt Petition (Civil) No. 1 of 2017, In the Matter of Hon'ble Shri Justice C S Karnan* (2017) 7 SCC 1.

(A) Removal

From 1701 the Act of Settlement provided security of tenure to judges during good behaviour, subject to a power of removal by the sovereign upon an address presented by both Houses of Parliament. There was much learning about the power, but it was rarely invoked. We saw in Chapter 1 that similar protections against removal were adopted elsewhere.[66] In broad terms removal under these powers applies in two situations, misconduct and incapacity.

Misconduct involving 'moral turpitude' has been asserted as the prerequisite for removal of a judge under the Act of Settlement. It has been applied to conduct prior to being a judge.[67] It was long stated that the type of misconduct covered matters concerning the office of the judge—improper exercise of the functions of the office, non-attendance, or neglect of or refusal to perform the duties of the office—but also extended to a conviction for 'any infamous offence', even if not committed in connection with the office but rendering the person unfit to serve.[68] There is now a summary process for initiating removal in England and Wales where a judge has been sentenced to imprisonment or been convicted or cautioned in relation to an offence involving dishonesty, deception, theft, or perverting the course of justice, or to sexual or violent offending.[69] Removal under the parliamentary address system in section 72(ii) of the Australian Constitution for 'proved misbehaviour' has been said to extend to conduct beyond the performance of judicial office: it must represent so serious a departure from the standards of proper behaviour that it destroys public confidence that the judge will perform their duty under the Constitution.[70]

There have been few dismissals of a judge under such provisions. Every attempt to remove a judge in Britain under the parliamentary address system has been unsuccessful except for Barrington's removal in 1830 for corruption.[71] Exceptionally, in March 2024 the president of South Africa formally

[66] PP. 16–17 above.

[67] *Ayers-Caesar v Judicial and Legal Service Commission* [2025] UKPC 15 [32] (Lord Reed) (PC, Trinidad and Tobago); *Therrien v Minister of Justice* [2001] 2 SCR 3.

[68] *Halsbury's Laws of England* (Butterworth & Co 1909) vol 7, para 24.

[69] Judicial Conduct Rules 2023, r 47(a)–(b), (d)–(f), made by the LCJ under Constitutional Reform Act 2005, ss 115, 117 (hereafter Judicial Conduct Rules) and Judicial Discipline (Prescribed Procedures) Regulations 2023, SI 1005/2023, r 7 (hereafter Judicial Discipline Regulations).

[70] Parliament of the Commonwealth of Australia, *Parliamentary Commission of Inquiry, Special Report Dealing with the Meaning of 'Misbehaviour' for the Purposes of Section 72 of the Constitution* (Parliamentary Papers, No 443, 1986) 18, 32, 45.

[71] See p. 130 above.

removed two senior judges from office under section 177 of the Constitution following the required resolutions of the National Assembly. The length of time taken in both cases underlines the difficulty in removing judges when the approval of the legislature is required. In the first case the Judicial Service Commission had recommended that a judge president be removed following a complaint by judges of the Constitutional Court that in 2008 he had attempted to interfere with a case before that court involving Jacob Zuma, soon to be the country's president.[72] In the second case a High Court judge was removed following an order of the Supreme Court of Appeal directing the Judicial Service Commission to refer the case to the National Assembly.[73] The court refrained from defining 'gross misconduct' in section 177; they would recognize it, they said, when they saw it.[74] In that case, the court held, the judge's behaviour was egregious. He had been convicted of drunk driving in 2007 and his behaviour at the scene of the accident was characterized by racism, sexism, and vulgarity. The judge had then conducted a dishonest defence at his trial and on appeal and had lied to the disciplinary tribunal. His conduct was inimical to his office, the court concluded: as long as he was entitled to call himself 'judge' the judiciary would continue to be stained in the eyes of the public.[75]

Judges may not recognize their own incapacity. From the nineteenth century senior judges in Britain have been eased out when their performance fell short through age, physical or mental illness, or the effects of accident.[76] Because this occurred informally, there was no need to grapple with the issue whether misconduct in the Act of Settlement sense—the sole ground for removing a senior judge in Britain—encompasses judicial incapacity. 'Good behaviour' seems to connote conformity to ethical or conventional standards rather than physical or mental capacity. Moreover, misconduct is generally intentional, whereas depression, senility, and physical infirmity are inadvertent. In jurisdictions like Australia and South Africa removal following a parliamentary address extends specifically to incapacity as well as misconduct.[77] Defining incapacity is not easy. The approach of the UN Basic Principles on the Independence of the Judiciary is to treat removal for

72 P. 128 above.

73 *Freedom Under Law v Judicial Service Commission* [2023] ZASCA 103, [2023] 3 All SA 631 [90] (Poonan JA).

74 ibid [29].

75 ibid [90].

76 eg, Lord Denning, *The Due Process of Law* (Butterworths 1980) 58–62.

77 Australian Constitution, s 72(ii); South African Constitution, s 177(1)(a).

incapacity and misconduct as equivalent—does it renders the judge unfit to discharge judicial duties.[78] Physical or mental incapacity may sometimes manifest itself in misconduct. Examples are the judge with depression being unable to complete the work, or the judge suffering from sleep apnoea disrupting hearings. A difficulty is that what appears to be incapacity may be treatable and temporary. It may be possible to deal with the problem informally by allocating non-sitting days or giving the judge leave for treatment and recuperation.

In England legislation from 1973 has sought to address incapacity where, as a result, the judge is unable to make a decision to resign. It enables the lord chancellor, with the concurrence of the senior judiciary, to declare a judicial office vacated. The lord chancellor must be satisfied, on the basis of a medical certificate, that a judge is disabled from performing judicial duties by reason of 'permanent infirmity' and is for the time being 'incapacitated' from resigning.[79] The provision goes far in that only one medical certificate is required, and the doctor need not have expertise relevant to the judge's condition. On the other hand, 'permanent infirmity' might not cover the situation where, say, a judge is suffering illness which medical evidence suggests is manageable, but at some indefinite point in the future. What seems to be needed is the possibility of requiring a judge to undertake a medical or psychological examination to decide (as with contemporary employment and discrimination law) whether reasonable adjustments are possible to accommodate the judge's incapacity.

(B) Disciplinary Procedures

Just as the decisional accountability of judges is provided for through an effective system of appeals, and institutional accountability through measures such as reasoned decisions and open justice, behavioural accountability requires a framework for dealing with the errant judge which is sufficient to secure public confidence. The question is, what would a reasonable member of the public regard as the appropriate course and sanction (if any) in light of the judge's conduct? The system's design and operation must be in line with principles such as judicial independence, access to justice, fairness,

78 UN Basic Principles (n 2) para 18.
79 Now Senior Courts Act 1981, s 11(8)–(9); Constitutional Reform Act 2005, s 36.

efficiency, and justice. There also needs to be a proper balance between transparency and confidentiality.

Fundamental to the design and operation of the machinery is the principle of judicial independence. The machinery must not be used to intimidate judges regarding their decision-making. In some jurisdictions disciplinary power over judges has been misused to exert improper pressure over a judge's 'decisional conduct'. Judges have been accused of misconduct or even corruption to justify their transfer or removal, or to force their resignation, when the real reason is that they are not regarded as government-friendly. Consequently, the disciplinary machinery must be independent of the executive government. Placing the disciplinary machinery in the hands of the judges lessens the threat to judicial independence. However, it raises two possible concerns. In some jurisdictions one would be the individual independence of the judges since senior judges might improperly invoke the machinery against them.[80] The other is the more general concern that if judges are in charge the public may regard the disciplinary machinery as too forgiving of judicial misconduct. The importance of public confidence supports the establishment of a body independent of both the judiciary and the executive but with significant judicial input.

A popular model has been an independent conduct commission comprising judicial and non-judicial members with a power to delegate decision-making to panels and investigatory staff.[81] The machinery in England deviates somewhat from this. The independent Judicial Conduct Investigations Office (JCIO) rejects out of scope and hopeless complaints and makes recommendations to the lord chancellor and chief justice (joint decision makers under the system) for action regarding less serious and clear-cut matters. Otherwise it makes no findings on misconduct itself but supports senior judges who are appointed to conduct inquiries and who will either dismiss a complaint or recommend a sanction. The central role of judges in the English system is justified on the basis of their knowledge of the context in which a judge works. It is only if a matter gets as far as a disciplinary panel that lay persons (who will be in a majority and cannot be lawyers) are involved.[82] Panels will not be convened unless the judge requests it, the lord chancellor and chief justice seek further consideration of a case, or suspension or removal is possible. If there is a disciplinary panel judges have

80 PP. 20–21 above.
81 New York was early in the field in 1976: Judiciary Law, art 2-A, § 41.1.
82 Judicial Discipline Regulations 2023, rr 11(1).

a right to an oral hearing and to be accompanied by a judicial colleague for support.[83]

The second principle is access to justice. The disciplinary machinery must facilitate complainants, who will be a significant source of information about the conduct of judges. That means that the public must be informed about its availability. If not properly signposted or encouraging, litigants, lawyers, court staff, and members of the public with meritorious complaints might not come forward. Publicizing a complaints procedure inevitably produces hopeless and out of scope complaints. That has to be accepted and addressed through a robust and efficient filtering process. There is an issue about whether anonymity should be allowed if a complaint can still be properly investigated.[84] Without anonymity lawyers in particular may not complain because they do not want to alienate a judge before whom they regularly appear. On the other hand, anonymity encourages the vexatious, the vindictive, or worse.

As well as through complaints by litigants, lawyers, and the public, a second way that judicial misconduct may be identified is within the court itself. An issue may not be public, at least initially, but judicial colleagues or the disciplinary body may learn about it. An example is where a judge's abilities are affected by substance abuse or mental health problems. There is a third potential source of information about misconduct. The emergence of the #MeToo movement led to revelations of harassment by some judges of close staff, especially their clerks. Factors conducive to this type of misconduct remaining hidden are the power which a judge has over the future careers of the victims, their consequent reluctance to complain, and the relative autonomy and confidentiality of judicial chambers which some senior judges have. All this points to workplace policies including whistleblowing which enable complaints to be raised and taken seriously.[85]

A third principle in framing the disciplinary machinery is fairness. This has two aspects, fairness for complainants and fairness for the judge under investigation. Complainants have to be treated fairly and may require assistance in advancing their case. Typically, the disciplinary machinery itself will undertake the investigation of a complaint. Fairness is the reason that the *Commonwealth Model Law on Judicial Service Commissions* provides that if

[83] Judicial Conduct Rules 2023, part 7.
[84] Anonymity is not allowed under the Judicial Conduct Rules 2023, rr 8, 10.
[85] eg, High Court of Australia, *Justices' Policy on Workplace Conduct* (13 November 2023).

a complaint is dismissed summarily the complainant can appeal.[86] Fairness to complainants does not mean the tolerance of late, unfounded, vexatious, or trivial complaints. It is a common phenomenon that losing parties, especially litigants in person, blame the judge. They confuse a ruling adverse to themselves with misconduct or mistake a judge's attempts to progress matters efficiently with judicial rudeness or a denial of justice.

Fairness for the judge has long been the standard of the common law for the handling of disciplinary complaints.[87] The (mis)treatment of judges by some European governments has led the ECtHR to develop a jurisprudence requiring that the disciplinary machinery for judges meet the fair trial standards of article 6.1 of the ECHR: there must be an independent and impartial tribunal established by law (or its decisions must be reviewable by a body meeting those requirements); it must be able to establish the facts; and judges must have notice of the case against them and the opportunity of being heard in their own defence.[88] Under the *Commonwealth Model Law* the judge may be represented before the tribunal by counsel, cross-examine witnesses, call evidence, and make submissions.[89] The other side of the coin to the disciplinary body acting fairly vis à vis the judge is that the judge must be frank and disclose relevant information to it relating to the matter being investigated. A failure in this regard may itself constitute misconduct.[90]

Related to this aspect of fairness is a fourth principle, that the disciplinary machinery must determine allegations efficiently and expeditiously, especially if the judge has been suspended or the matter has become public. In *Durity v Attorney General of Trinidad and Tobago* the Privy Council said that a consequence of judicial independence is that a judge cannot be suspended from duties indefinitely without good cause.[91] Efficiency also enters in ensuring that the disciplinary machinery is not clogged with hopeless complaints. There must be a strong filter to dispose of them. Disciplinary machinery without a robust approach to hopeless complaints could lead judges to become excessively indulgent to litigants in person,

[86] *Commonwealth Model Law on Judicial Service Commissions* (Commonwealth Secretariat 2018) 11(4)(b) (hereafter *Commonwealth Model Law*).

[87] *Willis v Gipps* (1846) V Moore, PC 379; 13 ER 536. See also *Moreau-Bérubé v New Brunswick (Judicial Council)* [2002] 1 SCR 249 [75]–[83]; *Archie v Law Association of Trinidad and Tobago* [2018] UKPC 23 (PC, Trinidad and Tobago) [38]–[39].

[88] eg, *Baka v Hungary* (2017) 64 EHRR 6 (GC); *Ramos Nunes de Carvalho e Sá v Portugal* App nos 55391/13, 57728/13, and 74041/13 (ECtHR, 6 November 2018) (GC); *Denisov v Ukraine* App no 76639/11 (ECtHR, 25 September 2018) (GC).

[89] *Commonwealth Model Law* (n 86) Schedule 4, paras 3, 6, 8.

[90] See *Wilson v Attorney-General* [2010] NZHC 1678, [2011] 1 NZLR 399 [90]–[91].

[91] [2008] UKPC 59 (PC, Trinidad and Tobago) [29].

or to counsel who fail to address a point or otherwise fall below standard. That is because of the fear of being subject to complaints, however unmeritorious, and the opportunity cost of refuting them. The result would be proceedings being unnecessarily lengthened and a potential chilling effect on decision-making.

A fifth principle, justice, is that errant judges must be subject to appropriate and proportionate sanctions if public confidence in the judiciary is to be maintained. Where the only punishment available is dismissal under the parliamentary address procedure, less serious behaviour will escape sanction since removal cannot be justified. A judge may be informally admonished in this situation, but that may leave a complainant unmoved, and with some judges it may not have a sufficient impact on behaviour. Consideration needs to be given to adopting a range of measures, interim and final, proportionate to the nature of judicial misconduct. Interim measures could include ordering a judge to undergo a medical examination.[92] An interim suspension might also be imposed, for example, during criminal investigations or proceedings.[93] There is a gradation of disciplinary sanctions for judges in England and Wales, in increasing order of severity formal advice, a formal warning, a reprimand, suspension, and removal.[94] The *Commonwealth Model Law* adds denying the judge a salary increment or promotion, and having to apologize to the complainant.[95]

Sanctioning should not be primarily as punishment of the judge but to maintain public confidence in the judiciary. The formal machinery should not affect the ability of leadership judges to speak informally to a judge about a matter of concern.[96] The most effective way to deal with an issue may be by quick and unofficial action, not through the disciplinary machinery. A delayed judgment, for example, may indicate that the judge needs judgment writing time. Judges may not realize that their behaviour is unacceptable but, if alerted, may be receptive to change. If in ill health, suffering from an addiction, or unable to do the job, a nudge may induce the judge to retire. Serious misconduct, however, needs formal sanctioning. Several incidents, none in themselves serious, may when cumulated constitute serious misconduct.

[92] eg, Judicial Commission of Victoria Act 2016, s 97.
[93] eg, Constitutional Reform Act 2005, s 108(4), (7).
[94] Constitutional Reform Act 2005, s 108(3). See also Judicial Conduct Investigations Office, *Judicial Discipline. Misconduct and Recommending Sanctions* (JCIO 2024) [25] (guidance on which sanction is appropriate) (hereafter *Recommending Sanctions*).
[95] *Commonwealth Model Law* (n 86) s 12(4).
[96] see Constitutional Reform Act 2005, s 108(3).

In some contexts the principles of judicial independence, access to justice, fairness, efficiency, and justice may not indicate a clear and satisfactory path for aspects of the disciplinary machinery. Take the principle of transparency and its bearing on whether there should be publicity around a disciplinary matter. On one view transparency can contribute to public confidence, especially with a serious allegation, as well as protecting the judge involved from misunderstandings based on suspicion and rumour. It also imposes a discipline on the tribunal's decision-making.[97] On another view publicity threatens the integrity of the judiciary as a whole, as well as undermining a judge's functional authority and reputation.[98] Publicity can have a lasting impact on a judge's career even if a complaint proves unfounded or is relatively minor. Fairness does not always require that disciplinary proceedings be public. Under the *Commonwealth Model Law*, disciplinary proceedings against judges are heard in private unless the judge elects publicity, but a reasoned decision must be published (although only of the allegation and the findings if a case is not proved).[99] In England disciplinary proceedings and reports are private, but an outline of the conduct, the name of the judge, and the sanction imposed are published. Publication on the JCIO's website is removed after a period, the length of time depending on the seriousness of the misconduct.[100]

IV Terms of Service

The logic of judicial independence is that judges should not be employed by the legislature, the executive, or any other part of the state, or by a senior judge such as the chief justice. Consistently with this, in some jurisdictions the judges will be in a contractual relationship as regards their terms of service with the judicial branch itself, or with an independent body like a judicial council. The position in England is that judges are independent statutory office holders, and there is no contractual relationship with the executive government (or any member of it), or with any presiding judge like a chief justice. Nor are English judges in Crown employment, civil servants, or the equivalent of civil servants.[101] The separateness and independence

[97] *Meerabux v Attorney General of Belize* [2005] UKPC 12, [2005] 2 AC 513 [39] (PC, Belize).
[98] *Attorney General (Canada) v Slansky* 2013 FCA 199, [2015] 1 FCR 81 [152] (leave refused SCC).
[99] eg, *Commonwealth Model Law* (n 86) Sch 4, para 2, 9.
[100] *Recommending Sanctions* (n 94) [13].
[101] *Gilham v Ministry of Justice* [2019] UKSC 44, [2019] 1 WLR 5905.

of judges in England is underlined in their appointment by the Crown—senior judges by letters patent under the great seal and other judges by royal warrant.[102]

In England, historically, there were a few terms and conditions for judicial service contained in statute law. There was the protection governing tenure and removal in the Act of Settlement. Legislation provided for judicial salaries and pensions from the first part of the nineteenth century, once suitor's fees and the sale of offices were abolished as a source of remuneration. And there was the occasional statutory condition, notably that full-time judges were disqualified from being Members of Parliament.[103] Otherwise, the terms of service for judges remained in non-statutory form. There was some variation in the early twenty-first century, when the reforms to the system of appointing and disciplining judges took statutory form as regards these matters. However, much in England is contained in conventions and understandings. In other jurisdictions, judicial terms and conditions may be enshrined to a greater extent in legislation, regulations, or contract.

(A) Remuneration

It has long been the principle governing the remuneration of judges that this should reflect the importance of the work, and be pitched at a level to attract good candidates from well-remunerated legal practice. In some circumstances the independence and integrity of a judge can turn on their remuneration.[104] Not only can a poorly paid judiciary fail to attract good candidates, but some of its members may be susceptible to temptations from outside interests seeking to corrupt them. As well as its effects on recruitment and integrity, the level of remuneration may have a bearing on the morale of judges and thus on retention. Judges must feel that the level of their salary, pension, and other allowances adequately reflects their responsibilities, compensates them for what they may have relinquished in private legal practice, and takes account of the restrictions on what they can do in office and on retirement. In some jurisdictions, allowances for housing, vehicles, education, entertainment, and so on are key components of a judge's remuneration.[105]

[102] *Halsbury's Laws of England* (LexisNexis 2023) vol 20 [489].
[103] Now House of Commons Disqualification Act 1975, s 1(1)(a), Sch 1, Pt I. See also Courts and Legal Services Act 1990, s 75, Sch 11 (ban on legal practice).
[104] For the relationship of salary with judicial independents see p. 17 above.
[105] See, eg, *All India Judges Association v Union of India* [2024] 1 SCR 327.

The current discussion is limited to remuneration by means of salaries and pensions.

Salaries

The legal and policy framework as regards a judge's salary takes one of at least four forms. First is the statutory model where judicial salaries are set by parliament passing legislation or increased by parliament amending it. Then there is the mixed executive–parliamentary model where judicial salaries are fixed in delegated legislation. In this model the executive government places a proposal about judicial salaries before parliament, and parliamentary approval must be given. Thirdly, under the ministerial model parliament is out of the picture and a government minister takes the decision about judicial salaries, possibly in consultation with other members of the government, especially the minister of finance. Finally, there is the judicial model, where the judges themselves wield a great if not a conclusive influence on the level of judicial salaries.

At one time in England judicial salaries were fixed by Parliament—the first, the statutory model. The Judges' Salaries Act 1832 set the annual salary of a puisne judge at an extremely generous £5,000, and it was pegged at that level for well over a century. Taking account of their generous pensions, judges were very highly rewarded. The County Courts Act 1846 empowered the Treasury to pay county court judges up to £1,200, later increased from 1867 to £1,500. Although the cost of living in the nineteenth century was stable, there was a dramatic increase in the early part of the twentieth century. Judges argued that their remuneration should be increased. They invoked what was to become the familiar argument, that otherwise leading barristers would not consider appointment to the bench. Finally, the Judges' Remuneration Act 1954 increased the salary of a High Court judge from £5,000 to £8,000 per annum, with similar increases for other senior judges. In the meanwhile legislation had increased the salaries of county court judges on several occasions.

The need for legislation to set judicial salaries meant inflexibility when they had to be increased in light of changed economic conditions. That led to the second, the mixed model, in the Judicial Offices (Salaries and Pensions) Act 1957. It empowered the lord chancellor with the consent of the Treasury to increase the salaries of county court judges by statutory instrument, which had to be approved by a resolution of each House of Parliament. That model was followed by the Judges' Remuneration Act 1965 for High Court judges, enabling an increase in their salaries by order in council, subject as with the county court judges to an affirmative resolution by both Houses of Parliament. The procedure was used on several occasions to increase judicial salaries in line with a changing economy.

The rapid inflation of the 1970s, and the need to increase judicial salaries more frequently, led to the adoption in England of the third model, of having senior judges' salaries determined by ministerial decision alone.[106] As a matter of law judicial salaries are a charge on the Consolidated Fund, which means that they need not be voted on annually by Parliament and their enactment in the Appropriation Act.[107] As well as greater flexibility, the ministerial model has the advantage of reducing the scope for political controversy in Parliament. The ministerial model is underpinned by placing responsibility for advising on the level of judicial salaries into the hands of an expert public body, the Senior Salaries Review Body (SSRB). The SSRB is attuned to setting judicial salaries in the interests of judicial recruitment and retention. Detailed financial analysis is included in its reports. Representations from the judges are considered. The legal position is that judicial salaries are still determined by the lord chancellor, with the agreement of the Treasury. The SSRB's recommendation is not always adopted. Among the advantages of having an independent body to advise on judicial salaries is that to an extent it depoliticizes the process and avoids any appearance of the judges bartering their independence for a salary increase.

Having an independent advisory body on judicial salaries does not remove all wrangling. In its controversial *Provincial Judges Reference Case*[108] the Supreme Court of Canada decided that the principle of judicial independence not only invalidated a reduction in judicial salaries but required that commissions be established to advise on judicial compensation for provincial judges. The commissions have both ministerial and judicial representation.[109] Although not bound by the Supreme Court's decision, the federal government established a Judicial Compensation and Benefits Commission for the judges it appoints. The work of some of the provincial commissions has been characterized by conflict and litigation as judges' associations have challenged the proposals put forward about salary. The Supreme Court sought to limit the damage in a later decision where it held that judicial review on rationality grounds of a government's response to a Commission

[106] eg, Senior Courts Act 1981, s 12(1); Constitutional Reform Act 2005, s 34(2).
[107] Senior Courts Act 1981, s 12(5); Constitutional Reform Act 2005, s 34(5).
[108] *Reference re Remuneration of Judges of the Provincial Court (PEI)* [1997] 3 SCR 3.
[109] eg, Judicial Compensation Act 2003 (British Columbia), s 2(2).

recommendation should be based on whether there was a legitimate reason and factual foundation for departing from it, and whether, viewed in the round, the Commission process ensured judicial independence.[110]

Perhaps India comes closest to the fourth, the judicial model for setting judicial salaries. Under the Indian Constitution, the salaries, allowances, and pensions of Supreme and High Court judges are to be fixed through legislation.[111] Enacted in the 1950s, the relevant legislation was amended whenever the rates were revised.[112] Although formally a mixed executive–parliamentary model, in practice there is a heavy judicial input as regards senior judges. In 2018 the government and then the Parliament approved the recommendations of a committee of three sitting judges appointed by the chief justice of India regarding the level of remuneration of Supreme and High Court judges.[113] With Indian district judges, in other words judges below Supreme and High Court levels, the judicial model is full-blown. In relation to them the Supreme Court appoints a judicial pay commission, chaired by a judge, to make recommendations regarding salary, pensions, and allowances. The Supreme Court has held that the Union government must implement its decisions regarding the Commission's recommendations and cannot raise any defence of undue financial burden to prevent it doing so. The Supreme Court has justified this on the ground of ensuring the independence and effectiveness of the district bench in dispensing justice throughout India.[114]

Judicial pensions

As a matter of law an occupational pension is often treated as a form of deferred salary, with the entitlement to it accruing over the length of a person's service. It is therefore not surprising that in international instruments concerning judicial independence the justification for adequate and secure salaries and pensions for judges should run together.[115] In practice the justification for adequate judicial pensions has often been more mundane than the

[110] *Provincial Court Judges' Association of New Brunswick v New Brunswick* [2005] 2 SCR 286.

[111] Articles 125, 221.

[112] Supreme Court Judges (Salaries and Conditions of Service) Act 1958; High Court Judges (Salaries and Conditions of Service) Act 1954.

[113] High Court and Supreme Court Judges (Salaries and Conditions of Service) Amendment Act 2018.

[114] See, eg, *All India Judges' Association v Union of India* [1992] 1 SCC 19, 1992 AIR SC 165; *All India Judges Association vs Union of India* (2023) INSC 564; *All India Judges Association v Union of India* [2024] 1 SCR 327 [14].

[115] eg, *Commentary on the Bangalore Principles of Judicial Conduct* (UNODC 2007) para 26(b) (hereafter *Commentary on the Bangalore Principles*)

contribution they make to judicial independence. They have been used as part of a strategy to influence the composition of the bench, at different times to facilitate the recruitment, retention, and removal of judges. The generosity of non-contributory judicial pensions has attracted the attention of policy-makers, concerned with pressures on the public finances. That concern has been highlighted by a comparison with other less generous occupational pensions, the demographic change of people living longer, and by former judges obtaining well-remunerated employment in retirement in addition to their pension.

The position in England is illustrative. In the nineteenth century the possibility of a relatively generous pension after fifteen years' service was introduced in 1799, and the amount increased in 1825. It was designed as an encouragement to judges (who had life tenure) to leave the bench before they lost their faculties. There are several occasions where lord chancellors used pensions to encourage judges to retire. Since a judge serving less than fifteen years did not qualify for any pension, there were some who despite their incapacities remained in office until they had served the full fifteen years. Pensions on a sliding scale geared to years served were eventually introduced. When life tenure was replaced in 1959 by a fixed retirement age of seventy-five years for all new judges, part of the package was an increase in pensions to encourage existing judges with life tenure to retire.[116] A first step in England of bearing down on judicial pensions because of their cost to the public purse occurred in the 1990s when judges appointed after 1995 needed to serve twenty, not fifteen years, before qualifying for a full pension (half the final salary).[117] This may also have had an effect on retention, although a counter-balance was that at the same time the retirement age for judges was reduced to seventy.

Another major change in England was the Judicial Pension Scheme 2015, which in line with changes for others in the public sector provided pension benefits based on career average earnings rather than final salary, linked the pension age to the state pension age, and limited the tax-relieved benefits which a member could accumulate. There was significant disquiet within the judiciary and to some outside observers, who foresaw adverse consequences for judicial recruitment. Transitionally protected judges were able to remain in their existing scheme, but this did not include younger judges. A group of them challenged the transitional arrangements for the scheme on

[116] Judicial Pensions Act 1959.
[117] Judicial Pensions and Retirement Act 1993.

age discrimination grounds. The Court of Appeal agreed that there was unlawful age discrimination.[118] Combined with the adverse impact of the 2015 scheme on recruitment and retention this led the government to introduce a new pension scheme for judges in 2022, having features of the 2015 scheme but reverting to the pre-2015 tax position.[119]

(B) Non-Financial Terms and Conditions

As well as remuneration, there can be any number of terms governing a judge's appointment and the conditions to which they are subject. These can be analysed along various lines. As with remuneration, the benefits and conditions may be contained in legislation or, in some jurisdictions, contract. For example, statute provides that senior judges in England are entitled to a clerk, and that some leadership judges qualify for additional administrative support.[120] Otherwise the terms and conditions may be in codes, soft law, or administrative practice. Next, the terms and conditions may be set out in explicit language, others may constitute nothing more than an unspoken understanding. Thirdly, there is implementation. Non-compliance with the conditions governing a judge's conduct may be dealt with by an informal warning, but may ultimately be effected through disciplinary machinery. As with discrimination, harassment, and victimization, enforcement may have the backing as well of the ordinary law.

'Terms of employment'

The terms and conditions for judges are generous compared with those enjoyed by many in public service. The UK Supreme Court decision in *Gilham v Ministry of Justice*[121] illustrates, however, two important dimensions to these terms and conditions, at least in the English context. First, what can be conveniently characterized as the individual 'terms of employment' are a jumble. In *Gilham* there were two aspects to this. One aspect was that the terms were contained in at least three different documents. First, the district judge had received a letter offering her appointment which contained stipulations as to duration, salary, pension on retirement, and other matters.

[118] *Lord Chancellor v McCloud* [2018] EWCA Civ 2844, [2020] 1 All ER 304 (leave to appeal to SC refused) (hereafter *McCloud*).
[119] Public Service Pensions and Judicial Offices Act 2022.
[120] Senior Courts Act 1981, s 98.
[121] *Gilham v Ministry of Justice* (n 101).

Enclosed with the letter was next, a detailed memorandum entitled 'District judges—Memorandum on conditions of employment and terms of service'. This included terms as to sitting days, sick pay, maternity, paternity, and adoption leave, training, the prohibition of legal practice, relations with the press and media, outside activities, and much more. Then, thirdly was the judge's instrument of appointment, which authorized her to sit at all the county courts in a certain part of the country. The second aspect to the 'terms of employment' jumble was their variable legal base, as explained in Lady Hale's judgment. None were expressed in contractual terms. Some, for example those relating to maternity, paternity, and adoption leave, had no basis in statute either, by contrast to the position with ordinary employees. Other terms, Lady Hale observed, were not binding but expressed as what was to be expected. With terms regarding matters like deployment ultimately, as we see shortly, the chief justice has the upper hand by virtue of statute. As to the essential components of the relationship—salary, pension rights, retirement age, and removal—these were derived from statute and not a matter of choice or negotiation between the parties.[122]

Secondly, *Gilham* illustrates a second dimension to these terms and conditions, at least in the English context, that legislative advances in individual employment rights for 'workers' and those in 'employment' do not necessarily apply to judges unless that is expressly provided for in legislation. In England this is because judges are statutory office holders and as such do not fall into the category of either 'worker' or 'employee', which are the categories usually used in legislation for the conferral of employment benefits. Express provision can occur, as where legislation is extended to public office holders, which would include judges. An example is the Equality Act 2010: some prohibitions there against discrimination, harassment, and victimization extend beyond those in employment to public office holders.[123] Moreover, as in *Gilham*, gaps in legislation in its application to judges may sometimes be overcome through human rights and equal treatment principles. In *Gilham* the whistleblowing protections in the Employment Rights Act 1996 did not on their face apply to statutory office holders, but the UK Supreme Court held that the judge was being treated less favourably than others in analogous situations regarding her right in article 10 of the ECHR to freedom of expression through whistleblowing. Her occupational classification was the reason, article 14 of the ECHR prohibited discrimination on that ground, and there

[122] ibid [17]–[18].
[123] ss 50–51.

was no legitimate aim in excluding judges from whistleblowing protection. Consequently, the court held, the legislation had to be interpreted to extend to judges.[124]

The story of plugging gaps in the individual employment rights of English judges had begun earlier with pension entitlement. *Ministry of Justice v O'Brien*[125] concerned recorders—those working mainly in legal practice who are paid a daily fee for sitting three or four weeks a year as judges in the Crown and county courts. The judicial pensions legislation did not apply to recorders. They were assumed to be making provision for a private pension like any self-employed person. In *O'Brien* the UK Supreme Court held that the Part-time Workers (Prevention of Less Favourable Treatment) Regulations 2000, transposing EU law into UK law, applied. Because of EU law—the EU Framework Agreement on part-time work—recorders were to be treated as 'workers' for the purposes of those regulations. The denial of a pro rata judicial pension to them on grounds mainly of cost did not justify the discrimination they experienced. Consequently, they were entitled to a pro rata pension.

Gilham and *O'Brien* concerned terms and conditions which following the Supreme Court's interpretation of the legislation now lie in statute. In other areas the rights of individual judges are contained in soft law, which can take various forms. Take the example of part-time and flexible working. In Britain the Employment Rights Act 1996 facilitates this for employees so that they have the legal right to request flexible working in terms of the number of hours they work, when they start or finish work, and the days they will work.[126] Those provisions do not apply to judges who we have seen are not employees but statutory office holders. Instead, there is a policy document providing the framework for the appointment of part-time permanent judges up to Court of Appeal level and for existing judges to apply to reduce their working pattern. Judges who have a fractional appointment are subject to the same terms and conditions as full-time judges—the same benefits (salary, pension, leave, and so on, calculated on a pro rata basis) and the same obligations (for example, to give up legal practice). The policy document provides that senior judges may decide that a fractional appointment

[124] Human Rights Act 1998, s 3.

[125] *Ministry of Justice v O'Brien (Council of Immigration Judges intervening)* [2013] UKSC 6, [2013] 2 All ER 1. See also Case C-432/17 *O'Brien v Ministry of Justice* [2019] 1 CMLR 40 and *McCloud* (n 118) (unlawful age discrimination in transitional provisions governing changes in the judicial pension).

[126] s 80F.

is not conducive to efficient judicial administration, limiting for instance the court's ability to list cases, or that it would hinder a judge's exposure to the cases and activities instrumental to maintaining judging skills. Under the policy there are internal avenues of appeal spelt out if applications by judges for part-time working are refused.[127]

Conditions: allocation of work and case assignment

As well as benefits, a judge's terms and conditions will entail duties. In general terms a judge must judge and must do so competently, efficiently, and well, and must exhibit the accepted standards in behaviour at and away from court—performance obligations ultimately enforceable through disciplinary powers.[128] As regards their adjudicative functions, a judge is protected by the principle of judicial independence from being directed as regards, for example, the outcome of a case.[129] However, a judge can be legitimately directed by a senior judge in other ways. For instance, there is an express provision in the UK Constitutional Reform Act 2005 for the chief justice to maintain appropriate arrangements for the deployment of judges and the allocation of work within the courts.[130] As in general employment, the implications of this may be the subject of some negotiation between the individual judge and the leadership judge. Ultimately, the essential components of the relationship are derived from statute and the judge must comply.[131] Subject to any stipulation in their terms of appointment, judges can therefore be required to sit in particular jurisdictions and to hear particular cases.

In practice this type of provision is mediated through routine administrative arrangements. With respect to the distribution of work there are, in broad outline, three models of case assignment—random, discretionary, and pragmatic. None match exactly what happens in practice in any particular jurisdiction. Random assignment must give way in the face of unexpected absences of judges through illness or out of court judicial business, conflicts of interest thrown up by the assignment process, and the refusal of a judge to sit on a panel with another judge for personal reasons. Discretionary assignment—as with the power of the chief justice of India as master of the roster—is an impossibility with the high caseloads facing many courts. Case assignment in discretionary systems has to be a routine matter in most cases,

[127] Ministry of Justice, *Judicial Salaried Part-time Working Policy* (MoJ, October 2021).
[128] PP. 119, 123, 137 above.
[129] PP. 12, 72 above.
[130] Constitutional Reform Act 2005, s 7(2)(c).
[131] *Gilham v Ministry of Justice* (n 101) [18].

administered along well-established lines by court officers with only occasional judicial intervention.

Pragmatic assignment focuses of availability, expertise, and fairness—'horses for courses' as it is sometimes known. A judge may be assigned to hear a case because of their expertise or experience given the legal issues a case raises, its complexity, or its nature (for example, it may be high-profile). Yet the expert or experienced judge may not be available if, for instance, their previous case has overrun its estimated time and another judge is pragmatically assigned. Judges also vary in the competence and the efficiency with which they resolve matters. That can influence case assignment. Workloads may be informally weighted in the interests of the court in addressing or preventing backlogs. That raises the issue of fairness. The *Commentary on the Bangalore Principles of Judicial Conduct* provides that there should be fairness and an equitable distribution to judges of the work of a court.[132] In other words all judges should have the opportunity to sit on interesting cases. It also means not overburdening efficient judges in the assignment process simply because they can get through the work.

Training, welfare, and judges' associations

In many jurisdictions judicial training has matured from after-court, occasional lectures into the institutional form of a judicial training institution or college.[133] Led by judges, these offer a variety of courses, ranging from substantive law, evidence, and procedure, through inclusion and diversity, to digital skills, judgecraft, and leadership. The judicial training institution may also produce bench books and other aids for judging. Principles developed internationally place a responsibility on the individual judge to undertake their own learning, but also on judiciaries to ensure that judges receive regular training throughout their professional lives and time off for them to do so.[134] In most jurisdictions there are financial and human constraints on judicial training. As an example, the statutory responsibility in England placed on the chief justice to maintain arrangements for training contains an express caveat that it is to be exercised within the resources made available by the executive government.[135] Given the resource handicaps, a judge's

[132] *Commentary on the Bangalore Principles* (n 115) para 216.
[133] eg, Judicial College (England and Wales), National Judicial Institute (Canada), National Judicial Academy (India), Judicial Education Institute (South Africa).
[134] International Organization for Judicial Training, *Declaration of Judicial Training Principles* (2017) principles 4, 6, 7 <www.iojt.org/> accessed 13 June 2025.
[135] Constitutional Reform Act 2007, s 7(2)(b).

'terms of employment' as they are characterized here are unlikely to contain absolutes, such as the right of judges to spend a specified number of days each year participating in professional development activities. Apart from mandatory induction programmes for new judges (and perhaps incoming leadership judges), and providing that judges cannot sit in some specialist jurisdictions or hear certain types of case without minimum preparation and annual refreshers, training provision is most likely to respond to specific needs such as new legislation or issues of current concern.

Judicial welfare was recognized in the *Commentary on the Bangalore Principles of Judicial Conduct* as affecting judicial performance. 'A judge should have sufficient time to permit the maintenance of physical and mental well-being', it said, underlining the stress associated with fulfilling judicial duties.[136] There is continuing international concern about the stressful, demanding, and isolating features for judges faced with excessive workloads, time constraints, outside pressures, unfounded criticism, or working without support in remote locations. In a sense judges are susceptible to the same problems that affect other professions, although given the context it can be described as litigation fatigue. Not only can judicial stress affect individual well-being but it can adversely affect the quality of judicial decision-making, a judge's sensitivity to biases, and ultimately public confidence in the judicial system.[137] Vague policy responses referring to the need to raise awareness among judges about well-being and to develop preventive strategies lack traction. Concrete measures such as helplines, counselling, and other services need to be identified and made available.

International standards recognize the role played by associations of judges in promoting judges' professional interests and defending judicial independence.[138] In particular they perform a role in highlighting welfare and other work-related issues to leadership judges. International standards are often couched in terms of judges having the right to freedom of association. As the *Commentary on the Bangalore Principles* acknowledges, there are limits to this right for judges. In exercising the right they must act in accordance with the values of impartiality and integrity and ensure internal and individual independence from other judges. In particular, the *Commentary* says,

[136] *Commentary on the Bangalore Principles* (n 115) para 194.

[137] United Nations Office on Drugs and Crime, *Exploring Linkages between Judicial Well-Being and Judicial Integrity* (UNODC 2022) 6–7.

[138] eg, UN Basic Principles (n 2) para 9; *Bangalore Principles of Judicial Conduct* (United Nations 2018) value 4, paras 4.6, 4.13; International Association of Judges, *The Universal Charter of the Judge* (rev edn, IAJ 2017) art 3.5.

restrictions may be placed on their right to strike.[139] Consistently with the importance of the right to freedom of association, judges are represented by a range of bodies, sometimes divided on jurisdictional lines (for example, senior judges, lower court judges, immigration judges). Associations of women judges have been especially active. There can be difficulties when associations of judges press for changes in the terms and conditions of service and that ends up in court. There are potential conflicts of interest for those judges who decide the issue. One way of addressing this is to have judges sitting who are not affected by the outcome, or to appoint on a temporary basis those from a different jurisdiction who are not affected by any ruling.

Community engagement

Community engagement is a feature of modern judging. If it ever existed, the notion has well and truly faded that on appointment a judge is in all but name entering something like a monastery or nunnery. Community engagement by judges is justified first, in enhancing societal confidence in the judiciary. It gives the public an awareness of who judges are and an insight into their work. Their humanity is revealed and perhaps the difficulties they face better understood. Secondly, community engagement is said to have a role in enabling judges to understand and reflect better the society in which they judge. Judges leading professional lives do not necessarily have a clear insight into other corners of the complex and variegated societies in which they work. Thirdly, community engagement can contribute to a judge's personal well-being. Participation can offer individual satisfaction and resilience.

Judges may be expected to be proactive about community engagement. In some jurisdictions judges are appointed to engage with the media, although on a day to day basis the task may be delegated to a judiciary's specialist communications officials. Diversity and community relations judges are appointed in England and Wales to undertake outreach work with legal professionals, community groups, and educational establishments, with the aim of explaining judging work and dispelling myths surrounding the judiciary.[140] The *Guide to Judicial Conduct* for justices of the UK's Supreme Court informs them that 'it is important' for them to deliver lectures and speeches, to take part in conferences and seminars, to write and teach, and generally to contribute to debate on matters of public interest in the law, the administration of justice, and the judiciary.[141] The selection criteria for the appointment of

[139] *Commentary on the Bangalore Principles* (n 115) paras 134, 176.
[140] *The Lady Chief Justice's Report 2024* (Judiciary of England and Wales 2024) 26, 39.
[141] *Guide to Judicial Conduct* (UK Supreme Court 2019) [3.4].

Supreme Court justices reinforces this expectation that those appointed will engage with the community in these ways. The reason for a proactive view, the *Guide* suggests, is to enhance the professional and public understanding of the issues facing the Supreme Court and its role.[142]

As we saw in Chapters 2 and 3, however, judges must take care with community engagement.[143] Association with controversial social, political, and religious causes is off-limits. A cause célèbre in England was a judge of the Family Division of the High Court who established the Marriage Foundation, a charity with the aim of furthering stable relationships within marriage. He was given a formal warning under the judicial disciplinary procedures following a public statement about marriage, in particular questioning the government's plans for gay marriage. Moreover, judges are only too aware that some types of community engagement provide an opportunity for challenges on the grounds of bias. A Canadian example concerned a trial judge who was a governor of a charity for the benefit of the French community in Alberta.[144] The judge heard a claim by the only French-language school in Yukon and found that the Yukon government was in breach of minority language education rights in section 23 of the Canadian Charter of Rights and Freedoms. The Yukon Court of Appeal considered that the judge's position in the charity gave rise to an apprehension of bias, but the Supreme Court of Canada disagreed. Canada, said Abella J, had devoted much effort to creating a more diverse bench and that diversity should not operate as a presumption of bias. Based on the evidence, the judge's position in the charity did not foreclose an ability to approach the case with an open mind.[145]

V Conclusion

The legal and policy framework for judging is a patchwork. First, it varies in its legal base. In most jurisdictions security of tenure and salary is firmly grounded in statute. Legislation may have a role with terms of service, but in important respects these are contained in contract, conventions, or understandings if, as is the case in England, ordinary employment law does not extend to judges. Then there is soft law governing matters such as how to

[142] ibid.
[143] See pp. 90–92 above.
[144] *Yukon Francophone School Board, Education Area #23 v Yukon (Attorney General)* [2015] 2 SCR 282.
[145] ibid [61]–[62]. But there was apprehended bias for other reasons: [55].

determine good character and merit in selecting judges and as regards some standards of expected conduct. Soft law may range from detailed policy documents, relate to the delineation of procedures, or involve recommendations about desirable outcomes.

Secondly, there is the manner in which the legal and policy framework for judging is given effect. Whereas in some respects it may be contained in clear and explicit instruments, in others there may be an uncertainty as to its content, enabling wide discretion to be exercised. An example is the principle of fairness in case assignment so that all judges have the opportunity to sit on interesting and a range of cases: fairness ought to be inherent with random assignment systems, but with other methods it might constitute nothing more than an unspoken assumption that it will happen. Another dimension to how the legal and policy framework of judging is given effect concerns how it is now given expression institutionally compared with the informality of the past. Examples are the bodies which have been created in many jurisdictions to appoint, promote, and discipline judges.

Thirdly, there is implementation. The availability of some benefits such as pensions may be claimable as a matter of law, while others may turn on the non-reviewable discretion of leadership judges or the ministry of justice. Similarly, non-compliance with the standards of judicial conduct may be dealt with informally since nothing short of dismissal is available in the jurisdiction, but elsewhere may be visited with tailored sanctions and, as with discrimination and harassment, the backing of the general law. Enforcing standards of 'efficiency' in judging has proved controversial. There has been a greater bureaucratization and centralization of power in senior judges to manage the judiciary. This reflects factors such as the growth in the number of judges, the transfer of administrative responsibilities from ministries of justice to the judiciary, and the notion that judges have career paths with the attendant provision of training and welfare. Another aspect of this has been the introduction of what critics characterize as 'managerialism'. Judges are regarded as part of the public sector which delivers services, and how efficiently this is done needs to be measured. A strong culture of individualism among common law judges, a scepticism that justice can be measured, and a concern with judicial independence have all led to a resistance to this type of performance management.

The patchwork in the legal and policy framework for judging is attributable in part to the absence of universal truths for the selection, disciplining, and terms of service for judges. Depending on the institutional and political context, measures which in one jurisdiction are essential for the independence, impartiality, and integrity of judges are unwarranted in another. For instance in some places having an independent commission to select judges will have an important bearing on whether the judiciary is independent and impartial, both in reality and appearance. However, the experience in some established democracies is that, while selection by the executive does not preclude less than satisfactory appointments, it does not undermine judicial independence. The justification for an independent commission to select judges in these jurisdictions may lie with other goals such as furthering judicial diversity, although in theory there is no reason that this cannot be achieved by strategic appointments by the executive. Another example concerns judicial appointments on a short-term or part-time basis. Deplored by some, the practice enables shortages in the judge-power in some jurisdictions to be addressed; expatriate judges to sit occasionally in small jurisdictions on sensitive, high-profile trials or the periodic appeal; and potential appointees to the bench in other jurisdictions to be tested and to evaluate for themselves the suitability of a judicial career.

The values of judicial independence, impartiality, and integrity account for a great deal of the legal and policy framework for judging. However, there are three caveats to invoking these values as justification for specific policies and laws regarding judging. First, they may be paraded as a justification for a policy or legal change, whereas there is a different underlying rationale. That separate rationale might be perfectly justifiable. However, wrongful use of these values in this way, rather than advancing the measure on its own terms, may only undermine these values in circumstances which demand a policy or legal response. Secondly, protections such as judicial tenure are not a privilege of the individual judge but primarily for the benefit of the judiciary as a whole. A simple example is that a sanction for a judicial transgression is imposed not primarily as a punishment of the judge, but in furtherance of preserving the reputation of the judiciary as a whole for its independence, impartiality, or integrity. Thirdly, times change. For example, a favourite nostrum of European judges and lawyers is that these values ground the establishment of a judicial council, with the selection of judges, their careers, and the operation of the judiciary being among its functions. Critics now argue that change is needed in some jurisdictions with judicial councils, since they have become politicized, or that court presidents have been able to become rival centres of power. The lesson is that a legal and policy framework for judging, once justified, may need reform if the continued independence, impartiality, and integrity of the judges and a judiciary are to be ensured.

5
Judgecraft

I Introduction

Judgecraft is the art of judging, the successful employment of practical skills associated with good judging. While the law, procedural and evidential rules, and the values of judging examined in Part I of the book all bear on judicial work, these may have a 'taken for granted' quality in particular situations. It is judgecraft which ensures the success of the judge in court, the efficient processing of their caseload, the making of good decisions, and the advancement of their reputation. Judgecraft encompasses the practical skills used on a daily basis as judges produce written orders, conduct hearings, find facts, make decisions, give their reasons in judgments, and perhaps provide leadership. These practical skills involve a range of techniques, strategies, and work practices as judges manage workflow; engage with litigants, lawyers, court staff, and judicial colleagues; deploy legal and other knowledge; deliberate over cases; resolve problems they encounter in the course of their work; communicate with others during legal proceedings or in other ways in their role as a judge; and if a leadership judge, manage the administration of justice. To consider judging without giving attention to judgecraft would be to oversimplify judicial work and overlook the full picture of judging.

The chapter opens in section II with an outline of judgecraft, with illustrative areas where judgecraft enters the everyday work of the judge. Section III of the chapter relates to managerial judging, where judges become involved in case management and possible attempts to facilitate the settlement of cases. Collegiality and the related topic of judicial leadership are addressed in section IV of the chapter, before a discussion of judgment preparation in section V.

II Dimensions of Judgecraft

This section begins with some general elements of judgecraft, including that in handling high-volume applications, speedily and effectively, before

Judging. Ross Cranston, Oxford University Press. © Ross Cranston 2025.
DOI: 10.1093/9780191890994.003.0005

turning, secondly, to the skill of fact-finding. Thirdly, there is the important judgecraft in decision-making without oral argument. The pressure of case-loads has meant that much judging now occurs away from hearings in court. One aspect is that more argument concerning a case is in written form. Another aspect, relevant here, is that important decision-making occurs 'on the papers'. Fourth, there is the *ex tempore* judgment, which demands a high level of judgecraft. There the judge does not reserve judgment to be handed down in writing at some later point, but rather gives it orally, almost immediately after the hearing, or perhaps the next sitting day. Finally, a quite different level of judgecraft is required when the judge is faced with a litigant in person—a party without legal representation—now a regular feature of everyday judging, even in the senior courts.

(A) Judgecraft in Outline

Judgecraft is essential to judging. Judges learn judgecraft from observation, experience, and self or taught instruction. That learning will have little to do with a judge's legal training, although some may have been assimilated when the judge appeared in court as a lawyer prior to appointment, and in the process observed the practice of other judges. Once on the bench judges draw on how other judges perform the work and from their own experience accumulated over time. As with all entrants to a profession, judges are socialized into the judiciary and internalize certain norms of behaviour. They draw on guidance from other judges both prior to and following their appointment. Learning can occur informally as judges seek out colleagues for immediate advice about a problem, and discuss issues and cases during the day if possible, and before and after court. It is facilitated if they are sitting with other judges on a panel. Learning by doing is crucial as judges pragmatically resolve problems which arise. Training for judges and prospective judges includes aspects of judgecraft such as conduct in court, judgment writing, and communicating with the media. This fosters a greater uniformity in judicial practice notwithstanding a diversity in judicial backgrounds. Judgecraft is sometimes contained in maxims, which distil practical wisdom. An example is the maxim for appellate judges, when disagreeing with the judge below: 'Let the judge down gently.' Over time the skills of good judgecraft become second nature to the judge and are applied as habit without thinking.

Judges are evaluated on their judgecraft. Often this is simple and informal, but in some jurisdictions it is more elaborate and organized. As with any craft there are good, bad, and indifferent practitioners. The judge well respected for aspects of judgecraft, such as presiding in court or getting through the work, may not be as positively evaluated in other spheres such as the quality of written judgments. External measures such as cases overturned on appeal may not be reflective of a judge's high reputation among colleagues for judgecraft or indeed their judgments. The proficient judge may have a bad day. As with any craft, judges measure their colleagues' performance against standards which may escape outsiders. In the face of uncertainty, for example, a judge may improvise so that a hearing proceeds without incident. Another example is that the judge producing well-crafted judgments may do so by taking excessive time, compelling colleagues to shoulder a disproportionate share of the court's work. Consequently, internal evaluation of the judge may not match the external.

In important respects there are discrete judgecrafts along the judicial spectrum. An orienting focus for the judgecraft of more senior judges is hearing cases and then preparing persuasively written judgments to justify their decisions. Some managerial judging will feature in their lives, as it does in those of other judges, but to a far lesser extent. For judges at the other end of the spectrum judgecraft involves managing large caseloads under tight time constraints. These judges may regularly encounter the grim realities of life, make decisions fundamental to the future of those before them, labour in relatively isolated conditions, and work under physical strain and psychological pressure. Judgecraft for them means applying established and simplified routines and intuitive decision-making to cope efficiently with the relentless stream of similar cases, the threat of a backlog, and disillusionment. It might also involve coping with the dynamics of what can be emotionally fraught hearings, conducted perhaps in their rooms, rather than in a courtroom.

Routinization, simplification, and speed as judges handle the caseload does not mean that uncertainty is eliminated. Things can and do go wrong. One aspect is that high-volume courts over-list cases on any day since many will settle or drop out. To assume that all will 'stand up' would lead to wasted resources. However, in courts which over-list there is the risk that not all cases in the list will be heard: some cases may require a disproportionate amount of attention, or sometimes a judge, a member of the court staff, or a courtroom has unexpectedly become unavailable. The judge may need to assuage the consequent disappointment of litigants whose case is not heard. Routinization and speed are not inevitably to the exclusion of judges being sensitive to how a case diverges from the norm, proactive in resolving sudden troubles, or innovative in fashioning more efficient work patterns for the future. Judges handling high-volume caseloads need to strike a balance between on the one hand getting through the work by making speedy decisions, given *ex tempore*, and on the other not sacrificing procedural fairness and the just resolution of the parties' disputes. All of this demands a high level of judgecraft, not least as judges attempt to convey a sense of empathy for a party's case, and that it has been properly considered, despite what might appear to be a truncated process. Judgecraft in this regard requires high skills. It is essential to maintaining respect for the judiciary more generally.

(B) Fact-Finding

A leading English judge underlined the importance of fact-finding by characterizing judging 'as an educated reflex to facts, though always within the framework of established legal principle'.[1] The common experience of first instance judges is that once the facts are relatively clear, issues of law fall into place. 'In eight cases out of ten, deciding the facts decided the case', recounted a former president of the NSW Court of Appeal of his experience as a first instance judge, based on the records he had kept.[2] The formal position is that the judge makes findings of primary facts based on the evidence before the court. As well as the evidence of lay witnesses there may be documentary and expert evidence. The law has principles as to whether evidence is admissible and therefore taken into account. These may differ between courts. The seriousness with which the principles are applied also varies. Once the evidence is admissible there is the task of evaluating it as it relates to the key factual issues in dispute on matters such as what happened, why, how, and a party's state of mind (their knowledge, intention, or belief). Some facts will be certain, or almost certain, and some not disputed. There may be an agreed statement of facts and a chronology covering some, possibly all, the crucial factual issues. In public law cases in England, the burden of fact-finding is

[1] Lord Goff, 'Judge, Jurist and Legislature' (1987) 2 Denning LJ 79, 82.

[2] Dennis Mahoney, 'Judgment Writing: Form and Function' in Ruth Sheard (ed), *A Matter of Judgment: Judicial Decision-Making and Judgment Writing* (Judicial Commission of New South Wales 2003) 104.

lessened because government agencies are under a duty of candour and must provide a full and accurate account of all the relevant facts.

Where the facts are in dispute, the formal position is that the judge must consider all the evidence and evaluate each item against the whole of the evidence in the case. Facts may be established when placed alongside known or agreed facts. A witness's interest in the outcome of a case is relevant to their evidence because it may lead them consciously, or more likely unconsciously, to distort matters. Consistency is also important, internal consistency in the witness's evidence, and consistency with evidence they have given on the same matter on other occasions. Once the primary facts are established, the judge may then draw inferences (or deductions) from them. In practice there can be real difficulties associated with fact-finding. Fact-finding can be the most difficult part of the judge's task. The difficulties have been highlighted as the work of social psychologists has percolated into judicial consciousness.

Seven points relating to fact-finding are worth highlighting. The first relates to demeanour, in other words how witnesses present themselves when giving evidence. The traditional view in civil cases was that fact finders—the jury and, once the civil jury's role waned, the judge—could discern reliable witnesses from their behaviour, hesitations, tone, nuances, and facial expressions.[3] Psychological research has long demonstrated that it cannot be assumed that the confident witness, with a vivid recollection, is more likely to be accurate than the less confident or hesitant witness. Not only can appearances be deceptive but judges can overestimate their ability to recognize those who are truthful.[4] Cultural background and giving evidence in a foreign language may well bear on a witness's presentation. Rather than assessing whether evidence is truthful from the manner in which it is given, it is now recognized that the judge must focus on its content and consider whether it is consistent with other evidence, including the witness's previous evidence, and with known or probable facts.[5] At one time appellate courts would not generally interfere with a trial judge's findings of fact since the judge had seen and heard the witnesses, but once demeanour is discounted other justifications are needed for non-intervention.

Secondly, truthfulness and reliability are not necessarily synonymous.[6] The honest witness can be unreliable because their memory is fallible. They

[3] eg, *Clarke v Edinburgh & District Tramways Co Ltd* 1919 SC (HL) 35, 36–37 (Lord Shaw).
[4] eg, *Taniwha v R* [2016] NZSC 121, [2017] 1 NZLR 116 [1] (Arnold J for the court). See also *Trawl Industries v Effem Foods Pty Ltd* (1992) 27 NSWLR 326, 348 (Samuels JA).
[5] eg, *Fox v Percy* [2003] HCA 22, (2003) 214 CLR 118 [30]–[31]; *R (SS) (Sri Lanka) v Secretary of State for the Home Department* [2018] EWCA Civ 1391 [39]–[41] (Leggatt LJ).
[6] *Gilbert v Bottle* 2011 BCSC 1389, [9] (Dickson J).

can honestly believe that something happened which did not happen because, as with others, their memory is vulnerable to a range of unconscious influences.[7] Experience and expertise shape what is encoded into a witness's memory at the time of an event. Moreover, recalling that event is affected by their current beliefs, attitudes, approach, and worldview which can differ from those at the time of the event. Both encoding and recollection of the past can be affected by the human tendency to want to portray one's participation in events in the best possible light. There are also the risks associated with reconstruction from semantic memory, in other words assuming that what a witness expects to have happened did happen. One obvious risk is that on this occasion it did not. Another is that the present semantic memory schema is being applied to a different time. There is also the pride and wishful thinking in a witness supposing that what they ought to have done and thought was what in fact they did and thought.[8] Given this background about memory, the judge must carefully evaluate a witness's recollections about conversations, events, and understandings. Factual findings about them will need to be based as well on the documentary evidence, known or probable facts, and the inferences which can be drawn from them.

That leads to the third point, documentary evidence. In some cases there will be few if any documents, or the documents which exist will be silent on the issues in dispute. The case will turn on oral and other evidence. If there are documents, these can be invaluable in establishing facts, especially with documents prepared before the dispute arose or documents unconnected with the dispute. A premium is placed on contemporary internal documents including emails and instant messaging since it is assumed that this is where a witness's guard is down and their true thoughts are expressed.[9] Yet even documents created near the time of an event are potentially lacking. There are the memory failings during the encoding process described earlier, which can affect document creation. Evidence bearing on the judge's determination of a document's accuracy will also include the motives of those creating it, their closeness or distance from events, what was important to them at the time, the (re)interpretation of any manuscript notes used in the document's creation, and the ambiguities within it. All these factors must be considered

[7] *Watson v Foxman* (1995) 49 NSWLR 315, 318–319 (McClelland CJ in Eq).

[8] Popplewell LJ, 'Judging Truth from Memory: The Science' (COMBAR Lecture, 16 November 2023).

[9] *Gestmin v Credit Suisse* [2013] EWHC 3560 (Comm) [22] (Leggatt J); *Simetra Global Assets Ltd v Ikon Finance Ltd* [2019] EWCA Civ 1413, [2019] 4 WLR 112 [48] (Males LJ).

alongside other factual issues and the inherent probabilities in establishing the facts relevant to the critical issues.[10]

Inherent probabilities, fourthly, are the probabilities (or improbabilities) of an event in question having happened. Inherent probabilities are based on common sense assumptions about behaviour in a particular context. The difficulty is that a judge's experience is limited in knowing what is typical behaviour in many situations and therefore what are the inherent probabilities.[11] Moreover, what might seem improbable in general terms can seem probable when considered along with other evidence. For example, if a child alleges sexual abuse by a parent it is common sense to start with the assumption that most parents do not abuse their children, but this assumption may be swiftly dispelled by other compelling evidence in a case concerning the relationship between parent and child or parent and other children.[12] Finally, there are the heuristics such as confirmation bias and hindsight bias canvassed earlier, which can distort a witness's understanding of the facts just as they can distort the judge's.[13]

Fifthly, appellate courts generally defer to a trial judge's findings of fact. There are a number of reasons for this: first instance judges are assigned the task of fact finder; reopening questions of fact for redetermination on appeal would be an additional cost to the parties and divert judicial resources for what would often be negligible benefit in terms of factual accuracy; and it is likely that the judge who has heard the evidence over an extended period will have a deeper insight into the facts than the appellate court with its perception focused on the challenge to particular parts of the evidence.[14] Accordingly, English law is that an appellate court should only interfere with a finding of fact made by a trial judge if satisfied that the decision is plainly wrong, or that there is a material error of law, a critical finding of fact with no basis in evidence, or a demonstrable misunderstanding of or failure to consider relevant evidence.[15] As well, in some cases conclusions of fact will not be conclusions of primary fact, but will involve an assessment of a number of

[10] *Jaffé v Greybull Capital LLP* [2024] EWHC 2534 (Comm) [229], [232], [265], [285] (Cockerill J).

[11] Tom Bingham, 'The Judge as Juror' in *The Business of Judging* (OUP 2000) 14.

[12] *Re B* [2008] UKHL 35, [2009] 1 AC 11 [15] (Lord Hoffmann).

[13] PP. 80–81 above.

[14] *Carlyle v Royal Bank of Scotland plc (Scotland)* [2015] UKSC 13 [22] (Lord Hodge).

[15] *Henderson v Foxworth Investments Limited* [2014] UKSC 41, [2014] 1 WLR 2600 [67] (Lord Reed) citing *HL v Canada (Attorney General)* [2005] 1 SCR 401 [55]–[56] and *Anderson v City of Bessemer* (1985) 470 US 564, 573–74.

different factors which have to be weighed against each other. This is often a matter of degree upon which appellate and trial judges can legitimately differ.

Sixthly, in addition to primary facts there are facts based on common knowledge. Under the doctrine of judicial notice these do not need to be proved in the normal way. The doctrine has the benefit of efficiency. As well as facts widely known, judicial notice can be taken of facts which are notorious in a locality as well as historical facts, such as those relating to constitutional history. English case law is replete with curious examples: human gestation is impossible in a fortnight; cats are domestic animals; the value of money depreciates over time (with inflation); goldfinches are wild British birds; and certain waters are tidal.[16] It would seem good practice for the judge to inform the parties that judicial notice will be taken of a fact so that they can raise objections. The limits to judges taking judicial notice of a fact turn on the function the court is performing. There may be a greater reluctance to assume facts in some cases compared with others. Thus facts relating to the development of law and legal policy, such as whether certain activities are insurable, may be more readily assumed than facts about which parties did what, and whether in doing so they acted rationally or intentionally.

Finally, there are social facts, which are general statements about the world, society, and the nature and behaviour of individuals, institutions, and society. Social facts may be admitted into evidence in the usual way, perhaps through expert evidence. Often, however, there is a taken-for-granted quality in the social facts invoked, for example, that the majority of victims of all forms of domestic violence are women, that the social and psychological realities of the doctor–patient relationship inhibit most patients from asking questions, and that certain restraints in examining the acts of a foreign state are justified because of the potential impact on international relations.[17] All these social facts may be, and probably are, true, but there is the risk that some of the social facts judges draw upon are contestable. An example is the social fact of defensive policing, that imposing further liability on police forces in favour of claimants will threaten vigorous investigations because of the disincentive engendered, and the diversion of resources and effort associated with being sued.[18] The Canadian Supreme Court declined to accept the

[16] *Halsbury's Laws of England* (LexisNexis 2021) vol 28, para 467.

[17] *Yemshaw v Hounslow LBC* [2011] UKSC 3, [2011] 1 WLR 433 [1]; *Montgomery v Lanarkshire Health Board* [2015] UKSC 11, [2015] AC 1430 [58]; *Belhaj v Straw* [2017] UKSC 3, [2017] AC 964 respectively.

[18] *Hill v Chief Constable of West Yorkshire* [1989] AC 53, 63.

social fact of defensive policing because of the lack of empirical evidence.[19] At the least, if the judge is to rely on a social fact in their reasoning, fairness generally requires that it is raised with the parties beforehand so that they have the opportunity to challenge it.

(C) Decisions Without a Hearing ('on the Papers')

The previous section on fact-finding has assumed that the parties and their advocates are in court. That is the common conception of how legal disputes are resolved. But judges make many important decisions in the absence of the parties and without the benefit of a hearing with them or their advocates. These decisions are sometimes described as being made 'on the papers', although in the modern era the relevant file is often sent to the judge electronically and the decision recorded digitally. Of course this does happen with certain matters. For example, if credibility is in dispute on a material issue, the judge will conduct a hearing. However, a wide range of matters are decided 'on the papers'—directions on case management for the future conduct of litigation, the approval of an order where the parties are agreed, and the resolution of interlocutory applications. In some courts, work of this nature is called 'box work', since at one time it was presented to the judge in a box. District judges in England and Wales spend a great deal of time on box work: case management directions, applications for the adjournment of a hearing, online financial consent orders in the case of family law work, orders to enforce a court's judgments, and so on.

Permission from a judge to proceed with a case will sometimes be required by a court's procedural rules. This is an area where matters will often be handled without the oral hearing which at one time was standard practice. An illustration is that in England and Wales a party must obtain a judge's permission to proceed to a substantive hearing with a judicial review or a statutory appeal from a tribunal or a planning inspector.[20] The threshold is relatively low, being whether the applicant has an arguable case. Typically, the application will be made in writing and the decision given in writing. If permission is refused, an applicant may request that the matter be reconsidered at an oral (a renewal) hearing.[21] Renewal hearings from a refusal of permission

[19] *Hill v Hamilton-Wentworth Police Services Board* [2007] 3 SCR 129. See *Michael v Chief Constable of South Wales Police* [2015] UKSC 2, [2015] AC 1732 [122].

[20] eg, Senior Courts Act 1981, s 31(3); CPR 54.4.

[21] CPR 54.12(3).

are, however, limited in scope and time, thirty minutes for the typical judicial review.[22]

Appeals are a second illustration if there is no automatic right to appeal and permission of a judge to appeal is a required. In England and Wales, an application for permission to appeal will initially be made to the court which has decided the case. The threshold is whether an appeal has a real prospect of success, or whether there is some other compelling reason for an appeal to be heard.[23] If the application is refused, a party may apply to the appellate court. At least initially an appellate court's decision in England will typically be made 'on the papers'. Oral renewal of a refused application may then occur, but these are no longer the norm with the English Court of Appeal, where oral renewals require a judge to decide that the application cannot otherwise be fairly determined.[24]

The rationale for limiting oral hearings for permission applications to proceed to a substantive hearing, or an appeal, is primarily to provide relief from the pressure of heavy caseloads.[25] The practice can place a significant responsibility on the judge, since a refusal means that the chances of taking the case further are diminished, if not extinguished. The experience of common law judges is that oral argument is capable of clarifying matters, even changing a judge's mind. There are at least three potential dangers when a judge makes decisions 'on the papers' without an oral hearing. The first is that a point can be missed or its significance overlooked, when it would be identified or highlighted if the parties appeared in person before the judge. The second is the adverse impact of cognitive biases in the absence of the more deliberative environment of an oral hearing where judges might slow their thinking rather than relying on assumptions and rules of thumb.[26] Thirdly, since matters are away from public gaze when matters are determined 'on the papers', there is scope for the adoption of slack practices which undermine a party's right to fairness in the consideration of their case.[27]

Mitigating the impact of these dangers lies in judgecraft. At the forefront is care in decision-making. Procedural rules may assist in situations of

[22] *Administrative Court Judicial Review Guide 2024* (Courts and Tribunal Judiciary 2024) 9.5.1, 9.5.4.

[23] CPR 52.6(1). With second appeals there must also be an important point of principle or practice: CPR 52.7(2).

[24] CPR 52.5(1)–(2).

[25] eg, Lord Briggs, *Civil Courts Structure Review: Interim Report* (Judiciary of England and Wales 2015) 9.21–9.32; *Final Report* (Judiciary of England and Wales 2016) 9.3.6, 9.4.3, 9.10.

[26] P. 245 below.

[27] eg, *Taito v R* [2002] UKPC 15, [2003] 3 NZLR 577 (PC, New Zealand).

uncertainty. Exceptionally the judge may be able to order an oral hearing of a permission application or may be able to give permission for an appeal, even if the prospect of success is low, by using another gateway (for example, there is some other compelling reason for an appeal). Exercising these powers requires judgement, since it has implications for the court's workload and possibly the judge's reputation, for example, if granting permission for hopeless appeals.

Essential if permission is refused is the preparation of a concise, reasoned decision. As well as enabling the parties and, if needs be, others to understand the decision's justification, it acts as a check on the judge's assumptions and unconscious biases.[28] Its detail depends on the circumstances of the case, but where the application raises specific points pro forma reasons are unacceptable, for example, 'the grounds are unarguable', 'the judge applied the correct legal principles, and it is not arguable that her conclusion is wrong', or 'for the reason given in the respondent's [written] submissions the applicant is not likely to succeed'. None of these pro forma reasons demonstrate that the judge has addressed the applicant's points or has properly engaged with them to refuse the application. The demands for adequate reasoning may be greater where the judge's decision means that a party has reached the end of the road.[29]

(D) *Ex Tempore* Judgments

At one time judgments in England were often *ex tempore*, delivered either immediately after the hearing or in the next day or so. At first instance Sir George Jessel MR never reserved a judgment—including one case with over one hundred witnesses heard over twenty-three days[30]—and in the Court of Appeal only very occasionally, then at the request of his colleagues.[31] The strict doctrine of precedent for the House of Lords, which lasted until 1966, was laid down in an *ex tempore* speech of Lord Halsbury.[32] Lord Denning

[28] *R (Goring-on-Thames Parish Council) v South Oxfordshire District Council* [2018] EWCA Civ 860, [2018] 1 WLR 5161 [35].

[29] *Wasif v Secretary of State for the Home Department* [2016] EWCA Civ 82, [2016] 1 WLR 2793 [19]–[20].

[30] *Commissioners of Sewers v Glasse* (1874) LR 19 Eq 134.

[31] Gareth H Jones, 'Jessel, Sir George (1824–1883)' in Colin Matthew and others (eds), *Oxford Dictionary of National Biography* (OUP 2004) vol 30, 85, 86.

[32] *London Street Tramways Co Ltd v London County Council* [1898] AC 375, (1898) 78 LT 361.

MR regularly gave *ex tempore* judgments, or gave oral judgments after a weekend's reflection. These days the senior courts in England would not survive without judges giving many *ex tempore* rulings and judgments.[33] *Ex tempore* judgments are often the product of circumstances. First are the cases where a decision is pressing. Occasions include applications for interim relief, procedural rulings during a hearing, and decisions on contempt in the face of the court. The alternative would be to announce the decision and hand down written reasons later, but in many cases the pressure of the workload makes an *ex tempore* judgment sensible, if not inevitable. That is, in effect, the second reason for *ex tempore* judgments, efficiency. Pre-trial and interlocutory applications, relatively short, straightforward hearings, and decisions on consequential issues such as costs—all these are illustrative of situations where an oral judgment is appropriate so that the pressing caseload is dealt with proficiently.

The risks with *ex tempore* judgments are threefold. The first is that *ex tempore* judgments can give the appearance that the judge has determined the outcome before the hearing.[34] Judges anticipating that an *ex tempore* judgment may be given will have pre-read the parties' case and submissions, identified the main issues, and be prepared with at least a structure for a judgment. The key requirement is that the judge with a preliminary view on outcome should keep an open mind for another possibility until the moment oral submissions are complete.[35] In many cases where an *ex tempore* judgment is anticipated, the judge (or judges) will retire for a decent interval to reflect on the parties' arguments, to consider whether these lead to the revision of any preliminary view, and to clarify their reasoning. The principle of fairness demands that the parties appreciate from the judge's conduct and judgment that their case has been properly considered.

An aspect of this, as well as an element of accountability, is that the *ex tempore* judgment be properly reasoned, reflecting the parties' arguments and how they are addressed. Herein lies the second risk. In giving an *ex tempore* judgment, the judge may lose their way or make mistakes (albeit slips can generally be put right). Appellate courts are generally sympathetic to the pressures facing judges giving *ex tempore* judgments and the need for

[33] See *Attorney General v Crosland* [2021] UKSC 58, [2022] 1 WLR 367 [82] (*ex tempore* judgments 'commonplace').
[34] ibid.
[35] *Newton v Public Prosecutor* [2023] SGHC 266, [2024] 2 LRC 151 [50] (Sundaresh Menon CJ).

expedition (and brevity). They will overlook language which ranges more widely than necessary. Even if a key matter is omitted, they may take the view that the judge's familiarity with it, or its prominence at the hearing, means that it is safe to assume that it was taken into account.[36] Judges are entitled to revise the transcript of their *ex tempore* judgments, polishing the expression, and clarifying both the findings and reasoning. Allowing this is justified on grounds of principle (it is fairer to the parties and assists them, especially with an appeal) and practice (to discourage judges improving *ex tempore* judgments would lead to more reserved judgments, and the consequent delay and additional time for judges to prepare them). Introducing wholly new or contradictory points in revising the transcript is a different matter: in making changes judges cannot act arbitrarily, but as with any discretion must exercise it judicially.[37]

The third risk of *ex tempore* judgments is the unguarded, even impulsive or hubristic comment. An example occurred in an *ex tempore* judgment by the only black judge in Nova Scotia at the time, who remarked that police officers had been known to mislead the court in the past and to overreact, particularly with non-white groups. She had acquitted a fifteen-year-old African Canadian in the Youth Court. The only prosecution evidence was from the white police officer, who had arrested him for offences associated with interfering with the arrest of another youth. The defendant was the only defence witness. The case reached the Supreme Court of Canada, which split six–three in holding that the comments did not give rise to a reasonable apprehension of bias, or taint the judge's earlier findings on credibility.[38] Four of the six majority judges held that, when read in their entirety, the reasons indicated that the judge had approached the case with an open mind, used her experience of the community to understand the reality of the case, and applied the fundamental principle of proof beyond a reasonable doubt, although the other two judges were troubled by the remarks and thought them close to the line.[39] Perhaps more guarded findings based in the evidence, rather than what the four judges characterized as 'contextualized judging', would have passed unremarked.

[36] *Piglowska v Piglowski* [1999] 1 WLR 1360, 1372 (Lord Hoffmann).

[37] *Shirt v Shirt* [2012] EWCA Civ 1029 [33]–[38]; *Minister for Immigration, Citizenship, Migrant Services and Multicultural Affairs v AAM17* [2021] HCA 6, (2021) 272 CLR 329 [30]–[31] (Steward J).

[38] *R v S (RD)* [1997] 3 SCR 484.

[39] ibid [59], [148], 152].

(E) Litigants in Person

Litigants in person are not new and there are examples of their appearing in the senior courts in the nineteenth century.[40] From the mid twentieth century small claims courts were designed around litigants in person. However, with reductions in public funding for legal services, litigants in person now appear regularly in the higher courts as well. Either they cannot afford legal assistance, or in some cases do not trust lawyers, or consider that they can do a better job. Litigants in person come from diverse backgrounds, with different levels of knowledge of litigation, and in various emotional states. By definition lawyers are not on hand to overcome their confusion and stress, nor to exercise a moderating influence on what might be their frustrations and resentments. Judges must perform the task. The overall aim, explains the *Equal Treatment Bench Book* for England and Wales, should be to ensure that litigants in person leave with the sense that they have been listened to and had a fair hearing, whatever the outcome. Judges, it continues, must be aware of the feelings and difficulties experienced by litigants in person. They must be ready and able to help them with the court's process, especially if a represented party is being confrontational. At the same time they must protect their represented opponent against the challenges that can be caused by their lack of legal and procedural knowledge.[41]

Judges may need to deploy a variety of strategies with litigants in person—explanation, indulgence, performance, assistance, and ultimately, in some cases, discipline. At the outset the judge may attempt to defuse anxiety or frustration on the part of a litigant in person by a calm explanation of the process, and what is expected of them, in language they can understand, together with an assurance that they will be given adequate time to argue their case. A full explanation may be needed if the judge grants a represented party what to the litigant in person might seem like an advantage. Secondly, there is indulgence, which involves affording a degree of latitude to the litigant in person to put their case. The judge will be aware that the litigant in person is unlikely to be in the same position as the professional advocate to handle interruptions, dialogue, indications of a preliminary view, and the cutting short of an argument. If the trial is to be fair, judges should temper their conduct accordingly.[42] Indulgence in this way may reduce the time taken in the

[40] *Fray v Blackburn* (1863) 3 B & S 576, 122 ER 217 was an action by a litigant in person against Lord Blackburn, then a Queen's Bench judge.

[41] *Equal Treatment Bench Book* (Judicial College 2024) 10–11.

[42] *Serafin v Malkiewicz* [2020] UKSC 23, [2020] 1 WLR 2455 [46].

long run and gain litigant satisfaction and a greater chance of compliance with any order. Thirdly, performance, since the judge exhibiting courtesy, patience, and empathy may dampen emotions and include the litigant in person more fully in the process. A pause or even a short adjournment may calm heightened emotions. Alluding to institutional values may assist—the need for both sides to comply with procedural requirements and that the principle of fairness is for the benefit of all. At some point the judge may need to 'perform authority' through facial demeanour, tone of voice, or a (strategic) display of irritation. At some point the judge may need to cut short the litigant in person in presenting their case.

As to fourthly, assistance, the judicial obligation to remain impartial limits what judges can do. The judge may need to explain these constraints. Under the Civil Procedure Rules in England, the judge is expressly authorized to assist the litigant in person in identifying relevant evidence and cross-examining witnesses.[43] It seems that assistance to the litigant in person does not include strategic advice.[44] Depending on the jurisdiction, a litigant in person may be assisted by a non-lawyer such as a member of their family, a friend, or a student from a law clinic. In the civil courts in England, the judge will need to grant permission for a litigant in person to be assisted or represented by a layperson. There is a presumption that permission will be granted under the well-known system for a so-called 'McKenzie Friend', who sits with a litigant in person, providing moral support, taking notes, and quietly offering advice. The judge may also grant a McKenzie Friend permission to address the court, including situations where that person is a close relative of the litigant; health problems preclude the litigant from doing this; and if the litigant is relatively inarticulate and proceedings would otherwise be unnecessarily prolonged.[45]

Finally, discipline, which apart from orders against a litigant in person for non-compliance with the judge's directions can go as far as limiting their access to the court. The sad reality is that the occasional litigant in person becomes a vexatious litigant, persistently taking proceedings against others which are totally without merit, or in some cases engaging in unacceptable behaviour against court staff, despite requests and warnings. In England judges are empowered to make orders forbidding vexatious litigants from starting civil proceedings without permission, and orders to desist

[43] CPR 3.1A.
[44] *Ontario v Criminal Lawyers' Association of Ontario* [2013] 3 SCR 3 [54].
[45] *Practice Guidance: McKenzie Friends (Civil and Family Courts)* [2010] 4 All ER 272 [21].

in unacceptable conduct against staff.[46] Bad conduct such as lying in evidence, producing fraudulent documents, or putting forward defences in bad faith—none of this justifies an order, but it may cast light on the need for one, assuming other prerequisites are satisfied such as persistence in vexatious behaviour.[47] An order must be necessary, proportionate, and reasonable. The litigant in person persistently bringing without merit proceedings causes costs both to the court itself and to the defendant, and leads to judicial resources being allocated to address unmeritorious applications at the expense of other litigants.

III Managerial Judging

Managerial judging is the term used primarily to refer to the special procedural techniques judges use proactively to manage cases with the aim, as the Civil Procedure Rules of England and Wales (the CPR) puts it, of furthering the overriding objective of dealing with cases justly and at proportionate cost.[48] Under the rules, active case management includes 'helping the parties to settle the whole or part of the case'.[49] Judges therefore need to have the judgecraft to manage litigation as well as to assist in the settlement of cases. It is self-evident that the skills for case management and for facilitating the settlement of cases do not equate with those for adjudicating them. If judges do not have these skills on appointment, they must obtain them as practising judges.

(A) Case Management

Case management requires procedural activism on the part of the judge. The judge is not only a legal decision maker in the traditional sense, but is also a decision maker in managing the progress of cases through the legal process. This control over the resources allocated to individual disputes is supported by a philosophy of distributive justice, ensuring judicial resources are allocated fairly and efficiently to litigants and would-be litigants, and that the

46 Senior Courts Act s 42; CPR 2.3, 3.11, PD 3C.
47 *Sartipy v Tigris Industries Inc* [2019] EWCA Civ 225, [2019] 1 WLR 5892.
48 CPR 1.1(1).
49 CPR 1.4(2)(f).

allocation of resources is proportionate to the importance of each dispute. The overall aim of case management is to conserve judicial resources, and consequently to enable more people to access the courts.[50] The judge decides what procedure is suitable for each case, sets realistic timetables, and ensures compliance. The judge is active, not passive, in the conduct of litigation. One objective of case management is to concentrate on the real issues between the parties, and also to encourage the resolution of cases at the earliest possible stage. There is early and continuous judicial control of cases, by contrast with what was the traditional laissez-faire approach of the adversarial system. If settlement is not achieved, case management ensures that a case is tried as quickly and economically as possible.

There is a distinction between case management and the more traditional procedures for handling litigation in an efficient manner. The latter include a judge refusing an unjustified adjournment; striking out a pleading if it appears that it discloses no reasonable grounds for bringing or defending a claim; and granting summary judgment. A judge's decisions as regards these measures must be exercised in accordance with law and justified with reasons (however brief). These decisions are subject to appeal in the ordinary way. By contrast, the judge has a wider discretion with case management, and reasons for a case management order can be relatively short. An appellate court will not interfere with a judge's case management decisions unless it considers that it is based on irrelevant considerations, has not considered relevant considerations, or is plainly wrong.[51]

Case management is effected through both structural and case-specific methods. Structural case management does not require intense judicial attention. One aspect is differential case management, where cases of different complexity are placed on different tracks governing procedure and trial. Under the Civil Procedure Rules for England and Wales, ordinary civil cases are allocated to one of three tracks—the small claims track, the fast track, and the multi-track. In the small claims and fast tracks, court control generally follows routinely under the relevant rules and practice directions, without much in the way of specific judicial intervention. In the multi-track, which is for the larger or more complex claims, there are standard directions as well. However, judges may be more involved in managing multi-track cases as

[50] *Ashmore v Corporation of Lloyd's* [1992] 1 WLR 446, 448, 454 (Lord Roskill and Lord Templeman).

[51] *BPP Holdings Ltd v Revenue and Customs Commissioners* [2017] UKSC 55, [2017] 1 WLR 2945 [33].

they progress through the court. Another structural method of case management is the individual 'docketing' of cases. With individual docketing each case is placed under the supervision of the same judge from the outset and throughout its progress to trial. That judge may conduct the trial as well. The reasoning is that if judges have continuous oversight of a case, they will become familiar with the issues and can therefore more efficiently make decisions about it.

Case-specific management focuses on the case itself and connotes greater judicial participation. A common technique is the case management conference, where the judge reviews progress in the various steps the parties have or should have taken, and can give directions on matters such as disclosure, expert evidence, and the future timetable for the case. As regards the issues in the case, the parties can be pressed to identify them, and decisions can be made as to which need full investigation and trial (with others being summarily disposed of), and in what order they are to be resolved.[52] Shortly before trial the court may require the parties to inform it whether the directions have been complied with and, if not, how the case is to be managed up to and including trial. With mega-litigation such as a group (class) action, the degree of judicial attention to managing the case will be considerable. Instead of the one trial at the end of the process, in effect there may be a series of mini-trials, which will in many cases end in settlement. Along with their case management powers, judges under the Civil Procedure Rules for England and Wales also have costs management powers with a view to keeping litigation costs reasonable and proportionate. The judge will manage the case so that it proceeds within the approved budget, and on its conclusion assesses costs in favour of a winning party in light of that.[53]

The exercise of case management powers requires experience and judgement. That may be acquired as a litigator, or after appointment as a judge. Case management does not imply that judges are not prepared to reach a reasonable accommodation with the lawyers and parties as to what orders are appropriate in a case. Parties will make submissions about particular case management orders, which can lead the judge to a decision. Nor does it signify judges micromanaging litigation. Case-specific management may involve standard directions, enabling the parties to agree matters without the judge having to be involved. However, experience will make judges wary about allowing a breach of the case management orders to which the parties

[52] CPR 1.4(2)(b)–(d). See also CPR 3.1 (the court's case management powers).
[53] CPR 3.12–18.

are subject, without good reason. Orders need to create the expectation among the parties and their lawyers that events will occur as ordered, and when scheduled. Breach can be visited with severe sanctions such as striking out a claim, or the refusal of permission to appeal. A particular proficiency the judge must exhibit at case management hearings is to avoid comments which would lead the fair-minded and informed observer to conclude that there was a real possibility that they had formed a concluded view on an issue without having heard full argument on the point. Sometimes there is a thin line between case management and premature adjudication, which the judge must not cross.[54]

(B) Facilitating Settlement

Legal disputes are frequently settled without any judicial involvement. Settlement takes place, as the literature puts it, in the shadow of the law. Settlement may occur without a party commencing proceedings. Settlement also occurs once court proceedings have begun. Parties decide, sometimes at the door of the court, that litigation is unnecessary. Cases may even settle during trial if, for instance, a witness does not 'come up to proof' (fails to give evidence in line with their witness statement). Moreover, a judgment in a particular case may lead to settlements in a tranche of similar cases which are in prospect. The substantial attrition of cases as they pass through different stages of court proceedings makes it wrong to draw too strict a line between settlement on the one hand, and adjudication on the other. None of this is to say that judges have no influence on these types of settlement. A judge's decision at interim points in the conduct of litigation may lead indirectly to the parties reaching settlement. Decisions whether certain issues can be raised or the pleadings amended, when and what documents need be disclosed, or when or what evidence is admissible may stimulate consideration by the parties as to whether to proceed further. Always hovering in the background are the further legal costs which proceeding to trial will incur as a result of such decisions.

The movement for greater case management has run in parallel with more focus on case settlement. One dimension is that case management orders can lead to litigants evaluating whether it is better to settle the case. Having the

[54] *Stubbs v The Queen* [2018] UKPC 30, [2019] AC 868 [17] (PC, The Bahamas); p. 98 above.

parties define the issues at an early stage is one way this occurs. Conducting case management conferences which fix the steps to trial is another. The judge simply setting the trial date may concentrate the minds of the parties as to whether to continue to trial. A second dimension is more direct, with case management orders which are directly concerned with facilitating settlement. There is a twin-tracked approach to this as recognized in the Civil Procedure Rules for England and Wales, first, the judge ordering, encouraging, and facilitating alternative dispute resolution (ADR) and secondly, the judge helping the parties to settle the whole or part of the case.[55]

Referring cases to ADR

In the United States judges have actively promoted settlements since at least the 1970s, by referring cases to court-annexed mediation or settlement programmes, which in different forms exist throughout US courts. The judges may undertake the mediation process although, if they do, they may then have to disqualify themselves from further involvement in the case because of the conflict of interest which might arise. A common rationale for promoting settlement is 'the familiar axiom that a bad settlement is almost always better than a good trial'.[56] Since with mediation and conciliation the parties will have had a hand in the outcome, it is also said that they are more likely to be satisfied and adhere to any obligations under a settlement agreement. Other jurisdictions have emulated the US experience and in various guises adopted court-annexed settlement programmes.

Judges referring cases to ADR has had a more chequered history in England and Wales. Lord Woolf's inquiry into Access to Justice in the 1990s gave a boost to the practice, encouraging its use in appropriate circumstances, while not recommending that it be compulsory.[57] As a result, judges used their power under the new rules to order costs when a party refused to mediate. There was a reaction against this when, in 2004, the Court of Appeal said that a judge could not order compulsory mediation since this would breach the right of access to the courts enshrined in article 6 of the European Convention on Human Rights.[58] Following this decision, judges ordered temporary stays to give the parties breathing space to settle proceedings voluntarily, or to narrow the issues by mediation or some other form of

[55] CPR 1.4(2)(e)(f). See also ELI/UNIDROIT Model European Rules of Civil Procedure, r 10(3), Commentary (hereafter ELI/UNIDROIT Model Rules).
[56] *In re Warner Communications Securities Litigation* 618 F Supp 735, 740 (SDNY 1985).
[57] *Access to Justice Interim Report* (1995) 136.
[58] *Halsey v Milton Keynes General NHS Trust* [2004] EWCA Civ 576, [2004] 1 WLR 3002.

ADR.[59] Then in 2023 the Court of Appeal changed tack and held that compulsory ADR was not in breach of article 6—it would pause, but not prevent, access to the courts—an approach incorporated in the Civil Procedure Rules. Under this approach a judge has discretion to order ADR if they consider that it is proportionate to achieving the legitimate aim of settling a dispute fairly, quickly, and at reasonable cost.[60]

Among the factors which the judge may regard as relevant in exercising this discretion are the form of ADR being considered; whether the parties are legally assisted; whether ADR is likely to be effective; whether it is clear to the parties that, if they do not settle, they are free to pursue their case; the urgency of the case and the reasonableness of the delay involved in going to ADR; its cost; the prospect of success; the balance of power between the parties; the reasons against ADR; and the reasonableness and proportionality of any sanction in the event that a party declines ADR.[61] In referring cases to ADR, judges will also be concerned about the suitability, quality, independence, and ethical standards of the ADR to which the parties will have recourse, and whether it can guarantee matters such as an equality of arms between the parties, non-pressured settlements, and trained and sensitive decision makers.[62]

Concerns remain about judges referring cases to ADR, especially mandatory ADR. The first relates to the private interests of the parties, that the resulting settlement may have no relationship to what a party would obtain at law. If undertaken at the early stage, it may be difficult to know the strength of a party's case or the proper value of a claim. Instead of having their cases tried by a judge on the merits, parties may capitulate to what is regarded as the pressure to settle, even if that pressure is unspoken. On the other hand, settlement may mean receiving quicker redress at less cost than if a case proceeded to trial, although it is wasteful for the parties if a judge mandates ADR in cases which in any event are likely to settle, or those where the chance of settlement is remote, for example a point of principle is involved. There is also the advantage for a party of finality and closure if ADR is successful. As to outcome, it is difficult to compare the quality of settlement and adjudication

[59] *Unwired Planet International Ltd v Huawei Technologies (UK) Co Ltd* [2020] UKSC 37, [2021] 1 All ER 1141 [99].

[60] *Churchill v Merthyr Tydfil CBC* [2023] EWCA Civ 1416, [2024] 1 WLR 3827. See CPR 1.1(2)(f), 1.4(2)(e), 3.1(2)(o), 28.7(d), 28.14(f).

[61] ibid [61], [66] (Sir Geoffrey Vos MR).

[62] *The Relationship between Formal and Informal Justice: The Courts and Alternative Dispute Resolution* (European Law Institute and the European Network of Councils for the Judiciary 2018) 9–11 ('Statement of European Best Practice').

outcomes when parties may rationally choose what might be a sub-optimal outcome through settlement, because of the uncertainties, time taken, and cost if there is a trial.

Secondly, there are concerns that settlements through ADR deny public interests. Open justice and accountability are two public interests. ADR occurs in private, no public judgment or reasons are given, and there is no appeal. On the other hand it could be said that the parties' consent validates any settlement if it is freely given. Parties are not obliged to pursue a case to trial; they have always been able to withdraw on making suitable arrangements. Perhaps the most important public interest is if there is less law creation through diverting cases away from the courts to ADR. Instead of the public, reasoned resolution of disputes by judges giving force to the values embodied in law, referring cases to settlement downgrades civil justice. Closely associated with this criticism is what has been termed the phenomenon of the 'vanishing trial', in other words a lower proportion of civil cases proceeding to judgment and precedent creation. In England and Wales, despite the fall off in civil trials—which seems to have levelled off in the early years of the twenty-first century—the number of appellate court judgments has increased and hence the bank of precedent cases. Moreover, referring a case to ADR is one way to advance the public interest of 'freeing court resources for other cases'.[63]

The 'settlement judge'

A judge's involvement in promoting settlement can occur in various ways. At one level a judge may simply suggest that the parties settle based on the evidence and arguments available at different points in the process. The parties may be before the judge for case management purposes, or on an application by one or both parties. At the next level, judges may use their case management and other powers at both the pre-trial and trial phases to promote settlement. These powers may enable a judge to leverage settlement when fixing the timetable to trial, ruling on various interlocutory matters, setting the time available at hearings, and managing the trial itself. At a third level, judges may actively pursue settlements. Where this occurs judges develop different styles and use a variety of soft and hard power to that end. Settlement conferences are a familiar feature of US courts, where in broad terms judges offer a non-binding evaluation of the legal merits to modulate the parties'

[63] *Mionis v Democratic Press SA* [2017] EWCA Civ 1194, [2018] QB 662 [89] (Sharp LJ).

expectations. In some US state courts judges hold 'settlement weeks', where they convene numerous settlement conferences to hammer out resolutions. Mediation is also possible, which begins with a joint initial session, followed by the parties separating, and the judge assuming the role of intermediary. Judges may assist in drafting a settlement agreement.

Other jurisdictions have followed the US lead. The ELI/UNIDROIT Model European Rules of Civil Procedure permit judges to become actively involved in settlement attempts including mediating between the parties.[64] In contemplating that in a judicial mediation the judge may receive information in the absence of one of the parties, the Model Rules provide that in this situation the judge should not hear the case if it goes to trial because of the possibility of bias.[65] The higher judiciary in England and Wales have not generally promoted settlements in civil cases in the same overt manner. The Winn committee rejected formal settlement conferences presided over by a judge, since they could result in a judge without knowledge of the facts or evidence, pressing the parties to reach an inappropriate compromise. Moreover, the committee considered that settlement conferences could cause delay and increase the cost of litigation.[66] The Woolf inquiry steered away from recommending direct judicial involvement in facilitating settlement, although it recommended experimenting with the non-binding judicial mini-trial of Alberta and British Columbia, where judges give an early evaluation of the merits.[67] As a result, the post-Woolf Civil Procedure Rules provide for early neutral evaluations by a judge.[68] In practice this is not often used, perhaps because of the cost and delay associated with it.[69]

For reasons similar to those touched on earlier, the notion of judges actively promoting case settlement has not escaped criticism. Three aspects deserve attention. One concerns judicial resources and ability. A judge's time and effort will have been wasted if in any event a case will settle (as many do), or if the judge lacks the aptitude (facilitating settlement is not necessarily part of a judge's repertoire or interests). The response to this point would be to caution judges to concentrate their efforts, and for the need for learning, as with the adjudicative function itself. Another aspect is judicial impartiality, and how that can be threatened when a judge becomes an active promoter of

[64] ELI/UNIDROIT Model Rules (n 55) r 10(3).
[65] ibid r 10(4).
[66] *Report of the Committee on Personal Injuries Litigation* (Cmnd 3691, 1968) paras 353–355.
[67] *Access to Justice Interim Report* (n 57) 142.
[68] CPR 3.1(2)(p).
[69] eg, *Lomax v Lomax* [2019] EWCA Civ 1467, [2019] 1 WLR 6527.

settlement. The answer would be that any threat to judicial impartiality can be addressed by judicial recusal under the accepted principles discussed in Chapter 2.[70] Perhaps the most important aspect is whether in stepping outside the judicial role of adjudicating cases, the 'settlement judge' threatens the legitimacy and dignity of the institution. Instead of adjudication, the judge performs the different (and in the view of some critics, less elevated) function of problem-solver. While this concern cannot be completely discounted, the counter-argument would be that the judicial role, especially in the modern age, stretches beyond adjudication. Case management is one example, assisting litigants in person another. Settlement promotion, with the cloak of authority of the Civil Procedure Rules, would be another.

IV Leadership and Collegiality

Judicial leadership is not confined to presiding in court but may include responsibility for a court's general operations, albeit that many tasks will be delegated. To varying degrees chief justices and other judges in leadership positions have long done this, but in the modern era the burdens of administration on them have increased. The background and experiences of judges do not necessarily equip them for the quite different tasks of leadership and administration. Related to leadership is collegiality. Leadership judges may foster collegiality in an effort to further a court's morale, enhance its decision-making, and project a positive image to the world. Collegiality is not the same as friendship or fellowship.

(A) Leadership

Judicial leadership can be categorized as jurisprudential, administrative, and institutional. Jurisprudential leadership is perhaps the most important, in ensuring that the law responds to the community's needs. Jurisprudential leadership has various manifestations. Much written about is where the presiding judge of a country's highest court has the skills to persuade colleagues that in a significant, usually constitutional case, a unanimous (or near unanimous) judgment is necessary to enhance its authority and impact. A well-known

[70] *Southwark LBC v Jiminez* [2003] EWCA Civ 502, [2003] ICR 1176.

example is the leadership of Chief Justice Warren of the US Supreme Court in avoiding dissents or concurring opinions in the anti-segregation case of *Brown v Board of Education*,[71] drawing on skills he refined as governor of California. In the UK, in the important constitutional decision *Miller I*[72]—where the UK Supreme Court upheld the Divisional Court that Parliament (and not the executive) needed to authorize notice to the EU of the UK's withdrawal under the Treaty on European Union—the then president of the court (Lord Neuberger) used his collegial style to nudge his colleagues to sit *en banc*, and then for the eight/three majority to agree a single judgment.[73] Brexit also gave rise to *Miller II*, where the president and deputy president of the court (Lady Hale and Lord Reed) prepared the judgment agreed to by all eleven justices regarding the unlawfulness of proroguing Parliament just prior to Brexit.[74] There are similar examples of jurisprudential leadership in other jurisdictions, where significant constitutional or social issues were dealt with in a unanimous judgment.[75]

Jurisprudential leadership may extend beyond single decisions to the generality of a court's jurisprudence. This may be exhibited where the presiding judge is regularly in the majority and delivers a high proportion of judgments, with which the others agree. That suggests a presiding judge able to bring colleagues into a coalition so that the court as an institution speaks with a clear voice. Another type of jurisprudential leadership is where the presiding judge persuades colleagues to adopt particular jurisprudential approaches, although this depends as well on the ideological affinity of the judges and the length of service of the presiding judge. In the United States, scholars associate Supreme Court eras with the name of the relevant chief justice, for example 'the Warren Court', which is associated with a caselaw expanding individual constitutional rights and the 'Rehnquist court', to describe a jurisprudence of greater judicial restraint. This US categorization of Supreme Court eras by the chief justice illustrates that a court's jurisprudence during a period does not necessarily flow solely or mainly from their own work. Warren CJ had instinctive qualities of leadership, and goals consistent with

[71] 347 US 483 (1954).

[72] *R (on the application of Miller) v Secretary of State for Exiting the European* Union [2017] UKSC 5, [2018] AC 61 (hereafter *Miller I*).

[73] Alan Paterson, 'Creating a Group Oriented Supreme Court–Lord Neuberger's Legacy' (2021) 28 Int'l J Leg Profession 107.

[74] *R (on the application of Miller) v Prime Minister* [2019] UKSC 41, [2020] AC 373 (hereafter *Miller II*).

[75] eg, *Cole v Whitfield* [1988] HCA 18, (1988) 165 CLR 360; *Reference re Senate Reform* [2014] 1 SCR 704; *Justice KS Puttaswamy (Retd) v Union of India* (2017) 10 SCC 1, AIR 2017 SC 4161.

the dominant spirit of the time, but he lacked intellectual weight. That in the Warren Court derived largely from other justices, notably William Brennan. Both Warren and Brennan shared the same overall goals, but Brennan was often responsible for the opinions giving expression to them, and for forging a block of supporting justices.

In Britain presiding judges of the apex court have provided jurisprudential leadership in a variety of ways. Lord Reid and Lord Bingham were outstanding senior law lords: Lord Reid in the 1960s and early 1970s led moves bringing common law doctrines in line with the times and furthering judicial review; Lord Bingham in the 2000s oversaw the successful incorporation of the European Convention on Human Rights into domestic law. Both Reid and Bingham led through their intellectual ability to identify and analyse the issues in a case, which when stated was frequently accepted as correct by a majority or the whole of the court. Both relied on the power of their reasoning in conference and in their draft judgments. They led by example and would not otherwise attempt to persuade their colleagues. That contrasts with another senior law lord, Lord Diplock, who would lobby other judges about the correctness of his view. Diplock might decide the case before hearing it, write his judgment before the hearing was complete, and then persuade his colleagues to agree with a mesmeric ability.[76]

In exercising jurisprudential leadership, judges employ a variety of techniques. Knowing the predispositions of colleagues to the subject matter of a case, a leadership judge may choose the judge or judges to hear it.[77] At the pre-hearing stage, a presiding judge may lead the panel in deciding that one or more points either are preliminary and should be dealt with as such; are weak, so counsel need not address them; or alternatively, are the nub of the case, on which the argument should concentrate. During the hearing a presiding judge may be able to set the agenda with colleagues, and guide counsel's submissions in directions favouring their view of the issues. During the post-hearing conference, as in the US Supreme Court, a chief justice may be the first to speak, so steering the discussion in a particular direction. By contrast the convention in the UK Supreme Court (as previously in the House of Lords) and in the English Court of Appeal is that deference is minimized at the post-hearing conference if initial positions are stated with the most junior judge beginning, then proceeding up the order of seniority to

[76] Garry Sturgess and Philip Chubb, *Judging the World: Law and Politics in the World's Leading Courts* (Butterworths 1988) 275 (interview with Lord Wilberforce).

[77] P. 29 above.

the presider. Finally, with the judgment, there may be the power to allocate the writing of the lead judgment: in the US Supreme Court that lies with the chief justice if in the majority. In the UK Supreme Court, the presiding justice may decide to allocate the lead judgment to themselves.

The impact of judicial leadership through the use of tools like case assignment and the allocation of judgment writing in a multi-member panel can be mitigated by convention and the context in which a court operates. The result may be that these amount to little in driving the analysis in particular cases, or the jurisprudence of the court as a whole. Presiding judges may be able to allocate judges to specific cases, but the practice of doing this to achieve a particular result may be widely deprecated. If a court comprises judges with a strong character, unafraid to assert their own views, it is unlikely that a presiding judge will be able to control the agenda. In any event, persuading colleagues involves a range of social skills, such as a willingness to compromise. A presiding judge may not have or be willing to exercise these skills. The power to allocate judgment writing may be bound by convention favouring a fair allocation among colleagues of lead judgment writing. Even if a presiding judge writes the single or majority judgment for the court, they may need to narrow their analysis or weaken it to enlist their colleagues' continued support for their draft.

Turning from jurisprudential to administrative leadership we see that, broadly speaking, there are two facets. The first concerns the narrow task of administration in support of decision-making. That includes allocating cases and tasks to individual judges, deciding on the composition of panels and other issues affecting multi-judge courts, and ensuring that adequate time is available for judgment writing. The second facet of administrative leadership is the wider operation of a specific court or courts. Part of this is maintaining and improving judicial performance and ensuring the satisfaction and welfare of colleagues. In the case of some chief justices, leadership will extend to the whole judicial branch.[78] As well as strategic guidance for all the judiciary, there will be a responsibility (at least in part) for matters such as judicial training and welfare, judicial discipline, and the judges' working conditions. This cannot be undertaken alone, and tasks will be devolved to other leadership judges. Against a background of judicial independence, judicial leadership is far removed from leadership as command. Since leadership judges, with a background in advocacy, may not have led organizations previously,

[78] eg, Constitutional Reform Act 2005, s 7(1) (chief justice head of judiciary of England and Wales).

skills will be imparted to potential leaders through the delegation of tasks and as part of judicial training. There is a broader context of administrative leadership in the judiciary's composition and workings. In some cases this may be a formal power based in statute as where leadership judges have a defined role in appointments.

Finally, there is institutional leadership, which concerns protecting and enhancing institutional values such as judicial independence, impartiality, and integrity, along with public confidence in the courts and the judges. Institutional leadership is on public display in the regular dealings of judicial leaders with parliament, the executive, the media, foreign judiciaries, and more broadly the public. As with jurisprudential leadership, judges other than those with formal positions may emerge as de facto leaders in distinct areas of judicial activity or perhaps as role models. Institutional leadership is both inward and outward looking. Each requires different skills. Internally, leadership judges need to build institutional values through a range of measures designed to facilitate open justice and accountability, procedural reform and efficiency, and a more representative and responsive judiciary. Much outward facing institutional leadership entails judges participating in professional and public gatherings, interacting with political authorities, and making contact with foreign judiciaries. These activities will generally concern the legal issues of the day—access to justice, law reform, and diversity in judicial appointments are examples. More broadly, judges' speeches and activities in the community and internationally are designed to explain the nature of judicial power, build public support, and promote the importance of an independent judiciary.[79]

(B) Collegiality

Judges work in a social organization, a court or related courts, and the degree to which they cooperate will vary with the history, practices, size, personnel, and even geography of the court(s). Judicial leadership has a role. Personality obviously enters. So does the institutional setting, since matters like the distribution of resources, the assignment of cases, promotion processes, and the allocation of non-judicial benefits and tasks can all have a bearing on the collegial culture. Collegial practices need not threaten judicial

[79] On the limits see p. 135 above.

independence: collaboration can enhance the quality of a court's decision-making. Collegiality can be analysed in various ways. A threefold division is collegiality as civility, collegiality as collaboration in the efficient operation of a court, and collegiality in judicial decision-making.

First, collegiality as civility means judges behaving respectfully to each other. As in other walks of life, there will be those with inflated notions of their work or worth, those who vent personal or other displeasure, and those simply careless of the feelings of others. In the US Supreme Court the combative language of justices regarding the judgments of other justices is notorious. Ideological division has now infected judging beyond the Supreme Court, as it has elsewhere in society, and the consequences for civility are evident in some judgments.[80] Judges are not obliged to like their colleagues, although in many cases will. Judges will (and should) disagree with each other as to the fabric and application of the law; in the long term a judiciary where conformity reigns cannot be conducive to a healthy jurisprudence. But there are ways of dealing with disagreements over the outcome of a particular case, the shape of legal doctrine, or personal animosities which are not destructive of a judiciary's reputation in the public eye, or which threaten the integrity of its decision-making.

A context where civility is especially important is with appeals. Through their judgments appellate judges can corrode the morale of judges whose decisions are being appealed, and impair mutual respect between courts. The judge appealed will not be present or represented to explain the judgment and how it was affected by defects in the way the appellant's arguments were advanced, or the pressures they were under for reasons outside the case. In the ordinary run of cases, civility means that the approach of the appellate judge will be to temper criticism of the judge below. There is certainly no call for personally offensive remarks. Appellate judges need to remind themselves about judging at the coalface (if they experienced it), or in a busy intermediate appellate court. There is also the danger of a higher court choking off beneficial legal developments with the dead hand of self-satisfied conformity.

Secondly, collegiality as collaboration recognizes that judges must work collaboratively, if a court is to be efficient and successful in undertaking its basic task of timeously deciding cases. At one level judges share information, opinions, and expertise. For example, a judge may seek an off the cuff view from a colleague as to whether in particular circumstances they should

[80] Just one example: *New York v US Department of Justice* 964 F 3d 150 (2d Cir 2020).

recuse themselves, or a judge relatively unfamiliar with an area of law might seek the assistance of a specialist judge as to where they should focus their attention or seek useful commentary. At another level collegiality as collaboration is the extent to which judges cover for each other in the interests of the institution, for example, when one is ill or hard pressed with outstanding judgments or other commitments. As in other walks of life fairness limits the extent to which a judge can be expected to undertake too many of the burdens of another judge in addition to their own work, especially if without others joining in to help.

Thirdly, collegiality in decision-making is especially pertinent when judges sit in panels. It is an extension of collaboration. It is said by its proponents that collegiality in this context creates the conditions for principled agreement among judges by allowing for courteous deliberation in an attempt to reach consensus on the best decision in a case.[81] In practice, collegiality in decision-making operates with differing degrees of formality. Informality is characteristic of collegiality in the Supreme Court of India, where nearly all judgments are unanimous, with dissents and concurring opinions being unusual, even with five-judge benches hearing the more difficult cases. Suggested explanations for this are that Supreme Court judges are appointed by the court itself, meaning that all members of the bench are likely to have a broadly similar outlook, and the strong convention that junior judges defer to more senior judges. There is also the very practical consideration that the high workload of the court leaves little time to prepare dissents or concurring judgments. Near the other end of the spectrum have been some US Courts of Appeals, where formal internal methods have been designed to promote collective decision-making, beyond deliberations between the judges. These have included ensuring each judge sits with every other judge on a regular basis, not using visiting judges absent a grave emergency, strict time limits within which judges must comment on the draft opinion of the lead judge or prepare a separate opinion, early circulation of opinions to the entire court so all judges are kept abreast of its work, and organized professional and social activities.

The English Court of Appeal and the UK Supreme Court seem to fall along this spectrum of formality. At one time judges in these courts heard cases without much if any pre-reading and then delivered their judgments seriatim without formal discussion about the details of the other judges' reasoning.

[81] eg, Harry T Edwards, 'The Effects of Collegiality on Judicial Decision Making' (2003) 151 U Pa LR 1639.

Now in the Court of Appeal there will be discussion at both a pre- and post-hearing conference. If all judges agree as to outcome the judge designated by the presiding judge as the lead judge will prepare the draft judgment, and the judges will then negotiate any changes of expression or substance to the draft. Typically, when the lead judgment is handed down, the other judges will simply state their agreement. Dissents are unusual; the pressure of work is an important reason for this. Judges usually sit in panels of three for three-week periods, which enables a fair allocation of work and draws on the different expertise of the judges on the panel. The process of collaboration in the UK Supreme Court is broadly similar to that in the Court of Appeal: a post-hearing conference, assignment by the presiding judge of judgment writing (maybe to themselves), and negotiations and compromises over its expression and substance. At the conference all the judges are expected to give a substantial opinion on the case.

Collegiality does not imply that judges are not above attempting to have their way with the outcome of a case or its reasoning. Most straightforward is when judges rely on argument in conference, a memorandum, or a draft judgment. The experience in the House of Lords and the UK Supreme Court has been that some judges have used more energetic techniques to persuade colleagues. A draft judgment in advance of the lead judgment has been one, although that can generate irritation, as well as giving the writer of the lead judgment the opportunity to meet the opposing arguments in their own draft. Another technique has been overt lobbying, but that can generate counter-lobbying. In addition, it may be futile if the lobbyist is renowned for being reluctant themselves to yield to attempts at persuasion. Lord Neuberger's leadership skills in the UK Supreme Court were collegial: he would appear hesitant and open to persuasion, and on occasions would support the majority judgment to make it more solid as a precedent. His overall goal was to enhance goodwill internally and the standing of the court externally.[82]

V Judgments

Judges explain their decisions in their judgments ('opinions' in the Privy Council, US courts). In this way judgments perform important functions. In the main judges are not writing for the general public although in publishing

[82] Paterson (n 73).

their judgments they make them available for all to read. In apex courts, and with high profile matters, the practice has developed of publishing summaries of judgments, possibly prepared by judicial assistants, for easier digestion by the profession, the press, and the public when they are handed down.

(A) Reasons for Reasons

Judgments perform an important function of accountability for the power judges exercise.[83] As well there are related considerations behind the duty on judges to give a reasoned justification for their decisions. These considerations are partly instrumental. The first is to facilitate challenges to a judge's decision. This might be through the avenue of an appeal. If the outcome is unexplained the parties will not know why they have won or lost, or whether they have a basis for an appeal. An aspect of this is fairness: without reasons the losing party can be deprived of an appeal, unless permission to appeal can be given on the basis that there are no (or no adequate) reasons. Another aspect is to prevent resources being spent on fruitless appeals. Secondly, reasons demonstrate that the judge has taken the parties' arguments into account and not acted arbitrarily. In particular, reasons may render a decision more acceptable to an unsuccessful party.[84] The fact that the judge has addressed the evidence, arguments, and submissions which they have advanced demonstrates a respect for them. A corollary is that a judge should not be deciding a case based on considerations of which the parties are not aware, or which are irrelevant to the legal issues.

A third 'reason for reasons' is their educative effect. 'Through reasoned decisions', said Binnie J in the Supreme Court of Canada, 'members of the general public become aware of rules of conduct applicable to their future activities'.[85] Planning can occur on that basis: judgments function to enable lawyers to advise their clients as to how to conduct their activities, structure their transactions, or, if necessary, litigate. More generally, reasons enable the public to see that justice is done impartially and with integrity. In this way judgments serve community interests. Fourthly, reasons can enhance decision-making. Preparing a reasoned judgment concentrates the mind

[83] PP. 52–53 above.
[84] *Osborn v Parole Board* [2013] UKSC 61, [2014] AC 1115 [70] (Lord Reed), referring to empirical evidence.
[85] *R v Sheppard* [2002] 1 SCR 869 [22].

and can result in a better justification of a decision, if not the decision itself. A fifth 'reason for reasons' is that they better enable the law's development. Decisions not only resolve disputes but also have a forward-looking character. Reasons encourage consistency in judicial decision-making and further equality before the law. In common law systems reasons perform an additional function, since the system of precedent requires later courts to apply earlier authoritative judgments. As Sir George Jessel MR put it, 'where no reasons are given for a particular decision, it becomes extremely difficult for a Judge to follow it, because he does not know the principle on which the decision proceeded'.[86]

In their reasons judges must demonstrate that they have directed their mind to the important issues between the parties and how they have determined them.[87] It is a familiar mantra that reasons should enable the losing party to understand why they have lost. In fact readily understandable reasons are required for both winners and losers, and so that the public more generally can understand how a case was decided. The reasons following a trial must explain the judge's findings of fact, contain a statement of the relevant principles of law, and explain how the judge has applied these to the facts. A judgment must disclose the process of reasoning so that a party can assess whether the judge was in error. In the event of conflicting evidence, the judge will need to spell out why one party's evidence has been accepted. If the critical issue was one of fact, it may be enough to say that one witness was preferred to another because they had a clearer recollection of the material facts, or that the answers were more consistent with the documentary evidence.[88] With expert evidence the explanation may be that the evidence of one expert accorded more satisfactorily with facts found by the judge, or was more inherently credible than that of the other, or that that expert was better qualified, or manifestly more objective, than the other. Findings on credibility need an explanation in terms, say, of the (in)consistency of a witness's evidence with documentary or other evidence. A judge is under no duty to deal with every argument presented in support of a party's case: it is sufficient that the reasons given offer sufficient detail of the underlying principles and the basis for the decision on the crucial issues.

[86] *In re Merceron* (1877) 7 Ch 184, 187.
[87] *South Buckinghamshire DC v Porter* [2004] UKHL 33, [2004] 1 WLR 1953 [36].
[88] *English v Emery Reimbold & Strick Ltd* [2002] EWCA Civ 605, [2002] 1 WLR 2409 [19].

(B) Clarity, Structure, and Content

Clarity is a key virtue of good judgment writing so that the reasoning can be understood, whatever the jurisdiction or subject matter. The judgment must explain why one party has won and the other lost. Clarity has various dimensions, including plain language, direct and uncomplicated expression, manageable paragraphs, and the avoidance of cliches—the requirements of any good writing. Clarity is a virtue for each of the different audiences for a judgment. First, clarity enables a view to be taken by the losing party, whether it is worthwhile to appeal if there is still an avenue of appeal open. Even if it has won, on reading the judgment the successful party may learn of the need to tweak its practices in light of comments in the judgment. Secondly, clarity makes it easier for other judges to apply any relevant principle the judgment contains, for lawyers to advise their clients about it, for students learning the law, for academics and others wanting to understand it, and possibly for the government and legislature concerned with law reform. Thirdly, members of the public, unhappy at the outcome of a judgment, will be better enlightened about whether and how the law may be reformed to achieve the result they desire. That can then inform any campaign of law reform. In these various ways clarity contributes to open justice, which is a building block of judicial accountability.

Along with clarity is the need for a structured approach if a judgment is to explain, persuade, and have the requisite certainty, especially if lawmaking is involved by the enunciation in it of legal principle. The reader must be able to follow the logic of the analysis. From the late twentieth century common law judgments began using paragraph numbering and headings as an aid to understanding. Few common law judgments outside the US follow the penchant there for footnotes, apart from case and statutory citations, and certainly not for footnotes containing important propositions of law, such as the famous footnote 4 in the US Supreme Court's decision in *United States v Carolene Products Company*, which said that the court would apply stricter scrutiny of laws aimed at 'discrete and insular minorities'.[89] In broad terms the judgment will likely have an introduction, identify the issues, set out the facts, discuss the legal principles to be applied, and contain a summary of the parties' submissions, all culminating in the crucial analysis of why the judge reaches their result, to put it in simple terms, by applying the law to the facts.

[89] 304 US 144 (1938).

Within these parameters of the judgecraft required is a certain amount of contested territory. There is limited support for stating the result at the outset, since that would circumvent what could be some complex analysis to reach it. Setting out the issue(s) to be decided in the introduction attracts pronounced favour, along with some scene-setting about the origins of the dispute. While the first instance judge will need to address all these issues in the course of the judgment, the principle of judicial economy may confine an appellate court to determining only those issues which it considers dispositive of the appeal. This promotes judicial efficiency and ensures that pronouncements on contested issues of law are limited to those that have the status of precedent.[90] A disappointment for a judge being appealed can be that, having in the view of the appellate court analysed five, say, of the issues correctly, they are regarded as falling short on the sixth issue, which hardly featured in the case advanced before them.

As to the facts there will usually be an account, albeit concise, of the background facts. Key features of the evidence, written and oral, will usually be delineated, together with findings of fact. On each issue reasons must be given as to why the principal relevant evidence is accepted or rejected, in particular if there is apparently compelling evidence contrary to the judge's proposed conclusion.[91] Evaluation might also involve the judge explaining why, on the evidence as a whole, more or less weight is given to key features relied on by the parties.[92] Findings on credit may bear on the major issues in dispute, and are commonly given separate treatment, although if relevant to single issues may be conveniently dealt with at that point. The English judge is reluctant to make findings of dishonesty against a witness and will simply indicate that they prefer one person's evidence over another's, giving reasons for this (for example, documentary support; inherent probabilities).[93]

Practice differs about whether to set out each side's case on the dipositive issues. Judicial economy suggests that outlining the party's case which on any issue fails is sufficient, along with the reasoning which the judge has for rejecting it. Those reasons may reflect the submissions of the other side. Especially against a background of caseload pressures, judges may adopt them as their own, especially when giving an *ex tempore* judgment. Copying is a long-standing practice; it is a mistake to regard it as plagiarism.

[90] *Boensch v Pascoe* [2019] HCA 49, 268 CLR 593 [7]–[8], [101].
[91] *Simetra Global Assets Ltd v Ikon Finance* (n 9) [46].
[92] *Re B (A Child)(Adequacy of Reasons)* [2022] EWCA Civ 407, [2022] 4 WLR 42 [59]–[60].
[93] Bingham (n 11) 15.

Attribution in the academic, artistic, and scientific spheres does not apply to reasons for judgment: 'The judge' said McLachlin CJ for the Supreme Court of Canada on one occasion, 'is not expected to be original.'[94] In many cases the parties will have thought about their case over what will generally have been a lengthier period than the judge. It is not, of itself, bad practice for a judge, having decided that the arguments of one side in relation to an issue are to be preferred, to also decide that they have been expressed in terms which cannot be improved upon, and which can therefore be incorporated, with acknowledgement, in their judgment.[95] However, the reasonable person reading a judgment must be able to conclude that the judge has engaged with the critical issues in an independent and impartial manner. The threshold for any challenge is high, although the safer course is to explain in the judge's own words how the issues have been analysed, and the reasons for rejecting one side's case.

Against this background of the need for the judge in their judgment to focus on relevant issues, to evaluate the evidence, and to set out the reasoning for their conclusions, it is no surprise that long deprecated has been the judgment containing a lengthy recitation of the evidence, the parties' submissions, and long quotations from precedents, especially if followed by a brief conclusion that judgment for one side inevitably follows (or words to that effect).[96] A related issue is the lengthy judgment, which also gives rise to criticism. There is no doubt that judgments have increased in length, especially compared with a time when the facts were decided by juries, so did not need a lengthy explanation. Reasons for longer judgments are increased complexity and features of legal and social change. Since matters are open to varying approaches and interpretations, fuller explanations and analysis are required. There are also more mundane explanations for long judgments, such as the first instance judge covering issues at length to avoid criticism by a higher court, the judge new to an area, learning for a first time its underlying legal principles by writing, and the pressure of time which preclude editing the text into something more concise and rigorous. Some courts have provided for short form judgments in cases which raise no issue of principle, and where the facts are not in dispute.[97]

[94] *Cojocaru v British Columbia Women's Hospital and Health Centre* [2013] 2 SCR 357, 357, DLR (4th) 585 [65].

[95] *Ramnarine v Ramnarine* [2013] UKPC 27 (PC, Trinidad & Tobago) [13].

[96] See *Hariram Bhambhi v Satyanarayan* [2021] 8 SCR 855 [23] (Dr DY Chandrachud J).

[97] eg, Supreme Court Act 1970 (NSW), s 45(4).

(C) Style

Style is concerned not with the substance of a judgment but how it is expressed. As some writers have put it, style is anything in the judgment which cannot be paraphrased. Style can be characterized as the judge's 'voice'. It is part of the persuasive aspect of the judgment, seeking to convince the reader of the correctness of the conclusion. There are both individual and institutional dimensions to style. Historically in the common law the tradition has been one of individuality. At one time judgments were delivered by judges orally either on the spot (*ex tempore*) or read out later. That has led to individual judges expressing themselves in various ways. With written judgments, different judges convey substance with varying sentence structure, grammar, vocabulary, paragraphing, formality, and complexity. Judges also differ in the extent to which ideas are simplified, quotations from precedents and statutory material summarized, and epigrams, metaphors, and other literary devices employed (although the pressure of work precludes most judges from employing literary embellishments).

Judgment style has been classified along various lines. In 1925 Cardozo identified six judicial styles, in summary the magisterial, laconic, conversational, refined, persuasive, and 'tonsorial or agglutinative'.[98] Karl Llewellyn contrasted the formal style of the late nineteenth-century judgment—an authoritative statement of propositions and logical reasoning leading to an inevitable conclusion—with the grand style represented by judges such as Lord Mansfield and Judge Cardozo, who addressed social needs and related the law to them in their reasoning.[99] Templeman LJ used three categories for judges and their judgments, the philosopher, the scientist, and the advocate, and associated each with some of his contemporaries.[100] Chief Judge Richard Posner contrasted pure and impure styles of judgment writing.[101] The pure style is solemn and highly polished, uses technical legal terms, quotes heavily from precedents, avoids levity, conceals the author's personality, prefers familiar and ready-made formulations to novelties, and conforms closely to professional expectations about the structure and style of a judgment. The

[98] Benjamin N Cardozo, 'Law and Literature' in Margaret E Hall (ed), *Selected Writings of Benjamin Nathan Cardozo* (Fallon Law Book Co 1947) 342.

[99] Karl N Llewellyn, *The Common Law Tradition: Deciding Appeals* (Little, Brown 1960) 36–39, 465–66.

[100] Quoted by Justice Michael Kirby, 'On the Writing of Judgments' (1990) 64 ALJ 691, 696.

[101] Richard Posner, 'Judges' Writing Styles (And Do They Matter)' (1995) 62 U Chi L 1421, 1426–30.

impure judicial stylist is the opposite, its users preferring to be conversational, writing for the ear rather than for the eye, and avoiding quotations from previous decisions so the judge can speak with their own tongue.

The direct style is a favourite of those teaching judgment writing. Judges should write like journalists, the lesson runs, for an audience including nonlawyers. Afterall, it is said, judgments have the public as their ultimate audience. In this teaching, this requires short sentences, or if there are to be long sentences these are to be constructed cumulatively so that there are frequent points of closure marked by commas, which could be replaced by full stops. Judgments should avoid legal jargon and use basic syntax. A different type of direct style is displayed in the small number of judgments for children which explain the decisions affecting them. The judgment in *Re A: Letter to a Young Person*[102] is seminal, a custody dispute about the 14-year-old anonymized Sam. The opening lines are illustrative: 'Dear Sam . . . This case is about you and your future, so I am writing this letter as a way of giving my decision to you and to your parents.' There then follows in clear and concise terms the law the judge had to apply, his role, the issues, the matters he considered, and his decision.

There is some association of a judge's style with their approach to judging.[103] Legalism is generally connected with an abstract and complex style, the application of legal principle, and logical and rational analysis. As a 'merits judge' Lord Denning cultivated his distinctive, direct style to command the attention of readers, and to persuade them that his conclusion reflected the justice of the case.[104] Minimalist judges, who believe in deciding one case at a time, might set out concisely the relevant legal principles; the precedents from which they are derived and perhaps their rationale, but without lengthy (if any) discussion or quotation; reasoning with as much brevity and economy of language as possible; and a conclusion which those principles produce in the circumstances of the case. These different approaches to judging are abstract in character, and it is not suggested that any one judge invariably adopts one style. Judgment writing style may vary over a judge's career, indeed between judgments as the judge moves from giving judgment with a litigant in person, to a highly complex commercial or public law case. Individual style is hemmed in to the extent that the judge is writing a joint judgment or a judgment with which others have indicated they will

[102] [2017] EWFC 48 (Peter Jackson J).
[103] For different approaches to judging pp. 261–267 below.
[104] Lord Denning, *The Family Story* (Butterworths 1981) 216.

agree. The judge's characteristic style may be disrupted by the discordant amendments and additions which must be accepted to retain support for the judgment's substance.

As well as being individual to the common law judge, judicial style is also institutional. A court's history, culture, and location in the judicial hierarchy mould how decisions are expressed. There are at least two aspects about the institutional norms of common law courts relevant to style. First, they generally allow individual judicial styles in judgments. Within limits the judge is able to expresses the substance of a decision and its justification in their own way, possibly as a concurring or dissenting judgment. Elsewhere institutional norms dampen individual styles or eliminate them completely, as in courts such as the Court of Justice of the European Union where there is one judgment of the court, without concurrences or dissents, leading to a rigidity in style, resort to abstraction, but the authoritative voice of a court in a federal system. Secondly, the institutional norms of the common law court are that judgments are generally rooted in the circumstances of the case, rather than at a level of high principle, although flexibility enables discourse about the meaning and reach of legal principle and policy. The antithesis to this is the stereotypical French judgment, summarizing the parties' cases, followed by a list of shortly stated reasons, leading logically to the judicial ruling, all stated concisely, without dissent, and generally absent any discussion of alternative interpretations or underlying legal policy.

(D) Separate, Joint, and Dissenting Judgments

The approach to giving judgment in common law appellate courts varies with the practices and policies of the court, the presence (or absence) of dominant personalities, the sense of judicial individualism, and the pressure of work. There are a number of broad possibilities, with variations and overlap. One approach is for separate judgments, including concurring and dissenting judgments. Another is the joint judgment, where two or more judges agree on a judgment. Joint judgments represent either a collaborative or collectivist approach. The trend from separate to joint judgments has generated considerable controversy. The joint judgment is mainly justified in utilitarian terms, the demand by lawyers and others for greater clarity in the law which the joint judgment gives, the need for expedition in publishing the court's judgment, and the volume of work making separate judgments impractical (unless they are of the 'I agree' variety). The defence of separate judgments is more high-minded: each judge has a duty to state their own view of a case, and the pressure to issue joint opinions is subversive of judicial independence. Each of these approaches merits further attention.

First, separate judgments. Given consecutively, in order of the judge's seniority, they have been (and in some cases remain) the traditional common law approach in appellate courts. If judges do not agree on a draft beforehand, and give judgment *ex tempore*, separate judgments are more likely. That is also the case in the absence of a judge to whom the others are prepared to defer. In their separate judgments the judge may agree on outcome, but not entirely (if at all) with the reasoning of the others. These separate judgments may be concurrences or, if not, may still fall short of an outright dissent. Separate judgments are justified on the basis that the function of the court is to enunciate principle, and if there is only one judgment the tendency is to treat what is said as a hard and fast rule, indeed as if it were statute.[105] If each appellate judge gives their own reasons, the obvious risk is that there may be an absence of common principle, even among those who agree on the conclusion. That makes difficult the task for later courts to apply precedent, for lawyers to advise clients as to what the law demands, and for students in learning the law. On occasions, even if separate judgments are the norm, there may be an acceptance among the judges that clarity in relation to a point of law requires that the other judges simply agree with the lead judgment.

Secondly, the collaborative approach is represented by the joint majority judgment. One or more judges produce a judgment and other judges agree to put their name to it. So long as there is a majority, there is room for concurring and dissenting judgments, without this confusing the basis for the court's decision.[106] The joint judgment deals with the factual background and the case's history up to that point, so that there is no need for any concurring or dissenting judgment to cover the same ground at any length unless there is a disagreement about their significance. Pressure of work is an important reason for this type of collaborative approach, especially in intermediate appellate courts, since a judge will not have time to set out in writing their independent reasons for each case. Experience suggests, however, that even though a judge might agree with the conclusion set out in the joint judgment,

[105] *Cassell & Co Ltd v Broome* [1972] AC 1027, 1085 (Lord Reid).

[106] eg, *Stanford International Bank Ltd (In Liquidation) v HSBC Bank PLC* [2022] UKSC 34, [2023] AC 761 (Lady Rose gave the lead judgment, with whom Lord Hodge and Lord Kitchin agreed; Lord Leggatt gave a concurring judgment and Lord Sales dissented).

a different complexion to the case might have emerged, or inchoate reasons taken an unexpected shape, were separate judgments to have been prepared.

Thirdly, there is the collective judgment, where there is one judgment of the court as a whole, which is published as such. A collective judgment may be written by one, possibly two judges, and other judges will agree with it. The collective judgment is unusual, but may be given in cases involving the most controversial issues the court faces.[107] With a collective judgment different parts may be divided between the judges for writing. Typically, however, there will be a main author, with contributions from the other judges, suggestions for amendment of the text accepted (at least in modified form), and sometimes compromises as to both expression and substance. The main author may not necessarily be the driving force behind the legal analysis adopted. A collective judgment lends legitimacy to a result, as well as providing a clear precedent. Criticisms of collective judgments are that nuances of analysis are glossed over, the judges are not individually accountable for the court's judgment, less active members of the court can free ride on the work of others, and the main author may not attract personal recognition for their work.

The separate judgment takes its most pronounced form in the dissent. At the level of legal policy judges have justified the dissent: as an important aspect of judicial independence; as the possible orthodoxy of tomorrow through later decision or legislation; as enabling the public to see that there can be honest disagreement about the law and therefore to appreciate justice more generally; and as a safeguard of the integrity of judicial decision-making by keeping the majority accountable for their decision.[108] Where the law is in a process of change, dissent is also said to assist through the range of judicial views expressed. Although the notion of stifling dissents in civil law cases has little if any support in the common law world—as opposed to criminal law, where certainty is at a premium[109]—the case for dissents can be overstated. Despite important examples where dissents have later become the orthodoxy, these cases are rare. Instead of contributing to the law's development, persistent dissents in an apex court can have an unsettling effect

[107] See *Miller I* (n 72) and *Miller II* (n 74).

[108] Respectively Lord Nicholls, 'Foreword' in Neal Geach and Christopher Monaghan, *Dissenting Judgments in the Law* (Wildy, Simmonds and Hill Publishing 2012); Lord Bingham, 'What is the Law' (2009) 40 Victoria U Wellington LR 597, 607; Claire L'Heureux-Dube, 'The Dissenting Opinion: Voice of the Future' (2000) 38 Osgoode Hall LJ 495; Michael Kirby, 'Judicial Dissent' (2005) 12 James Cook ULR 4; and William J Brennan, 'In Defence of Dissents' (1986) 37 Hastings LJ 427, 430.

[109] cf Criminal Appeal Act 1907, s 1(5).

on legal development, rather than assisting it. Persistent dissents may also diminish a court's authority, especially if divisions are ideologically based.

At the level of practice dissenting is an accepted practice in common law apex courts, although the reality is that it is influenced by institutional commitment, personality, and social factors. Institutional factors weigh heavily for some judges. In noting how Justice Brandeis suppressed some of his dissents in the US Supreme Court, Judge Jerome Frank remarked on Brandeis's institutional commitment and belief that 'dissents and concurrences need to be saved for major matters if the Court is not to appear indecisive and quarrelsome'.[110] Institutional commitment also explains that, whatever their record previously in dissenting in a court, once in leadership positions judges dissent less because it may undermine the court's standing as well as their own leadership. As to personality, some judges feel duty bound to express their view as a matter of course by way of a dissent. On the other hand the barrier for other judges is high, dissenting only where an important matter of principle is at stake, or the dissenting judge regards the majority as badly wrong. The composition of the bench may also enter in the sense that, given different colleagues, a judge would not feel as impelled to dissent because there would be more agreement with the others.

Among the social factors in dissenting is that judges recognize that dissents can irritate colleagues, especially important if a judge is likely to be sitting with them for many years. As a practical matter, the cause of irritation may simply be the delay in finalizing the court's consideration of a case, waiting for the dissenter's judgment, especially if the delay may contribute to public criticism of the court as a whole. If a judge is to dissent, collegiality demands that it be civil and without self-indulgence and false heroics.[111] Compared with apex courts, dissents are less common in intermediate appellate courts because of collegiality, workloads, and a possible concern with giving guidance on the law to first instance judges. As well as fraying collegiality, Judge Posner refers to the bother and futility of dissenting in what he describes as 'dissent aversion' in intermediate appellate courts.[112] Depending on the court structure, however, a dissent in an intermediate appellate court may be a signal to the apex court that a matter is deserving of their attention,

[110] 'The Unpublished Opinions of Mr Justice Brandeis by Alexander M Bickel' (1957) 10 J Legal Educ 401, 404.

[111] Susan Kiefel, 'Judicial Courage and the Decorum of Dissent' [2017] Qld Leg YB 96.

[112] Richard Posner, *How Judges Think* (Harvard University Press 2008) 32.

so that they should grant permission to appeal should the disappointed party pursue the matter to the apex court.

VI Conclusion

Judgecraft is the art of judging. It encompasses the practical skills of good judging. In lower courts it can encompass applying established and simplified routines and intuitive decision-making to cope efficiently with the relentless stream of similar cases. For first instance judges it includes fact-finding, a key ingredient of judging. Here the social sciences have had a significant impact on judicial practice by casting doubt on the weight to be given to the demeanour of a witness or their recollection of past events or states of mind, when set alongside other evidence such as known facts and documentary evidence. Another skill is making decisions 'on the papers', without the benefit of an oral hearing. Although the common law world has not on the whole emulated the US, where in federal district courts and courts of appeals oral argument is rare, the inexorable trend has been to give primacy to writing over speech. Decision-making without an oral hearing represents a significant but largely hidden development in the common law, where oral argument has been thought to be central. Judgecraft in these circumstances demands giving careful and concise reasons in any decision 'on the papers'. That forces the judge to identify and address the issues, as well as to mitigate error arising from 'heuristics', the tendency to adopt mental shortcuts and rules of thumb in decision-making. Similar considerations apply to *ex tempore* judgments, which call for preparation, as well as an intense focus in their execution, not least to avoid careless remarks which reach the media. As with handling litigants in person, a capable performance in open court is imperative to ensure both fairness and the appearance of fairness.

Managerial judging focuses on handling a court's caseload. It encompasses case management and settlement skills. Both require the judge to exercise judgecraft which is removed from that needed in adjudication. While case management can be incorporated into the court's procedures for standard cases, with larger and more complex litigation judicial skills will be engaged to ensure that the parties identify the issues, and proceed to trial in an orderly and efficient manner. Whereas settlement was traditionally in the hands of the parties, court rules now authorize the judge actively to facilitate settlement. The major impetus for this has been the need for the efficient and proportionate use of scarce judicial resources. Assisting settlement can be effected in various ways. One is to refer selective cases to ADR. More intrusive approaches include the judge commenting on the respective merit of the parties' case, highlighting settlement options and potential remedies, and prodding the parties in the direction of what the judge regards as a reasonable settlement. Each demands a careful assessment of whether it is an appropriate course and leads to a just outcome in the particular case.

Perhaps the most important facet of judicial leadership is jurisprudential leadership, which is concerned with the future of the law and its ability to respond to the needs of a community. Jurisprudential leadership is exhibited in the intellectual power of a judge in deciding pivotal cases and possibly, in doing so, guiding the direction of a court's jurisprudence. In part jurisprudential leadership can involve one or more judges setting the tone for decision-making and other judges (or at least a majority) backing it. In part this relates to the skills of a jurisprudential leader in persuading colleagues to agree or adopt the same analysis. As to administrative leadership, one aspect is that judicial resources must be managed efficiently and distributed fairly and proportionately. All judges have a responsibility in this regard, but leadership judges have the additional tasks of securing adequate resources in the first place, and then ensuring that their overall use meets these goals. A third facet of leadership is institutional leadership, one aspect being setting the tone for a court's internal operation and integrating different judicial personalities into its work. As important is the role in the wider society of affirming and strengthening judicial values. In this context the leadership judge needs ambassadorial skills when engaging with the profession, the media, and civil society.

Aspects of collegiality are necessary for a court to work effectively. One facet of collegiality is civility. It is relatively straightforward and evident when judges treat each other with courtesy and respect. That applies internally within a court, as well as in the way an appellate court treats judges elsewhere in the judicial hierarchy. Collegiality as civility can require conscious effort and is an aspect of judgecraft. A second level of collegiality, which can be described as collaborative, concerns the degree to which judges are able to work together to advance institutional goals such as efficient decision-making internally, as well as public confidence in the judiciary as an institution. It can require judges to assume additional burdens for a temporary period when a colleague is ill or overwhelmed. Related to collaboration is thirdly, collegiality in decision-making. This is mainly of concern in courts hearing cases in panels. Collegiality in decision-making is partly process (getting the court to adopt collegial decisions), partly product (can the court produce judgments containing clearly enunciated principles), and partly impact (is confidence in a properly functioning institution being maintained in the eyes of the community).

That leads to a crucial aspect of judgecraft, the production in a timely manner of clear and coherent decisions and judgments. The clarity, structure, and content of a judgment influences whether it conveys to the parties, any appellate court, and the legal community that the judge has correctly reasoned to the right outcome. Clarity has various dimensions, one being plain language and expression, the requirements of any good writing. Judges vary, however, in how they express their judgments, summed up in the notion of judgment style—the way a judgment is written and the manner in which a judge expresses a decision. Various styles can be identified and illustrate the point about judicial difference. Finally, there is judgment writing in appellate courts, in particular the contested issue of whether judges should write separate judgments, including concurring and dissenting judgments, or contribute to a collective effort with others to produce a judgment of the court. Separate judgments arriving at the same outcome by different reasoning can produce uncertainty in the law, although this may assist in a developing area of law where different judgments can help identify a better course for legal principle. In practice, there will often be institutional norms in appellate courts for formal and informal discussion among judges. There is often a culture that judges are open to persuasion and that, following an iterative process, disagreements can be resolved and a judgment produced which a majority can support.

6
Decision-Making

I Introduction

In *The Nature of the Judicial Process*, Benjamin Cardozo addressed how judges make decisions.[1] In his view the process was difficult to describe, but it involved following previous decisions, ensuring the law's symmetry, custom, and a consideration of the judge's and common standards of justice and morals. The mix was regulated by possibly unarticulated and subconscious principles. In some cases the source of the law to be applied was obvious in legislation or the constitution, he said, although there might be gaps to be filled or doubts or ambiguities to be cleared up. Otherwise, one had resort to precedents, the juridical conceptions at the back of them, or the habits of life or institutions of the society from which they are derived.[2] In Cardozo's account there was also the human dimension to judging. As he put it, not only do judges possess 'subconscious loyalties' to different social groups, but there are other forces, deep below consciousness, 'the likes and the dislikes, the predilections and the prejudices, the complex of instincts and emotions and habits and convictions'.[3]

Cardozo's portrayal of the judicial process in the higher courts has wide appeal. As is now accepted, judicial decision-making is a creative process. It is also a process where, as Cardozo put it, instincts and emotions have a role. None of this means that judges are in unchartered waters, forever having to navigate new ways and using hunch and speculation on the voyage. Despite these other forces, law matters to judges in practical decision-making—the law contained in legislation and in relevant precedent cases. The bulk of judicial business, as Cardozo acknowledged, turns on the application of the law to the facts, not on controversies about the law. This is especially the case when judges are engaged in routine decision-making. In this context, factors

[1] Cardozo, *The Nature of the Judicial Process* (Yale University Press 1921). (Cardozo was a judge of the New York Court of Appeals 1914–32 and US Supreme Court 1932–38.)
[2] ibid 10–19.
[3] ibid, 167, 175.

Judging. Ross Cranston, Oxford University Press. © Ross Cranston 2025.
DOI: 10.1093/9780191890994.003.0006

such as intuition can also have a bearing as judges seek to work through their caseload.

This chapter offers a variety of ways to understand how judges make judicial decisions. Section II begins with the individual judge and the social and psychological forces which can be at work. As long recognized by leading judges such as Cardozo, judicial decision-making cannot be divorced from extra-legal factors such as a judge's background, experiences, mental processes, and values.[4] The discussion employs the extensive literature where social scientists have sought to identify and measure these extra-legal influences on judicial decision-making and how they affect the individual judge. It is spelt out under three broad headings: first, psychological perspectives, in which factors like intuitive reasoning, unconscious bias, and emotion shape judicial decision-making; secondly, relational models, in which a judge's decisions are affected by their interactions with colleagues, counsel, and others; and thirdly, attitudinal models, in which a judge's personal preferences and values impact on their decision-making. Sophisticated statistical analysis is employed in some of these approaches to demonstrate the impact of extra-legal factors on decision-making. A certain caution is in order since a great deal of the attitudinal analysis is based on courts in the United States, where judging, especially at Supreme Court level, can be deeply ideological.

Judicial distinctiveness in decision-making is the theme of section III of the chapter. Judges, being human, vary in how they go about the task of determining the factual and legal issues at stake in a case and the law's demands. The subject of judicial difference is explored through the classic technique of the German social theorist, Max Weber, the 'ideal type'. Five ideal types of judges are identified—legalists, merits judges, minimalists, modernizers, and activists. Each ideal type is a construct drawing selectively on the practices and philosophies of different judges, but simplifying these to highlight important features. An ideal type does not purport to be a full description of how any one judge goes about the task of judging. There can always be a discrepancy between how a judge might characterize their decision-making on the one hand, and what they in fact do when faced with real-life litigants and the facts and issues in a specific case on the other. In reality judges share elements of different ideal types, although some elements will bring to bear a stronger influence than others. Despite the drawbacks, identifying ideal

[4] PP. 80, 82 above. See also Brenda Hale, *Spider Woman. A Life* (Bodley Head 2021) 243. (Lady Hale was president of the UK Supreme Court 2017–20.)

types is a useful tool in highlighting divergences in how judges make judicial decisions.

Section IV of the chapter leaves the world of the individual judge to consider 'practical judging'. With respect to decision-making the focus of practical judging is on the accepted patterns for this by all judges, what might be termed 'fidelity to law'. The discussion begins with the channelling effect of legislation and precedent. The sheer volume of legislation in the modern state means that it is a more definite structuring feature of judges' decisions than in Cardozo's day. Then there is case law. In the common law system previous decisions are a source of law and adherence to precedent is still central. In decision-making, judges use principles drawn from precedent to reason to a conclusion. Many cases can be decided only one way. Legislation and precedent can be a refuge, especially when judges are making routine decisions in high volume courts. They are also a guard in the exercise of judicial discretion against a 'forensic lottery', which depends on the idiosyncrasies of which individual judge decides a matter. Despite their channelling effect, legislation may be open to different interpretations, and precedent may not be fixed or require slavish following. Judges may be able to address new issues and social conditions through techniques of statutory interpretation and common law reasoning, or by reference to other legitimate factors.

II Models of Judging

In 1930 Jerome Frank (later a judge of the Second Circuit Court of Appeals) published his *Law and the Modern Mind*,[5] in which he argued that precedents were an illusion, that legal certainty was an infantile hope, and that psychological influences had a role in judges' decision-making. These psychological influences are the first strand of theorizing about judging considered. Frank's approach drew heavily on psychoanalysis. In the 1950s there was work on the psychology of jury behaviour, but little follow up about what psychology could say about judicial decision-making. That was despite a long concern with evaluating witness evidence and 'judicial temperament'. More recently there has been an outburst of work on the relevance of social psychology to understanding how a judge goes about making decisions. Of primary importance is what social psychology can tell us about intuitive

[5] Jerome Frank, *Law and the Modern Mind* (Brentano's 1930).

decision-making, but there is also the story of how emotion can enter into judging.

The second strand of theorizing about judicial decision-making is more sociological in nature. The focus is on those models which place an emphasis on the influences of the individual judge's role and their relationship with others. A collection of models has proposed ways that these mould decision-making. One aspect relates to the judge's socialization, which was explored earlier in the book.[6] Along with forces such as collegiality, other models concern coalition building to secure a majority judgment, social and environmental influences, and institutional norms. The relationship which a judge has with their colleagues when they sit together on a panel to hear a case might determine whether they suppress any disagreement (possibly after a colleague has amended a draft judgment to narrow or avoid an issue which initially concerned the judge), write a concurring judgment, or decide to dissent. Another line of analysis points to the strategic choices a judge makes vis à vis colleagues to advance their own interests. As well as with colleagues, a judge will have a relationship with their judicial assistants ('clerks' or 'associates'), which can also shape their decision-making.

A third strand of theorizing about judicial decision-making among social scientists puts centre stage the judge's personal attitudes (what are sometimes termed their ideological preferences). Originating largely with studies of the US Supreme Court, the methodology has been broadened to other courts both in the United States and elsewhere. The judge in these attitude models is typically labelled as conservative or liberal, based in the US on matters such as the political complexion of the nominating president. The polarized nature of appointments to the US Supreme Court, extended to other federal courts, gives a reasonable indication of the judge's own social and political attitudes, although it also raises questions about the applicability of the analysis elsewhere. Judicial outcomes are labelled depending on the legal issue in dispute. For example, anti-abortion decisions would be regarded as conservative, pro-abortion decisions, liberal. Sophisticated statistical analysis then produces correlations between judicial attitudes and case outcomes, significant in certain courts and types of cases. To the focus on the judge's attitudes has been added a concern with a judge's values and how these relate to the outcome of judicial decision-making.

[6] PP. 108–110, 111 above.

(A) Psychological Approaches

Psychological perspectives explore how different cognitive factors bear on a range of judicial decisions. There is no grand theory as in the attitudinal models where a judge's decisions are attributable to their so-called 'ideological preferences'. Social psychologists suggest that the motivations behind decisions might include the judge's inclination to conform, their need for approval, or their striving for recognition and prestige. Importantly they also suggest that along with the rest of humanity the decisions of judges might be flawed because of certain cognitive processes. With what has been called motivated reasoning (or motived cognition), for instance, judges will seek information supporting their beliefs about a case, give it greater weight than other information, and critically scrutinize and discount contrary information. Heuristics (mental short-cuts or rules of thumb) also lead to errors (termed 'cognitive biases') in judicial decision-making.[7] Along with this is the possibility of 'unconscious' or 'implicit' bias for or against certain persons or groups, which as the name indicates does not require any conscious awareness.[8]

Another issue where social psychologists have contributed is the variability in repeated decisions in the same subject area, what has been termed 'noise'.[9] The lack of consistency might be in the one judge's decisions on the same type of matter, or between different judges when making the same type of decision. Examples would be a lack of consistency in high volume matters such as when judges hear substantive asylum applications or consider the grant of permission for cases to proceed to a hearing or appeal. Reasons for noise include the focus on the instant case and the distortions induced by cognitive and implicit biases. Procedural rules offer some protection, such as the right of the asylum seeker to appeal and of a party refused permission to proceed or appeal to renew an application before another judge. With high volume matters noise should be evident in a court's internal statistics or a judge's own records, which they can use as a point of comparison. Once conscious of the issue corrective measures can be taken. In any event judges' decisions should be less prone to cognitive biases and to variability because they are guided by law, practices, experience, and training. This is not an

[7] PP. 80–81 above.

[8] P. 81 above.

[9] Daniel Kahneman, Olivier Sibony, and Cass R Sunstein, *Noise. A Flaw in Human Judgement* (William Collins 2021).

argument about judicial exceptionalism but a recognition of the confining effects of the judicial role.

Intuitive decision-making

No judge is likely to be satisfactory at any level, said Lord Simon of Glaisdale, unless they have 'acute intuitions', especially in making findings of fact and deciding on what he called 'matters of degree' (open textured standards such as reasonableness or fairness in civil and statutory contexts).[10] In examining intuitive decision-making, social psychologists refer to fast and slow thinking, and to two modes of making decisions. System 1 is where decisions are made intuitively, system 2, where decisions are reached after deliberation. Intuitive decisions are relatively effortless and quick; deliberative decisions are more rule-governed, require effort, and take time.[11] Reference was made in Chapter 2 to the heuristics and biases which can cause possible errors of judgment with intuitive decision-making. Social psychologists have also identified 'expert' intuitions, those which are more trustworthy and less prone to error. They fall on an intuition–deliberation continuum towards the deliberation end. Expert intuitions require regularities, which enable greater predictability. Regularities are learned though experience. Feedback about the quality of decision-making can assist.[12]

Judges use intuition or 'feel their way' to decisions in a wide range of situations. Intuitive decision-making is a pragmatic response to the pressures of judging. It is indispensable for judges working at speed to deal with a high volume of routine matters. Using intuition is neither arbitrary nor unsophisticated. Even at the highest level judges have an intuitive feeling for the outcome of cases, especially in their areas of expertise, although they may be persuaded that their initial, intuitive view should change.[13] After a time any judge should acquire a feeling for certain types of case if they have been assigned to hear them on a regular basis. Appeals against their decisions may also assist with feedback, as will a history of practising law in the area prior to appointment to the bench. Intuitive decision-making is appropriate for the judge facing a bank of routine, simple cases, which fit the pattern of those which have been before them many times previously. The judge then readily

[10] 'Judicial Processes in England Part II' LS Gaz, 11 July 1973, 2060, 2061.

[11] The account of the Nobel prize-winner, Daniel Kahneman, is well-known: *Thinking, Fast and Slow* (Penguin 2011).

[12] ibid 236–44.

[13] eg, views of Lords Neuberger and Sumption: Alan Paterson, *Final Judgment* (Hart 2013) 76, 196–97 (hereafter Paterson, *Final Judgment*).

applies the relevant rule or standard to what is an ordinary case. With intuitive decision-making the judge needs to pay careful attention to signs that a case does not match existing patterns and or that their intuitive view is not consistent with the facts or legal requirements. A condition to relying on intuition is that the judge should be able to check their intuited decisions and pause for further thought. In regard to this need for deliberative thinking Justice Albie Sachs uses a distinction from political science between the 'logic of justification' and 'the logic of discovery' to describe how the application of legal principles can cause a judge to abandon even the strongest initial intuitions.[14]

Emotions

Emotion, its display, and its social function varies across and within cultures. In the mid nineteenth century Mr Justice Willes had a fine reputation as a judge. Apparently as with others in the Victorian period, he was prone to crying in public, in his case during trials involving the death of children and passing the sentence of death.[15] Like Willes J, modern judges experience emotions when hearing cases although shedding tears may not be as common. The psychologist would say that judging and emotion run together: judges experience emotions since it is inherent in their humanity and a natural consequence of the social interactions which occur in a court setting. As well as compassion, other emotions a judge may experience are passion, empathy, sympathy, pleasure, courage, frustration, boredom, impatience, and anger.[16] Much depends on the level of court and the type of case the judge is hearing. The pressures and uncertainties in high volume courts can be emotionally draining and stressful. In specific cases judicial emotions may be triggered by the nature of the evidence, a litigant's plight, behaviour in court, and the difficulty of the decision. A commercial appeal between an owner and the charterer of a vessel is less likely to evoke emotions than a first instance dispute about whether a child should be removed from a parent's care. On appointment judges will not necessarily be equipped to deal with the range of emotional situations, some unpleasant, which they will encounter when judging.

The values of judging demand firstly that judges should not permit emotions to influence their decisions: emotional judging is generally an

[14] Albie Sachs, *The Strange Alchemy of Life and Law* (OUP 2009) 53–54.

[15] Thomas Dixon, 'The Tears of Mr Justice Willes' (2012) 17 J Vic Culture 1.

[16] There is no need to enter the debate on whether empathy is an emotion or a capacity for emotion and whether it implies action.

illegitimate exercise of judicial power. Striving to eliminate the influence of emotions on decision-making reflects the norms of Western legal culture that rationality and emotion are opposed, and that the introduction of emotion would undermine the objectivity and impartiality of judicial decision-making. Impartiality is sometimes the overarching justification for judges to put their emotions to one side in decision-making. Judging is according to law, not any sympathy felt for one of the parties. Secondly, judges should not display their emotions. Rather, they should adhere to what has been termed the 'cultural script of judicial dispassion'. Ethical codes exhort judges to listen patiently, to be dignified and courteous, especially when encountering difficult situations, and to maintain order and decorum in court.[17] Implicit in this is that judges must manage their own emotions. Anger on the part of a judge is an emotion which, if not kept in check, can lead to complaints from lawyers and others, and possibly to disciplinary proceedings against the judge. Demeanour and tone of voice in court are important in demonstrating calmness and emotional neutrality in reacting to typical provocations. Managing emotions is a facet of a good judicial temperament.

However, the modern judge is expected to exhibit some emotional qualities as part of that temperament. Empathy (described as 'sensitivity and compassion') has been listed as a standard which the English judiciary should demonstrate when judging, specifically through maintaining the court's authority, managing a hearing in a fair and efficient manner, and communicating effectively.[18] Empathy, however, has its limits. The standards went on to state that as regards professionalism and integrity judges must remain detached, and they must manage their reactions and emotions.[19] The boundaries to empathy's reach are set by the judicial function. If justice is to be done the judge must understand the litigants, the full implications of their dispute, and the social context in which it occurs. Empathy does not mean deciding a case on grounds of sympathy regardless of the law. However, adopting the words of Chief Justice Dickson of the Canadian Supreme Court, empathy is not an extra-legal factor magnanimously conveyed by a benevolent judge, but part and parcel of what we call law. Failing to understand fully—empathizing with—the situation faced by a litigant could constitute a partial

[17] eg, *Bangalore Principles of Judicial Conduct* (United Nations 2018) 6.6; *Guide to Judicial Conduct* (Courts and Tribunals Judiciary, July 2023) 9.

[18] Judicial College, *Framework of Judicial Abilities and Qualities* (October 2008) 9. See now p. 161 footnote 28.

[19] ibid 13.

or incomplete performance of the judicial function.[20] Moreover, being able to empathize with the parties and their predicament may enable the trial judge to decide which of the parties is giving the more accurate account of what happened.[21] In this instrumental sense of seeking to understand the perspectives and evidence of others, empathy is not a violation but an affirmation of the value of impartiality.

(B) Relational Models

'Relational models' is the portmanteau term used here to draw together different models about how a judge's relationships with the social environment in which they work can have a bearing on their decision-making. An example is that after appointment there is a socialization process in which the judge absorbs the mores of the judiciary both formally through training but also informally through associating with other judges.[22] Another example is that the judge sitting with other judges in a multi-member court is involved in collective decision-making, albeit that this can take a variety of forms. Not only may a judge's relationships with others judges have a bearing on judicial decision-making, the focus of this chapter, but they may also shape other matters such as their initial appointment and later, their promotion. A judge with a powerful judicial patron or network can go far. Another relationship deserving brief mention is that between the judge and the physical environment of their court. A striking example is the Constitutional Court of South Africa, built on the site of a prison whose inmates included Mahatma Gandhi and Nelson Mandela. A member of that court associated in its design, Justice Albie Sachs, has described his feeling that the 'terrible negative energy of the past was converted into positivity for the future . . . to defend the new Constitution'.[23]

'Situation sense'

'Situation sense' is the notion that a judge with a close relationship with the practices and ethics surrounding particular types of case is more able to make

[20] Dickson's views are quoted in Robert J Sharpe, *Good Judgment: Making Judicial Decisions* (University of Toronto Press 2018) 264–66.
[21] Lady Rose, 'What Makes a Good Judge?' (2023) 136 Graya 25–26.
[22] PP. 108–110, 111 above.
[23] Sachs (n 14) 91.

a sound decision when confronted with a problem in that area.[24] Situation sense is formed through knowledge, experience, and values. Experience supplies not only direct knowledge but also insights from others. With situation sense, a judge compares the specific situation for decision with other similar situations. That gives a general indication of the path to its sound resolution, with the peculiarities of the case being addressed at a later stage. The judge is not imposing abstract principles to resolve a case but using the insight acquired about particular fact situations to assist its resolution. Identification of 'situation types' may allow the formulation of tentative rules to be applied to them in daily practice. It equips the judge for sound intuitive decisions.

Situation sense is illustrated by judging in expert commercial courts. Judges in these courts with a background in commercial law and practice build up a knowledge of the customs, practices, and values associated with particular types of commercial transaction. They acquire a sense about how they should be conducted. When they have a transaction before them they also have a general sense of what outcome will be regarded as right, fair, and reasonable by the commercial community around the court. Situation sense means that the commercial judge appreciates that what might seem strange to the outsider should be regarded as lawful practice.[25] Conversely, the commercial judge is more able to identify what should be deemed as lax practice on the part of commercial parties. Situation sense works within the framework of legal principle, as applied to the facts of the individual case. It guides the judge as to how to read into it, especially when confronted with a commercial transaction in all its complexity, and gives the judge an intuitive feeling of where a solution may lie.

The notion of situation sense has purchase in other branches of the law where through long experience judges have a better than average understanding of the situation and what problems it presents. Over time the judge's confidence is enhanced enabling the assessment of the benefits and drawbacks of a possible decision. Thus the judge who has long practised in criminal law will be knowledgeable when on the bench not only about criminal law and procedure but also about the practices and values of those prosecuting and defending defendants. Their situation sense will better equip them to conduct complex trials since they are able to respond more readily to

[24] The idea is Karl Llewellyn's: *The Common Law Tradition: Deciding Appeals* (Little, Brown & Co 1960) 60.

[25] eg, *Arcos Ltd v EA Ronaasen & Son* (1932) 43 Ll L Rep 1, 5 (Scrutton LJ). On appeal [1933] AC 470.

unexpected twists and turns and the manoeuvring of the advocates. On one interpretation situation sense is more than expert intuition since it is based on the relationship which a judge has with relevant situation types and the concrete knowledge and understanding which flow from that. The judge is consequently in a better place to determine whether a party's account of, and interpretation of, a fact-situation is likely to be correct. However, the notion of 'situation sense' cannot be pressed too far. One reason is that even the wisest and most experienced of judges sitting in, say, a commercial court cannot know every conceivable part of (in that case) commercial practice. These days specialization sets in fairly early in a lawyer's career even within an area like commercial law.

'Dialogue'

Judging is a social process. Judges engage in dialogues with individuals and organizations which can shape their decision-making. A judge may be influenced within the context of their court through dialogue with its other judges and their judicial assistants (clerks), the social networks they have built within their wider judiciary, or the more formal contacts they have vertically with judges lower or higher in the hierarchy, or horizontally with those connected with their court (for example, judges in apex courts on the one hand and those in regional courts like the European Court of Human Rights on the other). Dialogue with the judiciaries in other countries is facilitated through bilateral visits, judicial training, and membership of an international organization of judges.[26] Then there is the discrete environment of the legal profession and the academy from which judges have come, and with which they may have continuing links. Dialogue in this respect is facilitated through judges attending conferences, giving speeches and lectures, and their membership of professional associations which include both judges and practitioners.[27]

Dialogue is undertaken for different reasons and takes different forms. Take the dialogue which judges engage in with lawyers and legal scholars. One dimension to this is the extent to which judges might seek the approval of these different groups through producing, for the former, practical decisions, even guidance, and, for the latter, reasoning which engages with or at least acknowledges academic contributions. Another dimension is the influence

[26] eg, Commonwealth Magistrates' and Judges' Association, International Association of Women Judges, Standing International Forum of Commercial Courts.

[27] eg, the Inns of Court in England; the Federalist Society in the US.

these groups have on judicial decision-making. With lawyers, for example, there is the sway which oral and written advocacy can have on the outcome of a case. Judges and counsel in the UK's apex court (House of Lords/Supreme Court since 2009) have reported that in specific situations advocacy may affect both the outcome and reasoning of the court's decisions.[28] As for legal academics, judges have acknowledged that they can influence change. An oft quoted example in English law is the impetus which legal scholarship has given to the development of unjust enrichment as a method for advancing restitutionary claims.

Dialogue suggests a degree of mutuality, but for some counterparties there may be a temporary or prolonged silence. Dialogue may sometimes be controlled by one side. Dialogue between the judges and advocates in a particular case may be constrained because a repeat player has decided not to argue a specific point. It might take the view that the factual setting in the present case or the sequence of litigation means that it is not conducive to its longer-term goals to do so now. This reflects the simple point that judges do not control the agenda but depend on parties to litigate points. Dialogue can be practised with different aims. Advocates in their dialogue with the judge aim to win the case; academics seek what they regard as the best formulation of legal norms. In some situations dialogue may produce a genuine cross-fertilization of ideas. In others it may be pretence: legal scholarship may be amply paraded in a judgment, inserted by a judicial assistant after the judge has approved the draft.

Collegiality and small group influences

The concept of dialogue melds into that of collegiality, discussed at greater length in the previous chapter.[29] Collegiality both motivates and constrains judicial behaviour. At first instance collegiality is evident when judges consult each other informally about problems encountered in their cases.[30] The obvious danger is that the judge may consult the like-minded rather than those who could challenge them. When judges sit with other judges, they cannot determine the outcome of a case by themselves: they need the support of others. To win support they may need to modify their views. Judges may change their positions after a post-hearing conference on a case. Even if they have not changed their views, there are rational reasons not to dissent

[28] Paterson (n 13) ch 2.
[29] PP. 222–224 above.
[30] Penny Darbyshire, *Sitting in Judgment: The Working Lives of Judges* (Hart 2011) 418–21.

or to prepare a concurring judgment—the additional work, especially if the judge is already overburdened; the likely futility of persuading colleagues to their view; and (with intermediate appellate courts) the low probability that the case will proceed further for their judgment to have an immediate impact on an appeal. Collegiality explains what has been called 'dissent aversion', where judges are reluctant to dissent even though they are not in complete agreement with the judgment they support.[31]

Along with collegiality, small group theories throw light on judicial decision-making. First, social psychologists recognize membership of a small group is more likely to give rise to an internalized sense of group membership and enhance the likelihood that a member will incorporate their group membership into their concept of themselves. As a result, judges as members of a court might be especially attentive to the norms and expectations of that court. Secondly, there can be an affective element to the relationship between members of a group. Thus judges in a particular court may have known each other from law school, been in the same legal chambers, worked together on the same cases, or sat with each other in a lower court. Even if none of this produces a friendship or even fondness for another judge it may at least lead to an instinctive appreciation of their astuteness and ability. That may result in a judge deferring to another judge, a judge having more influence on a panel of judges despite a lack of seniority, or a judge respecting the decisions of a judge below them in the judicial hierarchy. Thirdly, small group theorists refer to how, over time, social exchanges among group members produce collective ideas, perceptions, practices, interpretations, and recollections from shared events and activities. As regards judges in a particular court, these collective ideas and practices may be handed on to new judges as the correct way of doing things and mould how decisions are made.

A fourth point concerns how those in small groups are influenced by their colleagues. Members of a panel deciding a case may change their view following a discussion with colleagues, especially after hearing what the panel member experienced in the field has to say. The presence of a specialist on a panel may even change the perceptions of its non-expert members about their role, which becomes one of deference to the specialist's view unless it appears decidedly wrong. In a hierarchical environment like the judiciary there can be leadership or seniority effects. A chief justice, presiding judge, or experienced senior judge has potentially considerable clout on the outcome;

[31] PP. 235–236 above.

on the other hand, a judge sitting temporarily in a higher court is unlikely to wield as much influence. As a result of their familiarity with each other judges may feel freer in expressing their opinions and expect them to be heard. By contrast newcomers may be inclined to suppress their doubts to fit in. Their influence is consequently diminished. The influence of any one judge on decision-making can vary with the circumstances. Social psychologists have long distinguished between task and social leadership. Task leadership may mean that a leadership judge suppresses their view to maintain collegiality in the court. Their task leadership may centre on managerial or external matters more than on deciding cases so that their influence as regards the latter is diminished. As well some leadership judges provide more in the way of social leadership, with the intellectual leadership of the court residing elsewhere.

Finally, there is the so-called 'wisdom of the crowd', expressed in the adage 'two heads are better than one'. In other words, groups will make superior decisions than will individuals by themselves. Thus appellate courts, voting by majority, have a higher probability of making a correct decision because the errors of the judges are balanced out.[32] Indeed, the theory continues, collective decisions should be better than that of the smartest judge in the group because not only is the knowledge of the individuals aggregated and pooled but new knowledge is created through social interaction within it. In fact, environmental and social influences may undermine the wisdom of the crowd. First, in a busy appellate court judges may not have time to give equal and independent consideration to a matter. The judge assigned to write the main judgment works hard or is the expert and reaches a conclusion which the other judges are content to accept as correct. Secondly, there may also be a tendency to conformity especially when there is a strongly held view by a leadership or senior judge in favour of a particular outcome and its rationale. Thirdly, a persistent minority may wear down the majority. Fourthly, information known to all is amplified in group discussions and given disproportionate influence. Similarly, the like-minded may take more extreme positions than they would if faced with opposing voices. Fifthly, ill-will and dysfunction in a court may mean that the wisdom of the crowd is lost.[33]

[32] Chief Justice Gageler invokes in support Condorcet's jury theorem and Cardozo (n 1) 177: see 'Why Write Judgments?' (2014) 36 Sydney LR 189, 193–96.

[33] See Lord Neuberger, 'Twenty Years a Judge: Reflections and Refractions' (Neill Lecture 2017, Oxford Law Faculty, 10 February 2017) [42]–[43].

Strategic behaviour models

Strategic behaviour models meet reality in efforts by judges to build majorities in apex courts. Timing can be important in circulating a draft judgment to win support and in preventing followers from changing from a position supporting what until then was the majority position. Once a judge has committed themselves to a view in a draft judgment it becomes more difficult psychologically to move their position. Judges may approach colleagues directly for support during a case, over lunch, in the corridors, and in a judge's chambers. Some judges regard this as improper, and some refuse to engage in the practice. Their failure to do so explains how in some cases they end up in the minority when at an earlier stage they were in the ascendency.[34]

Strategic analysis also addresses a judge lower in the judicial hierarchy writing a judgment with an eye on what the appellate court might do, for example focusing on the facts to minimize the chance of being overturned (so-called 'reversal aversion'). A judge when sitting with others might indicate an intention to write separately to extract concessions from those in the majority. There is also what has been called the 'whistleblower effect', where a judge writes a judgment in a way to signal to a higher court that this is a case where they should hear an appeal. Strategic behaviour can also involve reciprocity to avoid reinforcing division on the court. There is some evidence from the Canadian Supreme Court and US Supreme Court where, rather than seeking to compromise and accept the majority judgment, a judge will chose to dissent or write a concurring judgment because in the past their colleagues have failed to accommodate them.[35]

Examination of strategic behaviour extends beyond case outcomes to issues such as agenda-setting through a judge granting permission for a case to proceed or to appeal so that a particular point can be aired. As well there are a judge's personal goals such as enhancing their reputation among colleagues or the public through their decisions. The term 'auditioning' has been applied to judges who choose to write judgments in a way which they imagine will advance their career. Judgments are crafted to catch the eye of those with the power over promotion or further appointments, perhaps consistently with the latter's known views. Strategic models have also been developed

[34] Paterson, *Final Judgment* (n 13) 132–35, 180–85, 191. See also Lord Millett, *As in Memory Long* (Wildy, Simmonds & Hill 2015) 176.

[35] Emmett Macfarlane, *Governing from the Bench. The Supreme Court of Canada and the Judicial Role* (UBC Press 2013) 116; James F Spriggs, Forrest Maltzman, and Paul J Wahlbeck, 'Bargaining on the US Supreme Court: Justices' Responses to Majority Opinion Drafts' (1999) 61 J Politics 485, 491, 501.

around judges seeking to maximize the chances of compliance by the parties and others with their decisions. The judge adopts reasoning with that end in view by setting out guidance or easing a legislative burden for the litigants and those in a similar position.

While strategic models accept that judges may make decisions in accordance with law, they assume that they also act strategically to further their attitudes and values. In the model judges consider the choices they expect others to make and the institutional context in which they are acting. The others to whom they have regard may be colleagues in the same court, appellate judges, or the legislature. Strategic behaviour might be short term in relation to achieving a specific outcome in a case or more long term in moulding the law or influencing the future of their court. Strategic behaviour can include attempting by oral interventions at a hearing to influence the thinking of the other judges on a panel; seeking if there is division in a panel to be in the majority, but with the judgment reflecting their views; and maintaining collegiality by not writing a separate judgment.

Most of the empirical work with strategic models revolves around judges sitting on panels with other judges and acting strategically in reaching decisions about judgments. Based on the reaction of the other judges, the judge acting strategically is ready to modify their approach when views are proffered about what should be the outcome and the reasons to support it. To win over its others members, a judge sitting on a panel may move from their most favoured position to one which overall is still acceptable to them. That may be because in the final judgment the issue is narrowed or hedged. A judge with an eye on the future of the law may be more concerned with the reasoning in the unanimous or majority judgment than with the specific outcome in the case before the panel. Leadership judges with the power to determine panel composition or to assign the writing of the unanimous or majority judgment are in a strong position to act strategically. In undertaking the judgment-writing task themselves or assigning it to an ally they can achieve their own goals as to a case's outcome and reasoning.

(C) Attitudinal Models

Attitudinal and value studies consciously challenge the notion that judicial decision-making is based on an objective analysis of the law and the facts of a case. The attitudinal model was developed against a background of the US Supreme Court's decisions in the 1930s. Initially the court ruled against

President Roosevelt's New Deal policies until he began appointing 'liberal' judges. The attitudinal model was lent support by the jurisprudence of American legal realism. Legal scholars and some judges such as Judge Jerome Frank contended that, broadly speaking, judges decide cases not primarily because of the law but because of their sense of what is fair on the facts of the case. From the 1960s proponents of the attitudinal model have suggested that the most significant independent factor explaining judicial decision-making is a judge's attitudes (ideological preferences) and that their legal reasoning is largely a rationalization of the result. In the attitudinal model a judge's attitudes are treated as external to the model and turn on their personal background and other social influences. Based on the empirical analysis involved, attitudinal models might predict the outcome of a case once the judges and issues are identified.

Attitudinal models began with decision-making in the US Supreme Court. There for many years it has been noticeable that the decisions of the individual justices will generally follow from their attitudes on the public policy issues coming before them. In its various guises the analysis boils down to the classification of a justice as conservative, moderate, or liberal bearing on the outcome of cases. In some studies justices are labelled as conservative or liberal using as a proxy their nominating president (Republican or Democratic), but in others there is more detailed analysis of their background to place them on a liberal–conservative spectrum. As to a justice's decisions, these are classified depending on whether they favour, for example, restrictive abortion laws, the business party in labour disputes, or the admissibility of evidence from police searches. Some models have a more sophisticated analysis, for example, whether the police search was under a warrant, its location (eg, home, business, personal), and how intrusive it was. Decisions on such issues are then correlated empirically with the conservative or liberal character of the justices. Conservative judges are found to favour conservative outcomes, liberal judges, liberal outcomes.

Although in the US the attitudinal model has concentrated on the Supreme Court, there have been studies of other courts. Analysis of decisions in the US Courts of Appeals over some forty years up to 1992 found a statistically significant association between judicial attitudes and the outcome of decisions.[36] For instance a panel of three judges appointed by a Democratic president dismissed an appeal against a 'liberal' decision of a district judge

[36] Frank B Cross, 'Decisionmaking in the U.S. Circuit Courts of Appeals' (2003) 91 Calif L Rev 1457, 1479–509.

well over three-fifths of the time, while a panel of three judges appointed by a Republican president dismissed this type of appeal only about half the time. The difference varied with the appointing president, in that judges appointed by the most ideologically conservative presidents reversed more of the liberal lower court decisions coming before them. However, the study found that other factors were also in play, such as legal constraints derived from precedent, so that judicial attitudes explained only a little over five per cent of the different outcomes overall.

Variations of the attitudinal model have been applied to courts outside the US. An attitudinal study of the Canadian Supreme Court concluded that the judges' own ideology influenced how they approached different policy issues when the court was divided but acknowledged that some judges resolved cases differently to what their ideology would otherwise indicate. The court was unanimous in about three-quarters of cases, and from their interviews with the judges the authors found a willingness to accommodate colleagues if this did not compromise their own principles too much.[37] Taking as the independent variable the strength of a judge's political affiliation on appointment, and measuring it against their decisions in criminal, family, and human rights matters (pro-defendant, pro-woman, or pro-claimant respectively), a study of the Ontario Court of Appeal—Canada's largest intermediate appellate court—found that political affiliation had some influence on the outcomes in criminal but not in family or human rights cases.[38]

Perhaps the earliest of the UK attitudinal studies was an empirical investigation of split decisions in the UK House of Lords between 1965 and 1978. It was based on the premise that where the law lords had a discretion their decisions would be influenced by their beliefs and attitudes inside a specifically legal and 'professional' ideology. Beginning with the degree of affinity between judges in some cases, the research then correlated this with differences in support for certain types of litigant. With some qualifications, the study found that judges could be characterized along several dimensions, notably those in criminal law matters who found for the prosecution rather than the defendant, and those in public law cases who favoured the state rather than

[37] Donald R Songer and others, *Law, Ideology, and Collegiality: Judicial Behaviour in the Supreme Court of Canada* (McGill-Queen's University Press 2012) 171–73.

[38] Lori Hausegger, Troy Riddell, and Matthew Hennigar, 'Does Patronage Matter? Connecting Influences on Judicial Appointments with Judicial Decision Making' (2013) 46 Canadian J Pol Sc 665, 678.

the other side. The upshot, it concluded, was that 'a serious case has been made out for the existence, in Britain, of a specifically judicial ideology'.[39]

Taking divided decisions of the UK Supreme Court between 2009 and 2017, Professor Hanretty transformed the judges sitting in these cases into a unidimensional scale based on rates of (dis)agreement. Lord Kerr and Lady Hale were grouped at one end of the scale, Lord Brown and Lord Rodger at the other. To interpret the scale, he then categorized case outcomes in left- or right-wing terms. For example, he categorized as left-wing a success for a party alleging a human rights violation or one for an individual or association claiming against a public authority or a company. The conclusion was that the best single interpretation of the scale was that it was separating judges into those more likely to reach left- or right-wing outcomes. However, the study concluded overall that legal factors were the best indicator of case outcomes, the surrogate for legal factors which the study used being the balance of opinion in the courts below.[40]

A further study of UK Supreme Court justices focused on their personal values rather than attitudes. The values most relevant to the study were characterized as tradition and conformity, self-direction (including liberty, autonomy, independence, and freedom), and universalism (including equality and social justice). Values were uncovered not through case outcomes but through a content analysis of the reasons given by the justices in their judgments. The study found that different judges had different values, and different judges were more forthright than others in expressing them. The study's premise was that decision-making was based on system 1 reasoning (values instinctively followed), modulated by system 2 reasoning (consideration of more deliberative factors). Analysing judgments in the early years of the UK Supreme Court, and drawing on the justices' extrajudicial speeches, the study concluded that in some hard cases where the law was uncertain, a justice's values could be detected notwithstanding system 2 reasoning. As well as having a bearing on whether to dissent, a justice's values influenced the outcome in split decision cases.[41]

With time, attitudinal models have become more sophisticated to accommodate influences in judicial decision-making, such as the legal issues raised,

[39] David Robertson, 'Judicial Ideology in the House of Lords: A Jurimetric Analysis' (1982) 12 Brit J Pol Sc 1, 25.

[40] Chris Hanretty, *A Court of Specialists: Judicial Behaviour on the UK Supreme Court* (OUP 2020) 208, 237, 271.

[41] Rachel Cahill-O'Callaghan, *Values in the Supreme Court: Decisions, Division and Diversity* (Hart 2020).

the legal limits on what a judge can decide, strategic choices, and the environment in which a judge operates. However, they still suffer from limitations. First, the classification in attitudinal models can appear crude. The political colour of the appointing president may be a good proxy for the attitudes of US Supreme Court and federal circuit court judges, assuming that there is no shift in their views during their judicial lifetime. It is not applicable in other jurisdictions, where there are different ways of appointing judges. Judges may be appointed on a non-party basis, perhaps appointed when one party is in government but promoted by the other major party. Appointment may be by non-political bodies. Judges may have no party-political alignment. Attitudes may have little salience in some cases and in some courts compared with others. Consequently, attitudinal models cannot throw light on significant parts of judicial decision-making. Moreover, classifying outcomes on a spectrum from left to right can be an oversimplification. Treating all human rights cases where the claimant succeeds as left-wing, for example, overlooks the reality that human rights cases are sometimes brought by businesses against regulations. In other contexts, such as most commercial disputes, a left–right spectrum has little traction.

III Varieties of Judges

Differences between judges in decision-making are marked, firstly, in the varying approaches in individual judgments, especially in appellate courts. In a famous article Lon L Fuller used the judgments of five hypothetical judges in an imagined appellate court to spell out their divergent legal philosophies—positivism, natural law, and legal realism.[42] Rarely, however, do judges articulate a legal philosophy, and even if they did it would be unlikely to offer a neat explanation of their decision-making in all their cases. Variations between judges may be evident, secondly, through observation of their everyday approach to court work. A study of Melbourne magistrates making domestic violence orders classified them as authoritative, lawmaker, mediator, proceduralist, and strict adherent.[43] Yet observation of court behaviour alone does not offer a complete picture of how judges make decisions. A third method of exploring variations among judges is through an examination of their decisions. An example is the analysis of the content

[42] Lon L Fuller, 'The Case of the Speluncean Explorers' (1949) 62 Harv LR 616.
[43] Rosemary Hunter, 'Styles of Judging' (2005) 30 Alternative LJ 231.

of judgments of the UK Supreme Court in its first ten years, which in ideological (or political) language yielded a range of differences between the individual judges when placed on liberal–conservative, activism–restraint, and institutional–independent scales.[44] Some proponents of feminist judging have suggested that it can make a difference to real-life judging by bringing a different experience to the task, but there are few cases where feminist judging has produced an outcome different from that which other judges reached.[45]

Instead of these approaches, variations in the decision-making of judges are pursued here through the technique of the ideal type. Max Weber developed the ideal type in the early twentieth century in the context of a theory of history and then applied it sociologically.[46] The ideal type is not an ideal in the sense of a desirable objective. To Weber the ideal type is a tool of analysis. It is not an average or a description of commonly found features in the real world. Rather, it is constructed by selecting elements which on artificial assumptions fit together in a rational way. The ideal type enables an understanding of reality, primarily through a comparison of reality with the ideal type. An example is Weber's three ideal types of authority, traditional, charismatic, and legal-rational. Weber accepted that the ideal type could not capture reality perfectly, and there is considerable debate about its application. There can be no denying, however, the insights ideal type analysis can bring.

(A) Ideal Types and Judging

The ideal types of judging explored below are not derived from legal philosophy or jurisprudence but are based on what judges have said about their approach to judging either in the context of particular cases or in separate speeches, articles, and memoirs. No doubt there are more, but five ideal types of judging are sketched out to assist in understanding the contrasting approaches which judges have to decision-making—legalism, merits judging, minimalism, modernizers, and activists. Each ideal type offers an exaggerated description of a more complex reality to distil the key aspects of

[44] Lewis Graham, *Judicial Individuality on the UK Supreme Court* (Hart 2025) chs 9–10.

[45] eg, see Lady Hale (a self-styled 'soft' feminist) in *Radmacher v Granatino* [2010] UKSC 42, [2011] 1 AC 534 [137]; *Re Northern Ireland Human Rights Commission for Judicial Review* [2018] UKSC 27 [6], [8]. See p. 74 above.

[46] Max Weber, *Economy and Society: An Outline of Interpretive Sociology* (Guenther Roth and Claus Wittich eds, Bedminster Press 1968) vol 1, 19–22.

existing practices and institutions. While the focus has been on ideal types of individual judges, there is no reason that the analysis cannot be extended to courts. For many years the High Court of Australia espoused legalism as its philosophy of decision-making;[47] the Canadian Supreme Court under McLachlin CJ shared characteristics of the modernizers; and the Indian Supreme Court when public interest litigation was at its height compared well with the ideal type of activist judging.

Legalism

Legalism as the basis for judging involves the judge ascertaining the relevant rule and legal principles and then applying these in accordance with the conventional standards of legal reasoning.[48] The judge proceeds upon the assumption that the law comprises a body of doctrine which governs decisions in particular cases. There is thus an external standard of legal correctness which determines the outcome and acts as a restraint on the judge. It is not a subjective standard or one personal to the judge but is to be found in the law. The judge cannot disregard the external standard provided by legal doctrine because of dissatisfaction with a particular outcome. The judge's duty, as Dicey put it in 1914, 'is not to remedy a particular grievance, but to determine whether an alleged grievance is one for which the law supplies a remedy'.[49] Adherents of legalism accept that cases and principles do not always yield a clear answer. Their volume is vast, different lines of authority can be inconsistent, and there can be honest disagreement about what principle is to be drawn from them to apply to the circumstances of a particular case. That does not give the judge a licence to decide a case at will. It may require a considerable intellectual effort, and the answer may be provisional, but the judge must work to determine the external standard and then apply it according to accepted standards of legal reasoning. Legalism requires intellectual effort to derive rules from existing legal principles and precedents, which are then applied to the new combinations of circumstances.

Legalist judging is not equivalent to mechanical jurisprudence, where a judicial decision is the product of syllogistic reasoning with the rule of law the major premise, and the facts the minor premise. Legalism accepts that new situations arise which will not be covered by existing principles or

47 (1952) 85 CLR xiii–xiv (Dixon CJ).

48 The following draws heavily on Sir Owen Dixon's address at Yale University in 1955: 'Concerning Judicial Method' (1956) 29 ALJ 468.

49 AV Dicey, *Lectures on the Relation between Law and Public Opinion in England During the Nineteenth Century* (2nd edn, Macmillan 1914) 365.

precedents. The outcome in such a case cannot be derived from a mechanical application of existing standards to its circumstances. But this does not entitle the judge to decide the case according to their own judgment of what is just and expedient. Judges inherit a body of law—legal principles and precedents—from which rules can be derived; they do not begin anew when deciding a case. For the sake of attaining uniformity, consistency, and certainty, said Parke J in a classic formulation, judges cannot reject those rules, and analogies to them, for new situations 'because we think that the rules are not as convenient and reasonable as we ourselves could have devised. It appears to me to be of great importance to keep this principle of decision steadily in view, not merely for the determination of the particular case, but for the interests of law as a science.'[50]

While accepting that change in the law is inevitable, legalism therefore requires that deliberate judicial innovation be approached cautiously. Otherwise, there is a risk that in changing the law the judge will produce adverse, unintended consequences. Law must develop, but judges must tread cautiously since they have only a limited capacity to foretell the future. Deciding only what is necessary to decide is one way to reduce the risk of unintended consequences. In addition, legal innovation may be regarded as usurping political authority. The judge must be attentive to judicial legitimacy. The judicial function is not to decide cases according to the judge's own personal standards or theories of justice. As important in decision-making is that the judge must exercise care about trespassing onto the territory of the legislature or the executive government. Legal reform is better left to Parliament.

Merits judging

At the other end of the spectrum from legalism is merits judging. The merits judge rejects legalism's rationality and its careful elaboration of principles for cases not covered by existing legal principles and precedents. The merits judge is focused on the parties and the facts before the court. Each case is treated as a dispute, and the merits judge decides what in their view is its sensible resolution. Then if needs be the merits judge will contrive a legal justification for that outcome. In reacting to the facts of a case, the merits judge is not primarily motived by legal principles or rules. These will often offer scope for the judge to pursue the merits of the case. If the law appears to

[50] *Mirehouse v Rennell* (1833) 1 Cl & F 527, 546; 6 ER 1015, 1023 (HL).

stand in the way of what seems to be the sensible resolution of a case, merits judges may reach their conclusion by a deftness of analysis. The facts drive the law. Merits judges deprecate what they regard as 'technical' legal arguments which run contrary to what they believe to be the merits of the case before them. Lord Mansfield identified the basis of merits judging when he advised the person of practical good sense, appointed governor of a colony and having to preside in its courts without judicial training, to give decisions boldly, for they would probably be right, but never to give reasons, for they would almost certainly be wrong.[51]

In simple terms merits judging is 'the individual judge's intuition as to which side ought to win'.[52] That intuition derives from what is perceived to be the 'common sense' resolution of a dispute when considering its background and the circumstances of the parties. In some cases indignation at the behaviour of one side means that a decision in their favour does not seem justified.[53] The issue then becomes whether the law constrains a decision on what the judge has identified as the merits. Essentially, merits judges regard their role as being to do justice between the parties: 'merits go to show where justice lies'.[54] They derive their sense of interpersonal justice from their own values, what they imagine is the consensus or majority view among judicial and professional colleagues, or what they conceive of as the way of thinking shared by reasonable members of the community. In some contexts, merits judges will also base their views about the sensible resolution of a dispute on its wider social merits. Their conception of merits then extends beyond those of the parties before them to the implications of a dispute for the society more generally, for instance, to the conclusion which to their mind will prevent serious loss or inconvenience to the community or thwart adverse economic consequences.[55]

Minimalist judging

Like the merits judge, the minimalist judge focuses on the case before them. But that is because to the minimalist judge the best way of avoiding harmful, unanticipated consequences in future is 'by confining decisions to concrete

[51] John Stuart Mill, *A System of Logic, Ratiocinative and Inductive* (8th edn, Harper & Brothers 1882) 144.

[52] *Guest v Guest* [2022] UKSC 27, [2024] AC 833 [156].

[53] *Rank Film Distributors Ltd v Video Information Centre* [1982] AC 380, 411 (Lord Denning).

[54] Lord Denning, *The Family Story* (Butterworths 1981) 207.

[55] eg, *Duport Steels Ltd v Sirs* [1980] 1 WLR 142, 154 (Lord Denning).

questions which have actually arisen in circumstances the whole of which are before the tribunal'.[56] For the minimalist judge cases ought to be decided on narrow grounds. Issues which are not necessary for the resolution of the case before them are put to one side for resolution in the future. The circumstances in future cases are unknown and are best left for future judges. If cases can be decided on the facts, all to the good. An exception is that the first instance minimalist judge may decide issues not central to their decision but in anticipation of a possible appeal, for example, the factual issues relating to quantum even though for legal reasons they have held that there is no liability. That is because if there is an appeal, the court may decide that there is liability and can then accept (or reject) the judge's basis for an award of damages.

By contrast with the merits judge, the minimalist judge accepts that legal principles should orient them in finding a solution in the present case. Those principles should be confined, however, to the existing stock of legal principles. Unlike the modernizers, the minimalist judge does not feel impelled to add to the stock of principles unless essential for deciding a case. There is no need for the judge to enunciate broader principles than those which are precisely on point for resolving the case at hand. Existing precedents are generally sufficient and should be respected. This leaves later judges a greater discretion to apply legal principles to the unforeseen fact patterns of the future.

There are several corollaries to the minimalist's approach to judicial decision-making. First, judicial minimalists eschew deciding hypothetical (or academic) questions where the outcome will not directly affect the rights and obligations of the parties. Not only is there an obvious public interest in not wasting court time or incurring unnecessary costs in ruling on a hypothetical question, but any such ruling also constitutes no more than *obiter dictum*, since it is expressed without the assistance of a concrete factual situation.[57] The minimalist judge takes the view that cases are fact sensitive and that their role is to resolve real disputes and not those of merely academic significance. Secondly, the minimalist judge does not believe in giving advisory opinions about the lawfulness or otherwise of proposed conduct. In their view decisions on pure questions of law and advisory opinions are inappropriate because they will be decided out of context. That is especially the case

[56] *John Deere Plow Co Ltd v Wharton* [1915] AC 330, 338 (Lord Haldane) (PC, Canada).

[57] cf *R v Secretary of State for the Home Department ex parte Wynne* [1993] 1 WLR 115, 119–20 (Lord Goff).

when a party seeks a declaration as to the lawfulness of conduct before it has occurred. Thirdly, minimalist judges take the view that it is not their function to keep the statute book up to date by means of advisory interpretations: that responsibility lies with the legislature and the executive.[58] At base minimalist judges are highly conscious of their limitations and ability to foresee the future; they prefer to leave matters undecided if they can.

Fourthly, the minimalist judge steers clear of giving general guidance for the future for similar reasons as those which apply where a question is hypothetical or a party seeks an advisory opinion. Guidance suffers because issues lie ahead, and the events to which it will relate have not occurred. There are risks for a judge in grappling with issues divorced from the context which require their determination. There is also the judicial time and cost in seeking to cover in guidance all potentially relevant circumstances. A danger is that the judge will enunciate principles without a full appreciation of their implications in practice. That could cause confusion among those who are obliged to apply those principles in real life. Judges lack the investigatory and consultative machinery which the executive and legislative arms of government have in formulating guidance. It is better, the minimalist judge would also contend, that future judges have the discretion to consider a matter unencumbered by any earlier guidance. A judge giving guidance cannot know with sufficient certainty what issues will arise in the specific circumstances to which it is supposed to apply.

Modernizers

Judges make law, not all the time, but more so the higher they are in the judicial hierarchy. At its simplest the application of an existing principle of law to facts not previously considered can constitute lawmaking: there is now a precedent that the principle extends in this way. The modernizing judge goes further in making law, believing that their role is to change it over time and that they should have a hand in innovating along with other lawmakers. In their view the law may be inadequate on its own terms for current needs because of its complexity or lack of coherence. Alternatively, it may be ill-fitted to a changing world and so 'must be developed to meet changing economic conditions and habits of thought'.[59] The modernizing judge considers that an aspect of the judicial function is to ensure that the law is up to date; in this regard judicial innovation is legitimate if change accords with underlying

[58] *R (on the application of Rushbridger) v Attorney General* [2004] 1 AC 357.
[59] *Myers v Director of Public Prosecutions* [1965] AC 1001, 1021 (Lord Reid).

trends. The modernizer takes the view that the task of change cannot be left to the legislature or the executive alone. Not only can these branches of the state not assist in the instant case but they are often slow to accomplish legal change even when change is recommended by the judges or law reform bodies.

The occasions for the modernizing judge to act are various. In the course of a hearing the modernizer may suggest a new line of argument for a party to adopt which will attract the judge's favour because it furthers their updating agenda. In decision-making the modernizer may reshape existing doctrine 'in adaptation to altering social conditions and standards'.[60] Consistently with principle, the modernizer may mould doctrine to changing social or economic conditions as with a principled development in the law to meet advances in commercial and financial practice or information technology. Exceptionally the modernizer may discard precedent where a judge-made rule is 'based on an assumption of fact which was true when the rule was formulated but which is no longer true and which now in many cases causes serious injustice'.[61] There are occasions where the modernizer is able to create new doctrine.[62]

The modernizing judge interprets statutory texts taking account of changing social conditions and purposes. The modernizing judge may read legislation purposively to fill gaps and bring its application up to date. With conflicting statutory provisions the modernizing judge will consider their wider context and purpose and reconcile them in a manner consonant with modern needs. The modernizing judge is able to use the 'always speaking' principle so that legislation is applied in circumstances which could not have been foreseen at the time it was enacted. To the modernizing judge a human rights or constitutional instrument is not to be interpreted according to the ordinary rules of statutory interpretation. Rather it is a 'living tree' or 'living instrument', which is 'capable of growth and expansion within its natural limits'.[63] In performing the interpretative task, the modernizer 'by way of progressive interpretation, accommodates and addresses the realities of modern life'.[64] In their view this ensures the continued relevance and

[60] *Donoghue v Stevenson* [1932] AC 562, 619 (Lord Macmillan).

[61] *Birmingham Corp v West Midland Baptist (Trust) Association Inc* [1970] AC 874, 898 (Lord Reid).

[62] eg, *Lipkin Gorman v Karpnale Ltd* [1991] 2 AC 548 (unjust enrichment); *Mabo v Queensland (No 2)* [1992] HCA 23, (1992) 175 CLR 1 (native title); *Carter v Canada (Attorney General)* [2015] 1 SCR 331 (physician assisted death); *S P Gupta v Union Of India* 1982 AIR SC 149 (public interest litigation).

[63] *Edwards v Attorney-General for Canada* [1930] AC 124, 136 (PC, Canada).

[64] *Reference re Same-Sex Marriage* [2004] 3 SCR 698 [22]–[23].

legitimacy of the instrument.[65] Treating the text as a living instrument may even result in the judge reversing an existing interpretation by reference to changing demands.

Activist judging

Activist judging is results-oriented judging. Activist judges decide cases to further their preferred social policy goals. Unlike the modernizers, who simply want to update the law to accord with current social needs, activist judges pursue their conception of social good through their decision-making. That may be a simple notion of achieving what they see as social justice in each case. On the political spectrum their social goals may be liberal at one end, conservative at the other. Activist judges may revel in their lawmaking. Lord Denning famously described the 'bold spirits who were ready to allow it if justice so required'—he placed himself in that category—by contrast with the 'timorous souls who were fearful of allowing a new cause of action'.[66] By contrast activist judges may pursue change, even a paradigm shift in legal doctrine, without fanfare. Ironically the justification of activists may be that they are thwarting (other) activist judges who are inserting their (different) ideas of social policy into legal decision-making.

Activist judging is also marked by its methods. The activist judge may decide a case in a manner that discounts the parties' submissions about how the case should be decided. The course of activist judging can entail bending existing law and adopting new doctrine. An aspect is the use of precedent. If needs be activist judges may ignore precedent which would frustrate them in achieving their social policy goals. Activist judges may read down the *ratio* of a previous decision or avoid it altogether on the basis that it is *obiter dictum*. Activist judges may decide that the precedent is somehow inapplicable, is inconsistent with previous decisions, or has been decided *per incuriam*.[67] Activist judges may even recast how the doctrine of precedent works and ignore precedents about precedent.[68] The scope for activist methodology as regards precedent varies with the level of court in which activist judging takes place. Judges in an apex court will generally be in a better position to circumvent precedents adverse to their goals or to overrule them.

Another feature marking out activist judging is the interpretation of legal texts—legislation, human rights instruments, and constitutions. To achieve

[65] ibid [23].
[66] *Candler v Crane, Christmas & Co* [1951] 2 KB 164, 178.
[67] eg, *Broome v Cassell & Co Ltd* [1972] AC 1027, 1054.
[68] eg, *Dobbs v Jackson Women's Health Organization* 597 US 215 (2022).

liberal policy goals an activist judge may argue for its wide and permissive interpretation in light of what they decide is the instrument's basic structure or the implicit values contained within it.[69] Alternatively, an activist judge may pursue conservative policy goals through a narrower interpretation of legal texts and in the process undermine liberal precedents. Under the doctrine of textualism (with statutory interpretation) or originalism (with constitutional interpretation) legal texts are construed to bear the meaning they had at the time they were drafted. Coupled with the interpretation of legal texts, activist judging might involve a willingness to strike down legislation where the constitution or human rights instrument enables this. As well as substantive law, activist judges might also rework procedural or remedial law to better achieve their social policy goals. Thus activist judges may seek to facilitate access to justice as with public interest litigation in India, which enabled those without means to file simple writ petitions for judicial relief; on the other hand, they may seek to limit judicial power by choking off claims through restrictive doctrines of jurisdiction and standing.

(B) Ideal Types and the Real World

Ideal types for judges and judging are not meant to be an accurate description of any one judge or what any one judge does. Although the ideal types draw on the practice of real-world judges, they are not intended to fully describe them. Rather they are an analytical tool by which real-life judging can be compared with an ideal type to illuminate specific features of judging. Comparison in this way is not necessarily straightforward. How a real-life judge is to be regarded may depend on the position of the observer. Reliance on what judges say they do faces the drawback, as with any informant, that how they rationalize their decision-making may differ from what they in fact do. A real-life judge may be similar in some respects to an ideal type but not in others, indeed a real-life judge may exhibit the features of two or more ideal types.

Legalism in real-life decision-making has three attributes. Predictability is one. Legalism provides a good degree of certainty enabling people to plan. A judge is held to a standard of legal correctness and constrained because the principles of the common law are binding. That ensures a greater

[69] eg, *Francis Coralie Mullin v Union Territory of Delhi* (1981) 1 SCC 608, 618 (Bhagwati J).

reliability to judicial decision-making than would occur if it were based, say, on each judge's assessment of the merits of the case or on social policy goals. Secondly, legalism eases the task of the judge in standard cases in that they apply existing principles to resolve disputes. That obviates the need to devise individual solutions for each case. Finally, legalism better insulates the judge from criticism. At least on the surface the outcome does not turn on the judge's perceptions of merits or their social or political attitudes. If the judge adheres to accepted methods of legal reasoning to reach a decision, it will turn on which side of the line a case falls in light of the law and the facts.

The downside to legalism is, first, that it does not respond sufficiently to an ever-changing legal order. New situations are accommodated as best as can be by extending existing principles to decide a specific case, but the judge is forbidden from expressly changing course because they are discontented with the results which flow from it. Next, legalism can mask a decision dependent on social values as the neutral application of established principles. Inherent in legalism as a method of judicial decision-making is, at the least, a conservativism derived from a caution regarding change. The upshot of legalism might also be to confine adjudication to applying rules to a narrow band of facts which excludes consideration of legal and social policies or the respective power of the parties. Finally, apart from the principle of *stare decisis*, legalism is ill-equipped to deal with the balancing and proportionality associated with adjudicating cases under human rights and other instruments containing multi-factorial standards. That involves reaching an evaluative judgment for which the notion of legal correctness through the application of legal principle is inadequate.

Merits judging is relatively common. The judge conceives of an outcome which will be generally accepted in the legal and wider community and then uses the law as a check.[70] In many areas a merits outcome will coincide with what the law requires. That may be because the judge's sense of where the merits of the case lie is itself informed by many years of reading cases as a student and practitioner and then deciding them as a judge. The other side of the coin to this is that the judge's view of the merits may therefore be different from a layperson's. Depending on the circumstances the judge may have a relatively free hand. The law confers a discretion, its tests of reasonableness, balancing, and proportionality are open-ended, or the available precedents do not address the issues at hand. In situations where there are precedents,

[70] See also intuitive judging at p. 245 above.

the merits judge can often distinguish them. Any applicable legislation may be sufficiently open textured to permit the judge to accomplish the desired end of a merits decision. Purposive interpretation can assist. Where the interpretation of a statute gives rise to an absurd and unjust outcome, the merits judge will avoid that with the justification that the legislature would never have intended it had they that situation in mind. That the law produces and can justify merits decision-making underpins it legitimacy. It is when judges decide cases on the basis of principle and the outcome is contrary to the merits as the community sees them that its authority is weakened.

The drawback to merits judging is that it can be too little bound by law. The judge's duty is not to administer justice in some general sense but to do so according to law. Justice in developed societies 'is not left to the unguided, even if experienced, sage sitting under the spreading oak tree'.[71] There is the obvious risk of merits decisions turning on the predilections and subjective values of individual judges. The judge confuses their own prejudices with the sensible resolution of a dispute, even worse, the demands of justice. Without self-doubt and reflection the judge may conceive that what they regard as a just outcome is precisely that. Other judges may have conflicting views so that which judge is allocated a case determines the outcome. Judicial decision-making becomes a forensic lottery. Society may regard the judge's merits as being out of touch or worse. Their decision might even be conceived as an exercise of arbitrary power. If perceived as simply adopting solutions which the judge thinks are right, the legitimacy of judicial power is eroded. Certainty and predictability may also be sacrificed if judges pursue the merits of individual cases. If judges are free of the restraint of principle, there may be no indication to the parties about what factors affect the ultimate outcome of their dispute. Parties will be uncertain as to how widely the judge will explore the circumstances of their case and therefore what evidence and submissions they should highlight. It becomes more difficult for others to settle cases in the shadow of the law.

Minimalist judging has long been the approach of many common law judges. Cases are decided consistently with legal principle but narrowing the facts and issues examined. There is no seeking to resolve non-essential matters of fact or to address legal issues not crucial to the resolution of a case. There are no legal or social musings, only what is crucial to the conclusion. The narrow focus enables cases to be despatched more efficiently. Leaving

[71] *Duport Steels Ltd v Sirs* [1980] 1 WLR 142, 168 (Lord Scarman).

matters unresolved is especially valuable when the law in the area is in flux and further litigation would enable a more rounded analysis of the underlying issues. If a case has been decided on the basis of what turns out to be an unusual set of facts, the judicial minimalist will more likely avoid setting a distortive precedent. This does not mean that the rulings of minimalist judges are not beneficial. Although closely circumscribed the resolution of discrete legal issues and points of statutory interpretation still has important radiating effects. Changes in social and economic circumstances are accommodated by the steady evolution of legal principle as cases are resolved one at a time.

A drawback to minimalist judging is that its narrow focus may not assist with the development of legal doctrine. Deciding one case at a time and focusing on the specific dispute at hand may not produce the broader legal principles needed for the public to plan their affairs. The consequent uncertainty imposes costs and burdens when parties are unable to settle their disputes in the shadow of the law. Minimalism in judicial decision-making could occasion legal stagnation. Whatever its value lower down the judicial hierarchy, legal minimalism may not always be fitting in the higher courts where a degree of legal innovation is expected. In some circumstances it may be appropriate for judges to make a ruling, even though the case can be disposed of on other grounds, because a large number of similar cases exist or are anticipated and it is likely that the issue will need resolving in the near future. By leaving it undecided, the minimalist judge causes uncertainty in the interim period and places a burden on other parties to relitigate the matter down the line although the case is ripe for decision now. Failure of an apex court to seize the opportunity to decide an important issue may leave the law uncertain for years to come, to the disadvantage of lower courts and the legal community.

Modernizers act within the traditions of the common law, developing and in some cases creating principles of law which accord with new social needs and values. Lord Mansfield was a prime example, forging aspects of commercial law consonant with Britain's position as an expanding commercial power. There are many cases since where common law judges have modified legal liability when faced with new legal and social problems. In extending the liability of manufacturers for faulty goods in an age of mass production *Donoghue v Stevenson*[72] is but one example. In deciding how the law should

72 [1932] AC 562.

respond to changes in social values one template for modernizers has been what reasonable people in the community would regard as acceptable (or unacceptable) behaviour.[73] This is one reason that modernizers face objections that they are injecting their personal values into decisions: not only do they lack knowledge of community values, they have no principled basis for reconciling competing values and preferring some over others. For modernizers in the real world there is also an uncertain boundary separating the legitimate development of the law by the judges compared with the legislature.[74] Modernizers are ill-equipped as law reformers with certain types of change. They lack the broader perspective, greater appreciation of economic and policy issues, and the tools for consultation and evaluation available to other branches of government, so that 'where the revision is major and its ramifications complex, the courts must proceed with great caution'.[75]

Activist judging in the real world is difficult to pin down, although that does not inhibit some commentators from attaching the label to any judge whose judgments they deplore. More considered criticism identifies as judicial activists those departing from the conventions of judging in applying precedent and interpreting statutes and constitutional instruments in the pursuit of their social and political goals. Acting in this way, say the critics, undermines the legitimacy of the judiciary in the eyes of the public. Especially in the areas of constitutional and public law, a standard criticism is that in overextending judicial power activist judges are effecting change at the expense of the legislative and executive branches of government which are the best means of balancing and reconciling conflicting interests in the community. The desirable role for the judge, the critics assert, is to follow precedent, exercise judicial restraint, and defer to society's democratically appointed decision-makers.

Judges labelled as activists would respond that their judging accords with the values and conventions of judging: they are no different from other judges in the techniques they employ, although in Lord Denning's phrase they may be 'bold spirits' in their approach. In this regard they would underline as a great attribute of the common law its capacity of renewal and change. In refuting the charge that they pursue their own conceptions of social good, they would draw attention with public law in England to what Lord Roskill

[73] *R v R* [1992] 1 AC 599, 616. See also *Shafin Jahan v Asokan* (2018) 16 SCC 368.

[74] *Woolwich Equitable Building Society v Inland Revenue Commissioners* [1993] AC 70, 173 (Lord Goff).

[75] *Watkins v Olafson* [1989] 2 SCR 750, 760–61 (McLachlin J for the court).

described as the 'upsurge of judicial activism' since the middle of the twentieth century, which resulted in a series of judicial decisions enlarging beneficially the scope of judicial review and the consequent accountability of public authorities for their exercise of powers affecting the public.[76] In the context of human rights in the UK, activists judges would add that it was the legislature through the Human Rights Act 1998 which encouraged greater activism on the part of the judges in giving effect to the rights recognized in the European Convention on Human Rights. In this area, as Simon Brown LJ expressed it, 'constitutional dangers exist no less in too little judicial activism as in too much'[77] so that the issue becomes in each case whether the decision or line of decisions of which it is part is 'too much'.

IV Practical Judging

Judges decide cases. In doing so they will have before them a specific fact-situation. At first instance the judge may need to establish the relevant facts based on the evidence.[78] Facts go a long way for the judge in decision-making. As well as finding the facts the judge must identify relevant legal principles. These will derive in large part from statute and precedent. Both statute and precedent need interpreting. In practice the tasks of establishing the fact-situation and the relevant legal principles run together. In conventional judging, the relevant legal principles are related to a fact-situation to produce a decision. Mostly the tasks of establishing the fact-situation and relevant legal principles, and relating one to the other, are routine. Well-accepted legal principles are applied straightforwardly to a fact-situation, easily established or agreed to by the parties, and a decision fairly readily follows. That does not mean that there is always a single correct view which will be upheld on any appeal.

Even in the higher courts the opportunities for legal creativity are limited, not least because parties have first to litigate an issue where creativity is demanded. Creativity cannot occur in a vacuum; in the common law system creativity takes place in the context of judges deciding specific issues put to them. Once the parties are before a judge the scope for legal creativity may

[76] *Council of Civil Service Unions v Minister for the Civil Service* [1985] AC 374, 414.
[77] *International Transport Roth GmbH v Secretary of State for the Home Department* [2002] EWCA Civ 158, [2003] QB 728 [54].
[78] PP. 198–200 above.

be narrow because the relevant legislation, constitutional or human rights instruments, precedents, or legal principles have been previously ascertained or interpreted. However, a specific fact-situation may in the judge's view throw a different light on an issue compared with how it was analysed in a precedent case. Legal principles may need qualification to accommodate a quite new fact-situation. Thus a platform for change may be available through legal techniques such as reasoning analogically or distinguishing a precedent. In some instances judges may be able to draw on considerations of legal or public policy, a concern with the consequences of adopting a particular course, or the demands of 'common sense' to resolve a case.

(A) 'The Institutional Character of the Judge'

In analysing the constraints and freedoms which judges enjoy in discharging their duties in a parliamentary democracy, Justice Bora Laskin of the Canadian Supreme Court characterized these as the 'institutional character of the judge'.[79] The doctrine of precedent institutionalized the judge, he observed, although a timorous judge might find more command in what a higher court had said than a closer examination of a precedent would carry. With a particular decision a judge's reasons might 'eddy out beyond its relation to parties and issues and provide a springboard for extension or contraction of the legal doctrine which underlies it'.[80] *Par excellence*, Laskin argued, this was an illustration of how the individual preference of the judge reacted upon the institutional system of which a judge was a member.[81] Laskin noted that with legislation a judge is faced with a manifestation of the 'popular will' and its interpretation should therefore reflect as much concern with realizing its purpose as with its literal expression.[82] Given, as Laskin suggests, that judges have an 'institutional character' derived from legislation and precedent, the question arises how they manoeuvre these when faced with the facts of a case and the issues the parties pose.

[79] Bora Laskin, 'The Institutional Character of the Judge' (1972) 7 Israeli L Rev 329. (Chief Justice, Canada 1973–84.)

[80] ibid 331.

[81] ibid 332–33.

[82] ibid 342.

The force of statute law

In common law systems judges apply legislation even if they regard it as unsatisfactory. The appropriateness or otherwise of the policy behind it is not a matter for the judge but for political determination. Nor can the judge make or remake legislation. The idea of an eminent American judge that judges may revise or update what might be regarded as obsolescent statutes conflicts with their constitutional role.[83] That task of clearing away the dead wood on the statute book lies with the legislature, possibly aided by a law reform body which can identify potential repeals.[84] Another idea—that legislation can act as a source for developing the common law—has never taken deep root jurisprudentially, although in practice statute may exert a 'gravitational force' on the ongoing development and application of legal principle.[85] In performing their task of applying statute law, however, judges must interpret it and this offers them opportunities for creativity within the bounds of legal principle.

Except as the principles of statutory interpretation permit, jurisprudential theories, linguistic conventions, and the philosophy of language have no purchase. But there can still be scope for judicial imagination in giving meaning to the words of a statute. One source of interpretive principle is contained in statute law itself. Apart from definitions in the legislation in dispute, from the time of the Interpretation Act 1850 there has been a limited dictionary which judges can draw on in interpreting legislation. Unless a contrary intention appears, for example, words importing the masculine gender include the feminine and vice versa, and words in the singular include the plural and vice versa.[86] Other legislation is more empowering. From 1981 section 15AA of the Australian Acts Interpretation Act 1901 has provided that in interpreting legislation the judge should prefer the interpretation which would best promote 'the purpose or object' of a statute whether or not it is expressly stated. Another example is the UK's Human Rights Act 1998. In general there is no power in English law for a judge to fill in gaps when interpreting legislation, and defects which the judge uncovers are to be cured by Parliament.[87] However, under section 3(1) of that Act a provision must be given effect

[83] cf Guido Calabresi, *A Common Law for the Age of Statutes* (Harvard University Press 1982) 164–66 (US Court of Appeals, 2nd Cir, 1994-).

[84] eg, Law Commission, *Statute Law Repeals: Twentieth Report. Draft Statute Law (Repeals) Bill* (Law Com No 357 / Scot Law Com No 243, 2015).

[85] eg, see Jack Beatson, 'The Role of Statute in the Development of Common Law Doctrine (2001) 117 LQR 247.

[86] s 4. See now Interpretation Act 1978, s 6.

[87] eg, *Magor and St Mellons Rural DC v Newport Corporation* [1952] AC 189.

compatibly if possible with the rights set out in the European Convention on Human Rights (ECHR). Exceptionally a compatible interpretation may result in the insertion of words into legislation.

Another source of interpretive principle is contained in precedent. There are precedents setting out general principles for interpretating legislation, and with some statutes an accumulation of precedents as to what their specific provisions mean. Tax law in Britain offers an example of both. In the *Duke of Westminster* case[88] the House of Lords laid down that tax statutes were to be interpreted literally and strictly and, so construed, applied to transactions analysed in a formalistic manner. The door was opened wide to tax avoidance. Despite the resistance of some judges, it took some forty-five years for the law lords to vary the approach, and another twenty-five years after that for the new position to be made unequivocally clear. The ultimate question, the law lords held in 2004, is whether the relevant legislation, construed purposively, is intended to apply to a transaction seeking to avoid tax when that transaction is viewed realistically rather than in the artificial manner of its designers.[89] That was not the end of the story, although the burden of addressing tax avoidance fell largely to legislation targeted against it.

Precedents regarding the interpretation of legislation have a long history. In the sixteenth century the idea of the equity of a statute was given expression in Plowden's Commentaries: the text of the statute was foundational but defects could be overcome by giving effect to the law's spirit.[90] The idea fizzled. In the early twentieth century a classification was popularized comprising the literal, golden, and mischief 'rules': the literal rule, as the name suggests, involving the judge giving the words of the statute their plain and ordinary meaning; the golden rule, enabling the judge to modify a plain meaning if it leads to absurdities or inconsistencies;[91] and the mischief rule, empowering the judge to construe a statute to 'suppress the mischief, and advance the remedy . . . and to add force and life to the cure and remedy, according to the true intent of the makers of the Act'.[92] By the beginning of the twenty-first century the threefold classification was disapproved and the stated approach was purposive rather than literal, so

[88] [1936] AC 1.

[89] *Barclays Mercantile Business Finance Ltd v Mawson* [2004] UKHL 51, [2005] 1 AC 684; *WT Ramsay Ltd v Inland Revenue Commissioners* [1982] AC 300.

[90] *Eyston v Studd* (1573) 2 Plow 459, 465–68; 75 ER 688, 695–700.

[91] *Grey v Pearson* (1857) 6 H L Cas 61, 106; 10 ER 1216, 1234 (Lord Wensleydale).

[92] *Heydon's Case* (1584) 3 Co Rep 7a, 7b; 76 ER 637, 638.

that in construing a statutory provision a judge has to be concerned with the policy behind it.[93]

This method of statutory interpretation is contextual: the judge must identify the meaning of the words of a statutory provision in their context to best give effect to the policy of the statute.[94] Broadly speaking the same approach of considering the text, context, and purpose of a statutory provision applies in other common law jurisdictions, with the exception of the United States.[95] It involves the judge considering the words of the relevant provision in the context of the section, the part of the statute in which the section is located, and the legislation as a whole. Previous versions of the provision and other legislation *in pari materia* (on the same subject matter) may occasionally assist, as may secondary material about the provision's legislative history such as explanatory notes, Law Commission reports, and government policy documents. Clear statements in Parliament by the minister or other promoter of the provision may be invoked, but only if the provision is ambiguous or obscure or, on a conventional interpretation, leads to quite unreasonable consequences.[96]

In addition to these general principles, the law of statutory interpretation contains a number of specific principles, presumptions, and canons of construction on which the judge may draw in giving meaning to the words of a disputed provision. If the provision bears more than one meaning, the one producing absurd outcomes is to be avoided. If a matter was not foreseen at the time a statutory provision was enacted, there is the 'always speaking' principle enabling words to be interpreted in the light of modern conditions.[97] Settled practice about the interpretation of a provision may inform its construction, justified by the reliance interests involved.[98] Recourse may occasionally be possible to canons of construction such as the *eiusdem generis* and *expressio unius* rules (respectively, that general words take their colour from specific words in a list; and that an express reference to a matter is taken to exclude others). Common law presumptions, containing substantive

[93] *R v Secretary of State for Health, ex p Quintavalle* [2003] UKHL 13, [2003] 2 AC 687 [8], [21].

[94] eg, *R (on the application of O (A Child)) v Secretary of State for the Home Department* [2022] UKSC 3, [2023] AC 255 [29]–[30].

[95] eg, *La Presse Inc v Quebec*, 2023 SCC 22 [22]–[24]; *Residual Assco Group Ltd v Spalvins* (2000) 202 CLR 629 [27].

[96] *Pepper v Hart* [1993] AC 593, 640, a controversial decision.

[97] eg, *News Corp UK and Ireland Ltd v Revenue and Customs Commissioners* [2023] UKSC 7, [2024] AC 89.

[98] eg, *Bloomsbury International Ltd v Sea Fish Industry Authority* [2011] UKSC 25, [2011] 1 WLR 1546 [58].

values, may apply. For example, what is now known as the principle of legality means that in the absence of an express indication legislation is to be interpreted so that it does not interfere with fundamental rights, contradict principles of international law, have retrospective effect, inhibit access to the courts, or operate extraterritorially.[99]

While the dispute in which a judge interprets a legislative provision may be mundane, at the other end of the spectrum it can be constitutionally significant.[100] Changes in the principles themselves, as with tax legislation, can have important social consequences. The principles can be put to contrasting use such as the presumption of non-interference with fundamental rights, now invoked to protect individual and human rights but used historically to curb the beneficial effects of social reform legislation when perceived as trenching on property rights. All this gives rise to debates about the force of legislation and whether judges assume for themselves too great a discretion in its interpretation, nowadays encouraged by the purposive approach and the search for the policy behind a contested provision.

With Justice Scalia of the US Supreme Court in the lead, textualism became a leading approach to statutory interpretation in the US (called 'originalism' with constitutional interpretation).[101] Textualism's stated aim is primarily to confine judicial discretion and to prevent judges from substituting their own ideas of what the policy behind legislation is for that of the legislator. It is also said that textualism encourages the better drafting of laws, and furthers certainty and predictability and the law's 'original public meaning'.[102] Textualism prioritizes the ordinary meaning of the legislative text at the time it was enacted. It promises a single right answer to what a statutory provision means. To assist in the task it allows reference to dictionaries, generally accepted canons of construction, related parts of the text, and the context in which the statute was enacted. Pursuing legislative intent is deprecated, since it is unlikely that legislators will have focused on the issue before the court, and if they did, they would probably have had differing views. Any quest for a statute's purpose must remain within the text and legislative history is to be avoided. In particular, textualism forbids a purposive approach or a concern with the mischief the legislation was designed to address since this

[99] eg, *R v Secretary of State for the Home Department, ex p Simms* [2000] 2 AC 115; *Saeed v Minister for Immigration and Citizenship* (2010) 241 CLR 252 [15], [58].

[100] eg, *R (on the application of Miller) v Secretary of State for Exiting the European Union* [2017] UKSC 5, [2018] AC 61 regarding Brexit.

[101] *Bond v United States*, 572 US 844, 860 (2014).

[102] *Kisor v Wilkie* 588 US 558, 621–22 (2019) (Gorsuch J).

encourages the judges to adopt their own policy preferences. While striking as a theory of statutory interpretation, there is no uniformity of approach among textualism's adherents.[103]

Absent textualism in England, the concern with judicial adventurism has given rise to the contention that in the interpretation of a statutory provision the judge's focus must be to give effect to the legislature's intention ('intentionalism') rather than its purpose ('purposivism').[104] The proponents of intentionalism argue that this is essential to parliamentary sovereignty and to limit judicial power. Responding to the difficulty of identifying a legislature's intention when members vote for legislation for different reasons, the intentionalists argue that it is possible to attribute an objective intention to a group like the legislature when its members act according to agreed procedures to change the law. The critics note that while this may produce a general intent for the legislation as a whole, that may not extend to a specific provision in dispute in litigation. Proponents of purposivism contend that the reality is of judges confronting legislation which may be vague, indeterminate, or needing to be applied in circumstances which could not have been contemplated at the time it was enacted. Judicial creativity is therefore necessary in giving it meaning and is better not concealed. As with intent, however, there can be problems in identifying a provision's purpose, the proper level of its operation, and its primary purpose if there are a number of (perhaps conflicting) purposes. For the judge the argument between the intentionalists and purposivists appears theoretical. What on one view is a provision's intention on another is its purpose.

Rules of precedent

Not only must the judge in a common law system apply statute law when deciding a case, they must also follow precedent. This is a key aspect in Laskin's analysis of the judge's 'institutional character'. Under the doctrine of *stare decisis* the judge is generally bound to follow the *ratio decidendi* of a precedent case. The *ratio* is the ruling on a point of law which the judge deciding the case has treated as the best or preferred justification.[105] In deriving the *ratio* of a precedent as well as separating it from non-binding *obiter dictum* lie pathways to flexibility and change. The *ratio* may not be 'textualized'—set

[103] eg, *Fischer v United States* 603 US 480 (2024).

[104] Justices of the Supreme Court participated in the debate: Compare Lord Sales, 'Legislative Intention, Interpretation, and the Principle of Legality' (2019) 40 Statute LR 53 with Lord Burrows, *Thinking about Statutes: Interpretation, Interaction, Improvement* (CUP 2018) 13–34.

[105] *R (Youngsam) v Parole Board* [2019] EWCA Civ 229, [2020] QB 387 [51] (Leggatt LJ).

out explicitly in the judgment—but needs to be drawn from the precedent's reasoning in light of its facts and the issues in dispute. Flexibility may be compounded if there are several judgments in the precedent case, or several precedents bearing on the point. Judgments are not to be read as canonical texts as with statutes.[106] Nor is following precedent like following tramlines. Later judges may consider that the true *ratio* of a case is different from that stated in the judgment or that it is better explained on a different footing, enabling it to be distinguished. Evaluating the *ratio* of a precedent case in this way turns on a consideration of the wider context including its consistency with other legal principles, its acceptance by the legal community, and whether it is responsive to current social needs and community values.

Vertical *stare decisis* is fundamental: judges must apply the decisions of the courts above them in the judicial hierarchy. There are exceptions. An apex court may provide expressly that a lower court can depart from a precedent where there has been a fundamental shift in the understanding of the legal question at issue.[107] On the other hand precedents about precedent can confine yet further the lower courts. An apex court may rule that the decisions of courts which are not strictly part of the hierarchy must be treated as binding by lower courts.[108] Moreover, an apex court may direct lower courts to apply the apex court's unanimously approved or 'seriously considered' *dicta* in preference to their own precedents.[109] This may be justified on utilitarian grounds if in light of those *dicta* an appeal to it would be a foregone conclusion. However, there may be difficulties in practice in identifying which apex court *dicta* are unanimously approved or seriously considered. More importantly the idea of binding *dicta* not only textualizes judgments, treating them like legislation, but is contrary to the accepted notion that judicial law-making is generally ancillary to adjudication.

As to horizontal *stare decisis*, judges generally apply the precedents of their own court unless the circumstances are exceptional.[110] Exceptional circumstances include where there are conflicting lines of precedent so one must be chosen over another, a precedent was decided *per incuriam* (in ignorance of another precedent or legislative provision—a rare event), or a precedent is

[106] eg, *Broome v Cassell & Co Ltd* [1972] AC 1027, 1085 (Lord Reid); *R v Henry* [2005] 3 SCR 609 [57] (Binnie J).
[107] eg, *R v Comeau* [2018] 1 SCR 342 [29]–[34].
[108] eg, *Willers v Joyce* [2016] UKSC 44, [2018] AC 843 [19]–[21].
[109] eg, *R v Barton* [2020] EWCA Crim 575, [2021] QB 685; *Farah Constructions Pty Ltd v Say Dee Pty Ltd* (2007) 230 CLR 89, 151–52.
[110] *Willers v Joyce* (n 108) [7]–[9].

now seen to be wrong in light of developments in legal principle or society.[111] The general rule is that the judge should not depart from the precedents of their own court simply because they disagree with them. In part that is to counter the risk that the outcome of cases might otherwise depend, or at least might appear to depend, on who happens to be sitting.[112] In some jurisdictions horizontal precedent is strengthened by a rule that only a larger bench can revisit the court's own precedents, for example a decision of a two-judge bench may only be reconsidered by a bench of three or more judges.[113]

Overruling precedent engages the reliance interests of those who have planned on the basis of the precedent. There can be arguments over the existence and extent of reliance interests. This arose in 2022 when the US Supreme Court overturned *Roe v Wade*,[114] which almost half a century previously had established a constitutional right to privacy and abortion. The legal soundness of *Roe v Wade* became part of the highly divisive political and religious debate in the United States. In *Planned Parenthood of Southeastern Pennsylvania v Casey*[115] the Supreme Court reaffirmed *Roe v Wade*, although based its ruling on the fourteenth amendment's due process clause. The justification was that people had reasonably relied upon the continued application in *Roe v Wade* in organizing intimate relationships and careers, and that overturning it would adversely affect their decisional freedom which was central to their dignity and autonomy. The court was also concerned with its own legitimacy if it overruled such a watershed decision when abortion was so highly controversial and the court could be seen to be giving way 'under fire' to one side of the debate.[116]

In overruling *Roe* and *Casey*, *Dobbs v Jackson Women's Health Organization*[117] held that there was no constitutional right to abortion and its regulation was up to the legislature in each state. Factors to be considered in deciding when a precedent should be overruled were the nature of its error, the quality of its reasoning, its workability, its effect on other areas of law, and reliance interests. In the majority's view the error in the precedents, *Roe* and *Casey*, was egregious in short-circuiting the democratic process, their reasoning was without grounding in the text of the constitution, history,

[111] see eg, *R v Kirkpatrick* [2022] 2 SCR 480 [201]–[244].
[112] *In re Dalton* [2023] UKSC 36 [47].
[113] *Central Board of Dawoodi Bohra Community v State of Maharashtra* (2005) 2 SCC 673 [12] (the larger bench rule in the Indian Supreme Court).
[114] 410 US 113 (1973).
[115] 505 US 833 (1992).
[116] ibid 866–67.
[117] 597 US 215 (2022).

or precedent, the undue burden test of *Casey* had generated conflicting case law in lower courts, and there was a distortive impact on other areas of law. As to reliance interests, the court held that there were none like those traditionally recognized, which involved property or contractual rights.[118] By contrast the dissenting justices referred to the reliance interest of all women of childbearing age who had grown up expecting to be able to avail themselves of *Roe*'s and *Casey*'s protections.[119]

Since overruling a precedent has retroactive effect, not only will it disappoint the expectations of a present litigant but also others who have relied on it to arrange their affairs. To mitigate what are seen as the disruptive and unfair consequences for those relying on a precedent being overruled, prospective overruling is used in a few common law jurisdictions. The court's order will be that the overruling decision only applies for the future.[120] Prospective overruling has been used by some apex courts in cases about constitutional invalidity.[121] Where apex courts acknowledge the possibility of prospective overruling in private law matters, the bar has been set so high that prospective overruling is not practicable.[122] Prospective overruling faces the objection of encouraging judicial activism if a ruling can be made without upsetting past arrangements. In some jurisdictions prospective overruling is rejected altogether: the judicial function is to adjudicate rights and obligations, not to create them, and it would be inconsistent to maintain in force the previous state of affairs for some which the court is deciding is not the law.[123]

Precedent institutionalizes judges (as Laskin put it) by setting boundaries to their decision-making. But that fosters relative consistency, certainty, and finality in judicial decision-making. It meets public expectations that the law should be stable, consistent, and predictable to enable planning for the future. It means that judges will treat like cases alike. Precedents are contained in reasoned public judgments, and that is an important factor in a judge's accountability. Adherence to precedent offers fewer incentives for parties to challenge settled interpretations and reduces the consequent cost of like issues being relitigated. Precedent also benefits judges. It means that they need

118 ibid 288.
119 ibid 409–10.
120 *Chevron Oil Co v Huson* 404 US 97 (1971).
121 eg, *Somaiya Organics (India) Ltd v State of Uttar Pradesh* (2001) 5 SCC 519; *Canada (Attorney General) v Hislop* [2007] 1 SCR 429.
122 eg, *Re Spectrum Plus Ltd (In Liquidation)* [2005] UKHL 41, [2005] 2 AC 680.
123 *Ha v New South Wales* (1997) 189 CLR 465.

not be forever reinventing the wheel. With pressing caseloads the application of precedent enables them to avoid having to reconsider every point afresh. Judges therefore economize on time and effort. The administration of justice consequently benefits through judicial efficiency. Precedent acts as a shield, particularly when judges decide difficult or contentious cases, if they can justify their decision by reference to it. Cases are resolved in legitimate ways, controversy is reduced, and public confidence maintained.

Yet following precedent has potential downsides. One is that the judge may be fettered when faced with new circumstances demanding a response at variance with what the precedents require. Another is path dependence, that once a path is chosen each choice along that path is limited by the earlier stages.[124] The upshot may be that the outcome of cases in a particular area is less desirable than if one were to begin with a blank sheet. With each decision related to what preceded it, self-correction and a change in course become more difficult. Decisions are locked in by the path initially taken. An initial precedent sets the law off in a particular direction, which is compounded by incremental decision-making as judges follow precedent. Path dependence with precedent, it might be said, leads to inflexibility and consequent inefficiency since legal rules fail to respond to a change in underlying conditions. Because final outcomes turn on the path first taken, the argument might continue, it is difficult to predict at the outset what it will be. The order in which cases arrive for judicial consideration can significantly affect the legal principles which emerge. The obvious question is how can the confining effect of precedent and resulting path dependence be mitigated.

(B) Responsive Judging

Although the institutional character of the judge limits their freedom of decision-making, responsive judging is still possible and part of the common law tradition. Judges respond to the facts of a case and social changes but maintain a degree of order in their decision-making by working within the framework of accepted principle. With legislation we have seen that the task is to attribute meaning to the text. Interpretation may be a straightforward exercise, but there are many cases where uncertainty surrounds the outcome. Frequently there will be no precedent as to what the language means, which

[124] cf Ronald Dworkin's chain novel metaphor: *Law's Empire* (Fontana Press 1986) 228–38.

is not surprising with the volume of new legislation. By contrast there may be an accumulation of precedents around the meaning of a statutory provision and path dependence ends up producing awkward results. Legislation may need to be applied to new circumstances or those which the legislature could not have anticipated. In all these cases the judge responds to the statutory text in light of its context and purpose. In some circumstances, as with new legislation, the judge may adopt a cautious approach for fear of stifling legal development.[125]

Compared with statute law, responding to the facts of a case and changed social conditions is a different exercise within the common law. Unlike statutory interpretation the judge is not confined by the language of a precedent case since it is not like a determinative text. With statutory interpretation every word of the relevant provision counts, but in the common law the focus is on the *ratio* of the precedent case or series of cases and this offers scope for fluidity and change. It is well accepted that the judge may need to bring the common law up to date because of new social conditions and expectations.[126] The common law method is typically incremental allowing for a variation of direction in the event of undesirable outcomes or path dependence. Legal principles are applied to new circumstances. Judges reason analogically from existing precedents or distinguish them to reach new conclusions, or the principles themselves are varied to address contemporary or unforeseen circumstances.

Precedent and practical judging

In practice the system of precedent structures decision-making but does not stultify it. Nor is path dependence inevitable or branching away from an existing path always prevented. First and foremost the judge complies with precedent because that is part of what good judging according to the rule of law supposes. There is no need for theories that a judge's adherence to precedent is attributable to reputational concerns or 'reversal aversion' (being reversed on appeal) even if these factors give added force to a vital element of good judging. In many cases the judge is content to apply existing precedent because it is regarded as 'rightly decided': it has produced acceptable outcomes in the past and will do so in the case before them. If existing precedent does not do that, the rules of precedent are flexible and can often justify the judge shaping it to accord with what appears to be the merits of the instant case or

[125] eg, *Qantas Airways Ltd v Christie* (1998) 193 CLR 280, 284 (Brennan CJ).
[126] *Re Spectrum* (n 122) [32] (Lord Nicholls).

the novel challenge it poses. Precedent does not have the equivalent binding quality of statutory language.

The tradition of the common law is that judges effect incremental extensions from the baseline of existing precedent by techniques like analogical reasoning that the factual situations in the previous and instant cases are legally similar.[127] In some cases precedent is absent or weak so that in effect the judge has a clean slate. That may also be because of an accumulation of unclear or conflicting precedents so the judge has some choice. Very occasionally an apex court will accomplish a quantum leap and break the path dependence of precedent. As with great cases like *Donoghue v Stevenson*, the landmark decision in English law about negligence, the law is then set in a new direction.[128] Precedents may be invoked in such cases as a cover for innovation but that cannot disguise the significance in doctrinal innovation.

Among the legitimate techniques enabling judges to use precedent creatively is first, through the interpretation (or reinterpretation) of the *ratio* of the relevant authorities. The *ratio* of a precedent may be restated at a higher level of generality to support the judge's analysis in the instant case, enabling the law to move forward. Occasionally the principle underlying a precedent may be reformulated in a way which in effect reverses it.[129] Secondly, a precedent may be 'distinguished' by identifying significant differences between its facts and those of the instant case to justify a different result. Although still binding, the impact of the precedent is being confined to a narrower basis than that used to decide it. What was thought to be the *ratio* of a precedent may be interpreted narrowly so that it is no longer regarded as binding in the broad sense it once was but in that regard is of persuasive authority only.

In practice judges rank precedents so that their 'legal strength' varies. If a precedent has been well received in subsequent cases it is more likely to be applied even though it is not strictly binding. On the other hand some precedents, even decided by distinguished judges, may never find favour and are eventually despatched with the justification that 'the law has moved on'.[130] Judges also justify following a precedent as broadly conceived since it was decided by a 'strong court', in other words it was the decision of judges highly regarded for their abilities or expertise or the positions they occupy. Less deference may be paid to other decisions because they are from a less impressive

[127] eg, *Paul v Royal Wolverhampton NHS Trust* [2024] UKSC 1, [2025] AC 459 [58], [106]. Often quoted is Brennan J in *Sutherland Shire Council v Heyman* (1985) 60 ALR 1, 43–44.

[128] [1932] 1 AC 562.

[129] *Osborne v Rowlett* (1880) 13 Ch D 774, 785–86 (Jessel MR).

[130] *Stack v Dowden* [2007] UKHL 17, [2007] 2 AC 432 [26], [60].

bench. Similarly, *dicta* have different weight, some being of such persuasive force that a judge will follow it even though not bound to do so. In some areas there may be a mass of precedents which in extreme cases may be regarded as little more than a mechanism to dispense palm-tree justice.[131] Faced with a number of precedents the judge may attempt to synthesize them into a principle or coherent pattern of factors for use in the instant and future cases.

One means judges use to upset path dependence is to identify a 'wrong turning' in what until then has been accepted as the leading precedent. The 'wrong turning' justifies the need to reformulate principle and set decision-making back on the 'right path'. The task is simpler if the leading precedent was based on a faulty premise, it has been wrongly assumed to have decided what in fact it did not decide, or its reasoning is flawed.[132] A 'wrong turning' analysis may also be explained on grounds that the leading precedent is unsound in the light of what is (or should be) the relevant underlying principle in an area of doctrine. A variation on this is to portray the leading precedent as being grounded in conditions of an earlier time which are no longer appropriate, or formulated such that it does not accord with new societal challenges such as (in the commercial context) developments in information technology.[133]

Legal and public policies

Alongside legal principles in judicial decision-making are legal and public policies. First, legal policies. Those that judges invoke range from the grand, such as furthering the rule of law or access to justice, through to the more mundane, such as finality and that 'fraud unravels all'. The meaning and reach of these policies may be uncertain. They may be in conflict. Finality as a legal policy offers an example. The implications of finality are that subject to any appeal once an issue is determined by a judge there are restrictions on the ability of parties to reopen the matter. Judges recognize that determinations of fact may be imperfect but having reached a solution with the best methods at their disposal the matter should be brought to an end. A strong justification is necessary for the reception of fresh evidence or to conduct a new trial. But there are exceptions where other legal policies trump finality. In the case

[131] eg, *United Policyholders Group v Attorney General of Trinidad and Tobago* [2016] UKPC 17, [2016] 1 WLR 3383 [80].

[132] eg, *Barclays Bank Plc v O'Brien* [1994] 1 AC 180, 192; *McRae v Commonwealth Disposals Commission* (1951) 84 CLR 377, 410.

[133] eg, *Broad Idea International Ltd v Convoy Collateral Ltd* [2021] UKPC 24, [2023] AC 389 [59]–[60] (Lord Leggatt).

of a miscarriage of justice in a criminal trial, Lord Atkin summed up the clash of policies: 'Finality is a good thing, but justice is a better.'[134] In civil cases litigants must generally advance all relevant matters before the court and are not normally permitted another opportunity in subsequent proceedings, but fraud is a thing apart. If not raised at trial there is no requirement imposed on the party now seeking to set aside a judgment infected by fraud that they should have exercised reasonable diligence at the time to uncover it.[135]

Certainty as a central policy of English commercial law can be traced to Lord Mansfield's dictum that 'it is of more consequence that a rule should be certain, than whether the rule is established one way or the other'.[136] As a touchstone for English commercial law certainty echoes to the present day.[137] It means bright-line rules which traders, shippers, brokers, and bankers can readily understand and apply in commercial practice. This ensures that parties can not only plan for their future relationship but also, as Lord Sumner put it, 'gather their fate then and there' if things go wrong.[138] A corollary of certainty is a strict application of rules. The merits in individual cases take a back seat. The policy of certainty accepts that adherence to bright-line rules may result in commercial parties using sharp practice or those with unmeritorious claims profiting at the expense of others. Despite this, bright-line rules mean that commercial parties know where they stand. Judicial decision-making is consistent and that promotes its own fairness.

Then secondly there are a variety of public policies playing a role in judicial decision-making. Public policies are at the forefront of human rights decision-making since judges must balance against the exercise of some rights what is necessary in a democratic society in the interest of matters like national security, public safety, economic well-being, public order, and public health or morals.[139] In private law decision-making public policy has a role in novel cases or those where existing law needs adapting to changed circumstances. Public policy has been especially important in determining the existence of a duty of care in new cases in tort. Over time policy arguments have sometimes transitioned into legal principles. For Lord Reid, public policy involved a responsiveness to community values. For this reason he

[134] *Ras Behari Lal v King-Emperor* [1933] UKPC 60, (1933) 50 TLR 1, 2.
[135] eg, *Takhar v Gracefield Developments Ltd* [2019] UKSC 13, [2020] AC 450.
[136] *Vallejo v Wheeler* (1774) 1 Cowp 143, 153; 98 ER 1012, 1017.
[137] eg, *Homburg Houtimport BV v Agrosin Private Ltd (The Starsin)* [2003] UKHL 12, [2004] 1 AC 715 [13] (Lord Bingham).
[138] *Bank Line Ltd v Arthur Capel & Co* [1919] AC 435, 454.
[139] eg, ECHR, art 10 (freedom of expression).

regarded it as valuable for judges to have given some public service before their appointment and for them to be aware of social problems.[140]

In judicial decision-making public policy is not immutable. Its implications for particular cases can be uncertain, an 'unruly horse' as it was famously described.[141] Public policy encompasses a wide field, on the one hand the broad policies of accommodating social values and community needs, on the other, specific goals such as protecting the health service, ensuring efficient policing, and facilitating finance for small businesses.[142] To the objection that judges have no particular expertise in public policy, Pollock CB gave the answer that this was no reason for their refusing to entertain it.[143] However, it does mean that judges should act with care. Although of narrower ambit than the public policy arguments considered by members of the legislature or the executive, some of the public policies judges invoke are contestable and not necessarily shared by the public as a whole.

Consequences

Consequence-based reasoning is a specific example of judges taking policy considerations into account. In reaching a decision they are concerned with its expected social and economic impact and whether this makes desirable the interpretation of a statute or precedent which is likely to bring it about. It is mainly a factor used against judges extending the boundaries of legal liability. The consequence-based reasoning of judges typically focuses on a single factor such as the response of others or the cost implications rather than on an overall balancing as with the economist's cost-benefit analysis of a decision. The extent of consequence-based reasoning varies with the subject matter. There is no scope for it where certain rights are at issue such as the right not to be subject to inhuman or degrading treatment or punishment. There protection is absolute and any sort of consequential balancing is excluded.[144] Consequence-based reasoning has a long history in the common law. *Ashby v White*[145] was a leading case about the right to vote and whether a claimant had a remedy when the returning officer denied it. To the objection

140 Lord Reid, 'The Judge as Lawmaker'(1972) 12 J Soc'y Pub Teachers Law (New Series) 22, 27.

141 *Richardson v Mellish* (1824) 2 Bing 229, 252; 130 ER 294, 303 (Burrough J).

142 *Rees v Darlington Memorial Hospital NHS Trust* [2004] 1 AC 309 [6]; *Hill v Hamilton-Wentworth Regional Police Services Board* [2007] 3 SCR 129 [56]–[58]; *Barclays Bank Plc v O'Brien* [1994] 1 AC 180, 188.

143 *Egerton v Brownlow* (1853) IV HLC 1, 151; 10 ER 359, 419.

144 eg, *A v Secretary of State for the Home Department* [2005] UKHL 71, [2006] 2 AC 221.

145 (1703) 2 Ld Raym 938, 92 ER 126.

that to grant a remedy in a case like that when the claimant suffered no loss 'will occasion multiplicity of actions', Holt CJ's retort (in dissent) was that 'if men will multiply injuries, actions must be multiplied too; for every man that is injured ought to have his recompence'.[146] Consequence-based reasoning regularly features when extensions of tort liability are in issue. In a negligence claim for pure financial loss Cardozo CJ gave the oft-repeated warning about adopting 'liability in an indeterminate amount for an indeterminate time to an indeterminate class'.[147] As liability has been extended for such claims, judges have been aware of the risk Cardozo CJ identified.

The consequences featuring in judicial reasoning take various forms. One—historically typified as the 'floodgates' argument—focuses on the consequence of a decision for the courts themselves and that they will be swamped by the claims which will result.[148] A second is the potential financial liability for the defendant and others in a similar position or for the public as a whole in terms of the negative impact on the public finances.[149] Similarly, judges may consider the potential impact of imposing liability on other beneficial activities. A third way that judges take consequences into account concerns the ramifications of a decision in other contexts. The instant case, it may be said, is relatively innocuous, but the real problem is that it creates a slippery slope to unknown dangers which, however careful the judge is, may not be prevented by their attempting to spell out clear boundaries in the judgment.[150] Fourthly, there is what has been called the 'overkill' argument. This is that the defendant and others in a similar position may engage in unduly defensive behaviour in the future by going beyond what the decision requires to insure against any risk of liability. Deterrence in this way, it is said, can lead to substantial and unnecessary costs as well as other disadvantages.[151]

With consequence-based reasoning a judge justifies a decision on the grounds of overall outcome. In some cases the likely beneficial or detrimental consequences of a decision will be fairly clear in the context of its facts or because of its obvious radiating effects. With others whether a decision will

146 at 955, 137. Upheld in the HL: (1703) 1 Bro PC 62, (1703) 1 ER 417.

147 *Ultramares Corp v Touche*, 255 NY 170, 179; 174 NE 441, 444 (1931).

148 eg, *Esanda Finance Corporation Ltd v Peat Marwick Hungerfords* [1997] HCA 8, (1997) 188 CLR 241 [110] (McHugh J).

149 eg, *Cooper v Hobart* [2001] 3 SCR 537 [55].

150 See *R (on the application of Finch on behalf of the Weald Action Group) v Surrey County Council* [2024] UKSC 20 [119]–[123].

151 *Rowling v Takaro Properties Ltd* [1988] AC 473, 502 (PC, New Zealand). See also pp. 202–3 above.

bring particular results is more uncertain. Decision-making in the legislature and by public authorities will often be accompanied by detailed cost-benefit analysis and evaluations of the outcome for the environment or human rights. That contrasts with consequence-based reasoning by judges which seldom has any comparable empirical base. Rather judges make assumptions based on what might be limited knowledge about social and economic arrangements and how people and institutions will respond to their decisions. Later decisions may demonstrate how awry such assumptions were, even in areas such as statutory amendment or doctrinal development where judges might be thought to have considerable insight.[152] Fairness requires that consequence-based assumptions which are a determining factor in judicial decision-making are exposed to argument, perhaps in some cases to expert scrutiny.

Common sense

Lord Atkin finished his speech in the pivotal case for English negligence law of *Donoghue v Stevenson*, by expressing satisfaction that 'the law in this matter, as in most others, is in accordance with sound common sense'.[153] This acknowledgement of the role of common sense in common law decision-making can be multiplied across time and jurisdiction.[154] Common sense is advanced as a ground for decision-making either by itself or along with other factors such as precedent. For some judges common sense may corroborate the outcome of legal analysis, provide content for legal concepts such as reasonableness, or address uncertainties at the margin where the law falls short. For other judges it is an informant that precedent is out of date and must be modified, or it acts as a check on whether legal analysis reaches a rounded and just solution in the instant case. For yet others it stands for shared community values and as such can be invoked in straightforward cases, but not where the community might be deeply at odds as to its demands. In each case there is a claim about the knowledge, insight, or values which common sense

[152] See *Prudential Assurance Co Ltd v Revenue and Customs Commissioners* [2018] UKSC 39, [2019] AC 929 [55]–[66].

[153] [1932] 1 AC 562, 599.

[154] eg, Reid (n 140) 25; *British Railways Board v Herrington* [1972] AC 877, 919 (Lord Wilberforce); *Collector of Customs v Agfa-Gevaert Limited* (1996) 186 CLR 389, 400; Terence Etherton, 'Liberty, the Archetype and Diversity: A Philosophy of Judging' [2010] PL 727, 730 (Etherton MR 2016–21); Lord Kerr, 'Striking the Balance Between Common Sense and Legal Reasoning' (Gresham College, 20 June 2019) (UK Supreme Court 2009–20); *R v Kruk* 2024 SCC 7 (Can SC).

brings in supporting, supplementing, or correcting the conclusions which legal principles produce.

The obvious difficulty is knowing what common sense requires. The concept can mean what everybody knows and that no special expertise is required because what is common sense is apparent from the practices of daily life. With judicial decision-making that might translate as what everyone knows to be fair and just in the context of a particular case. But that is problematic without elaboration and critical reflection. Common sense varies across social groups, societies, and time. The common sense and experience of judges can be limited by their bounded lives. As with all human beings judges are unconsciously impacted by cognitive limitations, and their notions of common sense are moulded by heuristics and biases.[155] While common sense can be based on sound knowledge, inherited wisdom, and experience, it can also be a collection of unsound facts, fixed attitudes, and popular prejudices. The common sense of the judge can be the nonsense of others.

Gosselin v Quebec (Attorney General)[156] illustrates how judges' notions of common sense are not universally held. There the Supreme Court of Canada rejected a class action challenge to a provincial social assistance scheme which reduced welfare payments to the under thirties unless they were in education or work experience programmes. The majority held that the scheme did not constitute discrimination or a denial of human dignity under the Canadian Charter of Rights and Freedoms. Logic and common sense, it said, supported giving young people the incentive to obtain skills.[157] Critics identified an unsupported 'common sense' assumption in the judgment that if younger people tried hard enough they could obtain work. One of the hallmarks of systemic discrimination, the critics argued, was the ability to cloak itself in 'common sense' and to erase the realities of those suffering from it.[158]

Common sense may have a surer foothold in specific contexts, but even here there are pitfalls. One example is the deployment of 'business common sense' in the interpretation of commercial documents. The practice has a distinguished history. In a claim under a contract for insurance Lord Mansfield observed that merchant contracts 'ought not to depend upon subtleties and niceties; but upon rules easily learned and easily retained, because they are

[155] PP. 244–245 above.
[156] [2002] 4 SCR 429.
[157] ibid [27], [44], [56].
[158] Natasha Kim and Tina Piper, 'Gosselin v. Quebec: Back to the Poorhouse' (2003) 48 McGill LJ 749, 780.

the dictates of common sense'.[159] In construing a charterparty over two centuries later Lord Diplock said that if a conclusion flowing from the detailed semantic and syntactical analysis of words in a commercial contract were to flout business commonsense, it would have to yield to the latter.[160] The accepted practice in English law is that in interpreting a contractual term a judge must ascertain the objective meaning of the language used against the background of the contract as a whole and its context, and that when there are rival interpretations weight can be given to the one more consistent with business common sense.[161] It is accepted that commercial common sense cannot be used to undervalue contractual language, or to remedy retrospectively what in light of the facts as they happened turns out to be a bad bargain.[162] The real problem, as Lord Neuberger put it, is that judges may not be 'the most commercially-minded, let alone the most commercially experienced' and so should not 'overconfidently [assume] the role of arbiter of commercial reasonableness or likelihood'.[163]

V Conclusion

In a lecture entitled 'What do Judges do?' Lord Mustill observed that the essential components of the judicial function are unobservable by the litigant or in many instances the skilled observer, who 'will not know which wheels turned, which chemical processes took place, when the judge formed the link between the material and the conclusion'.[164] Few judges would be so candid or so unwise to tell exactly what happened in their minds when arriving at a particular judgment, he observed, even in those cases where they were capable of reconstructing their thought processes after the event. Even with fully motivated judgments, Mustill continued, one could not always be sure, as regards the individual judge, that the reasons in the judgment were in fact the reasons for the decision: they may have been constructed to reconcile the

[159] *Hamilton v Mendes* (1761) 2 Burr 1198, 1214; 97 ER 787, 795.

[160] *Antaios Compania Naviera SA v Salen Rederierna AB (The Antaios)* [1985] AC 191, 201. Approved in *Enercon (India) Ltd v Enercon GmbH*, AIR 2014 SC 3152 [83].

[161] eg, *Wood v Capita Insurance Services Ltd* [2017] UKSC 24, [2017] AC 1173 [28], [40]. cf *Electricity Generation Corporation v Woodside Energy Ltd* [2014] HCA 7, (2014) 251 CLR 640 [35].

[162] *Arnold v Britton* [2015] UKSC 36, [2015] AC 1619 [17], [19]–[20].

[163] *Skanska Rashleigh Weatherfoil Ltd v Somerfield Stores Ltd* [2006] EWCA Civ 1732 [22] (Lord Neuberger). See also *J & P Marlow (No 2) Pty Ltd v Hayes* [2023] NSWCA 117, (2023) 112 NSWLR 29 [76] (Bell CJ).

[164] (1995–1996) 3 Juridisk Tidskrift 611, 613 (English judge and law lord 1978–97).

decision with legal materials which appeared to stand in the way, but played no part in the decision, or to call up support from favourable materials for a decision arrived at without recourse to them, for example one made intuitively or on grounds of policy.[165]

It is to the distinction that Mustill in effect draws between the reasons for, and the reasons given for, a decision that the models examined in section II of the chapter are directed. The traditional legal approach, focusing on matters like precedent, tells only part of the story of judging. The judge with whom the chapter began, Benjamin Cardozo, touched on some of the other parts, although over a century later we know so much more about what he characterized as the judge's subconscious loyalties, likes and dislikes, prejudices, instincts and emotions, and habits and convictions.[166] Models which address these matters draw from a variety of disciplines—social psychology, small group analysis, role theory, attitude theory, the concept of personal values, and so on. To varying degrees these enrich our understanding of judicial decision-making, although, like the legal approach, none can provide a full account. Depicting judging according to any one model is bound to fail given what we know about human complexity.

As we saw in section II, psychological models throw valuable light on the process of judging. Judges have long recognized the role of intuition in decision-making, where mental short-cuts are used to reach quick decisions. One judge has described it as 'reasoning from a given conclusion'.[167] Intuitive judging is a standard tool of decision-making. It enables judges to navigate the caseload, especially where they are dealing with high volume applications which follow a pattern. The lack of time and the need to proceed to the next case rules out fully deliberative decision-making. While intuitive decision-making is part of everyday judging, there are dangers. Social psychologists have identified potential errors because of the impact of cognitive biases. Among those to which intuitive decision-making is potentially prone is confirmation bias. A judge may adhere to the decision reached intuitively, which a little probing and scepticism would reveal to be wrong. A potential corrective to cognitive biases with judges is that they act in public, must explain themselves, and in most cases are subject to appeal (or review). Consequently, their impact should be dampened and the risk of error in decision-making reduced. When faced with situations where they

165 ibid 620.
166 PP. 244–245 above.
167 Stephen Sedley, *Ashes and Sparks: Essays on Law and Justice* (CUP 2011) 156.

need to make a decision, these factors focus the judge's attention on legally relevant matters and, to a varying extent, immunize them from distortive influences.

Emotion is a potential component when judges make certain types of decision. Depending on the context, the judge may positively use empathy—knowing and understanding another's experience—as part of the process of decision-making. Empathy can be especially important in trying to appreciate a litigant's case when the judge's own experiences are quite different. However, the judge must moderate other types of emotions, like sympathy, from influencing decisions. When the facts and law are uncertain, the social psychologist warns how judges, perhaps unconsciously, might assemble these into a compelling narrative to find in favour of the more sympathetic party. Judges must apply the law faithfully and impartially, even if it means reaching conclusions they dislike. Judges must also manage their emotions in public. To express them could undermine the integrity of the decision-making process, despite their frustration with the unprepared or impolite lawyer, or exasperation with the litigant in person taking a series of bad and lengthy points, despite judicial prompting that this will not advance their case. These constraints demand self-awareness on the part of the judge, along with a consciousness of appropriate boundaries. By contrast with the judge, there are not necessarily the same constraints on others in court showing anger, frustration, or boredom. As we saw in the previous chapter, part of the judge's judgecraft involves managing the emotions of others, along with managing their own.

Judging is a social process, the thread running through the relational models outlined in the second part of section II of the chapter. 'Situation sense' is where a judge's long association with a specific context of judging formed through training and experience relates directly to their decision-making. Along with the expertise gained comes a practical wisdom about patterns and practices in that area of legal practice, which assists in the despatch of the judge's caseload. Insights for the judge also derive from the 'dialogue' which the judge has, internally with a range of colleagues and judicial assistants, externally with the advocates in a case and those like academics who have written about the issue at hand. One aspect of dialogue concerns a judge's interactions with other judges. That in turn is an aspect of collegiality, and is typified by judges on a panel cooperating to fashion a judicial decision to be either the judgment of the whole court, or that of a convincing majority. Whatever one judge may think, if they cannot obtain support from other judges in an apex court their views go nowhere, at least in the short term.

Collegiality as a social process goes beyond collaboration in judgment writing to include for judges matters like the socialization of new judges into a court's culture, civility in everyday contacts within the court and with other courts, and the judges working cooperatively to enhance the court's reputation. Resentments and antagonisms may be concealed to preserve public confidence in the court's ability to resolve cases impartially. Finally, there are strategic behaviour models, which are based on the premise that to achieve their desired outcomes judges act in a calculated manner vis à vis other judges. Thus they take into account preferences and likely behaviours of other judges to attract favourable decisions from them. Like others, however, judges do not always act in a straightforward and rational fashion to attain their ultimate goals.

Finally in section II we examined attitudinal models of judicial decision-making, which have had great appeal among political scientists. They show how judges' attitudinally based preferences relate to the outcome of their own decisions (sometimes described as 'votes'). The focus on outcomes generally means that attitudinal models cannot account for how a case has been argued by the parties, the complexity of the issues, the impact on decision-making of collegiality and 'small group' discussions with other judges, and the subtleties in a judge's reasoning, revealing genuine disputes about what the law requires and what judges think they are doing. Favouring certain types of party or values may be because the judge is bound on a point by precedent or statute, so could not apply their own views even if they wanted. The overall conclusion of the models, that a judge's attitudes may bear on their decision-making, resonates with what can appear to be divisions between members of an apex court in their reasoning on issues of public policy. It is also evident in some cases, when one judge was assigned to sit on a panel, rather than another known to hold different views, with the consequent impact on outcome.[168]

The judicial values of independence, impartiality, and integrity oblige the judge to apply the law and minimize the influence of their attitudes and values, and any social or political agenda they may have. That includes representative judging, where a judge takes on the mantle of advancing certain outside interests through their decisions as judges. While judges can properly advance the interests of different groups in giving effect to a legislative mandate designed for this purpose, agenda judging and representative judging

[168] Lord Rodger, 'What are Appeal Courts For?' (2004) 10 Otago LR 517, 519; Paterson (n 13) 156–57.

are not compatible with the judicial role. Judges are subject to the force of legislation and the self-imposed limitation of precedent, which helps maintain confidence in the certainty and impartiality of the law.[169] As well, there is the expectation on the part of members of the community that the law should be clear and discernible so they can plan their affairs. Judges are therefore conscious of the need for legal coherence and the law's orderly development. None of this means that judges cannot bring to bear in their judging their different life experiences and understandings. A judge's decision-making can and will be informed by factors which may differ from other judges. Judicial decision-making is consequently enriched.

Section III of the chapter examined the variation between judges as decision-makers. After more than a quarter of a century on the bench, the former chief justice of Australia, Sir Anthony Mason, remarked that having sat with many judges over the years, he had not encountered any two who shared an entirely identical outlook.[170] There were judges who tended to be conservative in some areas of the law like property, commerce, and taxation, but less so in matters where social issues were involved. There were judges who interpreted a statute in the light of the pre-existing common law, but others more disposed to give the words full value. And there were judges, said Mason, who were known to give generous awards in personal injury cases, and others who were reputed to be niggardly. He added that the list of potential points of difference did not stop there.[171]

The method of exploring judicial differences, adopted in section III, is the classic social science technique of the ideal type. The ideal type is a construct based on a simplified and exaggerated version of reality which highlights key features for analysis when compared with real-world persons and practices. Five ideal types of judges and judging are identified—legalism, merits judging, minimalist judging, modernizers, and activists—but there could be more. The ideal types underline different approaches to the judicial function: legalism emphasizes the strict application of principle in line with conventional practice; merits judging places the sense of interpersonal justice at the heart of decision-making; minimalist judges decide one case at a time and avoid issues which do not need deciding; modernizers seek to ensure that the law accords with current social values and conditions; and activist judging involves the judge pursuing social goals when deciding individual cases.

[169] *Duport Steels Ltd v Sirs* [1980] 1 WLR 142, 168 (Lord Scarman).
[170] Sir Anthony Mason, 'The Art of Judging' (2008) 12 Southern Cross U LR 33, 38.
[171] ibid.

In the real world, each ideal type faces challenges. Legalism has to give way to practicality in particular circumstances where strict legal principles produce unacceptable results; the merits judge cannot decide cases outside the law; the minimalist may need to act more boldly if the law is not to become a collection of single instances, or reach a dead end; modernizers must accept that to ignore precedent or to rewrite legislation risks straying beyond the judge's legitimate function, and that in many contexts legislative change is more appropriate; and the activist risks undermining public confidence in judicial power.

Despite these drawbacks, the identification and use of ideal types raises important issues about judging. First, judicial difference is real, irrespective of where the judge is in the judicial hierarchy, and it can have an impact on litigants and the law. Lord Sumption is not the first judge to note differences in his colleagues' judicial outlook, although possibly more open than many in systematically describing them.[172] Secondly, although creative judging is always limited by time and place, the common law method confers the opportunity on judges to express their differences. In particular senior judges have scope to formulate and modernize the law. As we have seen this is effected through legitimate techniques, such as distinguishing a precedent or giving a legislative provision meaning. In some contexts judges lower in the hierarchy have conferred on them a considerable discretion and its exercise reveals differences in decision-making. Thirdly, there are limits on the expression of judicial difference. The extent to which judges may bend existing law, sweep away precedent, impose new doctrine, or strike at legislation (if this is permissible in a jurisdiction) is constrained by judicial values. Overextending judicial power threatens judicial independence through provoking a reaction by the other branches of government, and judging 'at will' is contrary to the judicial oath and undermines judicial impartiality.

Section II of the chapter began with the individual judge and the psychological and social forces which can bear on their judicial decision-making. In section III we explored different ideal types, to underline the differences which can occur between judges in decision-making. With section IV of the chapter we turned from the individual judge to judicial values, to interpreting legislation and precedent in accordance with established principle, and to proceeding incrementally, consistently with the values of judging. It is the value of fidelity to law. As we saw, the task of deciding cases often proceeds

[172] eg, Jonathan Sumption, *Trials of the State: Law and the Decline of Politics* (Profile Books 2019) 65–67.

fairly routinely, and without difficulty, as judges interpret legislation and apply precedent. With statutory interpretation, the answer will often lie in the ordinary meaning of the words when considered in their context. This interpretation of the text can be taken to reflect the intention or purpose behind the legislation. There is no need to resort to secondary materials, and doubly so to linguistic theories or philosophies of meaning (which themselves may be controversial). As to precedent, the judge accepts the need to apply legal principle established in previous decisions, those of judges higher in the judicial hierarchy (vertical precedent), and of those at the same level (horizontal precedent). When there are relevant precedents, the judge is not able to decide a case as if it raised a novel point. Determining a precedent's import is often straightforward, and the judge's conclusion from applying it typically delivers what would reasonably be expected.

As we saw in the discussion in section IV, both the principles for interpreting legislation, and applying precedent, ensure the responsible exercise of judicial power, but neither legislation nor precedent deny a judge agency. If the law faces new problems or is outdated, or if path dependence has led to an impasse, there are a number of legitimate techniques to assist the judge to reach an acceptable result in light of the circumstances of a case, or to accommodate social change. With statutory interpretation, the judge may resort to external sources regarding the purpose or intention behind a provision, drawing as well on established canons of construction and common law presumptions. With precedent, the judge may mould it to new situations by distinguishing it, or by extending its reach by analogy. In either case the judge may articulate a more general principle which encompasses the circumstances of the current dispute. In performing the task the judge may resort to legal and public policies, the consequences more widely of taking the course contemplated, and 'common sense' (if representing widely accepted community values).

This does not mean that judicial decision-making is straightforward. All judges face hard choices, challenging social issues, and intractable problems. The reality is that there can be more than one plausible interpretation of legislation, and the principles drawn from the precedent cases may not be self-evident, and may equally support divergent interpretations.[173] Precedents may also have fluctuated over time or be in conflict so that discrete outcomes can justifiably be chosen. Judges at different levels in the judicial hierarchy or

[173] See *Keighley, Maxsted & Co v Durant* [1901] AC 240, 246 (Lord Macnaghten).

sitting with other judges may conceptualize a case in distinct ways, leading to respectable debate about the proper analysis to be applied.[174] Path dependence may produce a line of precedent leading to sub-optimal results, yet it may appear impossible to break the mould without legislation.

Despite all this, the common law has proved remarkably adaptive. Its judges are not theoretical or doctrinaire. Interpreting legislation and precedent is a practical exercise, responsive to the submissions of the parties and the justice of a case. Judges engage in an exercise of evaluative judgment, spelt out in the reasons for their decisions. Disagreement with a judge's conclusion often remains, on a sliding scale of respectability. That is an inevitable feature of judging: not everyone agrees with the judge's decision. Social change can be accommodated, but typically incrementally, and possibly in fits and starts as judges confront different aspects of a problem. Judges may better deflect a contentious issue for future decision. The occasions for significant breakthroughs tend to be brief and intermittent. Given the nature of the issue the judge must accept that at times the legislature needs to step in with a solution. As Gaudron and McHugh JJ remarked in one case, it is 'a serious constitutional mistake to think that the common law courts have authority to "provide a solvent" for every social, political or economic problem'.[175]

[174] eg, compare *Attorney General v Blake* at [2001] 1 AC 268, [1998] Ch 439, and [1997] Ch 84.
[175] *Breen v Williams* (1996) 186 CLR 71, 115.

Bibliographical Essay

Preface

There are few works which present anything like the account of judging advanced here. *Good Judgment: Making Judicial Decisions* (University of Toronto Press 2018), by a leading Canadian academic and judge, covers some of the field, but as the subtitle indicates, is focused on decision-making. So is *The Business of Judging* (OUP 2002), by Lord Bingham, the greatest English judge of his generation. Judge Richard A Posner advances his theory of judging as practical reasoning (legal pragmatism) in a number of places including *How Judges Think* (Harvard University Press 2008) and to an extent, *Reflections on Judging* (Harvard University Press 2013). Among books by academics Shimon Shetreet and Sophie Turenne, *Judges on Trial* (2nd edn, CUP 2014) expertly covers matters such as the appointment, behavioural standards, and disqualification of judges for interest. Joe McIntyre's *The Judicial Function: Fundamental Principles of Contemporary Judging* (Springer Nature 2019) is a stimulating read, conceptualizing a great deal of material under his notion of judging as dispute resolution and social (normative) governance. Penny Darbyshire's *Sitting in Judgment: The Working Lives of Judges* (Hart 2011) (hereafter Darbyshire, *Sitting in Judgment*) is an outstanding ethnographic account of the realities of English judging at all levels, underlining its human character.

Chapter 1 Independence

I Introduction

Professor Shetreet has edited three volumes on judicial independence: Shimon Shetreet and Christopher Forsyth (eds), *The Culture of Judicial Independence: Conceptual Foundations and Practical Challenges* (Brill 2012); Shimon Shetreet (ed), *The Culture of Judicial Independence: Rule of Law and World Peace* (Brill 2014) (hereafter Shetreet (ed), *The Culture of Judicial Independence: Rule of Law and World Peace*); and Shimon Shetreet and Wayne McCormąck (eds), *The Culture of Judicial Independence in a Globalised World* (Brill 2016). See also the collection Guy Canivet, Mads Andenas, and Duncan Fairgrieve (eds), *Independence, Accountability and the Judiciary* (British Institute of International and Comparative Law 2006). Less conventional considerations of judicial independence include the public choice analysis of Landes and Posner, who argued that judicial independence is necessary to ensuring the application of legislation in accordance with the purposes promoted by the interest groups behind it: William M Landes and Richard Posner, 'The Independent Judiciary in an Interest-Group Perspective' (1975) 18 JL & Econ 875. In refuting this, Richard Epstein pointed out that judicial independence allows the judges to strike down interest group deals: 'The Independence of Judges: The Uses and Limitations of Public Choice Theory' [1990] BYU LR 827. Note that accounts of the Chinese legal system refute judicial independence (and the separation of powers) and contend that one must examine the empirical reality, including what Chinese courts achieve in its absence: see Minhao Benjamin Chen and Zhiyu Li, 'Courts without Separation of Powers: The Case of Judicial Suggestions in China' (2023) 64 Harv Int'l LJ 203. On how the CJEU read judicial independence into EU law: Michal Ovádek, 'The Making of Landmark Rulings in the European Union: The Case of National Judicial Independence' (2023) 30

J Eur Pub Policy 1119. Ruth Mackenzie and Philippe Sands, 'International Courts and Tribunals and the Independence of the International Judge' (2002) 44 Harv Int'l LJ 271 has suggestions on safeguarding the impartiality and independence of international judges.

II Principles and Practice

(A) An international value

Accounts of judicial independence by senior judges include Tom Bingham, 'Judicial Independence' in *The Business of Judging* (OUP 2000); Beverley McLachlin, 'Judicial Independence: A Functional Perspective' in Mads Andenas and Duncan Fairgrieve (eds), *Tom Bingham and the Transformation of the Law: A Liber Amicorum* (OUP 2009) (hereafter Andenas and Fairgrieve (eds), *Tom Bingham and the Transformation of the Law*); Ninian Stephen, 'Southey Memorial Lecture 1981: Judicial Independence—A Fragile Bastion' (1982) 13 Melb U LR 334; Anthony Mason, 'Judicial Independence and the Separation of Powers—Some Problems Old and New' (1991) 13 UNSW LJ 173; and Irving R Kaufman, 'The Essence of Judicial Independence' (1980) 80 Colum LR 671.

On a detailed overview of the issues, Jackson observes that elements favourable to judicial independence in one setting may have a different, indeed opposite valence in another: Vicki C Jackson, 'Judicial Independence: Structure, Context, Attitude' in Ajna Seibert-Fohr (ed), *Judicial Independence in Transition* (Springer 2012). Archibald Cox makes clear that the other side of the coin to judicial independence is that judges must decide cases according to law: 'The Independence of the Judiciary: History and Purposes' (1996) 21 U Dayton LR 565. Other academic accounts include Georg Vanberg, Benjamin Broman, and Christopher Ritter, 'The Rise and Protection of Judicial Independence' in Mark Tushnet and Dimitry Kochenov (eds), *Research Handbook on the Politics of Constitutional Law* (Edward Elgar Publishing 2023); Joe McIntyre, *The Judicial Function: Fundamental Principles of Contemporary Judging* (Springer 2019) ch 13; Mia Swart, 'Independence of the Judiciary' in *Max Planck Encyclopaedia of Comparative Constitutional Law* (OUP 2019); Roderick A Macdonald and Hoi Kong, 'Judicial Independence as a Constitutional Virtue' in Michel Rosenfeld and András Sajó (eds), *Oxford Handbook of Comparative Constitutional Law* (OUP 2012); Peter H Russell, 'Toward a General Theory of Judicial Independence' in Peter H Russell and David M O'Brien (eds), *Judicial Independence in the Age of Democracy: Critical Perspectives from around the World* (University of Virginia Press 2001); Kate Malleson, *The New Judiciary: The Effects of Expansion and Activism* (Dartmouth 1999) ch 3; and Stephen B Burbank, 'The Architecture of Judicial Independence' (1999) 72 So Cal LR 315. Arghya Sengupta has a good analytical account including Britain, India, and the US: *Independence and Accountability of the Higher Indian Judiciary* (CUP 2019) ch 6 (hereafter Sengupta, *Independence and Accountability of the Higher Indian Judiciary*).

(B) Framing judicial independence

The framework employed here draws on Charles Gardner Geyh, 'Judicial Independence as an Organizing Principle' (2014) 10 Annual Rev L & Soc Sc 185; Shivaraj S Huchhanavar, 'Conceptualising Judicial Independence and Accountability from a Regulatory Perspective' (2023) 9 Oslo LR 110; Mads Andenas, 'A European Perspective on Judicial Independence and Accountability' (2007) 41 Int'l L 1; Martin H Redish, 'Federal Judicial Independence: Constitutional and Political Perspectives (1995) 46 Mercer LR 697; and Jack Beatson, *The Rule of Law and the Separation of Powers* (CUP 2021) (hereafter Beatson, *The Rule of Law and the Separation of Powers*).

(C) External independence: outside threats and inducements

An account of the threats judges face is Alex Schwartz, 'Threats to Judicial Independence' in Lee Epstein and others (eds), *The Oxford Handbook of Comparative Judicial Behaviour* (OUP 2024) (hereafter Epstein and others (eds), *Oxford Handbook of Comparative Judicial Behaviour*). As to extreme threats, Gubbay CJ of Zimbabwe had his court invaded and Sir Salamo Injia CJ was arrested twice: see George Douvelos, *Anthony Roy Gubbay: A Judicial Life* (Wildy, Simmonds & Hill 2017) and John Logan, 'A Year in the Life of an Australian Member of the PNG Judiciary' (2014) 12 JR 79. There is an annual commemoration service for 'Martyrs of the Rule of Law', the three Ghanian judges mentioned in the text who were murdered: see Jeff Haynes, 'Human Rights and Democracy in Ghana: The Record of the Rawlings' Regime' (1991) 90 African Affairs 407, 418. On Lord Justice Gibson, murdered by the IRA in Northern Ireland, see 'Editorial' (1987) 38 N Ir LQ 219. As well as the IJA and CMJA, the private Dutch foundation Rechters voor Rechters (Judges for Judges) also reports on specific attacks on judges and judiciaries internationally.

On the constitutional crisis in Malaysia in 1988 and its aftermath: Björn Dressel and Tomoo Inoue, 'Politics and the Federal Court of Malaysia, 1960–2018: An Empirical Investigation' (2022) 9 Asian J Law & Soc 26; Andrew Harding and Amanda Whiting, 'Custodian of Civil Liberties and Justice in Malaysia. The Malaysian Bar and the Moderate State' in Terence Halliday, Lucien Karpik, and Malcolm M Feeley (eds), *Fates of Political Liberalism in the British Post-Colony: The Politics of the Legal Complex* (CUP 2012) (hereafter Halliday and others (eds), *Fates of Political Liberalism in the British Post-Colony*); RH Hickling, 'The Malaysian Judiciary in Crisis' [1989] PL 20. For the dismissal of Sri Lanka's chief justice see International Bar Association's Human Rights Institute, *A Crisis of Legitimacy: The Impeachment of Chief Justice Bandaranayake and the Erosion of the Rule of Law in Sri Lanka* (IBA 2014); Rehan Abeyratne, 'Rethinking Judicial Independence in India and Sri Lanka' (2015) 10 Asian J Comp L 99. The sacking and reinstatement of Chaudhry CJ, and his controversial legacy, are covered in Hamid Khan, *A History of the Judiciary in Pakistan* (OUP 2016) and Shoaib A Ghias, 'Miscarriage of Chief Justice: Judicial Power and the Legal Complex in Pakistan under Musharraf' in Halliday and others (eds), *Fates of Political Liberalism in the British Post-Colony.*

The subversion of judicial independence in Russia is described in Alena Ledeneva, *Can Russia Modernise? Sistema, Power Networks and Informal Governance* (CUP 2013) ch 5; Olga Schwartz and Elga Sykiainen, 'Judicial Independence in the Russian Federation' in Anja Seibert-Fohr and Lydia Friederike Müller (eds), *Judicial Independence in Transition* (Berlin 2012); Alexei Trochev, 'Regulating Judges in Russia's Dual State: Between Constitutional and Administrative Regimes' in Richard Devlin and Adam Dodek (eds), *Regulating Judges Beyond Independence and Accountability* (Elgar 2016); Maria Popova, *Politicized Justice in Emerging Democracies: A Study of Courts in Russia and Ukraine* (CUP 2012). Among the cases where foreign courts have had to assess the rulings of Russian courts: Neil Andrews, 'Judging the Independence and Integrity of Foreign Courts' in Shetreet (ed), *The Culture of Judicial Independence: Rule of Law and World Peace.* David Kosař and Katarína Šipulová identify three strategies to stack courts with loyal judges (1) the 'expanding strategy', increasing the size of the court; (2) the 'emptying strategy', decreasing the number of sitting judges; and (3) the 'swapping strategy', replacing sitting judges: 'How to Fight Court-Packing?' (2020) 6 Const Stud 133. See also David Kosař and Katarína Šipulová, 'Comparative Court-Packing' (2023) 21 Int'l J Const'l L 80. Tom S Clark explores the history of court-curbing measures considered in the US Congress in relation to the US Supreme Court: *The Limits of Judicial Independence* (CUP 2010).

(D) Internal independence: the role of other judges

The story of Lord Atkin's dissent in *Liversidge v Anderson* [1942] AC 206 is told in Geoffrey Lewis, *Lord Atkin* (Butterworths 1983) 138–40. The ECHR jurisprudence on internal judicial independence is analysed in Joost Sillen, 'The Concept of "Internal Judicial Independence" in the Case Law of the European Court of Human Rights' (2019) 15 Eur Const'l LR 104. In a number of studies David Kosař contends that Judicial Councils have not benefited individual judicial independence, and focuses on the power of court presidents in stifling it: eg, *Perils of Judicial Self-Government in Transitional Societies* (CUP 2016) ch 8. On remedies for this see David Kosař, Katarína Šipulová, and Ondřej Kadlec, 'Case for Judicial Councils as Fourth-Branch Institutions' (2024) 20 European Const'l LR 82. For an account of control by the chief justice and general secretariat over judges in the Japanese judiciary up to the mid 1990s, David M O'Brien and Yasuo Ohkoshi, 'Stifling Judicial Independence from within the Japanese Judiciary' in Peter H Russell and David M O'Brien (eds), *Judicial Independence in the Age of Democracy: Critical Perspectives* (University of Virginia Press 2001). In his 'Threats to Judicial Independence: The Enemy Within' (2013) 129 LQR 205, a former judge of the High Court of Australia, JD Heydon, argues that there are threats for individual judges from attempts to eliminate dissenting judgement in favour of composite or single majority judgments. For an assessment, referring to the views of other High Court judges, see Andrew Lynch, 'Keep Your Distance: Independence, Individualism and Decision-Making on Multi-Member Courts' in Rebecca Ananian-Welsh and Jonathan Crowe (eds), *Judicial Independence in Australia: Contemporary Challenges, Future Directions* (Federation Press 2016). An empirical analysis of the practice regarding dissents in the European Court of Justice, the International Court of Justice, and the European Court of Human Rights found that its effects on judicial independence were mediated by a third factor—the length and renewability of judicial appointments: Jeffrey L Dunoff and Mark A Pollack, 'The Road Not Taken: Comparative International Judicial Dissent' (2022) 116 Amer J Int'l L 340. Rory Kelly argues against the practice of no dissents in the Court of Appeal, Criminal Division, England and Wales in 'Criminalising Dissent' (2022) 138 LQR 432.

III Structural Independence: The Judge

(A) Security of tenure

The background to security of tenure for senior judges in the Act of Settlement is explained in Earl Russell, *Judicial Independence in the Early Seventeenth Century: Graya Occasional Paper* (Gray's Inn 1997) and Henry Brooke, 'The History of Judicial Independence in England and Wales' [2015] EHRLR 446. There is some evidence that its enactment had a positive effect on economic indicators: Daniel M Klerman and Paul G Mahoney, 'The Value of Judicial Independence: Evidence from Eighteenth Century England' (2005) 7 Amer L & Econ R 1. Those outside the higher judiciary have not enjoyed the same security of tenure: eg, Eddy D Ventose, 'Constitutional Protection for Magistrates in the Commonwealth Caribbean' [2009] PL 431; Sharyn L Roach Anleu and Kathy Mack, 'The Security of Tenure of Australian Magistrates' (2006) 30 Melb U LR 370; Judith Resnik, 'Interdependent Federal Judiciaries' (2008) 137 Daedalus 28. The context of *McCawley v King* [1920] AC 691 is examined at length in Ian Loveland, *McCawley and Trethowan: The Chaos of Politics and the Integrity of Law* (Hart 2021) vol 1. Colonial judges had no security of tenure: they could be removed by a colony's governor with the approval of the Colonial Office: eg, Martin J Wiener, 'Some Difficulties of Colonial Judging: The Bahamas 1886–93' in Paul Brand and Joshua Getzler (eds), *Judges and Judging in the History of the Common Law and Civil Law* (CUP 2012). On the dismissal of Turkish judges in 2016, Tom Ruys and Emre Turkut, 'Turkey's Post-Coup "Purification

Process": Collective Dismissals of Public Servants under the European Convention on Human Rights' (2018) 18 HRLR 539; Tarik Olcay, 'Firing Bench-Mates: The Human Rights and Rule of Law Implications of the Turkish Constitutional Court's Dismissal of its Two Members' (2017) 13 Eu Const LR 568; International Commission of Jurists, *Turkey: The Judicial System in Peril: A Briefing Paper* (ICJ 2016); and Venice Commission, Opinion No 875/201727 (Turkey) 27. On the use of the post-2016 judiciary against the media and the government's opponents: Merve Tahiroglu, 'How Turkey's Leaders Dismantled the Rule of Law' (2020) 44 Fletcher Forum W'ld Affairs 67. Analysis of the Polish situation from about 2016 is contained in an article co-authored by the chief justice of Poland's Supreme Court until 2020, Małgorzata Gersdorf, and Mateusz Pilich, 'Judges and Representatives of the People: A Polish Perspective' (2020) 16 Eu Const LR 345. See also Wojciech Sadurski, *Poland's Constitutional Breakdown* (OUP 2019); and Fryderyk Zoll and Leah Wortham, 'Judicial Independence and Accountability: Withstanding Political Stress in Poland' (2019) 42 Fordham Int'l LJ 875. The forced removal of Polish judges is discussed in Petra Bárd and Anna Śledzińska-Simon, 'On the Principle of Irremovability of Judges beyond Age Discrimination: Commission v. Poland' (2020) 57 CMLR 1555. The authors contrast the successful rule of law challenge to the Polish law with the European Commission's earlier response in Case C-286/12, *Commission v Hungary* [2012] EUECJ C-286/12, when the Hungarian government forcibly retired large numbers of judges. There the challenge was advanced on discrimination, not rule of law grounds: at 1570–72, citing Halmai, 'The Early Retirement Age of the Hungarian Judges' in Nicola Fernanda and Bill Davis (eds), *EU Law Stories: Contextual and Critical Histories of European Jurisprudence* (CUP 2017).

(B) Financial security

How judges in Britain resisted the reduction in their salaries during the Great Depression in the 1930s is told in Robert Stevens, *The Independence of the Judiciary: The View from the Lord Chancellor's Office* (Clarendon 1993) 50–63 (hereafter Stevens, *The Independence of the Judiciary*); Robert Stevens, 'Reform in Haste and Repent at Leisure: Iolanthe, the Lord High Executioner and Brave New World' (2004) 24 Leg Stud 1 (hereafter Stevens, 'Reform in Haste and Repent at Leisure'). In the latter Stevens records that in response to judicial paranoia, the government introduced the Judiciary (Safeguarding) Bill 1934. 'The Permanent Secretary to the Lord Chancellor, Schuster, urged the Statutory Draftsman: "Begin with a recital, which should be as long and pompous as possible, ... the independence and all the rest of it ... then declare that notwithstanding all this they are affected by the cut".' The Bill died: at 25. The Portuguese case, where the European Court of Justice upheld the reduction in judicial salaries, is analysed in Laurent Pech and Sébastien Platon, 'Judicial Independence under Threat: The Court of Justice to the Rescue in the ASJP Case' (2018) 55 CMLR 1854.

(C) Discipline, transfers, and court reorganization

The formal position with case assignment is discussed in Shimon Shetreet and Sophie Turenne, *Judges on Trial: The Independence and Accountability of the English Judiciary* (CUP 2013) 89–94. In practice, see the discussion of assignment in Lord Hope's Diaries: Lord Hope, *House of Lords 1996-2009* (Avizandum Publishing 2018) 213; *UK Supreme Court and Afterwards 2009-2015* (Avizandum Publishing 2019) 219. The background to the Polish disciplinary reforms is discussed in Katarzyna Gajda-Roszczynialska and Krystian Markiewicz, 'Disciplinary Proceedings as an Instrument for Breaking the

Rule of Law in Poland' (2020) 12 Hague J Rule of Law 451, and that of the transfer of the sixteen High Court judges during the Emergency in India in Granville Austin, *Working a Democratic Constitution: A History of the Indian Experience* (OUP 2003) chs 15, 25. Justice Kirby examines situations where judges and members of quasi-judicial bodies were removed by the abolition or reorganization of their courts and tribunals: 'The Abolition of Courts and Non-Reappointment of Judicial Officers' (1995) 28 Verfassung und Recht in Übersee 6; and see *Attorney General (NSW) v Quinn* (1989) 170 CLR 1.

(D) *Immunity from suit*

The starting point for considering judicial immunity is Professor Abimbola A Olowofoyeku's *Suing Judges: A Study of Judicial Immunity* (Clarendon Press 1993) (hereafter Olowofoyeku, *Suing Judges*), who critically examines judicial immunity covering UK, Commonwealth, and US authority. For the history of the English doctrine see J Randolph Block, 'Stump v Sparkman and the History of Judicial Immunity' [1980] Duke LJ 879, 881–96. Patrick Polden suggests that the firming up of judicial immunity at the end of the nineteenth century was attributable to judicial concern with the increase in litigants in person and parties suing in *forma pauperis*: 'Doctor in Trouble: Anderson v Gorrie and the Extension of Judicial Immunity from Suit in the 1890s' (2001) 22 J Leg Hist 37. US law is canvassed in Peter H Schuck, 'The Civil Liability of Judges in the United States' (1989) 37 Am J Comp L 655; Timothy M Stengel, 'Absolute Judicial Immunity Makes Absolutely No Sense: An Argument for an Exception to Judicial Immunity' (2012) 84 Temple LR 1071; Note, 'Judicial Immunity at the (Second) Founding: A New Perspective on § 1983' (2023) 136 Harv LR 1456 (examining the statutory immunity in 42 USC § 1983 and its history). Among those recommending a more limited judicial immunity are Olowofoyeku, *Suing Judges*; John Murphy, 'Rethinking Tortious Immunity for Judicial Acts' (2013) 33 Leg Stud 455; and Frank Way, 'A Call for Limits to Judicial Immunity: Must Judges be Kings of their Courts?' (1981) 64 Judicature 390. The recommendations in BV Harris, 'Remedies and Accountability for Unlawful Judicial Action in New Zealand: Could the Law Be Tidier' [2008] NZ LR 483 include a special tribunal to consider cases of judicial misconduct and compensation under it as well. Andrew Nicol, 'Judicial Immunity and Human Rights' (2006) 5 EHRLR 558 suggests qualified immunity but argues that human rights is a potentially counter-productive framework in which to address the issue. In a further contribution to the debate Olowofoyeku contends that, faced with judicial immunity, liability must rest with the state when judicial wrongdoing occurs: 'When Courts Get It Wrong: Judicial Errors and Common Law Underenforcement' (2018) 134 LQR 450.

IV Structural Independence: The Judiciary

In a seminal article, Owen M Fiss argued that judicial independence is not threatened by bureaucratization but that bureaucratization threatens the judicial function of engaging in a dialogue with litigants: see 'The Bureaucratization of the Judiciary' (1983) 92 Yale LJ 1442.

(A) *Constitutional and statutory protection*

On the contribution of the concept of the separation of powers to judicial independence see judicial contributions by Philip Sales, 'The Interaction of the Rule of Law and the Separation of Powers' [2022] PL 527; Beatson, *The Rule of Law and the Separation of Powers* ch 8; and Stephen Sedley, *Lions Under the Throne-Essays on the History of English Public Law* (CUP 2015) ch 9.

(B) Operational independence

Core functions: deployment, case assignment, and procedure

Robert Stevens and Shimon Shetreet describe occasions when Lord Halsbury, Lord Hailsham, Lord Hewart, and Lord Denning were said to have allocated judges to cases so as to achieve certain outcomes: respectively *Judges on Trial* (North-Holland 1976) 41–43 (hereafter Shetreet, *Judges on Trial*) and *The English Judges* (Hart 2002) 17–18, 87. Possible examples in more recent times are touched on in Lord Hope's diaries eg, Lord Hope, *House of Lords 1996-2009* (Avizandum 2018) 213–14; *UK Supreme Court. . .and Afterwards* (Avizandum 2019) 219.

Kate Malleson warns that assigning a case to a judge described as 'a safe pair of hands' may imply their commitment to particular social values: 'Safeguarding Judicial Impartiality' (2002) 22 Leg Stud 53, 68. Silje Hermansen argues that the president of the Court of Justice of the European Union builds the court's legitimacy by strategically allocating cases to select judges, in particular by appointing a rapporteur whose government holds moderate political preferences: 'Building Legitimacy: Strategic Case Allocations in the Court of Justice of the European Union' (2020) 27 J Eur Pub Policy 1215. A survey for the European Network of Councils for the Judiciary (ENCJ) revealed a concern among judges in several countries that case allocation is used to influence the outcome of cases: *ENCJ Survey on the Independence of Judges* (ENCJ 2022) 27–28. The ENCJ had published a set of principles for case assignment and a survey of practices in European countries: *Minimum Judicial Standards IV, Allocation of Cases Report 2013-2014* (ENCJ 2014). The selection of panels in the UK Supreme Court—'horses for courses' combined with random selection—is described in Lady Hale, 'Judges, Power and Accountability Constitutional Implications of Judicial Selection' (Constitutional Law Summer School, Belfast, 11 August 2017) (she underlines the need for neutral assignment); Alan Paterson, *Final Judgment* (Hart 2013) 70–73 (hereafter Paterson, *Final Judgment*); and Darbyshire, *Sitting in Judgment* 369–73. Philip M Langbroek and Marco Fabri (eds), *The Right Judge for Each Case: A Study of Case Assignment and Impartiality in Six European Judiciaries* (Intersentia 2007) is somewhat dated. Lori Hausegger and Stacia Haynie found that chief justices acted strategically in assigning judges to panels: 'Judicial Decisionmaking and the Use of Panels in the Canadian Supreme Court and the South African Appellate Division' (2003) 37 L & Soc'y R 635. Based on her study, Marin K Levy questions whether strict random selection operates in US federal appellate courts as is required: 'Panel Assignment in the Federal Courts of Appeals' (2017) 103 Cornell LR 65. The pragmatic way cases are assigned in Australian lower courts is explored in an empirical study: Anne Wallace, Sharyn Roach Anleu, and Kathy Mack, 'Evaluating Judicial Performance for Caseload Allocation' (2015) 41 Monash U LR 445. For a study covering New Zealand, Germany, and the US: Petra Butler, 'The Assignment of Cases to Judges' (2003) 1 NZ J Pub & Int'l L 83. The background to the controversy over assignments to panels in the Supreme Court of India is discussed in Chirag Balyan, 'Administrative Powers, Roles and Responsibilities of the Chief Justice of India' in Salman Khurshid, Lokendra Malik, and Yogesh Pratap Singh, *The Supreme Court and the Constitution: An Indian Discourse* (Wolters Kluwer 2020) 225–40; Sengupta, *Independence and Accountability of the Higher Indian Judiciary* 264–70; and Nick Robinson, 'Structure Matters: The Impact of Court Structure on the Indian and US Supreme Courts' (2013) 61 Am J Comp L 173, 186–87.

Judicial administration and budgets

Lord Browne-Wilkinson argued for greater administrative and financial autonomy in his FA Mann lecture 'The Independence of the Judiciary in the 1980s' [1988] PL 44 (a collegial body of judges to administer the system, a voice in formulating the policies affecting the legal system, and a greater involvement in preparing the estimates on which the total budget is voted by Parliament). Russell Wheeler was an early proponent of a separate administrative capacity for the courts to resist the encroachments of the other branches of government: *Judicial Administration: Its Relation to Judicial Independence* (National Center for State Courts 1988). The case for greater judicial autonomy in England and Australia is made by its longtime advocate, Professor Ian Scott, 'The Future of Judicial Administration' in Garrie J Moloney (ed), *Seminar on Constitutional and Administrative Responsibilities for the Administration of Justice: The Partnership of Judiciary and Executive* (Australian Institute of Judicial Administration 1986) and Guy Green, 'The Rationale and Some Aspects of Judicial Independence' (1985) 59 ALJ 135. The idea is critically examined in Graeme G Mitchell, '"Be Careful What You Wish For": Administrative Independence and Alternative Models of Court Administration—The New Frontier' in Adam Dodek and Lorne Sossin (eds), *Judicial Independence in Context* (Irwin Law 2010) (hereafter Dodek and Sossin (eds), *Judicial Independence in Context*). As well limited empirical evidence raises doubts that judicial independence is improved by the move from an executive model to a judiciary model of judicial administration: Katarína Šipulová and others, 'Judicial Self-Governance Index: Towards Better Understanding of the Role of Judges in Governing the Judiciary' (2023) 17 Regulation & Governance 22.

The ENCJ has identified principles for the funding of courts, as has the CMJA: *European Network of Councils for the Judiciary, Funding of the Judiciary Report 2015-2016* (ENCJ 2016); Commonwealth Magistrates' and Judges' Association, *Principles on the Funding and Resourcing of the Judiciary in the Commonwealth* (CMJA 2020). Shimon Shetreet recalls that the Bulgarian government cut the budget of the Constitutional Court because of a ruling against a political party: 'Judicial Independence, Liberty, Democracy and International Economy' in Shetreet (ed), *The Culture of Judicial Independence: Rule of Law and World Peace* 35. As to administrative autonomy, how this was established in the UK Supreme Court is explored in its early years by Kate Malleson, 'The Changing Institutional Politics of the UK Supreme Court' (2016) 7 UK Supreme Ct YB 54. See also William Arnold, 'The Supreme Court of the United Kingdom . . . the Roles of Judicial Officers and Court Administrators' (2014) 6 Int'l J Court Admin 19; Penny Darbyshire, 'The UK Supreme Court—Is There Anything Left to Think About? (2015) 7 UK Supreme Ct YB 148; Daniel Clarry, 'Watching the British: Keeping House and Resourcing in the UK Supreme Court' (2016–2017) 8 UK Supreme Ct YB 14. On the position elsewhere: eg, Tin Bunjevac, 'Court Services Victoria and the New Politics of Judicial Independence' (2015) 41 Monash U LR 299, which covers judicial administration in Victoria and in the Australian federal courts. The internal organization of the judiciary in England and Wales is discussed in the chief justice's Lionel Cohen lecture, Lord Thomas, 'The Judiciary within the State: Governance and Cohesion of the Judiciary' (2018) 51 Isr LR 127.

There is a considerable literature on the judicial councils in civil law countries: eg, Nuno Garoupa and Tom Ginsburg, 'Guarding the Guardians: Judicial Councils and Judicial Independence' (2009) 57 Am J Com L 103; Simone Benvenuti and Davide Paris, 'Judicial Self-Government in Italy: Merits, Limits and the Reality of an Export Model' (2018) 19 German LJ 1641; A Śledzińska-Simon, 'The Rise and Fall of Judicial Self-Government in Poland: On Judicial Reform Reversing Democratic Transition' (2018) 19 German LJ 1839. Pablo Castillo-Ortiz develops a theory about the relationship of judicial councils (and other forms of judicial administration) to the quality of democracy: *Judicial Governance and Democracy in Europe* (Springer 2023).

(C) Boundaries to extrajudicial functions

Nuno Garoupa and Tom Ginsburg review how judges perform nonjudicial functions in a range of common and civil law countries, how this is regulated, and the reputational damage it can cause: *Judicial Reputation: A Comparative Theory* (University of Chicago

Press 2017). This includes how a judge became interim prime minister in Greece in 2012 and how other judges became acting presidents in Pakistan, Bangladesh, and Bolivia on other occasions. Fiona Wheeler, 'Parachuting In: War and Extra-Judicial Activity by High Court Judges' (2010) 38 Fed LR 485 examines how Australian High Court judges acted as ambassadors and in other roles during the Second World War. The extensive participation by US Supreme Court judges in extrajudicial activities before the modern period is summarized in Peter Alan Bell, 'Extrajudicial Activity of Supreme Court Justices' (1970) 22 Stan LR 587. Stone CJ's views of the appointment of Justice Jackson as chief prosecutor at Nuremberg are referred to in Alpheus Thomas Mason, 'Extra-Judicial Work for Judges: The Views of Chief Justice Stone' (1953) 67 Harv LR 193. Cynthia Gray, *Ethics and Judges' Evolving Roles Off the Bench: Serving on Governmental Commissions* (National Center for State Courts 2002) summarizes advisory opinions about this.

The circumstances in which judges in Britain should serve on public inquiries, with some comparison of the position in Israel, is explored by Jack Beaton, then a serving judge: 'Should Judges Conduct Public Inquiries?' (2005) 121 LQR 221. See also Iain Steele, 'Judging Judicial Inquiries' [2004] PL 738; Lord Thomas, 'The Future of Public Inquiries' [2015] PL 225; and Sarah Cooper and Owen Thomas, 'Judge-led Public Inquiries in the UK: The Gold Standard?' in Scott Prasser (ed), *New Directions in Royal Commissions & Public Inquiries: Do We Need Them?* (Conor Court Publishing 2023). Historical information about judges conducting public inquiries is contained in Shetreet, *Judges on Trial* 354–64. See now Emma Ireton, *An Analysis of Legal and Political Influence on the Form and Nature of Post-2005 Public Inquiries and their Significance* (PhD thesis, Nottingham Trent University, 2020). Inquiries have been examined on their own terms, eg, Lord Scott's inquiry into arms sales to Iraq in the 1980s is dealt with in Ian Leigh and Laurence Lustgarten, 'Five Volumes in Search of Accountability: The Scott Report' (1996) 59 MLR 695. Critiques and criticisms of the role of judges conducting public inquires in Canada are contained in Adam Dodek, 'Judicial Independence as a Public Policy Instrument' in Dodek and Sossin (eds), *Judicial Independence in Context* and Patrick Monahan and Byron Shaw, 'The Impact of Extra-Judicial Service on the Canadian Judiciary: The Need for Reform' in HP Lee (ed), *Judiciaries in Comparative Perspective* (CUP 2011) (hereafter Lee (ed), *Judiciaries in Comparative Perspective*). The Canadian Justice Council adopted a *Protocol on the Appointment of Judges to Commissions of Inquiry* (Canadian Justice Council 2010). The restrictive view of judges participating in public inquiries in Australia, along with the historical background, is explained in Murray McInerney, Garrie Mooney, and DG McGregor, *Judges as Royal Commissioners and Chairmen of Non-Judicial Tribunals* (AIJA 1986). Fiona Wheeler, 'Constitutional Limits on Extra-Judicial Activity by State Judges: Wainohu and Conundrums of Incompatibility' (2015) 37 Sydney LR 301 explains the constitutional jurisprudence on institutional integrity enunciated by the High Court of Australia. The South African Constitutional Court drew on the jurisprudence discussed in Wheeler's article in *South African Association of Personal Injury Lawyers v Heath* [2000] ZACC 22, 2001 (1) SA 883 [23], [44].

V Behavioural Independence

(A) Personal independence: the judge's 'state of mind'

The resistance of the Polish and Hungarian judges to their populist governments is discussed, inter alia, in the special issue 'Judges under Stress' (2021) 22 German LJ 1147. Hans Petter Graver, 'Why Adolf Hitler Spared the Judges: Judicial Opposition Against the Nazi State' (2018) 19 German LJ 845 contains a range of examples of opposition by German judges, although the regime had loyal judges who transformed liberal German law into an instrument of oppression, discrimination, and genocide. Jewish judges were in a different category and fled the country early on. Regarding 'liberal' judges in apartheid South Africa, David Dyzenhaus, *Judging the Judges, Judging Ourselves* (Hart 1998). On the role of judges in sub-Saharan Africa, especially in disputed elections cases, see James Thuo Gathii and Olabisi D Akinkugbe, 'Judicialization of Election Disputes in Africa's International Courts' (2021) 84 L & Contemp Prob 181; Fombad Charles Manga, 'Taming Executive Authoritarianism in Africa: Some Reflections on Current Trends in Horizontal and Vertical Accountability' (2020) 12 Hague J Rule of Law 63; Duncan Okubasu, 'Lessons for Sub-Saharan Africa from Kenya on Electoral Reforms: The Role and Limitations of the Law' (2017) 16 Election LJ 306; Miriam Azu, 'Lessons from Ghana and Kenya on Why Presidential Election Petitions usually Fail' (2015) 15 Afr Hum Rights LJ 150.

Judge J Skelly Wright's role in implementing desegregation has attracted greater attention than that of other judges perhaps since he later served on the US Court of Appeals for the District of Columbia, some of the time as chief judge. See Richard H Fallon Jr, 'Greatness in a Lower Federal Court Judge: The Case of J Skelly Wright' (2015) 61 Loy L Rev 29; Randall Kennedy, 'Judge J. Skelly Wright and the Racial Desegregation of Louisiana' (2015) 61 Loy L Rev 57 (who also pays tribute to the litigants and attorneys who brought cases to Wrights' court).

(B) Cultural independence: society's support

The leading work on judicial independence and its political context in the UK is Graham Gee and others, *The Politics of Judicial Independence in the UK's Changing Constitution* (CUP 2015) (hereafter Gee and others, *The Politics of Judicial Independence in the UK's Changing Constitution*). The authors—Graham Gee, Robert Hazell, Kate Malleson, and Patrick O'Brien—conclude that despite the view of many judges, judicial independence emerged stronger from the constitutional changes of the early 2000s. Robert Stevens was a longtime critic of how English judges used the idea of judicial independence to cloak claims about their conditions and professional interests. Among the extravagant claims was also the judicial criticism of reforms of the English legal profession in the late 1980s: Stevens, *The Independence of the Judiciary* 173ff; Stevens, 'Reform in Haste and Repent at Leisure' 27; Robert Stevens, 'The Independence of the Judiciary: the Case of England' (1999) 72 So Cal LR 596. See also Graham Gee, 'Defending Judicial Independence in the British Constitution' in Dodek and Sossin (eds), *Judicial Independence in Context*. An econometric study of appointments of Court of Appeal judges to the House of Lords, 1951–86, confirmed common knowledge that deciding against the government was not a factor determining promotion chances: Eli Salzberger and Paul Fenn, 'Judicial Independence: Some Evidence from the English Court of Appeal' (1999) 42 JL & Econ 831.

John Bell explains how the different historical experiences in Spain and Sweden have led to different institutional patterns protecting judicial independence: 'Judicial Cultures and Judicial Independence' (2001) 4 Cambridge YB Eur Legal Stud 47. Charles Gardner Geyh highlights the importance of constitutional conventions to protect judicial independence in the US and the threat posed by what he describes as a neo-populist assault which rejects the concept: 'Judicial Independence at Twilight' (2021) 71 Case W Res L Rev 1045. See also his earlier 'Judicial Independence, Judicial Accountability, and the Role of Constitutional Norms in Congressional Regulation of the Courts' (2003) 78 Indiana LJ 153. Pedro Magalhãesa and Nuno Garoupa found that judicial trust in European countries with popular governments (Turkey, Hungary, Poland) was most adversely affected among those most ideologically distant from these governments, whereas with supporters the topic had less salience: 'Populist Governments, Judicial Independence and Public Trust in the Courts' (2023) 9 J Eur Pub Policy 2748.

TR Andhyarujina attributes the origins of the collegium system for judicial appointments in India to the Emergency: 'A Committed Judiciary: Indira Gandhi and Judicial Appointments' in Arghya Sengupta and Ritwika Sharma (eds), *Appointment of Judges to the Supreme Court of India* (OUP 2018). As well as the editor's chapter see especially the contrasting contributions in this collection by Gautam Bhatia, Madhavi Divan, Gopal Subramanium, and Suhrith Parthasarathy. See also Chintan Chandrachud, 'Constitutional Falsehoods: The Fourth Judges Case and the Basic Structure Doctrine in India' in Richard Albert and Bertil Emrah Oder (eds), *An Unconstitutional Constitution? Unamendability in Constitutional Democracies* (Springer 2018).

On whether the assertion of judicial independence by the Pakistan Supreme Court endangered fragile democratic governments: see Anil Kalhan, '"Gray Zone" Constitutionalism and the Dilemma Of Judicial Independence in Pakistan' (2013) 46 Vanderbilt J Transn'l L 33; Moeen Cheema, *Courting Constitutionalism The Politics of Public Law and Judicial Review in Pakistan* (CUP 2021) ch 8; Osama Siddique, 'The Judicialization of Politics in Pakistan' in Mark Tushnet and Madhav Khosla (eds), *Unstable Constitutionalism Law and Politics in South Asia* (CUP 2015). The important role of strong bar associations to shielding judicial independence is explored in Sadaf Aziz, 'Liberal Protagonists? The Lawyers' Movement in Pakistan' in Halliday and others (eds), *Fates of Political Liberalism in the British Post-Colony*.

VI Judicial Accountability

(A) Dimensions of accountability

It is now widely accepted among the judiciary that judicial independence and judicial accountability go together: see the lecture by Lord Burnett LCJ, 'Institutional Independence and Accountability of the Judiciary: Lionel Cohen Lecture 2022' (2022) 55 Isr LR 360. A popular way of analysing accountability is to ask questions such as who is accountable, to whom, for what, its purpose, the processes, and how it is effected. There is extensive discussion of the different dimensions of judicial accountability, on which the chapter draws: eg, David Kosař and Samuel Spáč, 'Conceptualization(s) of Judicial Independence and Judicial Accountability by the European Network of Councils for the Judiciary: Two Steps Forward, One Step Back' (2018) 9 Int'l J Court Admin 37; Arghya Sengupta, 'Judicial Accountability: A Taxonomy' [2014] PL 245; Mark Bovens, 'Analysing and Assessing Accountability: A Conceptual Framework' (2007) 13 European LJ 447. Bovens has also drawn attention to the division in the general literature between accountability as a virtue with the focus on normative issues—on the standards and the assessment of behaviour of public agents—and accountability as a mechanism where the focus is on the way institutional arrangements operate: 'Two Concepts of Accountability: Accountability as a Virtue and as a Mechanism' (2010) 33 West Eur Pol 946.

General accounts of judicial accountability include Tom F Bathurst, 'Who Judges the Judges, and How Should They Be Judged?' (2019) 14 TJR 1; John Lowndes, 'Judicial Accountability as an Evolving and Fluid Concept' (2017) 23 Cwlth Jud J 25; Gee and others, *The Politics of Judicial Independence in the UK's Changing Constitution* 16–22, 55–61, 99–101, 187–89, 257–59; James Harrison, 'Judging the Judges: the New Scheme of Judicial Conduct and Discipline in Scotland' (2009) 13 Edin LR 427; Francesco Contini and Richard Mohr, 'Reconciling Independence and Accountability in Judicial Systems' (2008) 3 Utrecht LR 26; Gleeson CJ, 'Judicial Accountability' in Ruth Sheard, *The Role of the Judge* (Judicial Commission of New South Wales 2004). Judicial accountability is often discussed in a constitutional context, eg Stephen B Burbank, 'Judicial Independence, Judicial Accountability & Interbranch Relations' (2008) 137(4) Daedalus 16; Andrew

Le Sueur, 'Developing Mechanisms for Judicial Accountability in the UK' (2004) 24 Legal Studies 73. Mark Tushnet consider the issue as regards apex courts: 'Judicial Accountability in Comparative Perspective' in Nicholas Bamforth and Peter Leyland (eds), *Accountability in the Contemporary Constitution* (OUP 2013). On the role of the free access to law movement making judgments and other legal materials available to the public at no cost: Graham Greenleaf, Andrew Mowbray, and Philip Chung, 'The Meaning of "Free Access to Legal Information": A Twenty Year Evolution' [2013] UTSLRS 5.

Judicial systems are assessed in terms of accountability under regional and international frameworks. For example, the ENCJ has developed indicators for the independence, accountability, and quality of judges, which have been applied through questionnaires to European countries. See Frans van Dijk and Geoffrey Vos, 'A Method for Assessment of the Independence and Accountability of the Judiciary' (2018) 9 Int'l J Court Admin 1. Performance, integrity, transparency, and accountability are included as part of United Nations, *Rule of Law Indicators: Implementation Guide and Project Tools* (United Nations 2011) 3.2, Judiciary.

On judicial performance programmes in the US for individual judges, including the American Bar Association's Guidelines for the Evaluation of Judicial Performance, see Penny J White, 'Judging Judges: Securing Judicial Independence by Use of Judicial Performance Evaluations' (2002) 29 Fordham Urb LJ 1053. In India, High Court judges evaluate judges in inferior courts: Geeta Oberoi, 'Need for Standardizing Performance Evaluation Criteria for Judicial Magistrates in India' (2018) 44 Cwlth Law Bull 251. Spigelman CJ of New South rejected the notion that courts deliver a service and urged reserve about performance indicators for the judiciary as an institution, since indicators could not account for the qualitative dimension of justice: 'Seen to be Done: The Principle of Open Justice' (2000) 74 ALJ 290 (pt 1), 378 (pt 2). To similar effect is Allsop CJ of the Federal Court of Australia: 'Courts as (Living) Institutions and Workplaces' (2019) 93 ALJ 375, who emphasizes the complexity of measuring and then evaluating the human task of judging.

(B) Reasons

There was no duty at common law for judges to give oral or written reasons: JL Montrose, 'Reasoned Judgments' (1958) 21 MLR 80; Michael Akehurst, 'Statements of Reasons for Judicial and Administrative Decisions' (1970) 33 MLR 154; Michael Taggart, 'Should Canadian Judges Be Legally Required to Give Reasoned Decisions in Civil Cases?' (1983) 33 U Toronto LJ 1; Max Radin, 'The Requirement of Written Opinions' (1930) 18 Calif LR 486. The practice in England in the 1950s (and later) of not giving reasons is described in Konrad Schiemann, 'The Movement Towards Transparency in Decision Taking' in Andenas and Fairgrieve (eds), *Tom Bingham and the Transformation of the Law* 477. The English and ECHR law regarding reasons and open justice are set out in Adrian Zuckerman, *Zuckerman on Civil Procedure: Principles of Practice* (4th edn, Sweet & Maxwell 2021) ch 3, what he calls the principle of publicity and the right to a fair hearing.

(C) Open justice

Bentham's views on open justice are canvassed in Jane Johnston and Leslie Moran, 'Three Phases of Courts' Publicity: Reconfiguring Bentham's Open Justice in the Twenty-First Century' (2018) 14 Int'l JL in Context 525. Despite the Star Chamber's reputation its hearings were conducted openly although witnesses were examined privately: Daniel L Vande Zande, 'Coercive Power and the Demise of the Star Chamber' (2008) 50 Amer J Leg Hist 326. The principle and scope of the open justice principle are discussed in Joseph Jaconelli, *Open Justice: A Critique of the Public Trial* (OUP 2002) and Burkhard Hess and Ana Koprivica Harvey (eds), *Open Justice: The Role of Courts in a Democratic*

Society (Nomos 2019). While Jaconelli does not deny the interests of the public in open justice, and its value as a check on the judges, he argues that its value lies rather as a guarantee of a fair trial. The edited collection of Hess and Harvey deals with the position in civil law. The anonymization of judgments in Europe is covered in Marc Van Opijnen and others, 'Online Publication of Court Decisions in Europe' (2017) 17 Legal Information Management 136. Advocates for greater anonymization of parties in England come from different quarters. Zoe Adams, Abi Adams-Prassl, and Jeremias Adams-Prassl contend that the publication online of employment tribunal decisions has risks such as the potential for automating blacklisting of employees which anonymization would address: 'Online Tribunal Judgments and the Limits of Open Justice' (2022) 42 Leg Stud 42. For an argument that the courts should do more to protect the privacy of litigants and should not bow to populist demands to pry into the affairs of others, particularly the wealthy: Gilead Cooper, 'Open (In)Justice: Privacy, Open Justice and Human Rights' (2019) 25 Trusts & Trustees 712. The extent of privacy in English family court proceedings is set out in Julie Doughty, Lucy Reed, and Paul Magrath, *Transparency in the Family Courts: Publicity and Privacy in Practice* (2nd edn, Bloomsbury Professional 2024). The national security incursions on the open justice principle are explored in Kieran Pender, 'Open Justice, Closed Courts and the Constitution: Australian and Comparative Perspectives' (2023) 42 U Qld LJ 155; Martin Chamberlain, 'Special Advocates and Amici Curiae in National Security Proceedings in the United Kingdom' (2018) U Toronto LJ 496; and Anthony Gray, 'A Comparison and Critique of Closed Court Hearings' (2014) 18 Int'l J Evidence & Proof 230.

(D) Public accountability

Joshua Rozenberg covers the criticism of the judges in the Divisional Court in the first Brexit case, as well as other aspects of public accountability in *Enemies of the People? How Judges Shape Society* (Bristol University Press 2020). The background to the contempt charges against Professor Barend van Niekerk, including that the first prosecution was apparently instigated by the Judge President of the Transvaal, is summarized in Iain Currie, 'The Judiciary and Freedom of Speech in South Africa' in Lee (ed), *Judiciaries in Comparative Perspective* 223–25. For the use of the contempt power in the Indian Supreme Court see Gautam Bhatia, *Offend, Shock, or Disturb: Free Speech under the Indian Constitution* (OUP 2016) and Abhinav Chandrachud, *Republic of Rhetoric: Free Speech and the Constitution* (Penguin Random House 2017).

VI Conclusion

As to the measurement of judicial independence, that can be on the basis of de jure factors (the institutional and decisional aspects considered) or de facto considerations (as assessed by judges, experts, or the public). As to the empirical literature, Drew A Linzer and Jeffrey K Staton suggest a cross-national measure of de facto judicial independence for 200 countries from 1948 to 2012: 'A Global Measure of Judicial Independence, 1948–2012' (2015) 3 J Law & Courts 223. Using data from 192 countries from 1960 to 2008, James Melton and Tom Ginsburg found that the rules governing the selection and removal of judges were the only de jure protections which actually enhanced judicial independence in practice, and then only when working together: 'Does De Jure Judicial Independence Really Matter?' (2014) 2 J Law & Courts 187. A study covering up to eighty-seven countries over many decades found a small correlation between de jure and de facto judicial independence: Bernd Hayo and Stefan Voigt, 'The Long-Term Relationship between De Jure and De Facto Judicial Independence' (2019) 183 Economics Letters 108603. As to the impact of judicial independence (or its absence) on economic development, Stefan Voigt and his colleagues found that improvements in de facto judicial independence were associated with higher economic growth: 'Economic Growth and Judicial Independence, a Dozen Years On: Cross-Country Evidence Using an Updated Set of Indicators' (2015) 38 Eur J Pol Econ 197.

Chapter 2 Impartiality

I Introduction

There is some history of the judicial oath in Ellison Kahn, 'The Judicial Oath' (1954) 71 South Africa LJ 22 and Enid Campbell, 'Oaths and Affirmations of Public Office under English Law: An Historical Retrospect' (2000) 21(3) J Leg Hist 1. Styles identifies a judicial indifference to the judicial oath, albeit that this may be isolated: Scott Styles, 'Judicial Impartiality: Involvement, Opinion and the Judicial Oath' (2009) 13 Edin LR 312.

II Impartiality and Its Reach

(A) Behavioural, institutional, and adjudicative dimensions

The institutional, behavioural, and adjudicative dimensions to impartiality used in the text have some overlap with the political, procedural, and ethical dimensions which Charles Gardner Geyh helpfully identifies in his 'The Dimensions of Judicial Impartiality' (2013) 65 Florida LR 493. For Geyh the political dimension of impartiality promotes public confidence in the courts, its procedural dimension affords parties a fair hearing, and its ethical dimension concerns a standard of good conduct which is the core to a judge's self-definition. There is little analysis of impartiality in the jurisprudential literature, although a welcome exception is chapter 3(II) of William Lucy, *Law's Judgement* (Hart Publishing 2017), drawing on his earlier 'The Possibility of Impartiality' (2005) 25 Ox JL Stud 3. The way that fair trial standards and using accepted methods of judicial decision-making contribute to impartiality is discussed in Denis J Galligan, *Due Process and Fair Procedures* (Clarendon Press 1996) 441–42 and Ofer Raban, *Modern Legal Theory and Judicial Impartiality* (Routledge-Cavendish 2003) 83, 111–12. Neil Duxbury canvasses *sua sponte* consideration in *Law's Sources* (OUP 2025) ch 7. The contribution of in-court judicial behaviour to impartiality is mentioned in Sir Alan Moses, 'The Mask and the Judge' (2008) 12 Southern Cross U LR 3, 22 and Sharyn Roach Anleu and Kathy Mack, 'Performing Impartiality: Judicial Demeanour and Legitimacy' (2010) 35 L & Soc Inquiry 137, 139, 169. The issue is discussed further in Chapter 3.

(B) Impartiality and the judge's background

Professor Martha Minow argues forcefully for the need to distinguish a judge's identity and perspectives based on matters such as race, ethnicity, class, and gender, from the ability to judge impartially. She sums up: 'If being implicated means bias . . . perhaps then no one can judge': 'Stripped Down Like a Runner or Enriched by Experience: Bias and Impartiality of Judges and Jurors' (1992) 33 William & Mary LR 1201, 1208. Thirty years after her article, Charles G Geyh highlights the extent to which, at least in the US, attention needs to be given to address the unacceptable influence of identity in clouding the exercise of judgment: 'Judicial Ethics and Identity' (2023) 36 Georgetown JL Ethics 233. Judge Motley's discrimination decision is examined as one part of her record as a lawyer and judge in Tomiko Brown-Nagin, *Civil Rights Queen: Constance Baker Motley and the Struggle for Equality* (Pantheon Books 2022) 302ff. For a strong argument that for justice to be done and seen to be done requires judges to be broadly reflective of the society they serve see Kate Malleson, 'Safeguarding Judicial Impartiality' (2002) 22 Leg Stud 53. There is little on impartiality and bias in international courts, but a useful corrective to this is Gleider Hernández, 'Impartiality and Bias at the International Court of Justice' (2012) 1 Cambridge J Int'l & Comp L 183, which suggests that theories of judicial behaviour based wholly on a national basis remain incomplete when there are other important influences such as training in a particular legal tradition; professional background of the judge in diplomacy, government, or practice; institutional loyalty; and an individual's judge's conception of function within the international order.

(C) Identifying bias: actual, apprehended, unconscious

There are cases of actual bias documented in colonial courts: see eg, John Lonsdale, 'Kenyatta's Trials: Breaking and Making of an African Nationalist' in Peter Coss (ed), *The Moral World of the Law* (CUP 2000). These days actual bias in Britain is unusual in practice. In 'Facing up to Actual Bias' (2008) 27 CJQ 32, James Goudkamp argues persuasively that although this may prevent a degree of judicial embarrassment there is a risk that far from promoting public confidence in the administration of justice it is likely to have the opposite effect. He cites *Howell v Lees Millais* [2007] EWCA Civ 720 as a case close to the line of actual bias which should have been characterized as such (judicial hostility to the lawyers on one side).

The test for apparent bias has given rise to a considerable volume of criticism. One line is that it is too uncertain in its application and statutory intervention is needed. That is the argument in a valuable article by Jula Hughes and Philip Bryden, 'From Principles to Rules: The Case for Statutory Rules Governing Aspects of Judicial Disqualification' (2016) 53 Osgoode Hall LJ 853. Another is that informed and fair-minded observers are endowed with so much knowledge that they share, in effect, the knowledge and beliefs of the judges themselves. Included in a penetrating discussion of the bias rule is the suggestion that a way of addressing this is for a greater level of transparency in the bias rule in which an additional step is for the judges to assess the reasonableness of a claim in a holistic manner: Matthew Groves, 'Clarity and Complexity in the Bias Rule' (2020) 44 Melb U LR 565, 587. Professor Abimbola Olowofoyeku would prefer to cut through the issue by reinstating the test for bias as the judgment of the court: 'Bias and the Informed Observer: A Call for a Return to Gough' (2009) 68 CLJ 388. And see suggestions for balancing different factors (Simon Atrill, 'Who is the "Fair-Minded and Informed Observer"—Bias after Magill' (2003) 62 CLJ 279) and for focusing on different contexts such as pre-judgment (Simon Young, 'The Evolution of Bias: Spectrums, Species and the Weary Law Observer' (2017) 41 Melb U LR 928). In 'Judicial Policy, Public Perception, and the Science of Decision Making: A New Framework for the Law of Apprehended Bias' (2019) 38 CJQ 376, Andrew Higgins and Inbar Levy argued that the gap must be closed between the case law on apprehended bias on the one hand and public attitudes and psychological research on matters like unconscious bias on the other. One way forward, they suggested, is the adoption of a code like that for international arbitrators which spells out specifically when judges should and should not sit. They then had the clever idea of testing what the general population thought about the results of reported decisions regarding the disqualification of judges for apparent bias. They found that the public considered that judges should have stood down in scenarios based on some of the leading cases where the courts had decided that recusal was unnecessary: 'What the Fair Minded Observer Really Thinks about Judicial Impartiality' (2021) 84 MLR 811.

Regarding unconscious bias, there is an excellent account in Australian Law Reform Commission, *Without Fear or Favour: Judicial Impartiality and the Law on Bias* (ALRC Report 138, 2021) ch 4 and *Judicial Impartiality: Cognitive and Social Biases in Judicial Decision-Making* (Background Paper JI6, 2021) 6.19–6.24. In a number of articles Chris

Guthrie, Jeffrey J Rachlinski, and Andrew J Wistrich used surveys of North American judges to show how they were influenced by biases such as anchoring, hindsight bias, and the representativeness heuristic when given hypothetical cases to answer: eg, 'Inside the Judicial Mind' (2001) 86 Cornell LR 777; 'Can Judges Make Reliable Numeric Judgments? Distorted Damages and Skewed Sentences' (2015) 90 Indiana LJ 695. See also Jeffrey J Rachlinski and Andrew J Wistrich, 'Gains, Losses, and Judges: Framing and the Judiciary' (2018) 94 Notre Dame LR 521. On how judges focusing on different aspects of a case come to different conclusions Jeffrey J Rachlinski, Andrew J Wistrich, and Chris Guthrie, 'Altering Attention in Adjudication' (2013) 60 UCLA LR 1586. There are helpful discussions of confirmation bias in Andrew J Wistrich and Jeffrey J Rachlinski, 'How Lawyers' Intuitions Prolong Litigation' (2013) 86 S Cal LR 571 and (despite its concern with the criminal side) Moa Lidén, *Confirmation Bias in Criminal Cases* (OUP 2023). Evidence of motivated cognition among judges is contained in Andrew J Wistrich, Jeffrey J Rachlinski, and Chris Guthrie, 'Heart versus Head: Do Judges Follow the Law or Follow Their Feelings' (2015) 93 Tex LR 855. Evidence of the gambler's fallacy in judicial decision-making is examined in Daniel L Chen, Tobias J Moskowitz, and Kelly Shue, 'Decision Making Under the Gambler's Fallacy: Evidence from Asylum Judges, Loan Officers, and Baseball Umpires' (2016) 131 QJ Econ 1181. The literature about whether judges of different backgrounds (race, gender, and so on) are 'biased' is brought together by Allison P Harris and Maya Sen, 'Bias and Judging' (2019) 22 Annual Rev Pol Sc 241. Implicit bias is addressed in Bernice Donald, Jeffrey Rachlinski, and Andrew Wistrich, 'Getting Explicit about Implicit Bias' (2020) 104 Judicature 75; Sarah E Redfield (ed), *Enhancing Justice: Reducing Bias* (American Bar Association 2017) (hereafter Redfield (ed), *Enhancing Justice*); and Anthony G Greenwald and Linda Hamilton Krieger, 'Implicit Bias: Scientific Foundations' (2006) 94 Cal LR 945. Michele Benedetto Neitz, 'Socioeconomic Bias in the Judiciary' (2013) 61 Clev St LR 137 deals with a much neglected field. Drawing on this literature about cognitive bias Gary Edmond and Kristy A Martire set out possible measures to address them: 'Just Cognition: Scientific Research on Bias and Some Implications for Legal Procedure and Decision-making' (2019) 82 MLR 633, 658–64. Addressing implicit bias is also addressed in Andrew J Wistrich and Jeffrey J Rachlinski, 'Implicit Bias in Judicial Decision Making: How It Affects Judgment and What Judges Can Do About It' in Sarah E Redfield (ed), *Enhancing Justice.*

(D) Competing values

The existence of values such as the efficient operation of the courts in the application of the law regarding disqualification for bias is touched on in Abimbola A Olowofoyeku, 'Inappropriate Recusals' (2016) 132 LQR 318. Waiver of bias is well accepted in the common law although critics have questioned whether parties should be able to do this: Bridgette Toy-Cronin, 'Waiver of the Rule against Bias' (2002) 9 Auckland U LR 850 and James Goudkamp, 'The Rule against Bias and the Doctrine of Waiver' (2007) 26 CJQ 310. The argument is that private litigants should not be able to sacrifice the public interest in maintaining the reality and appearance of impartial justice because they find it expedient to do so.

III The Disqualification Rules

DEC Yale, 'Iudex in Propria Causa: An Historical Excursus' (1974) 33 CLJ 80 and John Frank, 'Disqualification of Judges' (1947) 56 Yale LJ 605 contain good histories of the English rules on disqualification of judges for bias. Good overall accounts of the rules are Grant Hammond, *Judicial Recusal* (Hart 2009); John Tarrant, *Disqualification for Bias*

(Federation Press 2012); Charles Hollander and Simon Salzedo, *Conflicts of Interest* (6th edn, Sweet & Maxwell 2020) ch 11, 13; and part IV of Lee, *Judiciaries in Comparative Perspective*. In the United States the rules for disqualification for federal judges have their basis in statute and codes. Charles Gardner Geyh, 'Why judicial Disqualification Matters. Again' (2011) 30 Review of Litigation 671 sets out the distinct history of American disqualification rules. As to disqualification for interest, the historical background to the *Dimes* case is outlined in Frank A Sharman, 'Feudal Copyholder and Industrial Shareholder: The Dimes Case' (1989) 10 J Leg Hist 71. Regarding the judge's associations in *Hadley v Baxendale* (1854) 9 Ex 341, 156 ER 145 see Richard Danzig, 'Hadley v Baxendale: A Study in the Industrialization of the Law' (1975) 4 J Leg Stud 249, 266–67. Justice Scalia's approach to disqualification for association generated a great deal of discussion: eg, Monroe H Freedman, 'Duck-Blind Justice: Justice Scalia's Memorandum in the Cheney Case' (2004) 18 Geo J Leg Ethics 229, Abimbola Olowofoyeku, 'Regulating Supreme Court Recusals' [2006] Singapore J Leg Stud 60. On disqualification for opinion, the disqualification of Justice Robertson is discussed in James Cockayne, 'Special Court for Sierra Leone—Decisions on the Recusal of Judges Robertson and Winter' (2004) 2 J Int'l Crim Justice 1154 and [Judge] Richard Goldstone, 'International Judges: Is There a Global Ethic?' (2015) 29 Ethics & Int'l Affairs 249, 253. Ryan M Proctor, 'Catholic Judges Have No Obligation to Recuse themselves in Capital Cases' (2019) 42 Harv JL & Pub Policy 309 discusses an earlier article co-authored by Associate Justice Amy Coney Barrett of the US Supreme Court, who had argued that Catholic judges should recuse themselves in certain capital cases given Catholic teaching about the death penalty. Discussion of the issue of disqualification for pre-judgement through a judge's earlier involvement with a case includes Andrew Higgins, 'The BATAS v Laurie: Apprehended Bias and Actual Failure of Case Management' (2011) 30 CJQ 246 and Anna Olijnyk, 'Apprehended Bias and Interlocutory Judgments' (2013) 35 Sydney LR 761. It is here that considerations of effective decision-making and efficiencies must play their part in decisions on disqualification for bias. There is the analytically distinct situation where judges comment extra-judicially on cases, over which they preside, perhaps to meet personal criticism. For a discussion of the US rules and a defence of a no-comment approach see Mark I Harrison and Keith Swisher, 'When Judges Should Be Seen, Not Heard: Extrajudicial Comments concerning Pending Cases and the Controversial Self-Defense Exception in the New Code of Judicial Conduct' (2008) 64 NYU Ann Survey Am L 559. Whether when one member of a multi-member court is disqualified the others are contaminated and must step aside is considered in Abimbola A Olowofoyeku, 'Bias in Collegiate Courts' (2016) 65 Int'l & Comp LQ 895.

IV Procedure

Critics of the existing procedures for dealing with bias challenges include Gabrielle Appleby, Stephen McDonald, and Suzanne Le Mire: 'Pride and Prejudice: A Case for Reform of Judicial Recusal Procedure' (2017) 20 Legal Ethics 89 and 'Ethical Infrastructure for a Modern Judiciary' (2019) 47 Fed LR 335; and Zygmont A Pines, 'Mirror, Mirror, on the Wall—Biased Impartiality, Appearances, and the Need for Recusal Reform' (2020) 125 Dickinson LR 69 (who offers a procedural code).

Chapter 3 Integrity

I Introduction

Law as integrity is a distinct idea in the jurisprudence of Ronald Dworkin, in which decisions in a particular case flow from what best fits and justifies a community's legal and political practices as a whole, treating all members of the community as equals, as well as from the actual precedents and statues decided under those practices: *Law's Empire* (Harvard University Press 1986) 95–96. Integrity in adjudication in this Dworkinian sense is concerned with substantive decision-making, the subject matter of Chapter 6. This chapter is concerned with integrity in judicial behaviour as addressed, most evidently in written form in the ethical guidance and codes of judicial conduct such as the *Guide to Judicial Conduct* (rev edn, Courts and Tribunals Judiciary, July 2023), crucially as well the *Bangalore Principles of Judicial Conduct* (United Nations 2018). On adoption of the Bangalore principles see Tilman Hoppe, with Pedro Gomes Pereira, *The Road to Judicial Integrity* (Deutsche Gesellschaft für Internationale Zusammenarbeit 2018). Among commentaries on the *Guide to Judicial Conduct* is Yvette Genn, 'Ethics' in Godfrey Cole, Yvette Genn, and Mary Kane, *Making Decisions Judicially* (Hart Publishing 2023). Charles Gardner Geyh has a very fine overview of US ethical rules dividing the macro, micro, and relational elements, and discussing the diminished consensus about them exacerbated in the US by partisan and judicial self-interest: 'The Architecture of Judicial Ethics' (2021) 169 U Pa LR 2351. Geyh's 'macroethics' are roughly equivalent to this chapter's 'first principles' and judicial values, and his 'microethics' to the behavioural standards it discusses. 'Relational ethics' to Geyh are constraints on macro- and microethics; they are not treated separately in this chapter. Arguably they are part of macro- and microethics in some cases—or as with some US constitutional restraints, nothing to do with ethics at all. Using virtue ethics Professor Lawrence Solum lists as judicial vices corruption, civic cowardice, bad temper, incompetence, and foolishness: 'Virtue Jurisprudence A Virtue-Centred Theory of Judging' (2003) 34 Metaphilosophy 178. He lists as judicial virtues temperance, courage, temperament, intelligence, wisdom, and justice (justice comprising impartiality, integrity, and legal vision). Most of these fold into the discussion in this chapter. Jonathan Soeharno also uses virtue ethics in his *The Integrity of the Judge: A Philosophical Inquiry* (Ashgate 2009).

II Safeguarding Integrity

The voluminous social science literature on socialization is analysed in Connie Wanberg (ed), *The Oxford Handbook of Organizational Socialization* (OUP 2012). There is a limited literature on judicial socialization, mostly American, for example the panel discussion 'On Becoming a Judge: Socialization to the Judicial Role' (1985) 69 Judicature 139. There are also several US studies based on interviews and observations of judges, with an emphasis on the acclimatization process for new judges: eg, Susan Goldberg, 'Judicial Socialization: An Empirical Study' (1985) 11 J Contemp L 423; Paul B Wice, 'Judicial Socialization. The Philadelphia Experience', and Lenore Alpert, 'Learning about Trial Judging. The Socialization of State Trial Judges' in James A Cramer, *Courts and Judges* (Sage Publications 1981); Robert Carp and Russell Wheeler, 'Sink or Swim: The Socialization of a Federal District Judge' (1972) 21 J Pub L 359; Beverly Blair Cook, 'The Socialization of New Federal Judges: Impact on District Court Business' (1971) 49 Washington U LQ 253. Outside the US see Nicole De Silva, 'International Courts' Socialization Strategies for Actual and Perceived Performance' in Theresa Squatrito and others (eds), *The Performance of International Courts and Tribunals* (CUP 2018) and Diana Richards, 'Learning to Sentence: An Empirical Study of Judicial Attitudes towards Judicial Training in Romania' (2015) 7 Int'l J Court Admin 68. Evan Bell's 'Letter to a New Judge' (2014) 40 Comm L Bull 95 collects much of the wisdom which will be conveyed informally to a new judge in Commonwealth jurisdictions. The traditional method of 'on the job' ('experiential') socialization of judges in Ireland, but with resonance elsewhere, is described (and to an extent defended) in Niamh Howlin and others, '"Robinson Crusoe on a Desert Island"? Judicial Education in Ireland, 1995–2019' (2022) 42 Leg Stud 525.

Effective socialization into the culture of the judiciary in Britain is evidenced by the very high commitment to the judiciary which respondent judges report (eg, Cheryl Thomas, *2022 UK Judicial Attitude Survey* (UCL Judicial Institute 2023) 9, 17 and in the ethnographic study by Penny Darbyshire, *Sitting in Judgment*. Although not explicit about the concept of socialization, Conall Mallory and Hélène Tyrrell effectively use it to explain how the rules around judges exercising free speech rights limit what they do by a shared conception of what is appropriate: 'The Extrajudicial Voice' (2024) 44 Legal Studies 1.

On the prescriptive and proscriptive functions of guidance and codes for judges see Steven Lubet, 'The Search for Analysis in Judicial Ethics or Easy Cases Don't Make Much Law' (1987) 66 Nebraska LR 430. Arguments long lost in the US for greater self-regulation for judicial misconduct are set out by two judges in Irving R Kaufman, 'Chilling Judicial Independence' (1979) 88 Yale LJ 681 (1979) and Harry T Edwards, 'Regulating Judicial Misconduct and Divining Good Behaviour for Federal Judges' (1989) 87 Mich LR 765. The informal, pre-*Guide to Judicial Conduct* approach to judicial discipline in England is described in Henry Cecil, *Tipping the Scales* (Hutchinson 1964), the classic study of English judges, Shimon Shetreet, *Judges on Trial* (North-Holland 1976), and Tom Bingham, 'Judicial Ethics' in Ross Cranston (ed), *Legal Ethics and Professional Responsibility* (OUP 1995). There are few examples of criminal conduct by English judges, although in 'Judges in the Dock' (2022) 4 Amicus Curiae 185, Barrie Lawrence Nathan refers to a circuit judge who was dismissed when he pleaded guilty to customs offences in 1983, and to a recorder (part-time judge) who was convicted of perverting the course of justice in 2014. On the inadequacies of the code for US Supreme Court judges: Veronica Root Martinez, 'Supreme Impropriety? Assessing the Justices' Conduct' (2024) 87 L & Contemp Probs 147.

III Integrity in the Decision-Making Process

David Pimentel argues that judicial independence and judicial accountability are better framed in terms of a judge's courage and integrity, which enables a better appreciation of the implications for matters like judicial discipline, especially across different cultures: 'Reframing the Independence v Accountability Debate: Defining Judicial Structure in light of Judges' Courage and Integrity' (2009) 57 Cleveland State LR 1. In *Judicial Reputation: A Comparative Theory* (University of Chicago Press 2015), Nuno Garoupa and Tom Ginsburg examine the different levels of reputation (individual and collective, which depend on each other), how (other things being equal) judges make decisions to enhance their reputation, and how reputation is both cause and effect in court structures. There is an argument that well-executed legal processes support emotional and psychological repair in the face of highly traumatic and emotionally charged life experiences, and a consideration of the relationship between conventional judging, procedural justice, and therapeutic justice in Rosemary Hunter, Sharyn Roach Anleu, and Kathy Mack, 'Judging in the Lower Courts: Conventional, Procedural, Therapeutic and Feminist Approaches' (2016) 12 Int'l JL in Context 337.

(A) Fairness, competence, efficiency

Adrian Zuckerman, *Zuckerman on Civil Procedure: Principles of Practice* (4th edn, Sweet & Maxwell 2021) ch 3, discusses the legal provisions bearing on fairness. The implications of procedural fairness and equal treatment are explored in Lawrence Solum, 'Procedural Justice' (2004) 78 So Cal LR 181 and Frej Klem Thomsen, 'Concept, Principle, and Norm-Equality before the Law Reconsidered' (2018) 24 Legal Theory 103. From 2004 the Judicial College for England and Wales has published various editions of *The Equal Treatment*

Bench Book (Judicial College, July 2024), containing a mine of information on fair, equal, and sensitive treatment of the diverse range of litigants who appear before judges. Delay in the delivery of judgments, and the factors bearing on it, are analysed by the chief justice of Australia, Stephen Gageler, in 'Just versus Quick: Constructivist and Ecological Rationality in a Common Law System' (2022) 45 Melb U LR 830. Gageler evaluates US and New Zealand measures for publishing details of delayed judgments, favouring the New Zealand approach where the judge's name is not necessarily published.

(B) *Behaviour at court*

In his 'The Mask and the Judge' (2008) 12 S Cross U LR 1, [Lord Justice] Alan Moses sees the mask of the law—related to, but more than demeanour—as conveying authority. Jordan Tutton, Kathy Mack, and Sharyn Roach Anleu found that in Australia's highest court the judges adopted a detached demeanour, consistent with formal conceptions of the judicial role, occasionally leavened by a supportive manner to counsel, frustration, or laughter: 'Judicial Demeanour: Oral Argument in the High Court of Australia' (2018) 39 Justice System J 273. Variability of judicial demeanour in lower Australia courts to address different circumstances is cleverly analysed in Sharyn Roach Anleu and Kathy Mack, *Performing Judicial Authority in the Lower Courts* (Palgrave Macmillan 2017). Historic cases of judicial misconduct are canvassed in Shimon Shetreet, *Judges on Trial* (North-Holland 1976); David Pannick, *Judges* (OUP 1987); and Graeme Williams, *A Short Book of Bad Judges* (Wildy, Simmonds and Hill Publishing 2013). More recent incidents are canvassed in Barrie Lawrence Nathan, '"Ain't Misbehavin": Judicial Conduct and Misconduct' (2020) 2 (series 2) Amicus Curiae 8. What is good behaviour is addressed in the guides and codes of ethical conduct for judges, mentioned in the chapter, and the literature referred to in that regard. Ruth Sheard (ed), *The Role of the Judge* (Judicial Commission of New South Wales 2004) contains some timeless papers on judicial performance by those including former chief justices of Australia (Murray Gleeson, Sir Gerard Brennan) and other judges (John Doyle, Mahla L Pearlman). What might have escaped censure in the past will no longer be regarded as compliant with current ethical and professional norms. Contemporary examples of judicial misconduct are available in press reports and in England in the brief statements published by the Judicial Conduct Investigations Office, examined in Chapter 4. In the United States, the National Center for State Courts' Center for Judicial Ethics produces *The Judicial Conduct Reporter*, which summarizes recent decisions and advisory opinions on judicial misconduct, as well as articles on judicial ethics and discipline: <www.ncsc.org/>. The Canadian Judicial Council also publishes its reports on its publications page, <https://cjc-ccm.ca/en>.

Performance issues may be attributable to causes such as depression and other health conditions: for an argument that there needs to be an acknowledgement of capacity issues and principled measures to address them: Andrew Lynch and Alysia Blackham, 'Reforming Responses to the Challenges of Judicial Incapacity' (2020) 48 Fed LR 214. As a former judge, Michael Kirby offers a rounded account, explaining how the stress of the judge can lead to bad behaviour in court, sometimes moving over the line into the unacceptable: 'Judicial Stress and Judicial Bullying' (2013) 87 ALJ 516. In the United States the term 'benchslaps' is used for how it has become increasingly common for judges to control attorney behaviour by using public shaming and the power of their position to bully: eg, Joseph P Mastrosimone, 'Benchslaps' [2017] Utah LR 331. For a brave account by an alcoholic depressive, who later became a judge at the Old Bailey, London, see Graham Boal, *A Drink at the Bar: A Memoir of Crime, Justice and Overcoming Personal Demons* (Quiller Publishing 2021). Examples of judicial sleepiness in a number of countries, and the negative view taken by the media, are discussed in Ronald R Grunstein and Dev Banerjee, 'The

Case of Judge Nodd and Other Sleeping Judges: Media, Society, and Judicial Sleepiness' (2007) 30 Sleep 625. Perhaps surprisingly there is a considerable academic literature on judicial humour, canvassing its advantages and disadvantages and whether it is appropriate, for example Marshall Rudolph, 'Judicial Humour: A Laughing Matter?' (1989) 41 Hastings LJ 175; Adalberto Jordan, 'Imagery, Humour, and the Judicial Opinion' (1987) 41 U Miami LR 693; Sharyn Roach Anleu, Kathy Mack, and Jordan Tutton, 'Judicial Humour in the Australian Courtroom' (2014) 38 Melb U LR 621 (an empirical study based partly on interviews with judges); and Jack Oakley and Brian Opeskin, 'Banter from the Bench: The Use of Humour in the Exercise of Judicial Functions' (2016) 42 Aust Bar R 82. A study of humour at swearing-in ceremonies for new or promoted judges in the Royal Courts of Justice in London explores how it performs a variety of functions, such as underlining the hierarchical structure of the judiciary: Leslie J Moran, 'What's a Box of "Bakewell Tarts" Got to Do with It?' in Jessica Milner Davis and Sharyn Roach Anleu (eds), *Judges, Judging and Humour* (Palgrave Macmillan 2018).

Judicial harassment and bullying have attracted much attention. For the UK see eg, Darren Howe and Jo Delahunty, 'Recognising and Managing Oppressive Behaviour—In-Court and Out' parts 1 and 2, *Counsel* (March 2022 and April 2022). For the US see Abbe Smith in 'Judges as Bullies' (2017) 46 Hofstra LR 253, who identifies various categories of bullies, the ignorant and incompetent, the thin-skinned and ill-tempered, and the power hungry and the biased. See also Douglas Richmond, 'Bullies on the Bench' (2012) Louisiana LR 325. Instances of judicial bullying and sexual harassment are contained in cross-jurisdictional surveys such as Kieran Pender, *Us Too? Bullying and Sexual Harassment in the Legal Profession* (International Bar Association 2019). The Bar Council of England and Wales have produced guidance for barristers on judicial bullying on its 'Wellbeing at the Bar' website <www.wellbeingatthebar.org.uk/problems/bullying-barristers>. Specifically on discrimination and sexual harassment by judges of their own clerks and court employees, see Jaime A Santos, 'When Justice Behaves Unjustly: Addressing Sexual Harassment in the Judiciary' (2018) 54 Court Rev 156; Leah M Litman and Deeva Shah, 'On Sexual Harassment in the Judiciary' (2020) 115 Northwestern U LR 599; Susan Saab Fortney, 'Taking Courthouse Discrimination Seriously: The Role of Judges as Ethical Leaders' (2022) 70 Kansas LR 607; Aliza Shatzman, 'Untouchable Judges? What I've Learned About Harassment in the Judiciary, and What We Can Do to Stop It' (2022) 29 UCLA J Gender & L 161. For Australia, Kylie Nomchong SC, 'Sexual Harassment and the Judiciary' (2020) 32 Judicial Officers Bulletin 55; and Helen Szoke, *Review of Sexual Harassment in Victorian Courts: Report and Recommendations* (Court Services Victoria 2021).

(C) Abuse of position

Further details of the abuse of position cases briefly outlined in the text are available elsewhere. Much has been written during the long drawn out events surrounding Judge President Hlophe, for example, Hugh Corder and Calli Solik, 'Judge and be Judged: Judicial Discipline in South Africa' in Richard Devlin and Sheila Wildeman (ed), *Disciplining Judges: Contemporary Challenges and Controversies* (Edward Elgar 2021); Christopher Forsyth, 'The Failure of Institutions: The South African Judicial Service Commission and the Hlophe Saga' in Shimon Shetreet and Christopher Forsyth (eds), *The Culture of Judicial Independence* (Brill 2011). The background to the Murphy affair is covered in Enid Campbell and HP Lee, *The Australian Judiciary* (2nd edn, CUP 2013) 117–20; Geoffrey Lindell, 'The Murphy Affair in Retrospect' in HP Lee and George Winterton (eds), *Australian Constitutional Landmarks* (CUP 2003); Tony Blackshield, 'Murphy Affair' in *Oxford Companion to the High Court of*

Australia (OUP 2001); and Justice Roslyn Atkinson, 'The Chief Justice and Mr Justice Murphy: Leadership in a Time of Crisis' (2008) 27 UQLJ 221. For the resignation of the two Irish judges, see T John O'Dowd, 'The Sheedy Affair' (2000) 3 Contemp Issues in Irish Law and Politics 103.

(D) Corruption

The different categories of corruption are spelt out in *The International Bar Association Judicial Integrity Initiative: Judicial Systems and Corruption* (IBA 2016). Corruption as an obstacle to judicial independence is covered in Keith E Henderson, 'Global Lessons and Best Practices: Corruption and Judicial Independence' in Guy Canivat, Mads Andenas, and Duncan Fairgrieve (eds), *Independence, Accountability, and the Judiciary* (British Institute of International and Comparative Law 2006). Amongst international measures against judicial corruption is the Global Judicial Integrity Network under the United Nations Office on Drugs and Crime (UNDOC), which in line with Article 11 of the UN Convention against Corruption provides assistance to states by supporting the development of the *Bangalore Principles of Judicial Conduct* and producing tools to assist judiciaries: <www.unodc.org/ji>. The history of judicial corruption in England is covered in Wilfrid Prest, 'Judicial Corruption in Early Modern England' (1991) 133 Past & Present 67; Shimon Shetreet, *Judges on Trial* (North-Holland Publishing 1976) 387–88; Andrew Gibb, *Judicial Corruption in the United Kingdom* (W Green & Son 1957). On Barrington, see Patrick O'Brien, 'When Judges Misbehave: The Strange Case of Jonah Barrington' (*UK Const L Blog*, 7 March 2013) <http://ukconstitutionallaw.org>. A starting point for the state of play in modern times must be the 2007 report by Transparency International, *Global Corruption Report: Corruption in Judicial Systems* (CUP 2007). GRECO's [Group of States against Corruption of the Council of Europe] evaluation reports are available at <www.coe.int/en/web/greco/evaluations> and see Fabian Zhilla, 'Organised Crime and Judicial Corruption in the Western Balkans: Are Customary Norms Playing Any Role?' (2011) 18 J Financial Crime 387. Specific instances of judicial corruption in India and Indonesia are outlined in Shivaraj S Huchhanavar, 'Regulatory Mechanisms Combating Judicial Corruption and Misconduct in India: A Critical Analysis' (2020) 4 Indian LR 47; Tim Lindsey and Simon Butt, *Indonesian Law* (OUP 2018) ch 14. The 'clean hands' investigations in Italy are described in Raymond Fisman and Miriam Golden, *Corruption: What Everyone Needs to Know* (OUP 2017) 215. For the failed impeachment proceedings against Justice V Ramaswami of the Indian Supreme Court for financial improprieties in his administrative capacity when he was chief justice of the High Court of Punjab and Haryana see Sengupta, *Independence and Accountability of the Higher Indian Judiciary* 84–94.

IV Extrajudicial Conduct

(A) 'Free speech'

Freedom of speech is the subject of part III of Lee (ed), *Judiciaries in Comparative Perspective*, with chapters by John Williams (Australia), Kent Roach (Canada), Grant Hammond (New Zealand), Iain Currie (South Africa), Keith Ewing (UK), and Charles Gardner Geyh (US). The Kilmuir rules are discussed in AW Bradley, 'Judges and the Media—The Kilmuir Rules' [1986] PL 383, who argues that they became part of the 'untidy mass of non-legal rules, customary practices and political expectations' governing practice in the judiciary of England and Wales: 385. Lord Dyson has argued for a more liberal approach than under the *Guide to Judicial Conduct*: 'Beyond the Bench: What Can Judges Say Extra-judicially?' (2022) 26(2) Commonwealth Judicial Journal 11. The position in the US with campaign advertising for elected judges is different from elsewhere. The consequences of *Republican Party of Minnesota v White* 536 US 765 (2002) are outlined in Deborah Goldberg, 'How Much Speech for Judges' (2007) 28 Justice System J 335; Charles Gardner Geyh, 'Why Judicial Elections Stink' (2003) 64 Ohio St LJ 43; and Douglas Keith with Eric Velasco, *The Politics of Judicial Elections, 2019–20* (Brennan Center for Justice 2022). The Brennan Center's 'Buying Time' analysis examines the sponsorship, content, and costs of televised state supreme court campaign advertising: see <www.brennancenter.org>. There is a considerable Australian literature on public comment by judges: eg, Susan Bartie and John Gava, 'Some Problems with Extrajudicial Writing' (2012) 34 Sydney LR 637; Chris Finn, 'Extrajudicial Speech and the Prejudgment Rule: A Reply to Bartie and Gava' (2014) 34 Adelaide LR 267; Matthew Groves, 'Public Statements by Judges and the Bias Rule' (2014) 40 Monash LR 115; Jasmin Moran, 'Courting Controversy: The Problems Caused by Extrajudicial Speech and Writing' (2015) 46 Vict U Well LR 453. There was some comment in Canada about Thomas Berger, who while a member of the Supreme Court of British Columbia wrote a letter to the press arguing that the rights of Canada's First Nation peoples and women needed to be taken into account in the proposed Charter of Rights and Freedoms: J Webber, 'The Limits to Judges' Free Speech: A Comment on the Report of the Committee of Investigation into the Conduct of the Hon Mr Justice Berger' (1984) 29 McGill LJ 369.

(B) *Behaviour away from court*

Behaviour falling below community expectations is discussed in Shimon Shetreet and Sophie Turenne, *Judges on Trial* (2nd edn, CUP 2014) ch 6; Duncan Webb, 'Judicial Conduct in a very Small Place: Some Contextual Questions' (2003) 6 Legal Ethics 106; John Restano, 'Removal of the Rock's Chief Justice' [2020] PL 253; Laura Cahillane and David Kenny, 'Lessons from Ireland's 2020 Judicial Conduct Controversy' (2020) 51 Common L W'ld R 24. Material from the US is voluminous and categorized under numerous headings in Geoffrey P Miller, 'Bad Judges' (2004) 83 Tex LR 431. On associational activities see Richard Devlin and others, 'A Mixed Bag: Critical Reflections on the Revised Ethical Principles for Judges' (2022) 100 Can BR 325; Robert B McKay, 'The Judiciary and Nonjudicial Activities' (1970) 35 Law & Contemp Probs 9. Sexual indiscretion led to the resignation of a Scottish Court of Session judge in 1989: see WA Nimmo Smith QC and JD Friel, *The Report on an Inquiry into an Allegation of a Conspiracy to Pervert the Course of Justice in Scotland* (1993, HC 377) paras 5.1–5.4, 18.2–18.3. The use of social media is discussed in James J Alfini, 'Future Trends in Judicial Ethics: The Influence of Cyberspace' (2010) 51 S Tex LR 851, Cynthia Gray, 'Social Media Posts by Judges on Controversial Issues' (2021) 43 Jud Conduct Rep 2. A liberal approach to the use by judges of social media is advocated in Brian Hull, 'Why Can't We Be "Friends"? A Call for a Less Stringent Policy for Judges Using Online Social Networking' (2012) 63 Hastings LJ 595, who contends it can help educate the public about judges and judging. The contrary view is that it can lead to reputational damage for judges and the judiciary.

(C) *Judicial confidentiality*

There is a paucity of discussion, but see a valuable description in Stephen Pitel and Liam Ledgerwood, 'Judicial Confidentiality in Canada' (2017) 43 Queen's LJ 123. For the publication of Lord Hope's diaries, including the volumes when he was a member of the House of Lords and Supreme Court, see Ross Cranston, 'Lord Hope's Diaries' (2021) 137 LQR 170, justifying their publication in the public interest. There is an increasingly common practice of retired US Supreme Court justices releasing their private papers, including the exchanges of memoranda with other members of the court: it has been said that the deliberative process should remain confidential: see Kathryn A Watts, 'Judges and Their Papers' (2013) 88 NYU LR 1665.

(D) Former judges

Patrick O'Brien, Ben Yong, and Sam Anderson have an historical and empirical study of the position of former judges in England and Wales, containing references to the position elsewhere, with recommendations favouring professional regulation: 'The Decline of the Judicial Retirement Convention, 1950-2020' [2024] PL 623. Suggestions for a new ethical framework for former judges include Gabrielle Appleby and Alysia Blackham, 'The Shadow of the Court: The Growing Imperative to Reform Ethical Regulation of Former Judges' (2018) 67 Int'l & Comp LQ 505; Mark Mancini and Geoffrey Sigalet, 'Justice(s) out of Office: Principles for Former Judges' (2021) 46 Queen's LJ 243; and Stephen GA Pitel & Will Bortolin, 'Revising Canada's Ethical Rules for Judges Returning to Practice' (2011) 34 Dalhousie LJ 483. On the controversy surrounding the involvement of four former Canadian Supreme Court judges in the SNC-Lavalin affair: Richard Devlin and Sarah Frame, 'Economic Corruption, Political Machinations and Legal Ethics: Correspondents' Report from Canada' (2019) 22 Legal Ethics 94. The conviction of a former judge in Australia for behaviour unconnected with the bench (see *Einfeld v R* [2008] NSWCCA 215, 252 ALR 375) is dealt with in Fiona Harari, *A Tragedy in Two Acts: Marcus Einfeld and Teresa Brennan* (Melbourne University Publishing 2011). Based on a dataset of Supreme Court of India cases involving the government for 1999–2014, Madhav S Aney, Shubhankar Dam, and Giovanni Ko argue that Supreme Court judges in India ruled in favour of the government in the hope of receiving jobs after retiring from the bench: 'Jobs for Justice(s): Corruption in the Supreme Court of India' (2021) 64 J Law & Econ 479. There is a growing literature on former judges sitting in foreign courts. Alyssa S King and Pamela K Bookman see its roots in history and seek to explain, for example, the absence of US judges taking on the role (more attractive opportunities at home; former judges join law firms, precluding sitting; waning global US influence): 'Traveling Judges' (2022) 116 Amer J Int'l L 477. See also Anna Dziedzic, *Foreign Judges in the Pacific* (Bloomsbury Publishing 2021); Rosalind Dixon and Vicki Jackson, 'Hybrid Constitutional Courts: Foreign Judges on National Constitutional Courts' (2019) 57 Columbia J Transn'l L 283.

Chapter 4 Legal and Policy Framework

I Introduction

Some of the topics in this chapter are covered on a comparative basis by Richard Devlin and Adam Dodek (eds), *Regulating Judges: Beyond Independence and Accountability* (Edward Elgar 2016), although the framework adopted is different.

II Appointment and Length of Service

(A) Models of selection

Executive government

The history of executive government appointments of judges by lord chancellors in England is covered in Patrick Polden, 'The Legal Profession' in William Cornish and others (eds), *Oxford History of the Laws of England vol XI 1820-1914* (OUP 2010) 961–78; Stevens, *The Independence of the Judiciary* 40–45, 81–88, 179–81; and Shimon Shetreet and Sophie Turenne, *Judges on Trial* (2nd edn, CUP 2014). On political considerations in appointments in Britain see Robert Stevens, *The English Judges* (Hart 2002) 62–64 and Chris Hanretty, 'The Appointment of Judges by Ministers' (2015) 3 JL & Courts 305, 324–25. A leading judge, Michael Kerr, opined that two judges with Labour Party backgrounds would not have been appointed by the Conservative lord chancellor, Hailsham: *As Far As I Remember* (Hart 2002) 307. C Neal Tate, 'Paths to the Bench in

Britain: A Quasi-Experimental Study of the Recruitment of a Judicial Elite' (1975) 28 Western Pol Q 108 examined the social backgrounds and careers of the 317 higher court judges 1876–1972. The background to change in the system from 2005 is covered in Gee and others' invaluable *The Politics of Judicial Independence in the UK's Changing Constitution* 160–63. The case for parliamentary confirmation hearings for senior appointments in England is considered in Alexander Horne, *The Changing Constitution: A Case for Judicial Confirmation Hearings?* (Study of Parliament Group Paper, 2010).

Executive appointment is still the norm in the US (for federal and some state appointments), Canada, Australia, and New Zealand: see chapters in Lee (ed), *Judiciaries in Comparative Perspective*. The reduced extent of executive appointment in Commonwealth countries is identified in the Bingham Centre's report: J van Zyl Smit, *The Appointment, Tenure and Removal of Judges under Commonwealth Principles* (BIICL 2015). The essential distinction between executive appointments in established democracies on the one hand and new democracies and transitional states on the other is drawn in Kate Malleson and Peter H Russell (eds), *Appointing Judges in an Age of Judicial Power: Critical Perspectives from around the World* (University of Toronto Press 2006). That does not mean that there have not been unfortunate executive appointments in established democracies: for example Rebecca Ananian-Welsh, Gabrielle Appleby, and Andrew Lynch, *The Tim Carmody Affair: Australia's Greatest Judicial Crisis* (UNSW Press 2016) and the appointments of the Harper government in Canada: Rosemary Cairns Way, 'Deliberate Disregard: Judicial Appointments under the Harper Government' [2014] SCLR 67. For executive appointment at federal level in the US see Lee Epstein and Jeffrey Segal, *Advice and Consent: The Politics of Judicial Appointments* (OUP 2005). For partisan behaviour in considering nominees see Jon Rogowski and Andrew Stone, 'How Political Contestation Over Judicial Nominations Polarizes Americans' Attitudes Toward the Supreme Court' (2021) 51 Brit J Pol Sc 1251; Peter J Eckerstrom, 'The Garland Nomination, the Senate's Duty, and the Surprising Lessons of Constitutional Text' (2018) 21 U Penn J Constitutional L 33. Whatever might be said of vetting by the American Bar Association of nominees disfavouring Republican nominees in the past, the ratings 2001–20 do not exhibit any clear partisan bias: Austin R Nelson, 'Evaluating the Evaluator: Has the ABA Rated President Trump's Judicial Nominees Fairly?' (2020) 99 Texas LR 193.

Elections

The background to electing judges in the US, and the arguments for and against, are explored in a range of works, most succinctly Charles Gardner Geyh's *Who is to Judge?: The Perennial Debate Over Whether to Elect or Appoint America's Judges* (OUP 2019). An early critic of electing judges was the LSE's Harold Laski, who in 1926 condemned the election of judges because the public (or with choice by the legislature, its members) could not properly assess the qualifications of judicial office, proposing instead that judges be nominated by a judicial commission until retirement age, subject to good behaviour: 'The Technique of Judicial Appointment' (1926) 24 Mich LR 529. See, among many others, Steven P Croley, 'The Majoritarian Difficulty: Elective Judiciaries and the Rule of Law' (1995) 62 U Chi LR 689. In his article 'Economic Crisis and the Rise of Judicial Elections' (2010) 123 Harv LR 1061, Jed Handelsman Shugerman explains that strengthening the judiciary was the motive behind the mid nineteenth-century adoption of electing judges, but that adoption of the model was contingent on historical factors favouring it as well as other changes. For election of judges in Switzerland, Benjamin Suter, 'Appointment, Discipline and Removal of Judges: A Comparison of the Swiss and New Zealand Judiciaries' (2015) 46 Vict U Wellinton LR 267. On the defeat of Chief Justice Rose Bird and her colleagues in California's judicial elections in 1986 around the issue of the death penalty, see the account of former judge, Robert S Thompson, 'Judicial Retention Elections and Judicial Method: A Retrospective on the California Retention Election of 1986' (1988) 61 S Cal LR 2007. The defeat of three Iowan Supreme Court judges in 2010 over same-sex marriage is covered in Andrew J Clopton and C Scott Peters, 'Justices Denied: A County-Level Analysis of the 2010 Iowa Supreme Court Retention Election' (2013) 34 Justice System Journal 321. Other instances of judges being targeted and of attack advertising are examined in reports from the Brennan Center for Justice, for example Douglas Keith with Patrick Berry and Eric Velasco, *The Politics of Judicial Elections, 2017–18* (Brennan Center for Justice 2019). There is some empirical evidence that attack advertising in judicial elections does not have significant influence on election outcomes, certainly in partisan elections: Melinda Gann Hall, *Attacking Judges: How Campaign Advertising Influences State Supreme Court Elections* (Stanford University Press 2015). However, a number of studies have demonstrated that because judges are concerned about elections, and about attack advertising in the course of them, they tailor their judgments, especially in criminal sentencing and appeals, to improve their electoral prospects, adopting a harsher approach to criminal defendants: eg, Michael S Kang and Joanna M Shepherd, *Free to Judge?: How Campaign Finance Money Biases Judges* (Stanford University Press 2023). As well as the ABA, other bodies advocating changes in electing senior state judges include the Brennan Centre for Justice: Alicia Bannon, *Choosing State Judges: A Plan for Reform* (Brennan Center for Justice 2018).

Selection commissions

In the UK, the powerful voice of the judiciary in judicial selection despite the establishment of the Judicial Appointments Commission is covered in Gee and others, *The Politics of Judicial Independence in the UK's Changing Constitution* 184–85, 219; Alan Paterson, 'Power and Judicial Appointment: Squaring the Impossible Circle' in Graham Gee and Erika Rackley (eds), *Debating Judicial Appointments in an Age of Diversity* (Routledge 2018) (hereafter Gee and Rackley (eds), *Debating Judicial Appointments in an Age of Diversity*). For the consequent argument that the executive should have an enhanced role in judicial appointments in England see eg, Richard Ekins and Graham Gee, *Reforming the Lord Chancellor's Role in Senior Judicial Appointments* (Policy Exchange 2021). The role of affinity bias in judicial selection is mentioned in a report by a working party of Justice, *Increasing Judicial Diversity* (Chr: Nathalie Lieven QC, later Lieven J) (Justice 2017) 14, 36. The South African commission has attracted criticism because of the lack of clear criteria for appointment, the intrusion of political considerations, and its failure to appoint some well-regarded, independent-minded candidates: Freedom Under Law, *Serving the Judiciary? A Review of the Activities of the South African Judicial Service Commission 2009 to 2022* (Freedom Under Law 2002); Chris Oxtoby, 'The Appointment of Judges: Reflections on the Performance of the South African Judicial Service Commission' (2021) 56 J Asian & African Stud 34; Chris Oxtoby, 'Managing a Fraught Transition: the Practice of the South African JSC' in Hugh Corder and Jan van Zyl Smit (eds), *Securing Judicial Independence: The Role of Commissions in Selecting Judges in the Commonwealth* (Siber Ink 2017). (As well as chapters on other Commonwealth jurisdictions, *Securing Judicial Independence* contains the 'Cape Town Principles on the Role of Independent Commissions in the Selection and Appointment of Judges in the Commonwealth', drawn up by members of a project at the University of Cape Town's Department of Public Law and the Bingham Centre for the Rule of Law, London.) For further discussions of the South African position see Hugh Corder, 'Appointment, Discipline and Removal of Judges in South Africa' in Lee (ed), *Judiciaries in Comparative Perspective.* Martin L Friedland sets out the Canadian position in 'Appointment, Discipline and Removal of Judges in Canada' in Lee (ed), *Judiciaries in Comparative Perspective.* Thus at one time the Ontario commission simply vetted names that the government provided (qualified/not qualified); later they selected and presented closed lists from which the Attorney General could chose: 52–54. European standards for judicial councils are summarized in David Kosař and Attila Vincze, 'European Standards of Judicial Governance: From Soft Law Standards to Hard Law' (2023) 30 Journal für Rechtspolitik 491.

Judicialized selection

As for the collegium system for judicial appointments in India, TR Andhyarujina attributes it to the period of the Emergency: 'A Committed Judiciary: Indira Gandhi and Judicial Appointments' in Arghya Sengupta and Ritwika Sharma (eds), *Appointment of Judges to the Supreme Court of India* (OUP 2018). As well as the editors' chapter see especially the contrasting contributions in this collection.

(B) Selection processes

In telling the story of the ineligibility of a federal court judge for one of the Quebec seats on the Canadian Supreme Court, Carissima Mathen and Michael Plaxton go over much ground regarding the appointment processes for that court: *The Tenth Justice: Judicial Appointments, Marc Nadon, and the Supreme Court Act Reference* (UBC Press 2020). Chief Justice Beverley McLachlin in her *Truth be Told* (Simon & Shuster 2019) agrees with Canada's former prime minister, Jean Chrétien, that the attack on her over the issue was an unprecedented violation of respect for the court: 329. Professor Deborah L Rhode wrote much on legal ethics during her life. Chapter 1 of her *Character: What It Means and Why It Matters* (OUP 2019) has some discussion of the meaning of character. Professor Caroline Dick argues that a judge was the victim of gender bias in the evaluation of her pre-appointment conduct when she was a victim of revenge porn: 'Sex, Sexism, and Judicial Misconduct: How the Canadian Judicial Council Perpetuates Sexism in the Legal Realm' (2020) 28 Feminist Leg Stud 133.

There is a huge literature on diversity and merit. The different arguments for diversity and their implications are explored, for example, in Erika Rackley and Charlie Webb, 'Three Models of Judicial Diversity' in Gee and Rackley (eds), *Debating Judicial Appointments in an Age of Diversity*; Catherine Alberty, 'Judicial Diversity' in Cora Hoexter and Morné Olivier (eds), *The Judiciary in South Africa* (Juta 2014) (hereafter Hoexter and Olivier (eds), *The Judiciary in South Africa*); Brian Opeskin, 'Dismantling the Diversity Deficit: Towards a More Inclusive Australian Judiciary' in Gabrielle Appleby and Andrew Lynch (eds), *The Judge, the Judiciary, and the Court: Individual, Collegial and Institutional Judicial Dynamics in Australia* (CUP 2021) (hereafter Appleby and Lynch (eds) *The Judge, the Judiciary and the Court*). The seminal piece by a judge that women can have a (limited) impact on decision-making is by Bertha Wilson, of Canada's Supreme Court: 'Will Women Judges Really Make a Difference? (1990) 28 Osgoode Hall LJ 507. That argument was supported by Lady Hale, later president of the UK Supreme Court, in 'Equality and the Judiciary: Why Should We Want More Women Judges?' [2001] PL 489. The argument has been developed by a number of academics. Kate Malleson was early in the field in the UK; for subsequent analysis see Lizzie Barmes and Kate Malleson, 'Lifting the Judicial Identity Blackout' (2018) 38 Ox J Leg Stud 357. In her prize-winning monograph *Women, Judging and the Judiciary: From Difference to Diversity* (Routledge 2013) Erika Rackley developed the argument that women would enrich the judiciary: diversity and appointments on merit were mutually reinforcing. See also her 'A Short History of Judicial Diversity' (2023) 76 CLP 265. The critical analysis of Lord Sumption in 'Home Truths about Judicial Diversity' (Bar Council Law Reform Lecture, 15 November 2012) is in turn criticized in another book in the Clarendon Series, NW Barber, *The United Kingdom Constitution: An Introduction* (OUP 2021) 147–48. There is a large diversity gap in the Indian judiciary: Simashree Bora, 'Feminising the Indian Judiciary' in Melissa Crouch (ed), *Women and the Judiciary in the Asia-Pacific* (CUP 2021). An empirical study of US state courts suggests that the best method for the selection of women is executive appointment not judicial appointment commissions: Greg Goelzhauser, *Judicial Merit Selection: Institutional Design and Performance for State Courts* (Temple University Press 2019). Graham Gee suggests a greater role for executive government to address the diversity gap in the UK: 'Rethinking the Lord Chancellor's Role in Judicial Appointments' (2017) 20 Legal Ethics 4. On Canadian progress see Samreen Beg and Lorne Sossin, 'Diversity, Transparency & Inclusion in Canada's Judiciary' in Gee and Rackley (eds), *Debating Judicial Appointments in an Age of Diversity*.

(C) Length of service

There is extensive writing about life tenure for US Supreme Court and other federal judges. At the policy level there are arguments about whether life tenure is justified considering contemporary social and political conditions such as increasing longevity: eg, Roger C Cramton, 'Reforming the Supreme Court' (2007) Calif LR 1313. Judges in federal courts other than the Supreme Court respond, to an extent, to the measures encouraging them to work part-time. Stephen J Choi, Mitu Gulati, and Eric A Posner, 'The Law and Policy of Judicial Retirement: An Empirical Study' (2013) J Leg Stud 111 found that federal district judges took senior status (but did not retire) as expected when their pensions vested, although more able and wealthier judges were less sensitive to the financial incentives of the system, and some seemed to time this so that the president would appoint a like-minded judge. Because judges taking senior status create a vacancy, encouraging more judges to do so would add to the judge-power of the federal bench: Marin Levy, 'The Promise of Senior Judges' (2021) 115 NWU LR 1227. The issues associated with fixed retirement ages for judges are discussed in Alysia Blackham, 'Judges and Retirement Ages' (2016) 39 Melb U LR 738; Alysia Blackham, 'Judicial Retirement Ages in the UK: Legitimate Aims and Proportionate Means?' [2017] 2 PL 196; Brian Opeskin, 'Models of Judicial Tenure: Reconsidering Life Limits, Age Limits and Term Limits for Judges' (2015) 35(4) Ox J Leg Stud 627; and Mary L Clark, 'Judicial Retirement and Return to Practice' (2011) 60 Cath U LR 841. There is a valuable account of acting judges in Australia, with a summary of the position in New Zealand, the UK, and the US, in the report of Gabrielle Appleby and others, *Temporary Judicial Officers in Australia* (Judicial Conference of Australia 2017).

III Removal and Discipline

(A) Removal

Shimon Shetreet and Sophie Turenne, *Judges on Trial* (2nd edn, CUP 2014) 339–54 examines the cases for removal brought under the Act of Settlement. For impeachment in the US see Paul Carrington and Roger Cramton, 'Original Sin and Judicial Independence: Providing Accountability for Justices' (2009) 50 William & Mary LR 1105. As regards removal for incapacity, Alan Paterson was early in the field with his 'The Infirm Judge' (1974) 1 Brit JL & Soc'y 83, recounting that in at least fifteen instances since 1890 judges of the senior courts in Britain had been the subject of strong pressures or inducements to resign, ostensibly on the grounds of ill health which they were reluctant to face up to or were incapable of recognizing. Life tenure on the US Supreme Court has given rise to many instances of judges no longer mentally competent still serving, with the ramifications for the work and reputation of the court, and efforts (eventually successful in some cases) to prise them off the bench: for example, David Garrow, 'Mental Decrepitude on the US Supreme Court: The Historical Case for a 28th Amendment' (2000) 67 U Chi LR 995. Andrew Lynch and Alysia Blackham, 'Reforming Responses to the Challenges of Judicial Incapacity' (2020) 48 Fed LR 214 is a good discussion of the issues, which draws on discrimination law for insights into how a process to respond to judicial incapacity might be structured. See also Louis Blom-Cooper, 'The Age of Judicial

Responsibility: The Retirement and Resignation of Appellate Court Judges' in Shimon Shetreet and Christopher Forsyth (eds), *The Culture of Judicial Independence: Conceptual Foundations and Practical Challenges* (Martinus Nijhoff Publishers 2011).

(B) *Disciplinary procedures*

The issues in designing disciplinary machinery are thoughtfully analysed in Gabrielle Appleby and Suzanne Le Mire, 'Judicial Conduct: Crafting a System that Enhances Institutional Integrity' (2014) 38 Melb U LR 1. See also the editors' introduction in Richard Devlin and Sheila Wildeman (eds), *Disciplining Judges: Contemporary Challenges and Controversies* (Edward Elgar 2021), which contains descriptions of the processes for disciplining judges for misconduct in thirteen countries, including chapter 6, Graham Gee, 'Judicial Conduct, Complaints and Discipline in England and Wales: Assessing the New Approach'. Further descriptions of disciplinary machinery are James Harrison, 'Judging the Judges: The New Scheme of Judicial Conduct and Discipline in Scotland' (2009) 13 Edinburgh LR 427; Laura Cahillane, 'An Analysis of the Judicial Council Act' (2019) 42 Dublin U LJ 1, 11–25; BV Harris, 'The Resignation of Wilson J: A Consequent Critique of the Operation of the Judicial Conduct Commissioner and Judicial Conduct Panel Act 2004' [2011] NZLR 625; Morné Olivier and Cora Hoexter, 'The Judicial Service Commission' in Hoexter and Olivier (eds), *The Judiciary in South Africa*. The removal of nineteenth-century judges in the British Empire is covered in John McLaren, *Bewigged, Bothered, & Bewildered: British Colonial Judges on Trial, 1800-1900* (University of Toronto Press 2011).

The Commonwealth principles are analysed in J van Zyl Smit, *The Appointment, Tenure and Removal of Judges under Commonwealth Principles: A Compendium and Analysis of Best Practice* (Bingham Centre for the Rule of Law 2015); Commonwealth Secretariat, 'Model Law on Judicial Service Commissions' (2017) Comm L Bull 577. The position in the US is set out at the federal level in the report of a committee chaired by Justice Breyer of the US Supreme Court, *Implementation of the Judicial Conduct and Disability Act of 1980: A Report to the Chief Justice*, 2006, and in the states in Keith Swisher, *Judicial Discipline in the States* (Institute for the Advancement of the American Legal System 2018). In most states (44 of 51) there is broad representation on the commissions with non-judge majorities: James J Alfini, Shailey Gupta Brietzke, and James F McMartin IV, 'Dealing with Judicial Misconduct in the States: Judicial Independence, Accountability and Reform' (2007) 48 South Texas LR 889. On international and regional standards for disciplinary procedures for judges see, for example: UN Basic Principles (UNGA Res 40/ 32 (29 November 1985) and UNGA Res 40/ 146) arts 17– 20; Council of Europe Committee of Ministers Recommendation CM/Rec(2010)12 to Member States on judges: independence, efficiency and responsibilities, art 69; European Networks of Councils for the Judiciary, The Minimum Judicial Standards V, Standards for Disciplinary Proceedings and Liability of Judges, Adopted, The Hague, 2015.

Sanjay Jain and Saranya Mishra deal with an issue with international dimensions: 'Scandalizing the Judiciary: An Analysis of the Uneven Response of the Supreme Court of India to Sexual Harassment Allegations against Judges (2020) 18 Int'l J Const'l L 563. On the reluctance to complain about judicial misconduct see David Pimentel, 'The Reluctant Tattletale: Closing the Gap in Federal Judicial Discipline' (2009) 76 Tenn LR 909. Charles Gardner Geyh argues that informal discipline is administered regularly and effectively: the small number of complaints culminating in formal discipline does not translate into a significant volume of unaddressed incidents: 'Informal Methods of Judicial Discipline' (1993) 142 U Pa LR 243. Quietly easing out a judge with mental issues is described by Lord Hope when he was the senior judge in Scotland: JAD Hope, *Lord President, 1989-1996* (Avizandum Publishing 2018) 53–54, 57. The threat to judicial independence when judges face sanction for 'decisional conduct' is discussed in Steven Lubet, 'Judicial Discipline and Judicial Independence' (1998) 61 Law and Contemp Prob 59. The wider issue of disciplining judges on political grounds and undermining judicial independence is illustrated by events in Turkey following an attempted coup in 2016: *Turkey: The Judicial System in Peril: A Briefing Paper* (International Commission of Jurists 2016); Tom Ruys and Emre Turkut, 'Turkey's Post-Coup "Purification Process": Collective Dismissals of Public Servants under the European Convention on Human Rights' (2018) 18 Human Rights LR 539.

IV Terms of Service

(A) Renumeration

There has been a fluctuating concern in a number of jurisdictions over the reluctance of leading lawyers to apply for judicial appointment. One reason is the loss of income it would entail, but that is only part of the story: see for example Hazel Genn, *The Attractiveness of Senior Judicial Appointment to Highly Qualified Practitioners* (Judicial Office 2008). An example of the work of the Review Body on Senior Salaries on judicial salaries is *Forty-Sixth Annual Report on Senior Salaries Report No. 97* (CP 1120, 2024) ch 5. Sophie Turenne and John Bell prepared a report on the issue: *The Attractiveness of Judicial Appointments in the United Kingdom* (Report to the Senior Salaries Review Body, January 2018). For the *Provincial Judges Reference Case* in Canada, Peter W Hogg, 'The Bad Idea of Unwritten Constitutional Principles: Protecting Judicial Salaries' in Dodek and Sossin (eds), *Judicial Independence in Context* and Lori Hausegger, Matthew Hennigar, and Troy Riddell, *Canadian Courts Law, Politics, and Process* (2nd edn, OUP 2015) 190–93. On pensions, Brian Opeskin contends that it is inequitable and politically unsustainable for judges to have such generous provision, although his material is from Australia, where judicial pensions are especially generous with fewer restrictions on retired judges returning to legal practice: *Future-Proofing the Judiciary: Preparing for Demographic Change* (Palgrave Macmillan 2021) ch 4. As well as considering the impact of salary on the recruitment and retention of judges, the Review Body on Senior Salaries in Britain has considered how these have been affected by changes in judicial pensions: eg, *Forty-Third Annual Report on Senior Salaries 2021* (CP 494, 2021) ch 5.

(B) Non-financial terms and conditions

There is little written on this topic, but Alysia Blackham draws on a comparative analysis of the UK, Australia, and other common law countries to suggest a framework for considering some aspects, see 'Reconceiving Judicial Office through a Labour Law Lens' (2019) 47 Fed LR 203. Surveys of judges throw up a number of concerns which would fall under this head: for example, Cheryl Thomas, *2022 UK Judicial Attitude Survey* (UCL Judicial Institute 2023). For case assignment in the context of judicial independence see pp. 29–30 above. Random assignment is designed to ensure all judges receive a fair and diverse mix of cases, but a large dataset of panel assignments in the US Courts of Appeals questions whether this occurs. Random assignment is a structural block to specialization, which many regard as crucial as with commercial cases. Specialization may lead to judges becoming jaded by handling the same type of case or set in their attitudes to those specialist cases. Michael A Livermore, Nina Varsava, and Daniel N Rockmore, 'Gendered

Judicial Opinions' (2024) 1 JL & Empirical Analysis 1 found that gender was a significant predictor of the content of judicial opinions, but this result may have been confounded by the way cases are assigned.

For the more formal methods of judicial training internationally: Livingston Armytage, *Educating Judges: Towards Improving Justice* (Brill 2015); Diana Richards, 'Current Models of Judicial Training' (2016) 5 Int'l Org Judicial Training J 41. There is a comparative account of judicial education in Australian Law Reform Commission, *Judicial Impartiality: Ethics, Professional Development, and Accountability* (ALRC Background Paper JI5, 2021).

Stress in the judiciary is much discussed. A pioneering (and brave) discussion was Justice Michael D Kirby, 'Judicial Stress' (1995) 13 Aust Bar Rev 101. Academic studies include Jared Chamberlain and James T Richardson, 'Judicial Stress: A Topic in Need of Research' in Monica K Miller and Brian H Bornstein (eds), *Stress, Trauma, and Wellbeing in the Legal System* (OUP 2012). Carly Schrever, Carol Hulbert, and Tania Sourdin have several papers based on interviews with judges: 'The Privilege and the Pressure: Judges' and Magistrates' Reflections on the Sources and Impacts of Stress in Judicial Work' (2024) 31 Psychiatry, Psychology & Law 327; 'The Psychological Impact of Judicial Work: Australia's First Empirical Research Measuring Judicial Stress and Wellbeing' (2019) 28 J Jud Admin 141. See also Janet Chan, Suzanne Poynton, and Jasmine Bruce, 'Lawyering Stress and Work Culture: An Australian Study' (2014) 37 UNSW LJ 1062. Two judges, Pauline Spencer and Jamey H Hueston, consider the need for protective skills by judges, in particular compassion, to cope with vicarious trauma and burnout: 'The Power of Compassion: A Judicial Reflection on Wellbeing and the Court' (2024) 31 Psychiatry, Psychology & Law 320. Global Judicial Integrity Network, *Exploring Linkages between Judicial Well-Being and Judicial Integrity* (UNDOC 2022) has suggestions for effective actions and initiatives to promote the well-being of judges worldwide. See also Judiciary of England and Wales, *Judicial Wellbeing Survey 2021 Report and Action Plan* (Judicial Office 2022).

Jane Johnston covers the move to community engagement in 'Three Phases of Courts' Publicity: Reconfiguring Bentham's Open Justice in The Twenty-First Century' (2018) 14 Int'l JL in Context 525. For a Canadian perspective: Malcolm Rowe and Dahlia Shuhaibar, 'To Participate or not to Participate: Judicial Involvement in the Community' (2020) 71 UNB LJ 275. For the Family Court judge discussed in the text, see the account by the complainant in his case Rob Allen, 'Lessons to be Learned: Paul Coleridge' in Matthew Rogers and Penelope Gibbs (eds), *Rethinking Judicial Independence* (Transform Justice 2017). For activities aimed at affirmatively promoting improved public knowledge of courts and judicial work, Kathy Mack, Sharyn Roach Anleu, and Jordan Tutton, 'The Judiciary and the Public: Judicial Perceptions' (2018) 39 Adel LR 1. Although with a somewhat different perspective, much of what Conall Mallory and Hélène Tyrrell cover in their study of judges' external communications is relevant to judges' community engagement: 'The Extrajudicial Voice' (2024) 44 Legal Stud 1.

V Conclusion

The objections to performance management of judges are raised in James Allsop, 'Courts as (Living) Institutions and Workplaces' (2019) 93 ALJ 375; Francesco Contini and Richard Mohr, 'Reconciling Independence and Accountability in Judicial Systems' (2007) 3 Utrecht LR 26; James Spigelman, 'Seen to Be Done: The Principle of Open Justice' (2000) 74 ALJ 290, 378.

Chapter 5 Judgecraft

I Introduction

Early editions of the *Equal Treatment Bench Book* for judges in England and Wales defined judgecraft as the art of judging: it was about how judges went about performing their tasks, covering matters not necessarily found in the books on law, evidence, and procedure (eg, *Equal Treatment Bench Book* (Judicial College 2013)). See also Roy B Flemming, Peter F Nardulli, and James Eisenstein, *The Craft of Justice: Politics and Work in Criminal Court Communities* (University of Philadelphia Press 1992).

II Dimensions of Judgecraft

(A) Judgecraft in outline

One of the few general accounts of judgecraft is Herbert M Kritzer, 'Toward a Theorization of Craft' (2007) 16 Soc & Legal Stud 321, who offers some acute observations, including that the craftsperson will often be unable to explain their skills and techniques, which have become 'automatic'. Among the skills Kritzer identifies is judgment—the product of training, experience, and innate personal qualities. See also Nigel G Fielding, 'Judges and their Work' (2007) 16 Soc & Legal Stud 97 on 'learning by doing'. The judgecraft of problem-solving, active intervention, direct engagement, and careful communications in high volume, time-pressured lower courts in Australia is detailed in an accomplished account, Sharyn Roach Anleu and Kathy Mack, *Performing Judicial Authority in the Lower Courts* (Palgrave Macmillan 2017). Other studies of routinization and heuristics in courts like these include Dave Cowan and Emma Hitchings, 'Pretty Boring Stuff: District Judges and Housing Possession Proceedings' (2007) 16 Soc & Legal Stud 363, and Jessica Hambly and Nick Gill, 'Law and Speed: Asylum Appeals and the Techniques and Consequences of Legal Quickening' (2020) 47 JL & Soc 3 (a French court).

(B) Fact-finding

An early work identifying faulty judicial assumptions about fact-finding in light of the work of social psychologists was Sally Lloyd-Bostock and Brian R Clifford (eds), *Evaluating Witness Evidence: Recent Psychological Research and New Perspectives* (John Wiley & Sons 1983). From its twentieth edition there is a valuable account of the law relating to demeanour evidence, with reference to social science literature, in Hodge Malek and others (eds), *Phipson on Evidence* (Sweet & Maxwell 2021) 1737–41. The social science evidence casting doubt on whether anyone (including a judge or jury) is able to detect truth or falsity from appearances is canvassed in many places, including Max Minzner, 'Detecting Lies Using Demeanour, Bias and Context' (2008) 29 Cardozo LR 2557; Olin Guy Wellborn, 'Demeanour' (1991) 76 Cornell LR 1075; Loretta Re, 'Oral v Written Evidence: The Myth of the "Impressive Witness"' (1983) 57 ALJ 679. The psychological research on memory and it bearing on witness evidence is canvassed in Alan Baddeley and others, 'Legal Aspects of Memory: A Report issued by the Psychology and Law Sections of the British Academy' (2023) 11 J Brit Academy 95, Annex. The classic account of judicial notice is Kenneth Culp Davis, 'Judicial Notice' (1955) 55 Colum LR 945. On social facts see various contributions from Kylie Burns, eg, '"In this Day and Age": Social Facts, Common Sense and Cognition in Tort Law Judging in the United Kingdom' (2018) JL & Soc 226; Kylie Burns, 'The Australian High Court and Social Facts: A Content Analysis Study' (2012) 40 Fed LR 317. See also Justice Peter Applegarth, 'Deciding Novel and Routine Cases without Evidence' (2018) 11 J Tort L 173. For the need for social facts to be based on rigorous case-specific research: Gregory Mitchell, Laurens Walker, and John Monahan, 'Beyond Context: Social Facts as Case-Specific Evidence' (2010) 60 Emory LJ 1109.

(C) Decisions without a hearing ('on the papers')

There seems to be virtually nothing written about this despite the volume of work judges undertake 'on the papers'. The literature focuses on (i) written argument for cases; and (ii) the agenda setting, resulting from grants of permission to proceed or to appeal. On (i) the history of 'appellate briefs' and time-limited oral argument in US courts is set out in Suzanne Ehrenberg, 'Embracing the Writing-Centred Legal Process' (2004) 89 Iowa LR 1159. See also Mark R Kravitz, 'Written and Oral Persuasion in the United States Courts: A District Judge's Perspective on Their History, Function, and Future' (2009) 10 J App Prac & Process 247. On (ii) the seminal study is HW Perry, *Deciding to Decide: Agenda Setting in the United States Supreme Court* (Harvard University Press 1994). In 'Curation, Narration, Erasure: Power and Possibility at the U.S. Supreme Court' (2024) 138 Harv LR 1, Karen M Tani examines docket construction in the 2023 term and that, although they were available for the court's consideration, cases involving predatory economic practices did not feature prominently. The permission stage for appeals to the House of Lords and UK Supreme Court is explained in Brice Dickson, 'The Processing of Appeals in the House of Lords' (2007) 123 LQR 571 and Paterson, *Final Judgment* 29–31, 67–70. For the role of judicial assistants in preparing memoranda on permission applications see Tetyana Nesterchuk, 'The View from Behind the Bench: The Role of Judicial Assistants in the UK Supreme Court' in Andrew Burrows, David Johnston, and Reinhard Zimmermann (eds), *Judge and Jurist: Essays in Memory of Lord Rodger of Earlsferry* (OUP 2013) (hereafter Burrows and others (eds), *Judge and Jurist*). Concerning leave applications in other apex courts, eg, Denise Cooney, 'An Absence of Reason: Why the Supreme Court of Canada Should Justify Dismissing Applications for Leave to Appeal' (2012) 70 UT Fac L Rev 23. On permission to appeal to the Court of Appeal of England and Wales, written before the 2016 rule change: Charles Blake and Gavin Drewry, 'The Role of the Court of Appeal in England and Wales as an Intermediate Court' in Andrew Le Sueur (ed), *Building the UK's New Supreme Court: National and Comparative Perspectives* (OUP 2004). The introduction of a permission stage for judicial review and the move away from oral applications to an initial paper stage is discussed in Sarah Nason, 'The Administrative Court, the Upper Tribunal and Permission to Seek Judicial Review' (2012) 21 Nottingham LJ 1, and Tom Cornford and Maurice Sunkin, 'The Bowman Report, Access and the Recent Reforms of the Judicial Review Procedure' [2001] PL 11. Changes such as a permission stage, and making decisions 'on the papers', are attributed to public sector managerialism and the pursuit of cost-effectiveness in Brian Opeskin, 'Rationing justice: Tempering Demand for Courts in the Managerialist State' (2022) 45 UNSW LJ 531.

(D) Ex tempore judgments

The case for *ex tempore* judgments is made in Michael Kirby, 'Ex tempore Judgments: Reasons on the Run' (1995) 25 U West Aust LR 213. The article contains practical advice to judges on preparation for *ex tempore* judgments, as does *A Guide for the Magistrate in the Commonwealth: Fundamental Principles and Recommended Practices* (Commonwealth Magistrates' and Judges' Association 2021) ch 10 and Max Barrett, *The Art and Craft of Judgment Writing* (Globe Law and Business 2022) (hereafter Barrett, *The Art and Craft of Judgment Writing*) ch 13. Before rule changes reduced the right to an oral renewal, when permission to appeal to the English Court of Appeal was refused on the papers (see p. 204 above), almost all decisions were given *ex tempore*: Hazel Genn and Nigel Balmer, 'Court of Appeal, Time and Motion Data Analysis' in Lord Justice Briggs, *Civil Courts Structure Review: Final Report* (Judiciary of England and Wales 2016) Annex 4, 202.

(E) *Litigants in person*

The experiences of litigants in person are explored in Kate Leader, *Litigants in Person in the Civil Justice System* (Hart 2024), and Gráinne Mckeever and others, 'The Snakes and Ladders of Legal Participation: Litigants in Person and the Right to a Fair Trial under Article 6 of the European Convention on Human Rights' (2022) 49 JL & Soc 71. The leading proceduralist in England, Adrian Zuckerman, 'No Justice Without Lawyers—The Myth of an Inquisitorial Solution' (2014) 33 CJQ 355 suggests that judges cannot overcome the 'justice deficit' when one party is a litigant in person, through an inquisitorial approach or otherwise. Penny Darbyshire's ethnographic study of English judges describes how some judges conduct hearings with litigants in person: *Sitting in Judgment* 237–50, 309–13. See also Richard Moorhead, 'The Passive Arbiter: Litigants in Person and the Challenge to Neutrality' (2007) 16 Soc & Legal Stud 405.

III Managerial Judging

(A) *Case management*

The classic text on case management is Ernest C Friesen, Edward C Gallas, and Nesta M Gallas, *Managing the Courts* (Bobbs-Merrill 1971), and on the promotion of case management see the influential Maureen Solomon and Douglas K Somerlot, *Caseflow Management in the Trial Court* (American Bar Association 1987). Steven Baicker-McKee, 'Reconceptualizing Managerial Judges' (2015) 65 Amer U LR 353 is a useful tour de horizon in the US. On the adoption of case management in England and Wales following reports by Lord Woolf: Stephen Clark and Rupert Jackson, *The Reform of Civil Justice* (2nd edn, Sweet & Maxwell 2018), John Sorabji, *English Civil Justice after the Woolf and Jackson Reforms* (CUP 2014), and Adrian Zuckerman and Ross Cranston (eds), *Reform of Civil Procedure Essays on 'Access to Justice'* (Clarendon Press 1996). For discussion of how case management changes the judge's role: Robert F Peckham, 'The Federal Judge as a Case Manager: The New Role in Guiding a Case from Filing to Disposition' (1981) 69 Calif LR 770; Justice Ronald Sackville, 'From Access to Justice to Managing Justice: The Transformation of the Judicial Role' (2002) 12 J Judicial Admin 5. Anna Olijnyk, *Justice and Efficiency in Mega-Litigation* (Hart 2021) draws on interviews with English and Australian judges regarding case management in long-running, resource intensive litigation. At a more mundane level Penny Darbyshire contains a description of some district judges as they conducted case management in an English county court: *Sitting in Judgment* 234–36.

(B) *Facilitating settlement*

An experienced English judge describes how he was a 'settler': he tried to get a solution which would avoid the expense and possible acrimony of a court hearing: John Baker, *Ballot Box to Jury Box: The Life and Times of an English Crown Court Judge* (Waterside Press 2005) 155. See also the settlement attempts, when she was on the county court, of the first female High Court judge in England, Elizabeth Lane, *Hear the Other Side* (Butterworths 1985) 124–27. John Eekelaar and Mavis Maclean observed family judges acting as helpers, managers, and adjudicators as they spent their time facilitating agreements between parties—'moving cases along': *Family Justice: The Work of Family Judges in Uncertain Times* (Hart Publishing 2013). In only five of the forty-eight cases observed was there an adjudication following legal argument. On the basis of observations, Michal Alberstein and Nourit Zimerman found that English judges conducted case management conference in a formal manner and were reluctant to engage in settlement activities: 'Judicial Conflict Resolution in Italy, Israel and England and Wales: A Comparative Look on the Regulation of Judges' Settlement Activities' in Maria Federica Moscati, Michael Palmer, and Marian Roberts (eds), *Comparative Dispute Resolution* (Elgar 2020). See also Simon Roberts,

A Court in the City: Civil and Commercial Litigation in London at the beginning of the 21st Century (Wildy, Simmonds & Hill 2013) (case management conferences as an opportunity to discuss settlement). For the position in Canada, there is a more equivocal approach in Hugh F Landerkin and Andrew J Pirie, 'Judges as Mediators: What's the Problem with Judicial Dispute Resolution in Canada' (2003) 82 Can BR 249. Judicial involvement in facilitating settlement conferences is explained in Archie Zariski, 'The Multi-door Courthouse at Middle Age: Life in Canada' (2019) 38 CJQ 44 (Alberta). The argument of Tania Sourdin's 'Five Reasons Why Judges should conduct Settlement Conferences' (2011) 37 Monash LR 145 is evident in the title. There is a good history of how promoting settlement took hold among US judges in Robert G Bone, 'Settlement and the Good Judge' (2019) 38 Rev Litig 211. See also on the US, William P Lynch, 'Why Settle for Less: Improving Settlement Conferences in Federal Court' (2019) 94 Wash LR 1233 and Richard Marcus, 'The Litigation Superpower's Case Management Cure for Adversarial Ills' in Peter CH Chan and CH van Rhee (eds), *Civil Case Management in the Twenty-First Century: Court Structures Still Matter* (Springer 2021). There is a description of the range of techniques used by Tel Aviv judges to effect settlements: Hadas Cohen and Michal Alberstein, 'Power and Persuasion in the Courtroom: The Force of Law and the Settlement Dynamics of Judges' (2023) 6 Cardozo Int'l & Comp LR 767.

The seminal criticism of a settlement perspective for judges begins with Bentham, who abhorred compromise as a denial of justice: William Twining, 'Alternative to What? Theories of Litigation, Procedure and Dispute Settlement in Anglo-American Jurisprudence: Some Neglected Classics' (1993) 56 MLR 380, 385. That approach continued with Lon Fuller's classic 'The Forms and Limits of Adjudication' (1978) 92 Harv LR 353, with its praise of civil adjudication as a process conferring on the affected party a peculiar form of participation in the decision. Arguments against a settlement perspective were spelt out in Owen M Fiss's well-known 'Against Settlement' (1984) 93 Yale LJ 1073. He argued that the 'dispute perspective' of courts, as if they are to resolve quarrels between neighbours, 'trivialises' their power conferred by public law to give force to the public values embodied in law. The seminal critique of case management, settlement, and the decline of adjudication and its public benefits is Judith Resnik, 'Managerial Judges' (1982) 96 Harv LR 374. Resnick followed with a series of articles eg Judith Resnik, 'Mediating Preferences: Litigant Preferences for Process and Judicial Preferences for Settlement' [2002] J Disp Resol 155 (on judges favouring settlement—'docket pressures that are unending, lawyers that appear contentious, dissembling, and overpriced, and the profoundly challenging problems of rendering judgment': 165). There is a sophisticated analysis in David Luban, 'Settlements and the Erosion of the Public Realm' (1995) 83 Geo LJ 2619. Carrie Menkel-Meadow attempts a balance, observing that settlement offers a substantive justice that may be more responsive to the parties' needs than adjudication: 'For and Against Settlement: Uses And Abuses of the Mandatory Settlement Conference' (1985) 33 UCLA LR 485; 'Whose Dispute is it Anyway? A Philosophical and Democratic Defence of Settlement' (1995) 83 Geo LJ 2663. Alexandra Lahav *In Praise of Litigation* (OUP 2019) refutes notions of excessive litigiousness and elaborates the democratic benefits of litigation. Marc Galanter's name is most closely associated with the notion of the vanishing trial as settlement has taken hold: eg, 'The Vanishing Trial: An Examination of Trials and Related Matters in Federal and State Courts' (2004) 1 J Empirical Leg Stud 459. Galanter's 'vanishing trial' has given rise to a voluminous literature, eg, John Lande, 'Shifting the Focus from the Myth of "The Vanishing Trial" to Complex Conflict Management Systems. . .' (2006) 6 Cardozo J Conflict Resolution 191. For the evidence in England and Wales, see Linda Mulcahy and Wendy Teeder, 'Are Litigants, Trials and Precedents Vanishing After All?' (2021) 85 MLR 326.

Arguments for and against mandatory ADR appear in Richard Ingleby, 'Court Sponsored Mediation: The Case against Mandatory Participation' (1993) 56 MLR 441; Masood Ahmed, 'Formulating a More Principled Approach to ADR within the English

Civil Justice System' in Xandra Kramer, Jos Hoevenaars, and Erlis Themeli (eds), *Frontiers in Civil Justice: Privatisation, Monetisation and Digitisation* (Elgar 2022); Lola Akin Ojelabi, 'Legislating Appropriate Dispute Resolution for the Public Good' (2023) 42 CJQ 333; Nayha Acharya, 'Exploring the Role of Mandatory Mediation in Civil Justice' (2023) 60 Alberta LR 719; Barbara Billingsley and Masood Ahmed, 'Evolution, Revolution and Culture Shift: A Critical Analysis of Compulsory ADR in England and Canada' (2016) 45 Common L W'ld R 186; Vicki Waye, 'Mandatory Mediation in Australia's Civil Justice System (2016) 45 Common L W'ld R 214. In 'What is Civil Justice for—Reform, ADR, and Access to Justice' (2012) 24 Yale JL & Human 397, Hazel Genn notes that success is defined by mediators as a settlement that the parties 'can live with', and comments that therefore the outcome of mediation is not about just settlement, it is just about settlement. In the article and in her *Judging Civil Justice* (CUP 2009) she forcefully argues that the civil justice system is a public good that serves more than private interests, and that modern civil justice reform is mainly about neither more access nor more justice, but rather the diversion of disputants away from the courts and (echoing Fiss) the downgrading of civil justice.

IV Leadership and Collegiality

(A) Leadership

Deborah L Rhode draws on insights outlined in contemporary leadership research relevant to law in 'Leadership in Law' (2017) 69 Stan LR 1603. Adam Blisa & David Kosař, 'Court Presidents: The Missing Piece in the Puzzle of Judicial Governance' (2018) 19 German LJ 2031 identify seven components in judicial leadership: power over judges' careers, jurisprudential, administrative, financial, ambassadorial, media power, and ancillary powers (a residual category). Jurisprudential leadership in the House of Lords and UK Supreme Court have been studied over the decades by Alan Paterson: see *The Law Lords* (Macmillan 1982) (hereafter Paterson, *The Law Lords*); and *Final Judgment*. In 'Creating a Group Oriented Supreme Court–Lord Neuberger's Legacy' (2021) 28 Int'l J Leg Profession 107 Paterson describes Neuberger's leadership as collegial—while trying to nudge colleagues to his preferred solution—whereas Lord Diplock was coercive; Lord Reid and Lord Bingham were authoritative, Lord Phillips was detached, and Lady Hale offered a role model. On Lord Bingham see Brenda Hale, 'A Supreme Judicial Leader' in Mads Andenas and Duncan Fairgrieve (eds), *Tom Bingham and the Transformation of the Law: A Liber Amicorum* (OUP 2009). In Rehan Abeyratne and Iddo Porat (eds), *Towering Judges: A Comparative Study of Constitutional Judges* (CUP 2021) (hereafter Abeyratne and Porat (eds), *Towering Judges*), the editors invited contributions about judges who were 'towering' in the sense of making a substantial contribution to their jurisdiction's constitutional system. Chapters relevant to jurisprudential leadership include Gabrielle Appleby and Andrew Lynch on Mason CJ of the Australian High Court, Alon Harel on Aharon Barak P of Israel, and Rehan Abeyratne on PN Bhagwati CJ of India. Rosemary Hunter and Erika Rackley have a chapter on Lady Hale, who became President of the UK Supreme Court. In another contribution Hunter and Rackley use statistical information on judgments (eg, leading, concurring, dissent, simple agreement) and outside activities (eg, speeches, overseas engagements) to identify administrative, jurisprudential, social, and community leadership: Rosemary Hunter and Erika Rackley, 'Judicial Leadership on the UK Supreme Court' (2018) 38 Legal Stud 191. The importance of intellectual leaders having support is brought out in the experience of Bora Laskin CJ of Canada. He was appointed over the heads of more senior judges by Prime Minister Trudeau to transform the Supreme Court. In his early years his 'liberal' vision of jurisprudence was contrary to that of most of the court, and he was often in dissent. Later, with new appointments, he was able to lead a coalition for change: see Peter McCormick, 'Follow the Leader: Judicial Power and Judicial Leadership on the Laskin Court, 1973-1984' (1998) 24 Queen's LJ 237; 'Assessing Leadership on the Supreme Court of Canada: Towards a Typology of Chief Justice Performance' (1993) 4 SCLR (2d) 409.

Jurisprudential leadership in the US Supreme Court has given rise to a voluminous literature. The seminal discussion by David J Danelski in 1960, of the chief justice's use of the power of opinion assignment, was published in abridged form in Thomas P Jahnige and Sheldon Goldman (eds), *The Federal Judicial System: Readings in Process and Behaviour* (Holt, Rinehart & Winston 1968). See now David J Danelski and Artemus Ward (eds), *The Chief Justice: Appointment and Influence* (University of Michigan Press 2016). Other agenda setting powers are discussed in Frank B Cross and Stefanie Lindquist, 'The Decisional Significance of the Chief Justice' (2006) 154 U Pa LR 1665; G Edward White, 'The Internal Powers of the Chief Justice: The Nineteenth-Century Legacy' (2006) 154 U Pa LR 1463. The extent of Warren CJ's role in the unanimous decision in *Brown v Board of Education* 347 US 483 (1954) is contested: eg, Bernard Schwartz, *Super Chief: Earl Warren and his Supreme Court: A Judicial Biography* (New York University Press 1983); Dennis J Hutchinson, 'Hail to the Chief: Earl Warren and the Supreme Court' (1983) 81 Mich LR 922. Mark Tushnet covers a number of chief justices in 'The Landscapes that Towering Judges Tower Over' in Abeyratne and Porat (eds), *Towering Judges*.

As to administrative leadership, Linda Greenhouse contrasts what liberal Justice Ruth Bader Ginsburg called the most efficient and fairest boss she had ever had—conservative Chief Justice Rehnquist—with his predecessor, Chief Justice Burger, in the administration of the business of the US Supreme Court: 'How Not to Be Chief Justice: The Apprenticeship of William H. Rehnquist' (2006) 154 U Pa LR 1365. Administration of the judiciary involves skills ranging from thinking strategically through deciding on resource allocation, to appraisal, mentoring, complaints handling, whistleblowing, and personnel issues: see eg, Ernest Ryder and Stephen Hardy, *Judicial Leadership: A New Strategic Approach* (OUP 2019). Lord Thomas, 'The Judiciary within the State: Governance and Cohesion of the Judiciary' (2018) Isr LR 127 describes how, despite legal authority residing in the chief justice, the judiciary of England and Wales is administered in a collegial manner.

On institutional leadership there are chapters in *Towering Judges* eg, Dennis Davis on the first president of South Africa's Constitutional Court, Arthur Chaskalson, whose leadership played an important part in establishing the court's legitimacy. In New Zealand Richard Cornes describes the role of the chief justice as being a statesperson and guardian of the constitution, which may apply in other contexts as well: 'A Point of Stability in the Life of the Nation: The Office of Chief Justice of New Zealand—Supreme Court Judge, Judicial Branch Leader, and Constitutional Guardian and Statesperson' [2013] 2013 NZ LR 549. See also his 'Gains (and Dangers of Losses) in Translation. The Leadership Function in the United Kingdom's Supreme Court, Parameters and Prospects' [2011] PL 509. Gabrielle Appleby and Heather Roberts refer to the role of the chief justice in furthering judicial independence, accountability, transparency, efficiency, and representativeness: 'The Chief Justice under Relational and Institutional Pressure' in Appleby and Lynch (eds) *The Judge, the Judiciary and the Court*. Institutional leadership is not confined to the highest courts: District Judge Nicholas Crichton pioneered the creation of Family Drug and Alcohol Courts in England in 2008 to tackle parental substance misuse in care proceedings, see <https://fdac.org.uk>.

(B) Collegiality

Sarah Murray provides a good overall account of the subject, concluding that collegiality has emerged as a judicial value, contributing to the quality of the deliberative process at both individual and institutional levels: 'Judicial Collegiality' in Appleby and Lynch (eds) *The Judge, the Judiciary and the Court*. The contributions to Birke Häcker and Wolfgang Ernst (eds), *Collective Judging in Comparative Perspective: Counting Votes and Weighing Opinions* (Intersentia 2020) (hereafter Häcker and Ernst (eds), *Collective Judging*) draw out the contrast between collegial decision-making in civil law countries (and the Court of Justice of the European Union) where there must be one judgment, drafted by the judge rapporteur, and that in common law courts, where concurrences and dissents are permitted. There is a chapter by Harry T Edwards, Chief Judge Emeritus of the US Court of Appeals for the DC Circuit, a strong proponent of collegiality in decision-making: 'Collegial Decision-Making in the US Courts of Appeals', who has written extensively elsewhere on the subject. Häcker and Ernst (eds), *Collective Judging* contains chapters on the practices and procedures relevant to collegial decision-making in the UK Supreme Court (Lord Reed, then deputy president, later president of the court), the Court of Appeal of England and Wales (Jack Beatson, Launcelot Henderson, Keith Lindblom, all judges of that court), and the High Court of Australia (Susan Kiefel, chief justice of that court). In *Sitting in Judgment*, Penny Darbyshire describes the camaraderie and good humour among members of the English Court of Appeal, where none took precedence in discussion. See also Mary Arden, 'The Distinct Leadership Profiles of Intermediate and Final Appellate Courts' in Marcus Moore and Daniel Jutras (eds), *Canada's Chief Justice: Beverley McLachlin's Legacy of Law and Leadership* (LexisNexis 2018). The practice in the Canadian Supreme Court under a number of chief justices is dealt with in Emmett Macfarlane, *Governing from the Bench: The Supreme Court of Canada and the Judicial Role* (UBC Press 2013). For the Indian Supreme Court see Nick Robinson, 'Structure Matters: The Impact of Court Structure on the Indian and US Supreme Courts' (2013) 61 Am J Comp L 173; Aparna Chandra, William Hubbard, and Sital Kalantry, 'The Supreme Court of India. An Empirical Overview of the Institution' in Gerald N Rosenberg, Sudhir Krishnaswamy, and Shishir Bail (eds), *The Indian Supreme Court and Progressive Social Change* (CUP 2019).

Discourteous treatment and worse by judges of one another are the stuff of legal folklore: examples are the feud between Lord Brandon and Lord Templeman in the House of Lords, the refusal of Starke J to speak to Evatt and McTiernan JJ in the High Court of Australia, the rupture between Chief Justice Lamer and Madam Justice L'Heureux-Dubé in the Canadian Supreme Court, and the rivalry between Justices YV Chandrachud and PN Bhagwati of the Indian Supreme Court. Unjustified public criticism by appellate judges of judges whose decisions are being appealed was the heart-felt theme of Keith Mason, the President of the New South Wales Court of Appeal, in his paper 'Throwing Stones: A Cost/Benefit Analysis of Judges Being Offensive to each Other' (2008) 82 ALJ 260. There are other examples well known in the legal community of this sort of treatment. Sometimes this spills over in public, such as Scrutton LJ's spats with McCardie J (see David Foxton, *The Life of Thomas E Scrutton* (CUP 2013) 221–23) and Lord Simonds' criticism of Lord Denning (eg, in *Magor and St Mellons Rural DC v Newport Corp* [1952] AC 189, 190–91). In her concurring judgment in the Canadian Supreme Court case of *R v Ewanchuk* [1999] 1 SCR 330, Madam Justice L'Heureux-Dube criticized the outdated sexist myths and stereotypes contained in the judgment being appealed (from the Alberta Court of Appeal). Justice McClung, who had written it, sent a letter to a newspaper, the *National Post*, and gave a media interview condemning L'Heureux-Dube J. That in turn led to an inquiry by the Canadian Judicial Council which decided against further action against him: see Hester Lessard, 'Farce or Tragedy? Judicial Backlash and Justice McClung' (1999) 10 Cons'l Forum 65. There has been institutional concern by UK judges about the European Court of Human Rights (and before Brexit, of the Court of Justice of the European Union), for example, Lord Hoffmann, 'The Universality of Human Rights' (2009) 125 LQR 416.

There are calls for greater judicial dialogue between UK and European judges: see Mary Arden, *Human Rights and European Law: Building New Legal Orders* (OUP 2015) pt 7; Sir Peter Gross, *Independent Human Rights Act Review* (CP 586, 2020) ch 4.

V Judgments

As well as writing judgments, judges have also written (or spoken) a great deal about writing judgments, including Lord MacMillan, 'The Writing of Judgments' (1948) 26 Can B Rev 491; Lord Neuberger, 'No Judgment—No Justice' (First Annual BAILII Lecture, 20 November 2012); Lord Stephens, 'Writing and Judgecraft: A View From The Supreme Court' (2023) 7 Irish Judicial Stud J 117; Bora Laskin, 'A Judge and His Constituencies' (1976) 7 Man LJ 1; Debbie Mortimer, 'Some Thoughts on Writing Judgments in, and for, Contemporary Australia' (2018) 42 Melb U LR 274 (who makes the effective point that for judgments to be more accessible requires appellate courts to endorse shorter and more straightforward reasons); Linda Dessau and Tom Wodak, 'Seven Steps to Clearer Judgment Writing' in R Sherd (ed), *A Matter of Judgment: Judicial Decision-making and Judgment Writing* (Judicial Commission of New South Wales 2003); and Barrett, *The Art and Craft of Judgment Writing.*

While not directly relevant, it is important to note the feminist judgment writing projects, which argue how judgments could, and should, have been different through a feminist perspective. Judgments are rewritten to take this perspective into account, but within the constraints existing at the time of the original judgment. These include the doctrine of precedent, the facts as found in the original judgment, and the law at that time. There have been a range of feminist judgment writing projects in a range of common law jurisdictions: for example, Rosemary Hunter, Clare McGlynn, and Erika Rackley (eds), *Feminist Judgments: From Theory to Practice* (Hart Publishing 2010); Heather Douglas, Francesca Bartlett, and Trish Luker (eds), *Australian Feminist Judgments: Righting and Re-Writing Law* (Hart Publishing 2014); Máiréad Enright, Julie McCandless, and Aoife O'Donoghue (eds), *Northern/Irish Feminist Judgments* (Hart Publishing 2017); Elisabeth McDonald, Rhonda Powell, and Mamari Stephens (eds), *Feminist Judgments of Aotearoa/ New Zealand* (Hart Publishing 2017); Sharon Cowan, Chloe Kennedy, and Vanessa E Munro (eds), *Scottish Feminist Judgments* (Hart Publishing 2019). For Canada (where the movement began) see 'Special Issue: Rewriting Equality' (2006) 18 Can J Women & Law 1, and 'Rewriting Equality II' (2018) 30 Can J Women & Law 197. For India, see Aparna Chandra, Jhuma Sen, and Rachna Chaudhary, 'The Indian Feminist Judgements Project' (2021) 5 Indian LR 261. There has also been feminist judgment rewriting in specific subject areas, for example Bridget J Crawford and Anthony C Infanti (eds), *Feminist Judgments: Rewritten Tax Opinions* (CUP 2017); Loveday Hodson and Troy Lavers (eds), *Feminist Judgments in International Law* (Hart Publishing 2019). The approach with feminist judgement writing has been extended to other areas: see Eva Brems (ed), *Diversity and European Human Rights: Rewriting Judgments of the ECHR* (CUP 2013); Helen Stalford, Kathryn Hollingsworth, and Stephen Gilmore, *Rewriting Children's Rights Judgments: From Academic Vision to New Practice* (Hart 2017) (hereafter Stalford, Hollingsworth, and Gilmore, *Rewriting Children's Rights Judgments*); Nicole Watson and Heather Douglas (eds), *Indigenous Legal Judgments: Bringing Indigenous Voices into Judicial Decision-making* (Routledge 2021).

(A) Reasons for reasons

Apex courts often do not give detailed, if indeed any, reasons for refusing permission to appeal (or, in the case of the US Supreme Court, in refusing certiorari). For the practice of the UK Supreme Court and two Australian courts see respectively CJS Knight, 'The Supreme

Court gives its Reasons' (2012) 128 LQR 477 and Luke Beck, 'The Constitutional Duty to Give Reasons for Judicial Decisions' (2017) 40 UNSW LJ 923. 'Reasons for reasons' are examined in, for example: David Dyzenhaus and Michael Taggart, 'Reasoned Decisions and Legal Theory' in Douglas Edlin (ed), *Common Law Theory* (CUP 2007) and Bruce V Harris, 'The Continuing Struggle with the Nuanced Obligation on Judges to Provide Reasons for their Decisions' (2016) 132 LQR 216 (who also explains how the adequacy of reasons varies with context). For an account which sees the duty to provide reasons as flowing from the principle of open justice: Jason Bosland and Jonathan Gill, 'The Principle of Open Justice and the Judicial Duty to Give Public Reasons' (2014) 38 Melb U LR 482. Public justification is an aspect of contemporary liberal democratic political theory and public law scholarship: see Kai Möller, 'Justifying the Culture of Justification' (2019) 17 Int'l J Const L 1078. With increased caseloads US appellate federal courts are refraining from publishing detailed opinions in most of their cases: Mathilde Cohen, 'When Judges Have Reasons not to Give Reasons: A Comparative Law Approach' (2015) 72 Washington & Lee LR 483. That a judge's reasons may not be the 'real' reasons for a decision: David Shapiro, 'In Defence of Judicial Candor' (1987) 100 Harv LR 731.

(B) Clarity, structure, and content

William D Popkin, *Evolution of the Judicial Opinion: Institutional and Individual Styles* (NYU Press 2007) defines style as 'whatever in the judicial opinion seeks to persuade beyond the paraphrasable content of the decision'. He divides style into voice and tone, the judge's relationship to the source of law and to the audience respectively: at 143. An early and insightful comparison of common and civil law styles was J Gillis Wetter, *The Styles of Appellate Judicial Opinions* (AW Sythoff 1960). The judicial style in France is outlined in chapter 8 of Eva Steiner, *French Law: A Comparative Approach* (2nd edn, OUP 2018). Behind the relatively formal and magisterial civil law judgment are discursive features, exposed in the European Court of Justice with the more purposive opinions of the Advocates General. Eliza Walker, '"Terms of Heart": Judicial Style in Obergefell v Hodges' (2020) 61 Boston College LR 1935 argues that fundamental rights cases in the US Supreme Court have led to a style of speaking to the reader because these are the cases most likely to be seen by the public. In relation to *Obergefell v Hodges* 576 US 644 (2015), which held that same-sex marriages were constitutionally protected, she considers whether the majority judgment of Justice Kennedy elevated style over legal analysis: at 153. 'Child-friendly' judgments are explored in Helen Stalford and Kathryn Hollingsworth, '"This Case is About You and Your Future": Towards Judgments for Children' (2020) 83 MLR 1030, who argue that these promote children's access to justice. Stalford, Hollingsworth, and Gilmore's *Rewriting Children's Rights Judgments* contains law reports rewritten from a children's rights perspective. James A Raymond has taught judgment writing around the world and boils down his direct approach in *Writing for the Court* (Carswell 2010). In similar vein are Commonwealth Magistrates' and Judges' Association, *Guide for the Magistrate in the Commonwealth: Fundamental Principles and Recommended Practices* (CMJA 2021) ch 11; Ginger Briggs (ed), *Judicial Decisions: Crafting Clear Reason* (National Judicial College of Australia 2008); Edward Berry, *Writing Reasons: A Handbook for Judges* (5th edn, LexisNexis 2021).

(C) Style

Justice Cardozo seems to have been the first to classify judicial styles in 'Law and Literature' [1925] Yale LR 14. As well as identifying his pure and impure styles, Chief Judge Posner in his 'Judges' Writing Styles (And Do They Matter)' (1995) 62 U Chi L 1421 sought to link these two styles with two jurisprudential stances, the formalist and his own judicial philosophy, pragmatism. Lord Rodger, 'The Form and Language of Judicial Opinions' [2002] LQR 226 contrasts the pedestrian prose of Lord President Inglis, sitting day after day delivering judgment after judgment, with the mannered prose of Judge Cardozo, who would hear cases and then reserve judgments, which were consequently carefully prepared, written compositions. Lord Reed has similarly compared Lord Rodger's unremarkable judgments when he occupied Inglis's position as lord president with the more vivid and vigorous style of judgment, containing humour and literary illusions, when Rodger transferred to the House of Lords: 'The Form and Language of Lord Rodger's Judgments' in Burrows and others (eds), *Judge and Jurist*. Changes of style are discussed in Louis Blom-Cooper, 'Style of Judgments' in Louis Blom-Cooper, Brice Dickson, and Gavin Drewry (eds), *The Judicial House of Lords 1876-2009* (OUP 2011) and Matthew Groves and Russell Smyth, 'A Century of Judicial Style: Changing Patterns in Judgment Writing on the High Court 1903-2001' (2004) 32 Fed LR 255. The increasing length of judgments compared with earlier times is a recurrent theme: eg, Lady Justice Arden, 'Judgment Writing: Are Shorter Judgments Achievable?' (2012) 128 LQR 515; Ryan C Black and James F Spriggs II, 'An Empirical Analysis of the Length of US Supreme Court Opinions' (2008) 45 Houston LR 621. In fact judges write for different audiences—the classic account is Lawrence Baum, *Judges and their Audiences: A Perspective on Judicial Behaviour* (Princeton University Press 2006)—and that has an influence on judges' writing: eg, Vicki Waye, 'Who are Judges Writing For' (2009) 34 UW Australia LR 274 (writing for a legal audience means more detailed discussion etc); and David A Hoffman, Alan J Izenman, and Jeffrey R Lidicker, 'Docketology, District Courts and Doctrine' (2007) 85 Wash U LR 681 (lengthier, more reasoned judgments in commercial cases which have a higher risk of appeal). For the English approach to footnotes in judgments see Roderick Munday, 'Judicial Footnotes: A Footnote (with Footnotes)' (2006) 170(45) JP 864.

(D) Separate, joint, and dissenting judgments

The experience and arguments concerning joint, separate, and dissenting judgments in the House of Lords and UK Supreme Court are expertly canvassed in Paterson, *Final Judgment* 99–120. For the Court of Appeal see Roderick Munday, '"All for One and One for All" The Rise to Prominence of the Composite Judgment within the Civil Division of the Court of Appeal' (2002) 61 CLJ 321 and 'Judicial Configurations: Permutations of the Court and Properties of Judgment' (2002) 61 CLJ 612. In practice the reasons for one main judgment in the Court of Appeal are pragmatic, the pressure of work and lack of time: Darbyshire, *Sitting in Judgment* 343–57. The arguments are further considered in Mary Arden, 'A Matter of Style' in Mary Arden, *Common Law and Modern Society: Keeping Pace with Change* (OUP 2015) and James Lee, 'A Defence of Concurring Speeches' [2009] PL 305. Marie-Claire Belleau, Rebecca Johnson, and Christina Vinters contend that while there may be authorial names in particular judgments, they are products of larger collaborative ventures: 'Voicing an Opinion: Authorship, Collaboration and the Judgments of Justice Bertha Wilson' (2008) 41 SCLR 53. In Australia the debate has raged over joint or separate judgments. Sir Frank Kitto, 'Why Write Judgments?' (1973) (1992) 66 ALJ 787 argued that the latter were more likely to lead to correct judgments, as the judge refines and reformulates in the process of writing. The concerns of another High Court judge are evident in the title, JD Heydon, 'Threats to Judicial Independence: The Enemy Within' (2013) 129 LQR 205. On this approach see Andrew Lynch, 'Keep Your Distance: Independence, Individualism and Decision-Making on Multi-Member Courts' in Rebecca Ananian-Welsh and Jonathan Crowe (eds), *Judicial*

Independence in Australia: Contemporary Challenges, Future Directions (Federation Press 2016). Sir Anthony Mason as chief justice of Australia encouraged the practice of joint judgments to produce more certainty in the law and more timely judgments, while recognizing the duty of a judge who disagreed with colleagues to express his views: 'The Individual Judge' (2014) 88 ALJ 554. Justice Pat Keane of the High Court of Australia underlined the institutional reasons for joint judgments in providing clarity and coherence in the law, and in a timely fashion (noting that the judge who insists upon always writing separately is likely to cause delay in the court's work): 'The Idea of the Professional Judge: Multiple Versus Single Appellate Judgments' in Judicial Commission of New South Wales, *Handbook for Judicial Officers* <www.judcom.nsw.gov.au/benchbooks-resources>. The debate continues: James AJ Dunn, 'Should Judges Join In? A Normative Study of Joint Judgments in Selected Australian Intermediate Appellate Courts' (2021) 40 UQLJ 555. Benjamin Alarie and Andrew J Green, *Commitment and Cooperation on High Courts: A Cross-Country Examination of Institutional Constraints on Judges* (OUP 2015) ch 8, draws on empirical work on the apex courts of the US, the UK, Canada, India, and Australia to explore collaboration on judgments and dissents.

With dissents the starting point must be Neil Duxbury's essay in *The Intricacies of Dicta and Dissent* (CUP 2021). See also Cass R Sunstein, *Why Societies Need Dissent* (Harvard University Press 2003) ch 8. As well as the literature quoted at p. 235n.108 above, the views of other judges include Lord Kerr, 'Dissenting Judgments—Self Indulgence or Self Sacrifice?' (The Birkenhead Lecture, 8 October 2012) <https://supremecourt.uk/uploads/speech_121008_9b9a51e9ea.pdf> (dissenting involves prosaic considerations) and Bernice B Donald, 'Judicial Independence, Collegiality, and the Problem of Dissent in Multi-Member Courts' (2019) 94 NYU LR 317 (a pillar of judicial independence). Lord Brown argues for civility in dissent, which is not seen by English judges in the US Supreme Court: 'Dissenting Judgments' in Burrows and others (eds), *Judge and Jurist*. On dissenting in intermediate appellate courts, see for example Freda M Steel, 'The Role of Dissents in Appellate Judging' (2017) 67 U Tor LJ 142. For academic studies John Adler, 'Dissents in Courts of Last Resort: Tragic Choices?' (2008) 20 Ox J Leg Stud 221 (dissent may be as important as majority judgment in signalling principles immanent in the law). Michael Blackwell, 'Indeterminacy, Disagreement and the "Human Rights Act": An Empirical Study of Litigation in the UK House of Lords and Supreme Court 1997–2017' (2020) 83 MLR 285 shows that (with qualifications) there are higher rates of dissent in human rights cases. For apex courts in Australia, Canada, and India see Russell Smyth, 'What Explains Variations in Dissent Rates? Time Series Regression Evidence from the High Court' (2004) 26 Sydney LR 221; Andrew Lynch, 'Dissent: The Rewards and Risks of Judicial Disagreement in the High Court of Australia' (2003) 27 Melb U LR 724; Donald R Songer, John Szmer, and Susan Johnson, 'Explaining Dissent on the Supreme Court of Canada' (2011) 44 Can J Pol Sci 389; and Krithika Ashok, 'Disinclined to Dissent? A Study of the Supreme Court of India' (2017) 1 Indian LR 7 (the low rate of dissent in the Indian court, especially in two and three bench sittings, is explained by collegiality, deference to the senior presiding judge, and workload).

Chapter 6 Decision-Making

I Introduction

Benjamin Cardozo's *The Nature of the Judicial Process* (Yale University Press 1921) has been a regular topic of discussion since its publications. Among the many evaluations of its legacy are John Van Voorhis, 'Cardozo and the Judicial Process Today' (1961) 71 Yale LJ 202; Dan Simon, 'The Double-Consciousness of Judging: The Problematic Legacy of Cardozo' (2000) 79 Or L Rev 1033; and Joel K Goldstein, 'The Nature of the Judicial

Process: The Enduring Significance of a Legal Classic' (2018) 34 Touro LR 159. There is also Cardozo's biographer, Andrew L Kaufman, *Cardozo* (Harvard University Press 1998). For a short English commentary by a judge, Rabinder Singh, *The Unity of Law* (Hart 2021) Epilogue.

II Models of Judging

There is an invaluable overview of some of what is termed 'theories of judging' in Brian M Barry, *How Judges Judge: Empirical Insights into Judicial Decision-Making* (Routledge 2021) (hereafter Barry, *How Judges Judge*). It does not (and could not) cover the enormous (mainly) US literature. This is largely by social scientists and uses highly sophisticated statistical analysis of data about cases, which is often built on rather shaky premises when applied outside American courts. There are summaries of this literature in compendiums such as Lee Epstein and Stefanie A Lindquist (eds), *Oxford Handbook of US Judicial Behaviour* (OUP 2017) and Epstein and others (eds), *Oxford Handbook of Comparative Judicial Behaviour.*

(A) Psychological approaches

There are good summaries of the existing literature in Australian Law Reform Commission, *Without Fear or Favour: Judicial Impartiality and the Law on Bias*, ALRC Report 138 (ALRC 2021) ch 4; Barry, *How Judges Judge*; Jeffrey J Rachlinski and Andrew J Wistrich, 'Judging the Judiciary by the Numbers: Empirical Research on Judges' (2017) 13 Annual Rev Law & Soc Sci 203; and Doron Teichman and Eyal Zamir, 'Behavioural Economics and Court Decision-Making' (2021) 17 Rev Law & Econ 385. On motivated reasoning (sometimes called 'motivated cognition') see Avani Mehta Sood, 'Motivated Cognition in Legal Judgments. An Analytic Review' (2013) 9 Annual Rev Law & Soc Sci 307. As to 'noise', variations in asylum applications are covered in Jaya Ramji-Nogales, Andrew I Schoenholtz, and Philip G Schrag, 'Refugee Roulette: Disparities in Asylum Adjudication' (2007) 60 Stan LR 295; Sean Rehaag, 'Judicial Review of Refugee Determinations (II): Revisiting the Luck of the Draw' (2019) 45 Queen's LJ; Nick Gill and others, *Inconsistency in Asylum Appeal Adjudication* (2015) 50 Forced Migration Rev 50; and Robert Thomas, *Administrative Justice and Asylum Appeals: A Study of Tribunal Adjudication* (Hart 2011). For variations in grants of permission to apply for judicial review in England: Varda Bondy, Lucinda Platt, and Maurice Sunkin, *The Value and Effects of Judicial Review* (Public Law Project 2015).

Intuitive judging was first identified a century ago by Judge C Hutcheson, later chief judge of the US Court of Appeals for the Fifth Circuit, who included as a hunch the 'flash of understanding' in even difficult cases: 'Judgment Intuitive. The Function of the Hunch in Judicial Decision' (1929) 14 Cornell LQ 274. For intuitive judging by lower court judges based on limited interview and observation in Northern Ireland courts: Richard Young, 'Managing the List in the Lower Criminal Courts: Judgecraft or Crafty Judges?' (2012) 41 Common Law World Review 29. US studies include Chris Guthrie, Jeffrey J Rachlinski, and Andrew J Wistrich, 'Blinking on the Bench: How Judges Decide Cases' (2007) 93 Cornell LR 1; and see generally Diana Richards, 'When Judges Have a Hunch: Intuition and Experience in Judicial Decision-Making' (2016) 102 ARSP 245. Emma Cunliffe suggest a number of questions a trier of fact might ask to challenge the conclusions of intuitive reasoning based on stereotypes, unsafe assumptions about human behaviour, and preferred conclusions: 'Judging Fast and Slow: Using Decision-Making Theory to Explore Judicial Fact Determination' (2014) 18 Int'l J Evidence & Proof 139.

Emotions on the bench are the subject of large-scale empirical work (interviews, observations, surveys) involving lower court judges in Australia, where the data was expertly analysed: Sharyn Roach Anleu and Kathy Mack, *Judging and Emotion: A Socio-Legal Analysis* (Routledge 2021). See also their 'Emotion Work as Judicial Work' in Appleby and Lynch (eds), *The Judge, the Judiciary and the Court*. Another empirical study—100 judges were interviewed in four district courts in Sweden—found a legal culture where in the 'staged drama' of the courtroom emotion was suppressed, but if needs be the emotions of the parties were managed by a subtle exchange of cues and signals between judges and lawyers: Stina Bergman Blix and Åsa Wettergren, *Professional Emotions in Court: A Sociological Perspective* (Routledge 2018). They returned to court culture in 'Comparing Culturally Embedded Frames of Judicial Dispassion' in Susan A Bandes and others (eds), *Research Handbook on Law and Emotions* (Edward Elgar 2021). Terry A Maroney has been a leading US advocate of judges engaging with the psychology of emotion: 'The Persistent Cultural Script of Judicial Dispassion' (2011) 99 Calif LR 629; 'Emotional Regulation and Judicial Behaviour' (2011) Calif LR 1485; and '(What We Talk About When We Talk About) Judicial Temperament' (2020) 61 Boston Coll LR 2085. Andrew J Wistrich, Jeffrey J Rachlinski, and Chris Guthrie, 'Heart versus Head: Do Judges Follow the Law or Follow Their Feelings' (2015) 93 Tex LR 855 shows that among the judges they examined there was a susceptibility to emotion which many failed to recognize—the judicial heart carried the day—and suggested that to counter it judges should attempt to consider the opposite, a technique proven successful in mitigating some cognitive biases. There is an overview of the psychology of emotion in Monica K Miller and others (eds), *The Cambridge Handbook of Psychology and Legal Decision-Making* (CUP 2024). Samuel H Pillsbury reminds us that higher court judgments can contain expressions of a judge's passion for ideas: 'Harlan, Holmes, and the Passions of Justice' in Susan A Bandes, *The Passions of Law* (NYU Press 1999), a point Justice Brennan of the US Supreme Court made in his lecture 'Reason, Passion, and the Progress of the Law' (1988) 10 Cardozo LR 3. Julia JA Shaw's *Law and the Passions: Why Emotion Matters for Justice* (Routledge 2019) is an exploration of how emotions shape law through a study, inter alia, of judgments, legislation, and legal and non-legal literature (see esp chapter 5 on compassion). Empathy is discussed at length in Thomas B Colby, 'In Defence of Judicial Empathy' (2012) 96 Minn LR 1944.

(B) Relational models

A large volume of articles and judicial speeches address the academic influences on judgments. Neil Duxbury, *Jurists and Judges: An Essay on Influence* (Hart Publishing 2001) adopts an historical and analytical approach. For a specific example Keith Stanton traces the modern law of nuisance to an article in the LQR: K Stanton, 'Use of Scholarship by the House of Lords in Tort Cases' in J Lee (ed), *From House of Lords to Supreme Court: Judges, Jurists and the Process of Judging* (Hart Publishing 2011). Lord Burrows, 'Judges and Academics, and the Endless Road to Unattainable Perfection' (2022) 55 Israel LR 50 identifies the key literature at footnote 3. See also Susan Kiefel, 'The Academy and the Courts: What Do They Mean to Each Other Today?' (2020) 44 Melb U LR 447; Robert J Sharpe and Vincent-Joel Proulx, 'The Use of Academic Writing in Appellate Judicial Decision-Making' (2011) 50 Can Bus LJ 550. Burrows also comments on the decline in what he calls 'practical legal scholarship' usable to judges in favour of more theoretical musings. Jane Stapleton touches on this theme in *Three Essays on Torts* (OUP 2021). The seminal piece in the US on this theme was by Judge Harry T Edwards: 'The Growing Disjunction between Legal Education and the Legal Profession' (1992) 91 Mich LR 34.

Judicial concern about the approval and respect of audiences including legal scholars but ranging from fellow judges to members of the press derives from Lawrence Baum's work, based on social psychology: *Judges and Their Audiences: A Perspective on Judicial Behaviour* (Princeton University Press 2006). The literature on court architecture tends to concentrate on its role as a form of communication, conveying messages of authority, impartiality, and accountability rather than on its impact on decision-making: see Linda Mulcahy, *Legal Architecture: Justice, Due Process, and the Place of Law* (Routledge 2011) and Judith Resnik and Dennis Curtis, *Representing Justice: Invention, Controversy, and Rights in City-States and Democratic Courtrooms* (Yale University 2011).

There is a vast literature on dialogue between courts internationally, especially in relation to human rights. A seminal piece is Anne-Marie Slaughter, 'A Typology of Transjudicial Communication' (1994) 29 U Richmond LR 99. See also André Nollkaemper, 'Conversations among Courts: Domestic and International Adjudicators' in Cesare Romanò, Karen J Alter, and Yuval Shany (eds), *The Oxford Handbook of International Adjudication* (OUP 2014). The leading account of domestic dialogue is Paterson, *Final Judgment* on the UK's apex court and its dialogue with counsel, colleagues, judicial assistants, and, more widely, the Court of Appeal, academics, courts overseas (notably Strasbourg), parliament, and the executive. Alison L Young, *Democratic Dialogue and the Constitution* (OUP 2017) examines mechanisms of inter-institutional dialogue, including between UK courts and the European Court of Human Rights and Court of Justice of the European Union.

The notion of situation sense was developed by Karl Llewellyn and summed up in his *The Common Law Tradition: Deciding Appeals* (Little, Brown & Co 1960). Llewellyn's notion is somewhat difficult to understand, but see his leading interpreter, William Twining, *Karl Llewellyn and the Realist Movement* (2nd edn, CUP 2012) 224–27. David Foxton uses situation sense to understand a judge Llewellyn much admired in his *The Life of Thomas E. Scrutton* (CUP 2013) 267ff. Todd Rakoff has applied situation sense to identify default rules in contract ('The Implied Terms of Contracts: Of "Default Rules" and "Situation-Sense"' in Jack Beatson and Daniel Friedman (eds), *Good Faith and Fault in Contract Law* (OUP 1997) ch 8). Situation sense was used to explain the more ideologically neutral responses of some 250 state judges to factual problems compared with those of law students and the general public: Dan M Kahan and others, '"Ideology" or "Situation Sense"? An Experimental Investigation of Motivated Reasoning and Professional Judgment' (2016) 164 U Penn LR 349.

On collegiality see Harry T Edwards, 'The Effects of Collegiality on Judicial Decision Making' (2003) 151 U Penn LR 1639 and references for collegiality in Chapter 4. Small group theory in judicial decision-making is rather thin. The text draws on Cass R Sunstein, *Why Societies Need Dissent* (Harvard University Press 2003) ch 8 and Cass R Sunstein, David Schkade, and Lisa Michelle Ellman, 'Ideological Voting on Federal Courts of Appeals: A Preliminary Investigation' (2004) 90 Va LR 301; the possibilities canvassed in Wendy L Martinek, 'Judges as Members of Small Groups' in David E Klein and Gregory Mitchell (eds), *The Psychology of Judicial Decision Making* (OUP 2010); and Brian M Barry, 'Judging Better Together: Understanding the Psychology of Group Decision-Making on Panel Courts and Tribunals' (2023) 14 (1) Int'l J Ct Admin 1. Peter McCormick, '"Was It Something I Said?": Losing the Majority on the Supreme Court of Canada, 1984-2011' (2012) 50 Osgoode Hall LJ 93 speaks of a 'persuading court' to capture the persuasion deployed by judges to win over their colleagues. See also CL Ostberg and Matthew E Wetstein, 'Panel Effects on Courts Around the World' in Epstein and others (eds), *The Oxford Handbook of Comparative Judicial Behaviour*. Thomas G Walker, 'David J. Danelski: Social Psychology and Group Choice' in Nancy Maveety, *The Pioneers of Judicial Behaviour* (University of Michigan Press 2003) canvasses the work of an early scholar who used mainly historical material to analyse the US Supreme Court. Banks Miller and Brett Curry found that non-expert judges serving with specialists in search and seizure, anti-trust, environmental, and securities regulation in the US Courts of Appeals were especially likely to vote with the specialists' ideological position: 'Small-Group Dynamics, Ideology, and Decision Making on the US Courts of Appeals' (2016) 39 L & Policy 48. In UK tribunals Cheryl Thomas and Hazel Genn found that the more experienced and expert judges wielded more influence: *Understanding Tribunal Decision-Making: A Foundational Empirical Study* (Nuffield Foundation 2013) 14–15 (hereafter Thomas and Genn, *Understanding Tribunal Decision-Making*). In a limited study Michael J Nelson, Morgan LW Hazelton, and Rachael K Hinkle, 'How Interpersonal Contact Affects Appellate Review' (2022) 84 J Pol 573 found that judges in the US Courts of Appeals varied in the deference they gave to the decisions of district judges below depending on the frequency of their contact. A popular account of the superiority of groups in making decisions is James Surowiecki, *The Wisdom of Crowds* (Doubleday 2004) ie groups are better if members form opinions independently. However, some studies challenge the superiority of group decisions: the best individual may equal group accuracy, especially when free riders exist eg, Mario Fifić and Gerd Gigerenzer. 'Are Two Interviewers Better Than One?' (2014) 67 J Bus Stud 1771. Moreover, there is always the accuracy/efficiency trade-off to be considered. One study of the Court of Appeal, Civil Division for England and Wales centred on the impact of the specific association arising because high court judges sometimes join appellate judges to constitute a three-judge panel for that court. The study found that the proportion of appeals being dismissed was thirty per cent point higher where the appellate judges knew they were soon to sit with the high court judge relative to when such interactions were absent: Jordi Blanes i Vidal and Clare Leaver, 'Bias in Open Peer-review: Evidence from the English Superior Courts' (2015) 31 JL Econ & Org 431.

Alan Paterson's outstanding contributions to our understanding of the work of the law lords and the UK Supreme Court justices contains much of what could be classified as strategic behaviour: *The Law Lords* and *Final Judgment*. There is a summary of strategic theories in Lee Epstein and Jack Knight, 'Strategic Accounts of Judging' in Robert M Howard and Kirk A Randazzo (eds), *Routledge Handbook of Judicial Behaviour* (Routledge 2018) and Shai Dothan, 'Strategic Analysis' in Epstein and others (eds), *The Oxford Handbook of Comparative Judicial Behaviour*. For a history of strategic theory: Lee Epstein and Jack Knight, 'Walter F. Murphy: The Interactive Nature of Judicial Decision Making' in Nancy Maveety (ed), *Pioneers of Judicial Behaviour* (University of Michigan Press 2003). Forrest Maltzman, James F Spriggs II, and Paul J Wahlbeck, *Crafting Law on the Supreme Court: The Collegial Game* (CUP 2001) is a study of the US Supreme Court based on information from judges' private papers about negotiations between the justices over opinion writing, which is correlated with statistics from well-known databases. On negotiations in the Roosevelt court eg, Noah Feldman, *Scorpions: The Battles and the Triumphs of FDR's Great Supreme Court Justices* (Hachette Book Group 2010). Lee Epstein, William M Landes, and Richard A Posner, *The Behaviour of Federal Judges* (Harvard University Press 2013) use rational labour market theory for how judges pursue their personal goals, trading off the benefits (including non-pecuniary benefits such as prestige, power, and self-esteem) and costs (foregone leisure, threat of reversal by higher court, professional criticism). On the well-known 'tournament' of judges seeking promotion through their judgments: Stephen Choi and Mitu Gulati, 'A Tournament of Judges?' (2004) 92 Calif LR 299.

(C) Attitudinal models

Leading proponents of this model of judicial decision-making are Jeffrey A Segal and Harold J Spaeth, *The Supreme Court and the Attitudinal Model Revisited* (CUP 2002) 86: '. . . the Supreme Court decides disputes in light of the facts of the case vis à vis the ideological attitudes and values of the justices.' An overview of the US attitudinal literature is provided by Jeffrey A Segal and Alan J Champlin, 'The Attitudinal Model' in Robert M Howard and Kirk A Randazzo (eds), *Routledge Handbook of Judicial Behaviour* (Routledge 2018). A detailed account of how since the 1960s different scholars developed the attitudinal model is Nancy Maveety (ed), *Pioneers of Judicial Behaviour* (University of Michigan Press 2003) part I ('The Attitudinal Pioneers'). The background in realist jurisprudence to these behavioural studies is summarized in Brian Leiter, 'American Legal Realism' in Martin P Golding and William A Edmundson (eds), *The Blackwell Guide to the Philosophy of Law and Legal Theory* (Blackwell 2005). Critics of attitudinal studies include [Judge] Harry T Edwards, 'Pitfalls of Empirical Studies that Attempt to Understand the Factors Affecting Appellate Decision-making' (2009) 58 Duke LJ 1895. Attitudinal studies elsewhere are covered in Nuno Garoupa, Rebecca D Gill, and Lydia B Tiede (eds), *High Courts in Global Perspective: Evidence, Methodologies, and Findings* (University of Virginia Press 2021).

For the UK David Robertson built on the article cited in the text in his *Judicial Discretion in the House of Lords* (Clarendon 1998). Earlier than his *A Court of Specialists: Judicial Behaviour on the UK Supreme Court* (OUP 2020), Chris Hanretty had undertaken a similar analysis of split decisions in the law lords between 1969 and 2009 and concluded that their different views in cases could not be attributed to their 'political' attitudes: 'The Decisions and Ideal Points of British Law Lords' (2013) 43 Brit J Pol Sci 703. Although a study of human rights and rights-related cases in the House of Lords between 1994 and 2007 found a variation in individual judges' support for these types of claim, it could not attribute this to political ideology such as along a liberal/conservative axis: Thomas Poole and Sangeeta Shah, 'The Law Lords and Human Rights' (2011) 74 MLR 79. Contrast TT Arvind and Lindsay Stirton, 'Legal Ideology, Legal Doctrine and the UK's Top Judges' [2016] PL 418, which for public law cases in the House of Lords and UK Supreme Court 1985–2015 placed the judges on a scale from those limiting the discretion of public authorities (Lady Hale, Lord Kerr, and Lord Phillips) to those limiting their own discretion to interfere (Lord Brown, Lord Carnwath, and Lord Hodge). In 'More than Politics: Ability and Ideology in the British Appellate Committee' (2015) 32 JL Econ & Org 61, Matias Laryczower and Gabriel Katz use a model which attempted to add legal considerations to ideology to explain decision-making by the law lords 1969–2002. In addition to her *Values in the Supreme Court: Decisions, Division and Diversity* (Hart 2020), Rachel Cahill-O'Callaghan undertook similar analysis regarding the High Court of Australia, with similar results: 'Values and Judicial Differences in the High Court' in Appleby and Lynch (eds), *The Judge, the Judiciary and the Court.*

Thomas and Genn, *Understanding Tribunal Decision-Making* found that although male panel members were somewhat more inclined than female panel members to reject an appeal on a first assessment and at the final decision stage, there was no significant difference between final decisions of male and female panel members, and that seemed to apply even in gender-based issues. Analysis of over 300,000 opinions of US federal courts of appeals 2001–17 found that gender was associated with the content of judgments, but that this was as likely affected not by the gender of the judges hearing the cases but by how judges were selected to hear cases. The number of women on a panel was positively associated with some topics (eg, criminal law) and negatively associated with others (eg, administrative law): Michael A Livermore and others, 'Gendered Judicial Opinions' (2024) 1 JL & Empirical Analysis 1. Empirical evidence from Europe and the US suggests that female judges are more likely to rule in favour of a female claimant than male judges in sex discrimination but not it seems in other cases: eg, Erik Voeten, 'Gender and Judging: Evidence from the European Court of Human Rights' (2020) 28 J Eur Pub Policy 1453; Christina L Boyd, 'Representation on the Courts? The Effects of Trial Judges' Sex and Race' (2016) 69 Pol Research Q 788. See also Susan W Johnson, Donald R Songer, and Nadia A Jilani, 'Judge Gender, Critical Mass, and Decision Making in the Appellate Courts of Canada' (2011) 32 J Women, Politics & Policy 237. Gender sensitive judging by female judges in specific cases is addressed in eg, Erika Rackley, *Women, Judging and the Judiciary* (Routledge 2013) 172–77; Ruth B Cowan, 'Do Women on South Africa's Courts Make a Difference?' in Ulrike Schultz and Gisela Shaw (eds), *Gender and Judging* (Hart 2013) (hereafter Schultz & Shaw (eds), *Gender and Judging*).

III Varieties of Judging

On Weber's ideal type analysis: eg, Anthony T Kronman, *Max Weber* (Stanford University Press 1983); Richard Swedberg, 'How to use Max Weber's Ideal Type in Sociological Analysis' (2018) 18 J Classical Sociology 181, Appendix 1. Previous works have characterized the decision-making styles of judges, but not it seems in terms of Weber's ideal types. Lon Fuller's 'The Case of the Speluncean Explorers' (1949) 62 Harv LR 616 is much discussed, eg, 'The Case of the Speluncean Explorers: A Fiftieth Anniversary Symposium' (1999) 112 Harv LR 1834. For the US Supreme Court, Cass R Sunstein identified heroes (broad principles and little concern for democratic authority), soldiers (concerned about democratic authority and following its orders), mutes (avoidance of constitutional questions), and minimalists (one case at a time, apply precedent and shallow decisions): 'Constitutional Personae' [2013] Sup Ct Rev 433. One judge with a definite philosophy for judging was Judge Richard Posner, a US federal appellate judge 1981–2017 and former Chicago law professor who espoused legal pragmatism during most of his career: eg, 'Legal Pragmatism Defended' (2004) 71 U Chi LR 683; *How Judges Think* (Harvard University Press 2008) 230ff.

On feminist judging see Rosemary Hunter, 'An Account of Feminist Judging' in Rosemary Hunter, Clare McGlynn, and Erika Rackley (eds), *Feminist Judgments: From Theory to Practice* (Hart Publishing 2010) (note that this includes many features of feminist judging, which could be included in an ideal type); Rosemary Hunter, 'Justice Marcia Neave: Case Study of a Feminist Judge' in Schultz & Shaw (eds), *Gender and Judging*; Rosemary Hunter, 'More than Just a Different Face? Judicial Diversity and Decision-making' (2015) 68 Current Leg Prob 119; Rosemary Hunter and Erika Rackley, 'Feminist Judgments on the UK Supreme Court' (2020) 32 Can J Women & L 85 (identifying male judges who engaged in feminist judging); Rosemary Hunter, 'Feminist Judging in the "Real World" (2018) 8 Oñati Socio-legal Series 1275; and Rosemary Hunter, Sharyn Roach Anleu, and Kathy Mack, 'Feminist Judging in Lower Courts' (2021) 48 JL & Soc 595. For the writings and judgments of Lady Hale: eg, Lady Hale, 'A Minority Opinion?' (2008) 154 Proceedings of the British Academy 319, Rosemary Hunter and Erika Rackley, 'Lady Hale: A Feminist Towering Judge' in Abeyratne and Porat (eds), *Towering Judges*; Rosemary Hunter and Erika Rackley, *Justice for Everyone: The Jurisprudence and Legal Lives of Brenda Hale* (CUP 2022). For other judges in the Commonwealth see, for example, Constance Backhouse, *Claire L'Heureux-Dubé: A Life* (UBC Press 2017) 542–45. See also Daphne Gilbert, 'Unequalled: Justice Claire L'Heureux-Dubé's Vision of Equality and Section 15 of the Charter' (2003) 15 Can J Women & L 1; Michelle Boivin, 'Les Principles Feministes En Action' (2003) 15 Can J Women & L 73. Elsewhere see, for example, Schultz & Shaw (eds), *Gender and Judging*, pt 3 'Gender Perspectives in Judging'; Judith Olans Brown, Wendy E Parmet, and Mary E O'Connell, 'The Rugged Feminism of Sandra Day O'Connor' (1999) 32 Indiana LR 1219.

The discussion of legalism draws heavily on Sir Owen Dixon's 'strict and complete' legalism. Dixon was a member of Australia's highest court, the High Court of Australia, for thirty-five years, chief justice for twelve. Legalism was adopted as the mode of judging by other Australian judges: eg, John Gava, 'Dixonian Strict Legalism, Wilson v Darling Island Stevedoring and Contracting in the Real World' (2010) 30 Ox J Leg Stud 519 (which at 521–24 has a valuable account of legalism); Jeffrey Goldsworthy, 'Australia: Devotion to Legalism' in Jeffrey Goldsworthy (ed), *Interpreting Constitutions: A Comparative Study* (OUP 2006); Daryl Dawson and Mark Nicholls, 'Sir Owen Dixon and Judicial Method' (1986) 15 Melb U LR 543. Legalism fell into disfavour for a period, but in the early twentieth century there was a revival: see Frank Carrigan, 'A Blast from the Past: The Resurgence of Legal Formalism' (2003) 27 Melb U LR 163; William Gummow, 'The 2017 Winterton Lecture. Sir Owen Dixon Today' (2018) 43 UW Aust LR 30.

The text builds merits judging as an ideal type by drawing, in part, on Lord Denning and Judge Richard Posner. Denning is one of the few English judges to espouse a judicial philosophy, and 'merits judging' was part of it. His approach to achieving what he regarded as justice in adjudicating cases was set out early in *The Road to Justice* (Stevens 1955). Towards the end of his career, he described this, and his rationalization of the results, in Lord Denning, *The Family Story* (Butterworths 1981) 174. His 'palm tree' judging has been subject to extensive discussion: eg, Paul Watchman, 'Palm Tree Justice and the Lord Chancellor's Foot' in Peter Robson and Paul Watchman (eds), *Justice, Lord Denning and the Constitution* (Gower 1981); AWB Simpson, 'Lord Denning as Jurist' in JL Jowell and JPWB McAuslan (eds), *Lord Denning: The Judge and the Law* (Sweet & Maxwell 1984); Sean Raymond Curley, *The Judicial Decision Making Process of Lord Denning* (PhD Thesis, University of Huddersfield, 2016); James Wilson, *Lord Denning: Life, Law, and Legacy* (Wildy, Simmonds & Hill 2023). See also Charles Stephens, *The Jurisprudence of Lord Denning: A Study in Legal History* (Cambridge Scholars 2009); Wilfrid J Waluchow, 'Hart, Legal Rules and Palm Tree Justice' (1985) 4 Law & Phil 41. At the end of his career as a judge, Richard Posner espoused merits judging: judges should opt 'not to worry initially about doctrine, precedent, and the other conventional materials of legal analysis, but instead try to figure out the sensible solution to the problem': *The Federal Judiciary: Strengths and Weaknesses* (Harvard University Press 2017) 80. Chief Judge Skelly Wright of the US Court of Appeals for the District of Columbia also said that when he got a case the first thing he did was to think of what should be done and only then did he examine the law to see if he could do it: Jack Bass, *Unlikely Heroes* (University of Alabama Press 1990) 116 (1979 interview with Wright).

Minimalism has been employed by Cass Sunstein as a constitutional theory for the US Supreme Court, linking it with deliberative democracy in which the court enables the elected branches of government to resolve controversial issues, eg, *One Case at a Time: Judicial Minimalism on the Supreme Court* (Harvard University Press 1999); 'Burkean Minimalism' (2006) 105 Mich LR 353. The context is specific, but Sunstein's analysis is helpful. For example, he contends that judicial minimalists will make decisions which are 'shallow' rather than 'deep', 'narrow' rather than 'wide'—shallow decisions are pragmatic rather than philosophical, and narrow decisions are confined to the facts of the case rather than covering a range of situations. There is a considerable literature: eg, Christopher J Peters, 'Assessing the New Judicial Minimalism' (2000) 100 Colum LR 1454; Tara Smith, 'Reckless Caution: The Perils of Judicial Minimalism' (2010) 5 NYU JL & Liberty 347. Justice O'Connor, who served on the US Supreme Court 1981–2006, was said to have 'prized narrow opinions that emphasized the facts and left wiggle room in subsequent cases': Stewart J Schwab, 'Justice O'Connor as the Good Judge' (2024) 137 Harv LR 1809, 1810.

Among the English modernizers is Lord Bingham, who sought to reconcile precedent with social change: 'The Judges: Active or Passive' (2006) 139 Proceedings of the British Academy 55; 'The Judge as Lawmaker: An English Perspective' in *The Business of Judging*

(OUP 2000). Mason CJ had the view that the High Court of Australia should bring the law into line with Australian social conditions and community values: see Anthony Mason, 'The Judge as Law-Maker' (1996) 3 James Cook UL R 1 and Paul Kildea and George Williams, 'The Mason Court' in Rosalind Dixon and George Williams (eds), *The High Court, the Constitution and Australian Politics* (CUP 2015). The creative role of the judge was espoused by other members of Mason's court eg, Michael Kirby, *Judicial Activism* (Sweet & Maxwell 2004); Michael McHugh, 'The Law-Making Function of the Judicial Process (Pt 1)' (1988) 62 ALJ 15. In Canada McLachlin CJ saw the need for 'measured development' to adapt the law to changed social conditions: see Beverley McLachlin, 'The Role of the Supreme Court of Canada in Shaping the Common Law' in Paul Daly, *Apex Courts and the Common Law* (University of Toronto Press 2019) and Jamie Cameron, 'McLachlin's Law: In all its Complex Majesty' (2019) 88 Sup Ct LR (2d) 307. The Privy Council applies the 'living instrument' doctrine to post-independence constitutions (with qualifications): eg, *Chandler v State of Trinidad and Tobago* [2022] UKPC 19, [2023] AC 285 (PC, Trinidad and Tobago) [26]. Early on the European Court of Human Rights held that the European Convention of Human Rights is a 'living instrument' to be interpreted in the light of present-day conditions: *Tyrer v UK* (1978) 2 EHRR 1 [31]. See Sandra Fredman, 'Living Trees or Deadwood: The Interpretive Challenge of the European Convention on Human Rights' in NW Barber, Richards Ekins, and Paul Yowell (eds), *Lord Sumption and the Limits of the Law* (Hart 2016).

Activist judging as an ideal type suffers because judicial activism has become a pejorative term in many jurisdictions. The ideal type draws on various strands. There are the individual judges like Lord Denning: see Allan C Hutchinson, *Laughing at the Gods: Great Judges and How They Made the Common Law* (CUP 2012). Other individual judges in Commonwealth courts identified, to varying degrees, as (in Denning's terms) 'bold spirits', if not judicial activists, include Lady [Brenda] Hale, Madame Justice Claire L'Heureux-Dubé, and Justices Bhagwati, Kirby, and Sachs. On Hale and L'Heureux-Dubé see P. 348. For Bhagwati's activism: Abhinav Chandrachud, *Supreme Whispers* (Penguin Random House 2018) 28–40; Rehan Abeyratne, 'PN Bhagwati and the Transformation of India's Judiciary' in Abeyratne and Porat (eds), *Towering Judges*; PN Bhagwati, 'Judicial Activism and Public Interest Litigation' (1985) 23 Colum J Transnational L 561. Michael Kirby set out a modest view of activism in his Hamlyn lectures, *Judicial Activism*, above. For Albie Sachs' period on the South African Constitutional Court see his books *We the People: Insights of an Activist Judge* (Wits University Press 2016) and *The Strange Alchemy of Life and Law* (OUP 2009).

Courts collectively have tended to attract more attention for being activist than individual judges: see Brice Dickson (ed), *Judicial Activism in Common Law Supreme Courts* (OUP 2007). There is significant literature around the US Supreme Court: eg, Ernest A Young, 'Judicial Activism and Conservative Politics' (2002) 73 U Colorado LR 1139. An attempt to measure activism in that court between 1954 and 2004 is Stefanie A Lindquist and Frank B Cross, *Measuring Judicial Activism* (OUP 2009). As well as results-oriented judging, Lindquist and Cross regard as aspects of activism counter-majoritarianism, institutional aggrandizement, and interpretative fidelity (or its absence). As to the European Court of Human Rights, see Marko Bosnjak and Kacper Zajac, 'Judicial Activism and Judge-Made Law at the ECtHR' (2023) Human Rights LR 2023. Both the Indian and Pakistan Supreme Courts have been activist, in their different ways: eg, TR Andhyarujina, 'The Unique Judicial Activism of the Supreme Court of India' (2014) 130 LQR 53. The evolution of India's 'basic structure' doctrine regarding the Indian constitution is described in Manoj Mate, 'Priests in the Temple of Justice' in Halliday and others (eds), *Fates of Political Liberalism in the British Post-Colony*. Criticism of activist courts is common. Tanya Josev, *The Campaign against the Courts: A History of the Judicial Activism Debate*

(Federation Press 2017) reviews the critical literature in the US and Australia. An example of the critical tone sometimes adopted is a piece by a justice of the High Court of Australia, Dyson Heydon, 'Judicial Activism and the Death of the Rule of Law' (2004) 10 Otago LR 493. A defence of activism, especially in relation to the Canadian Charter of Rights and Freedoms, is Kent Roach, *The Supreme Court on Trial: Judicial Activism or Democratic Dialogue* (Irwin Law 2001). Dickson characterized UK Supreme Court judges as activist, moderate, or restrained in Brice Dickson, 'Activism and Restraint within the UK Supreme Court' (2015) 21 European Journal of Current Legal Issues 5. The rights and wrongs of judicial activism have been canvassed at some length in the British context. The Judicial Power Project (at the think tank Policy Exchange) contends that the court has wrongly extended the proper scope of the judicial power at the expense of legislative and executive authority: eg, Richard Ekins and Graham Gee, 'Putting Judicial Power in Its Place' (2017) 36 U Queensland LJ 375; Richard Ekins, *Protecting the Constitution: How and Why Parliament Should Limit Judicial Power* (Policy Exchange 2019). See also Paul Craig, 'Judicial Power, the Judicial Power Project and the UK' (2017) 36 U Queensland LJ 355.

IV Practical Judging

(A) 'The institutional character of the judge'

With statutory interpretation, a good starting point is Neil Duxbury, *Elements of Legislation* (CUP 2013). Discussions of statutory interpretation by judges include Michael Kirby, 'Towards a Grand Theory of Interpretation: The Case of Statutes and Contracts' (2002) 24 Statute LR 95; Johan Steyn, 'The Intractable Problem of the Interpretation of Legal Texts' (2003) 25 Sydney LR 5; Robert French, 'The Principle of Legality and Legislative Intention' (2019) 40 Statute LR 40; Lord Justice Sales, 'Modern Statutory Interpretation' (2017) 38 Statute LR 125; Stephen Gageler, 'Common Law Statutes and Judicial Legislation: Statutory Interpretation as a Common Law Process' (2011) 37 Monash U LR 1; and Thomas A Cromwell, Siena Anstis, and Thomas Touchie, 'Revisiting the Role of Presumptions of Legislative Intent in Statutory Interpretation' (2017) 95 Can BR 297. Academics who became judges have written about using statutes for developing common law principles: Paul Finn, 'Statutes and the Common Law' (1992) 22 U West Aust LR 7; Jack Beatson, 'The Role of Statute in the Development of Common Law Doctrine' (2001) 117 LQR 247. See also Mark Leeming, 'Theories and Principles Underlying the Development of the Common Law—The Statutory Elephant in the Room' (2013) 36 UNSWLJ 1002. The history of construing tax legislation in Britain is set out in Judith Freedman, 'Interpreting Tax Statutes: Tax Avoidance and the Intention of Parliament' (2007) 123 LQR 53, who also refers to the position in Canada, Australia, and the EU. Discussions of specific principles in interpretation include Jeffrey Goldsworthy, 'Lord Burrows on Legislative Intention, Statutory Purpose, and the "Always Speaking" Principle' (2022) 43 Statute LR 79 (who advances an intentionalist argument); Diggory Bailey, 'Settled Practice in Statutory Interpretation' (2022) 81 CLJ 28; and Karl N Llewellyn, 'Remarks on the Theory of Appellate Decision and the Rules or Canons about How Statutes Are to Be Construed' (1950) 3 Vand LR 395. Tim Sayer, 'Statutory Interpretation and the Administrative State: Refocusing the Purposivist/Intentionalist Debate' (2024) 44 Legal Stud 437 argues that there should be a greater deference by judges to administrative views on statutory interpretation.

The text for US textualism is Antonin Scalia and Bryan A Garner, *Reading Law: The Interpretation of Legal Texts* (Thomson/West 2012). A leading refutation is Stephen Breyer, *Reading the Constitution Why I Chose Pragmatism, Not Textualism* (Simon & Schuster 2024) and Stephen Breyer, 'Pragmatism or Textualism' (2025) 138 Harv LR 717. Tara Leigh Grove, 'The Supreme Court, 2019 Term—Comment: Which Textualism?' (2020) 134

Harv LR 265 outlines divisions among the textualists. Anita S Krishnakumar demonstrates statistically the difference over plain meaning in the US Supreme Court, indicating that textual analysis does not give one answer or retrain ideological decision-making: 'Dueling Canons' (2016) 65 Duke LJ 909, 984, 988n. There is controversy whether the major-questions doctrine of textualists—an interpretative canon that government agencies must have clear and specific authorization—is anti-textualist: Kevin Tobia and others, 'Major Questions, Common Sense?' (2023) 97 So Calif LR 1153. Contrasting views on intentionalism are Richard Ekins, *The Nature of Legislative Intent* (OUP 2012) and John F Manning, 'Without the Pretence of Legislative Intent' (2017) 130 Harv LR 2397. For theories of statutory interpretation see eg, David Miers and William Twining, *How to Do Things with Rules* (5th edn, CUP 2010) 230–67; Suzanne Corcoran, 'Theories of Statutory Interpretation' in Suzanne Corcoran and Stephen Bottomley (eds), *Interpreting Statutes* (Federation Press 2005); William N Eskridge, *Dynamic Statutory Interpretation* (Harvard University Press 1994); Einer Elhauge, *Statutory Default Rules: How to Interpret Unclear Legislation* (Harvard University Press 2008); Ronald Dworkin, *Law's Empire* (Harvard University Press 1986); Richard A Posner, *Reflections on Judging* (Harvard University Press 2013) ch 7.

With precedent Neil Duxbury, *The Nature and Authority of Precedent* (CUP 2008) carefully examines its nature and concludes that there is no overarching theory to explain why precedents guide and constrain. Timothy Endicott, Hafsteinn Dan Kristjánsson, and Sebastian Lewis (eds), *Philosophical Foundations of Precedent* (OUP 2023) contains forty contributions on the basic aspects of the nature and authority of precedent and its justification. A judicial view used in the text is Lord Leggatt, 'Precedent in English Law' (Harris Society Annual Lecture, Keble College, Oxford, 26 April 2024), and as regards his criticism of 'textualism' see Peter M Tiersma, 'The Textualization of Precedent' (2007) 82 Notre Dame LR 1187. Ali S Masood and Monica E Lineberger in 'United Kingdom, United Courts? Hierarchical Interactions and Attention to Precedent in the British Judiciary' (2020) 73 Pol Sc Q 714 analysed Court of Appeal responses to a stratified random sample of over 650 precedents of the House of Lords between 1970 and 2002 and found that legal, rather than strategic, factors influence the propensity to follow the precedents of the House. *Dicta* is discussed in Neil Duxbury, *The Intricacies of Dicta and Dissent* (CUP 2021) and for its binding effect see Bernice Chen, 'Seriously Considering Seriously Considered Dicta: Precedent after Farah Constructions' (2021) 95 ALJ 186.

For overruling horizontal precedent see Neil Finkelstein and Ronald Podolny, 'Canada v Craig—The Common Law as the Servant of Society' (2012) 91 Can Bar R 455. The conservative turn of the US Supreme Court in the first part of the twenty-first century has led to a pruning of earlier liberal decisions. A justification was given by Amy Coney Barrett, a justice of that court from 2020, in 'Originalism and Stare Decisis' (2017) 92 Notre Dame LR 1921 and see Hillel Y Levin, 'Justice Gorsuch's Views on Precedent in the Context of Statutory Interpretation' (2019) 20 Alabama LR 687. Nina Varsava, 'Precedent, Reliance, and *Dobbs*' (2023) 136 Harv LR 1846 considers how *Dobbs* overruled *Casey* not just as a precedent about abortion but as a precedent about precedent. On overruling precedent in the Supreme Court of India see Shrutanjaya Bhardwaj and Ayush Baheti, 'Precedent, Stare Decisis and the Larger Bench Rule: Judicial Indiscipline at the Indian Supreme Court' (2022) 6 Indian LR 58, which identifies important cases in which the larger bench rule has been breached in practice. On prospective overruling see Eva Steiner, *Comparing the Prospective Effect of Judicial Rulings Across Jurisdictions* (2015); Samuel Beswick, 'Retroactive Adjudication' (2020) 130 Yale LJ 276.

The seminal discussion of path dependence in law is Oona A Hathaway, 'Path Dependence in the Law: The Course and Pattern of Legal Change in a Common Law

System' (2001) 86 Iowa LR 601. John Bell, 'Path Dependence and Legal Development' (2013) 87 Tul LR 787 is concerned with path dependence in legal systems as a whole. See also Stefanie A Lindquist & Frank B Cross, 'Empirically Testing Dworkin's Chain Novel Theory: Studying the Path of Precedent' (2005) 80 NYU LR 1156 and Frederic G Sourgens, 'The Virtue of Path Dependence in the Law' (2016) 56 Santa Clara LR 303.

(B) Responsive judging

There are many descriptions of the common law method but among the classic expositions are Neil MacCormick, *Legal Reasoning and Legal Theory* (Clarendon Press 1978) and AWB Simpson, 'The Common Law and Legal Theory' in AWB Simpson (ed), *Oxford Essays in Jurisprudence* (Second Series) (Clarendon 1973), which remains one of the most challenging. Descriptions by serving judges include Lord Hodge, 'The Scope of Judicial Law-Making in the Common Law Tradition' (2020) 84 Rabels Z 211; Philip Sales, 'The Common Law: Context and Method' (2019) 135 LQR 47; Lord Goff's 1983 Maccabean Lecture 'The Search for Principle', reprinted in William Swadling and Gareth Jones (eds), *The Search For Principle: Essays in Honour of Lord Goff of Chievely* (OUP 1999); and Murray Gleeson, 'The Value of Clarity' in Mads Andenas and Duncan Fairgrieve (eds), *Tom Bingham and the Transformation of the Law* (OUP 2009). There is a considerable literature on the nature of analogical reasoning and the extent to which recognizing a similarity between the facts of a previous and the present case turns on principles, or at least knowledge and expertise: see Lloyd L Weinreb, *Legal Reason The Use of Analogy in Legal Argument* (2nd edn, CUP 2016); Frederick Schauer and Barbara A Spellman, 'Analogy, Expertise, and Experience' (2017) 84 U Chi LR 249, and see generally Cass R Sunstein, 'On Analogical Reasoning' (1993) 106 Harv LR 741; Paul Daly, 'Introduction' in Paul Daly, *Apex Courts and the Common Law* (University of Toronto Press 2019).

Concern with the role of public policy in English law is not new eg, Percy H Winfield canvassed the history in 'Public Policy in the English Common Law' (1928) 42 Harv LR 76. More recent accounts are Stavros Brekoulakis, 'The Evolution of Public Policy and Judicial Function in English Law' (2019) 10 J Int'l Disp Settlement 472; James Plunkett, 'Principle and Policy in Private Law Reasoning' (2016) 75 CLJ 366. There is a lively debate among academics, some arguing that principle should be determinative and policy should have no role in judicial decision-making, see Robert Stevens, *Torts and Rights* (OUP 2007). The reality is that public policy occasionally plays an important part in judicial decision-making: eg, Jane Stapleton, *Three Essays on Torts* (OUP 2021). John Bell, *Policy Arguments in Judicial Decisions* (Clarendon Press 1983 still bears study for how English judges use policy arguments in hard cases.

FKH Maher, 'Common Sense and Law' (1972) 8 U Melb LR 587 is an original contribution. Patricia Cochran, *Common Sense and Legal Judgment: Community Knowledge, Political Power, and Rhetorical Practice* (McGill-Queen's University Press 2017) examines common sense through the writings of philosophers and social scientists. There is a considerable literature on common sense and causation. Compare Jane Stapleton, 'Factual Causation' (2010) 38 Fed LR 467 with Andrew Summers, 'Commonsense Causation in the Law' (2018) Ox J Legal Stud 793. Peter Applegarth, 'Deciding Novel and Routine Cases without Evidence' (2018) 11 J Tort L 173 argues that the sheltered lives of most judges offer limited experience of the lives of individuals whose behaviour judges evaluate in both novel and routine cases. Kylie Burns highlights the potential cognitive biases in using common sense: 'Judges, "Common Sense" and Judicial Cognition' (2016) 25 Griffith LR 319. An essential beginning with consequence-based reasoning is Peter Cane, 'Consequences in Judicial Reasoning' in Jeremy Horder (ed), *Oxford Essays in Jurisprudence: Fourth Series*

(OUP 2000). Other contributions include Noam Gur, 'Ronald Dworkin and the Curious Case of the Floodgates Argument' (2018) 31 Can JL & Jurisprudence 323; Péter Cserne, 'Courts and Expertise: Consequence-Based Arguments in Judicial Reasoning' in Pierre Larouche and Péter Cserne (eds), *National Legal Systems and Globalization* (2013); and Frederick Schauer, 'Slippery Slopes' (1985) 99 Harvard LR 361 (focusing on freedom of speech).

Index

For the benefit of digital users, indexed terms that span two pages (e.g., 52–53) may, on occasion, appear on only one of those pages.